studies, guidelines, and excerpts from dialogues, as well as recommended readings for
mediators wishing to extend their knowledge and expertise. This book will not only
be of value to mediators and those interested in becoming mediators but also to
the various practitioners who use mediation
techniques in their daily work.

THE AUTHORS

JAY FOLBERG is professor of law, Lewis and
Clark Law School, and adjunct faculty
member, Department of Psychiatry, School
of Medicine, Oregon Health Sciences University. ALISON TAYLOR is adjunct faculty
member, Lewis and Clark Law School, and
has a private mediation practice.

✷ ✷ ✷ ✷ ✷

Jay Folberg
Alison Taylor

✻ ✻ ✻ ✻ ✻

Mediation

A Comprehensive Guide
to Resolving Conflicts
Without Litigation

The Jossey-Bass
Social and Behavioral Science Series

�֍ ✖ ✖ ✖ ✖

Mediation

A Comprehensive Guide to Resolving Conflicts Without Litigation

Jossey-Bass Publishers · San Francisco

MEDIATION
A Comprehensive Guide to Resolving Conflicts Without Litigation
by Jay Folberg and Alison Taylor

Copyright © 1984 by: Jossey-Bass Inc., Publishers
350 Sansome Street
San Francisco, California 94104

Jay Folberg
Alison Taylor
10015 S.W. Terwilliger Boulevard
Portland, Oregon 97219

Library of Congress Cataloging in Publication Data

Folberg, Jay (date)
    Mediation : a comprehensive guide to resolving conflicts without
litigation.

    Bibliography: p. 359
    Includes index.
    1. Conflict management.   2. Mediation.   3. Dispute
resolution (Law)—United States.   I. Taylor, Alison,
1950-   . II. Title.
HM136.F54   1984   303.6   83-49259
ISBN 0-87589-594-8

Manufactured in the United States of America

JACKET DESIGN BY WILLI BAUM

FIRST EDITION
    HB Printing   10 9 8 7 6

Code 8414

✸ ✸ ✸ ✸ ✸

Foreword

Conflict and dispute are inevitable and pervasive aspects of life. They have valuable individual and social functions—they provide the impetus for social change and individual psychological development. The question is not how to avoid or suppress conflict; doing so usually has harmful or stagnating consequences. Rather, the question is how to create the conditions that encourage constructive, enlivening confrontation of the conflict. A useful distinction can be made between lively controversy and deadly quarrel.

From the theoretical and practical work done on conflict resolution during the past several decades, there has begun to emerge a coherent set of ideas and a systematic technology for training people in how to foster the constructive rather than destructive potential in conflicts. These developments may have profound significance for promoting individual and social well-being. Although conflict is a pervasive aspect of life, most people have developed only meager skills for handling the difficult conflicts they confront in the course of their lives. This is true for conflicts in our personal and family lives, in groups and organizations, and even in international relations. The emerging theory and technology in the area of conflict resolution provide the possibility of training mediators to help people involved in a dispute manage their conflict more productively.

Jay Folberg and Alison Taylor have drawn extensively on the accumulated theoretical work and practical experience of scholars and practitioners in the field of conflict resolution in writing this very useful, comprehensive guide to the mediation process. Their book will not only be of value to mediators and would-be mediators but also to the various social practitioners—administrators, counselors, therapists, teachers, and so on—who are often called upon as neutral third parties to help disputants resolve their conflicts. It is an excellent, detailed handbook for those who are interested in becoming mediators, but it is more than a manual for practice. It articulates intellectual and ethical frameworks for mediation that are important contributions to the development of a profession of mediation.

March 1984   Morton Deutsch
                                            Edward Lee Thorndike Professor
                                            of Psychology and Education
                                            Teachers College
                                            Columbia University

※ ※ ※ ※ ※

Preface

Public and professional interest in mediation has increased dramatically in the last few years. Mediation is an intervention that is intended to resolve disputes and manage conflict by facilitating decision making. Because it differs from other conflict resolution processes—counseling, negotiation, arbitration, litigation—it has evolved a philosophical orientation and specific techniques appropriate to its particular goals. A growing number of practitioners in the helping services identify themselves as mediators, and mediation has become a course of study in many curricula. Although numerous journal articles and a few books have been published on aspects of mediation, such as its use in labor conflicts or family disputes, no one volume has provided a foundation of knowledge and skill in the emerging uses of mediation for a broad range of conflict situations. Our book has been designed to fill that gap.

In *Mediation: A Comprehensive Guide to Resolving Conflicts Without Litigation,* we present what is currently known about mediation practices and offer a framework for effective mediation. We trace the historical evolution of mediation and discuss its uses in various social and cultural contexts. We then spell out the stages in mediation, concepts useful in developing needed skills, and various approaches to the process. Throughout, we provide perspectives on both practical and policy issues facing mediators so they may share

xi

in the "professionalization" of mediation. By discussing the special techniques and specific applications of mediation, our book helps readers understand and put into practice those skills necessary for effective mediation. By emphasizing the importance of educational and ethical standards, this book contributes to the growth and development of mediation as a professional practice.

We have written this book for several groups. First are the helping professionals: therapists, counselors, psychologists, social workers, lawyers, and health care providers who must deal with interpersonal conflicts in order to do their jobs effectively. All will benefit from the knowledge and practice base provided. Those in public or private practice who wish to diversify their present services to include mediation will find practical, how-to advice and specific details on a range of topics, from improving communication to actually setting up a separate mediation service. Practicing mediators seeking to enhance both their understanding of mediation concepts and their techniques will also benefit from this volume.

Second, the book will serve as a training manual for beginning mediators from a variety of backgrounds. In addition, it can be used in academic programs in counseling, social work, psychology, education, law, health care, management, and business; it is ideally suited for interdisciplinary courses.

Third, the book is intended for persons who want to integrate mediation into their existing roles without necessarily becoming professional mediators. Those who will find the material complete and yet easily readable include teachers and school counselors, administrators and managers in various public and private settings, police officers and members of community boards or neighborhood dispute resolution centers. In short, the mediation process outlined can be used by everyone who is responsible for promoting cooperation among people.

The mediation process can be applied to a variety of personal, social, and economic problems—such as divorce, custody and visitation decisions, neighborhood differences, educational conflicts, minority and racial tensions, environmental concerns, business and labor disputes, and health care issues. Because mediation can be applied to so many different types of conflicts, we offer examples from several diverse situations for clarity and illustrative purposes. We have, however, chosen divorce and custody disputes for many of our examples in order to draw from our professional experience and because we anticipate the greatest immediate use of mediation in domestic conflicts. We have included many recommended readings, each with a short explanatory annotation, to encourage readers to learn more and to obtain a different perspective of the principles presented. References have been cited only when appropriate for attribution or helpful for those seeking more comprehensive coverage than might be supplied by the recommended readings.

Throughout the book we refer to those who are mediating their disputes as *participants* or occasionally *disputants*. The word *participant* better conveys the idea of involvement that is essential to the mediation process. The term *parties* implies the traditional legal adversarial system; the word *client* seems too closely connected to law and counseling practices. A mediator does not have just one "client," since *all* participants are to be served by the mediator, not as advocate or therapist but as facilitator. Those involved in mediation are not simply recipients of a service; they are actively involved in the process as participants.

Part One introduces the reader to mediation and conflict resolution, explaining what they are—and what they are not. Chapter One discusses the development of mediation, provides a working definition, and offers a set of assumptions that serve as the conceptual framework for the use of mediation. Chapter Two focuses on the nature of conflict and the alternatives for resolving it—mediators should understand how conflicts arise and be familiar with other conflict resolution processes.

Part Two presents our procedural approach and details skills and concepts necessary for effective mediation. In Chapter Three, we outline a generic seven-stage process that encompasses various applications and uses of mediation. Chapter Four provides mediators with a set of principles and practical theories about the behavior they will see in participants. Chapter Five considers the verbal and nonverbal skills required by all mediators. Chapters Four and Five might seem elementary to those who come to mediation from the fields of psychology and counseling; nevertheless, they summarize current concepts about motivation, empathy, behavior, internal conflict, stress, and loss, which every mediator can use. Even those who have had rigorous training in these concepts are invited to review them and consider their application to mediation situations.

Part Three describes various mediation styles and discusses the practical applications of the mediation process to many diverse conflict situations. Chapter Six examines in detail different styles and approaches to mediating conflict. Chapter Seven is devoted to the rapidly growing area of family mediation, particularly divorce and custody disputes. Chapter Eight looks at a number of other types of conflicts, from housing to environmental issues, where mediation offers a valuable intervention.

Part Four addresses the educational, professional, and practical considerations in preparing for and developing a mediation practice, as well as the special concerns that may arise in offering mediation services. Chapter Nine offers a blueprint for additional education and training to become a mediator. The standards and safeguards required for the practice of mediation may differ from those applicable to other professional services, as Chapter Ten explains; this chapter also lays out relevant legal issues. Chapter Eleven describes how to set up a mediation practice and the many practical and economic decisions that must be made. Considerations involved in receiving and referring participants are discussed in Chapter Twelve. Chapter Thirteen focuses on the important topic of ethnic differences, as well as resistance among participants.

We have included several resources at the end of the book to give readers some basic tools: a contract that outlines obligations and that can be modified to each mediator's practice, a set of guidelines that form basic assumptions and expectations for participants, and a mediated plan to illustrate the outcome of the process. A proposed code of professional conduct for mediators is reproduced, and a list of national organizations is provided for obtaining further information and developing professional contacts.

Mediation is preferable to the alternatives of resolving disputes by coercion or adversarial proceedings. The current interest in mediation is a reflection of both the conflicted times in which we live and the inherent human desire to act fairly with one another.

Acknowledgments

Many people have contributed their energy and expertise to this book. Like a reliable and skilled midwife, Lenair Mulford has helped to deliver this mindchild into the world with her patience and marvelous word processing skills. Janis Alton, Sandra Hansberger, Turid Owren, and Susan Andersen have provided research and editorial assistance. Valerie McCourt and Ronald Blosser attended to production details. This book was prepared with the facilities and staff assistance of the Lewis and Clark Law School, for which we are grateful.

Substantive review of some chapters was provided by William Glasser, John Geisler, Nell Babcock, Kim Kay, Bruce Mack, Ronald Lansing, and Steven Waksman. Special thanks for their information on environmental issues goes to Michael Blumm, Emil Berg, Katherine Coffin, James Herlihy, and Stanley Biles. Christopher Moore provided valuable comments on the entire manuscript. Finally, the workshop by the Neighborhood Justice Center of Atlanta helped us reconfirm the universality of the mediation process.

Portland, Oregon   Jay Folberg
March 1984   Alison Taylor

Contents

Part Two: Mediation Stages, Concepts, and Skills

Part Three: Varieties of Mediation and Applications to Practice

※ ※ ※ ※ ※

The Authors

Jay Folberg is a professor of law at Lewis and Clark Law School and serves on the adjunct faculty of the Department of Psychiatry at the School of Medicine, Oregon Health Sciences University. He is president of the Association of Family and Conciliation Courts, past chairman of the Mediation and Arbitration Committee of the American Bar Association–Family Law Section, consultant to the National Divorce Mediation Research Project, distinguished affiliate member of the American Association of Marriage and Family Therapists, and on the panel of arbitrators of the American Arbitration Association. He has served as a mediator for the past eight years. Folberg received his B.A. degree in economics from San Francisco State University in 1963 and his J.D. degree from the University of California at Berkeley (Boalt Hall) in 1968.

Alison Taylor serves on the adjunct faculty of Lewis and Clark Law School and has a private mediation practice. She is a partner of a consulting firm providing mediation training and services for business, education, and social services. She is a certified mediator of special education disputes for the Oregon Department of Education. She received her B.A. degree in interdisciplinary liberal arts from Coe College in 1972 and her M.A. degree in counseling and personnel from Western Michigan University in 1979. She has written on the subjects of mediation and interviewing techniques for practicing mediators and for attorneys.

　　Alison Taylor and Jay Folberg currently coteach a course in dispute resolution at Lewis and Clark Law School.

※ ※ ※ ※ ※

Mediation

A Comprehensive Guide to Resolving Conflicts Without Litigation

With deep appreciation for the support of our spouses, parents, and children, who all, in their own ways, taught us something about conflict resolution and without whom this book would not have been possible.

We dedicate this book to the promotion of peace.

1

Development, Definition, and Functions of Mediation

Mediation as an alternative to self-help or formal legal procedures is not entirely new. Forms of conflict resolution in which a third party helps disputants resolve their conflicts and come to their own decisions have probably been practiced since the existence of three or more people on earth. Mediation, like most concepts, is not a novel invention but an adaptation of that which has already existed in other cultures or in other times.

Historical and Cultural Roots

In ancient China, mediation was the principal means of resolving disputes (Brown, 1982). The Confucian view was that optimum resolution of a dispute was achieved by moral persuasion and agreement rather than sovereign coercion. Confucian beliefs proposed the existence of a natural harmony in human affairs that should not be disrupted. Unilateral self-help and adversary proceedings presume the end of a harmonious relationship and would thus be the antithesis of the peace and understanding central to Confucian thought (Cohen, 1966). Mediation on a grand scale continues to be practiced today in the People's Republic of China through the institution of People's Conciliation Committees. Even in the formal Chinese legal system, considerable importance is placed on self-determination and mediation in the resolution of all types of disputes (Ginsberg, 1978).

Conciliation and mediation have a rich history in Japanese law and customs (Henderson, 1965). The leader of the village community was expected to help community members settle their disputes. Provision for conciliation of personal disputes in Japanese courts was enacted prior to World War II (Schimazu, 1982). Many writers, analyzing the litigious quality of American society, have noted the relative absence of lawyers in Japan. The tradition of conciliation and mediation is so imbued in Japan that there are rumored to be more flower arrangers in Japan than attorneys (Vroom, Fossett, and Wakefield, 1981). However, this preference for mediation in Japan may reflect a system of procedural barriers to formal litigation as much as a popular preference for less formal dispute resolution (Haley, 1978).

In parts of Africa, the custom of assembling a *moot*, or neighborhood meeting, has long provided an informal mechanism for resolving a variety of interpersonal disputes. Any disputant or neighbor may call a moot where a respected notable or "big man" often serves as a mediator to help the involved parties resolve their conflict cooperatively. The role of the notable and the tradition of the moot vary from one community to another, but all appear to seek settlement without judge, arbitrator, or the use of sanctions (Gibbs, 1963). The success of the moot may be based, in part, on the extended kinship circles within many African communities (Gulliver, 1979).

The extended family and kinship circles have provided a mediation resource in many lands and cultures (Vroom, Fossett, and Wakefield, 1981). Patriarchal as well as matriarchal family leaders have offered wisdom, precedents, and models to assist family members in resolving their disputes. As rural families gathered together in villages, as villages grew into cities, and as the nuclear family supplanted the extended family, the family structure began to provide less of a resource for conflict resolution. People turned increasingly to formal rather than informal mechanisms to resolve their disputes (Merry, 1982).

The church or temple has played an important part in resolving conflict among its members for centuries. The local parish priest, minister, or rabbi was frequently called upon to serve as a mediator, particularly in family disputes, to suggest ways that the disputants might learn to live with each other or reorganize their relationships. There is a rich New Testament tradition of mediation stemming from the recognition that Paul talked to the congregation at Corinth, suggesting that they should not take their disputes to the court but ought rather to appoint people of their own community to settle their disputes (1 Corinthians 6:1–4). Mediation is consistent with, if not central to, the biblical values of forgiveness, reconciliation, and community (Brunner, 1947). There is both a biblical foundation and approval for mediators able to bring about peaceful coexistence: "Blessed be the peacemakers for they shall be called the sons of God" (Matthew, 5:9).

Ethnic and religious groups, as well as other subcultures, have historically established their own alternative systems for dispute resolution (Pospisil, 1967). They desired to avoid imposition of the majority government's values and sought to retain their own means of resolving conflicts. The Jewish Beth Din, a council of local rabbis, has existed for this purpose for many generations and in many different settings (Yaffe, 1972). Merchant groups, trade councils, gypsies, and even organized crime have all felt a common need to resolve disputes, one way or another, without the imposition of outside authority. Resolution of interpersonal and commercial conflicts between members of a subgroup with the assistance of respected third parties from the group was a way to retain a cherished independence and set of norms (Abel, 1973; Merry, 1982). Mediation, and to some extent arbitration, represented a form of personal, cultural, and religious empowerment without conceding the power to decide personal disputes to the king or other secular authority.

In the United States, Chinese immigrants set up the Chinese Benevolent Association to resolve by mediation disputes between members of the community and within the family (Doo, 1973). In 1920, the American Jewish community established its own mediation forum, the Jewish Conciliation Board, in New York City (Yaffe, 1972). The early Quakers in the United States practiced both mediation and arbitration to resolve their commercial disputes and marital disagreements without resorting to litigation (Ordione, 1954). More recently, the Christian Conciliation Service has established several pilot projects to train and provide church mediators for the resolution of personal disputes (Buzzard, 1982).

The most familiar model for mediation in the United States comes from the dispute resolution procedures in labor/management relations (Merry, 1982). Labor disputes—like family disputes, neighborhood conflicts, environmental issues, and other relation-based tensions—represent a "polycentric," or many centered, situation (Fuller, 1963). Labor relationships are long-term and depend on future cooperation of the parties, in contrast to isolated disputes dependent for resolution on findings of historical fact for the purpose of deciding upon a "winner" and "loser" who need have no further dealings with one another (Fuller, 1971). Some of the early writing proposing the adaptation of alternative dispute settlement techniques for interpersonal conflict drew heavily from the background and experience of labor and industrial dispute resolution (Kressel and others, 1977).

Beginning in the late 1960s, American society experienced a flowering of interest in alternative forms of dispute settlement, although there were antecedents (Harrington, 1982). This period was characterized by strife and discontent on many fronts. The Vietnam War protests, civil rights struggles, student unrest, growing consumer awareness, gender role reexamination, and statutory creation of many new causes of action appeared to produce less tolerance for perceived wrongs and frustrations (Sander, 1982). There was also a growing acceptance of divorce as a common life event. Conflicts that in the past might have been resolved by deference, avoidance, or resignation were directed to the courts.

Court filings of civil and criminal complaints expanded rapidly. Filings of domestic relations cases soared. Alarms about delay were sounded by the judicial and legal establishments (Burger, 1982; Kennedy, 1978). The public became increasingly disillusioned with the formality, expense, and slowness of judicial proceedings, and concerns were voiced about the denial of access to justice (Rosenberg, 1972).

In response to the litigation explosion, the popular dissatisfaction with the formal system of justice, and the growing American propensity to pursue grievances and claims, a number of existing organizations attempted to provide mediation services (Brown, 1982). New entities also emerged to fill the need for alternative forms of dispute resolution. In 1964 the Civil Rights Act established the Community Relations Service in the U.S. Department of Justice to aid in the settlement of racial and community disputes. The Federal Mediation and Conciliation Service (FMCS), established in 1947 to provide dispute resolution services for industry and labor, briefly experimented in 1978 with offering the considerable expertise of its professional staff for the resolution of nonlabor disputes.

The American Arbitration Association (AAA) began developing guidelines and training for the application of conciliation, mediation, and arbitration in consumer, community, and domestic disputes. Professionals from AAA and FMCS and others created the Society of Professionals In Dispute Resolution (SPIDR) in order to promote greater use of "neutrals" in resolving all types of disputes. A number of sections of the American Bar Association (ABA) established mediation and arbitration committees to explore the application of alternative dispute resolution to specific subjects. In 1976 the ABA established a Special Committee on Alternative Means of Dispute Resolution.

The Association of Family and Conciliation Courts, founded in 1963 to promote court-connected family conciliation, began promoting the use of mediation as an alternative to family court litigation. Family mediation has more recently become an active area of private practice that has given birth to several new national organizations, including the Family Mediation Association and the Academy of Family Mediators (Brown, 1982).

The Federal Law Enforcement Assistance Administration took an early interest in developing alternatives to the courts for resolution of personal and community conflicts that led to crimes. In 1980 Congress responded further to the growing interest in alternative conflict resolution by passing the Dispute Resolution Act, which called for the establishment of alternative dispute resolution programs nationwide to be administered by the Justice Department. Though passage of this act was heralded as a major triumph for advancement of alternatives to the courts, Congress has never allocated the money needed for its implementation (Vroom, Fossett, and Wakefield, 1981).

On the local level, many neighborhood justice centers and community boards blossomed, similar to the emergence in the 1950s of "Good Neighbor Committees" in Poland (Shonholtz, 1983; Harrington, 1982). Family mediation centers and clinics have also been established in many communities. Some of these local efforts have been connected to the courts; others have positioned themselves as the antithesis of anything related to established courts. Some are funded by the community or government, others are backed by foundations or established agencies, while some depend on fees for service. All are related in their efforts to help disputants resolve their own conflicts (Milne, 1982, 1983).

A few local, regional, and national organizations came into existence in the 1970s to mediate certain types of disputes. The Institute for Environmental Mediation in the Northwest and the Center for Environmental Conflict Resolution (Resolve), now part of The Conservation Foundation, are two examples involving natural resources. The Rocky Mountain Center for the Environment (ROMCOE), now called ACCORD Associates, was the first environmental mediation group and was founded in 1968 (Moore, 1983a). Special organizations that apply mediation and other dispute resolution techniques to settle institutional grievances and disputes between business entities have sprung up on both coasts. Other organizations provide mediation services to settle housing, health service, medical, and educational disputes. These specialized efforts often follow the example of labor/management dispute resolution panels and organizations.

All the current efforts for noncoercive dispute resolution were encouraged and enriched, directly or indirectly, by the writings of many scholars, theoreticians, and practitioners who studied alternative dispute resolution mechanisms. Cultural anthropologists such as Laura Nader (1969, 1978, 1979, 1980) and P. H. Gulliver (1979) have studied dispute settlement mechanisms in different settings and interpreted them so that others could apply the principles cross-culturally. Law professor Richard Abel (1973, 1982), a prolific author and editor, has helped focus interdisciplinary, theoretical thinking about conflict resolution. Legal scholars, most notably

Lon Fuller (1963, 1971), Frank Sander (1976, 1977, 1982), and Roger Fisher (1978, 1983), all of Harvard Law School, have helped shape professional and public thinking on the procedures, application, and techniques for the resolution of conflict outside the courts. Robert Mnookin and Lewis Kornhauser (1979) have analyzed the role of legal norms in the settlement of domestic disputes. David Trubek, Marc Galanter, and Stewart Macaulay of the University of Wisconsin Dispute Processing Research Program (1983) have given an empirical dimension to the study of legal dispute settlement. Three noted mediators with interdisciplinary backgrounds, O. J. Coogler (1978), Howard Irving (1980), and John Haynes (1981), have published books in recent years that have helped to guide and promote a rapid growth in the application of mediation techniques to family and divorce disputes. Probably the most influential and perceptive analysis of conflict resolution in general is that of Morton Deutsch (1973). His book, *The Resolution of Conflict,* examines constructive and destructive processes of dispute settlement and appears to have profoundly shaped the movement toward mediation and other cooperative conflict processes. Deutsch's work was also a significant inspiration in the preparation of this volume.

Definition

The history of mediation only begins to define what it is. Many questions about mediation are answered by understanding what mediation is and what it is not. The practice of mediation falls along a spectrum that defies a strict definition. The specifics of mediation depend on what is being mediated, the parties in dispute, who is doing the mediating, and the setting in which mediation is offered. Mediation is first and foremost a *process* that transcends the content of the conflict it is intended to resolve.

Mediation is an alternative to violence, self-help, or litigation that differs from the processes of counseling, negotiation, and arbitration. It can be defined as the process by which the participants, together with the assistance of a neutral person or persons, systematically isolate disputed issues in order to develop options, consider alternatives, and reach a consensual settlement that will accommodate their needs. Mediation is a process that emphasizes the participants' own responsibility for making decisions that affect their lives. It is therefore a self-empowering process.

The most useful way to look at mediation is to see it as a goal-directed, problem-solving intervention. It is intended to resolve disputes and reduce conflict as well as provide a forum for decision making. Even if all elements of the dispute may not be resolved, the underlying conflict can be understood by the participants and reduced to a manageable level. Thus some see the principal goal of mediation as conflict management rather than dispute resolution, and some of the literature refers to mediation as a process of conflict management (Haynes, 1981). This distinction between the manifest dispute to be resolved and the underlying conflict that may remain, perhaps in more manageable form, is discussed in subsequent chapters. For the time being, let us accept both dispute resolution and conflict management as complementary and realistic goals of mediation.

Mediation has definite stages involving a series of techniques for accomplishing necessary tasks (Taylor, 1981). It is a finite process that produces specific outcomes by utilizing the values, norms, and principles of the participants rather than those of mediators. The objectives of mediation are:

• Production of a plan (agreement) for the future that the participants can accept and comply
• Preparation of the participants to accept the consequences of their own decisions
• Reduction of the anxiety and other negative effects of the conflict by helping the participants devise a consensual resolution

Mediation is usually a short-term process rather than a long-term intervention. It is interactive rather than interpersonal. The participants' personality structures and behavior (including manipulation, overt anger, withdrawal, power struggles) that may have created the interactional problems may be discussed, but personality is not the primary focus unless the behavior blocks the mediation process. Mediation is more concerned with how the parties will resolve the conflict and create a plan than with personal histories. In this respect, mediation is cognitive and behavioral in perspective rather than existential. It is more concerned with the present and the future than with the past. Mediation helps to:

- Reduce the obstacles to communication between participants
- Maximize the exploration of alternatives
- Address the needs of everyone involved
- Provide a model for future conflict resolution

Trust and confidence by the parties involved, as in any helping relationship, are necessary for an effective mediation process. The development of a therapeutic relationship between the parties and the mediator is not a goal, however. The relationship that is formed may be an important means, but it is subordinate to the orientation toward tasks and goals. Participation in mediation may or may not have a therapeutic effect on the parties. It is not intended to bring insight into past behavioral patterns or change personality. Mediation is task-directed and goal-oriented. It looks at results rather than the internal causes of conflict. It discourages dependence on the professional rather than promoting it.

Mediation is not primarily didactic. It is an experiential process requiring active participation. While there may be "take-home" knowledge that is derived from the experience of mediation, its primary focus is on the solution of the task and the development of a plan of action for the future. Mediation is not a new therapy method, nor is it a panacea for all psychological and interactive problems. It should be seen as a set of skills and a process that can be used selectively by professionals when the problems demand a coherent agreement between conflicting participants. Mediation will not replace present theories of behavior or therapy; it will not replace long-term therapy of behavioral, perceptual, or personality problems; nor will it replace the need for legal information and advice. It can, however, be a useful intervention technique when the situation calls for a structured agreement to a conflict (see Chapter Three).

Rationale

Both the rationale for mediation as an alternative to the adversary process and the effect of mediated agreements appear to make it a promising, if not compelling, process when compared to the adversarial model. Mediation can educate the participants about each other's needs and provide a personalized model for settling future disputes between them. It can thus help them learn to work together, isolate the issues to be decided, and see that through cooperation all can make positive gains.

Mediation offers this advantage because it is not bound by the rules of procedure and substantive law, as well as certain assumptions, that dominate the adversary process. The ultimate authority in mediation belongs to the participants themselves, and they may fashion a unique solution that will work for them without being strictly governed by precedent or being unduly concerned with the precedent they may set for others. They may, with the help of their mediator, consider a comprehensive mix of their needs, interests, and whatever else they deem relevant regardless of rules of evidence or strict adherence to substantive law. Unlike the adjudicatory process, the emphasis is not on who is right or wrong or who wins and who loses, but rather upon establishing a workable solution that meets the participant's unique needs. Mediation is a win/win process.

By definition, a consensual agreement, whether reached through mediation or direct negotiation, reflects the participants' own preferences and will be more acceptable in the long run than one imposed by a court. In the process of mediation, participants formulate their own agreement and make an emotional investment in its success. They are more likely to support its terms than those of an agreement negotiated or imposed by others. The lack of self-determination in adversary proceedings helps account for the never-ending litigation surrounding some conflicts.

The reduction of hostility—by encouraging direct communication between the participants through the process of mediation—facilitates the permanence of a settlement. It naturally reduces the likelihood that a legal battle will continue beyond the mediation process. Mediation tends to diffuse hostilities by promoting cooperation through a structured process. In contrast, litigation tends to focus hostilities and harden the disputants' anger into rigidly polarized positions. The adversarial process, with its dependence upon attorneys on behalf of the clients, tends to deny the parties the opportunity of taking control of their own situation and increases their dependence on outside authority. The self-esteem and sense of competence derived from the mediation process are important by-products that help to provide self-direction and lessen the need for participants to continue fighting.

Mediation works very well for many types of disputes. Groups and individuals who attempt to resolve their differences by using this process generally respond favorably to postmediation evaluations about its fairness and value.

Preliminary studies on the effects of mediation, while primarily limited to divorce cases, indicate that the theoretical promises of mediation are real and measurable. In the Denver Custody Mediation Project (Pearson and Thoennes, 1982), the agreement rate for mediated cases was 58 percent. Of those couples who did not reach agreement during formal mediation, 65 percent later reached agreement prior to their court hearing. In other words, less than 16 percent of those who went through mediation in the Denver program ultimately relied on the court to decide custody and visitation issues. By contrast, 50 percent of those in the control group who did not engage in mediation had a contested court hearing on the custody or visitation issue.

The Toronto Conciliation Project (Irving and others, 1981) consisted of two interlocking studies focusing on the effectiveness of court-connected "mediational counseling" in custody and support disputes as a court service. Seventy percent of all couples who used the service and for whom complete data were available either reached a written agreement or reconciled.

The Family Mediation Center in Portland, Oregon, co-founded by one of the authors, is a fee-charging service that uses lawyer/therapist teams to mediate comprehensive divorce settlements involving custody, support, and property (Folberg, 1981). After three years of operation, the center reported that divorcing couples reached agreement on all issues in more than 80 percent of cases. In many cases where a comprehensive agreement was not reached, the parties came to agreement on at least some aspects of the divorce custody, support, or property division aspects.

Other reports on the incidence of agreements reached through mediation support its success, though the reported percentage of cases resulting in agreement varies. Mediation works, and it helps participants feel better about the outcome than do other dispute resolution methods. In some studies, even participants who did not sign a mediated settlement reported they would not change their decision to mediate if they had it to do over. Despite the outcome, they said that mediation as a process was a better option.

Most of those who use divorce mediation services are pleased with the process. In the Denver Custody Mediation Project, 93 percent of all the clients who agreed to mediate said they would mediate again in the future or recommend the process to a divorcing friend. Even 81 percent of those who were unsuccessful in mediation would recommend it to a friend. Eighty-five percent of the mediation clients reported that their agreements were "complete and thorough," and a majority felt that the mediated agreements they reached were "perfectly fair." In contrast, only 33 percent of the control group who went through the court process reported the process to be "perfectly fair" and only 20 percent of those who reached a stipulated nonmediated agreement thought it was "perfectly fair." (See Pearson and Thoennes, 1982.) A one-year follow-up survey in the Toronto Project revealed that 81 percent of those who reached a mediated agreement were "somewhat satisfied," "satisfied," or "very satisfied" with the total agreement (Irving and others, 1981).

Similar satisfaction has been noted in other studies of comprehensive mediation to resolve financial and custody issues upon divorce. A study of sixty-nine cases using private, structured mediation in Atlanta, Georgia, and Winston-Salem, North Carolina, was compared with sixty-two cases from Charlotte, North Carolina, in which two adversarial attorneys negotiated a separation agreement. It was reported that 91 percent using mediation were satisfied with their final agreement whereas only 50 percent were satisfied with the agreement reached adversarially (Parker, 1980). Steven Bahr reports that 53 percent of the divorce mediation clients he studied in Fairfax County, Virginia, were "very satisfied" with their final mediated decisions on money, property, and custody in contrast to 15 percent of "very satisfied" clients in a sample of nonmediated adversary cases. While none of the mediation clients was "very dissatisfied" and only 10 percent were "somewhat dissatisfied," 41 percent of clients using the traditional adversary system were either "very" or "somewhat" dissatisfied (Bahr, 1981).

Divorce mediation has been studied more than other applications but is not the only mediation use that has generated reports of user satisfaction. The significant satisfaction of participants in special education mediation is reported by Gallant (1982). Neighborhood justice centers also report high user satisfaction (Cook, Rochl, and Shepard, 1980). Popular media attention and the growth of mediation programs also attest to the user acceptance of this conflict resolution alternative.

In summary, then, mediation is a conflict resolution process which, when integrated with a supportive legal system, provides the participants with not only a plan of action for the future but also a greater sense of satisfaction about the process they have undergone than do other methods of settling disputes. It is ideally suited to polycentric disputes and conflicts between those with a continuing relationship, since it minimizes intrusion, emphasizes cooperation, involves self-determined criteria of resolution, and provides a model of interaction for future disputes.

Basic Propositions and Assumptions

Most mediators appear to share a set of principles, although these principles have rarely been systematically stated. The propositions outlined by Deutsch (1973) provide general truths about the resolution of conflict, whereas those offered by Taylor (1981) are more directed at the mediation process. The propositions listed below are intended to help form a framework of values and beliefs that will allow mediators to develop a shared theory of practice. Identifying, testing, and refining a set of principles upon which mediators can agree will allow mediation to grow into a separate and distinct profession. The "professionalization" of mediation will better serve the interests of the public as well as the needs of the mediator. These principles, which we shall call propositions, form the philosophy of mediation.

Propositions about mediation include beliefs about participants' abilities and motivation and beliefs about human processes in general. We propose the following eight propositions, further described in subsequent chapters, as the basis for a system of shared, unified beliefs for mediators:

- *Proposition 1.* People try to escape what they perceive as negative or destructive (pain) and go toward what they perceive as advantageous and positive (pleasure).
- *Proposition 2.* People make more complete, and therefore better, decisions when they are consciously aware of the feelings created by conflicts and deal effectively with those feelings. ("Dealing effectively" means integrating the feelings into decisions without allowing the emotions to overwhelm rational concerns.)
- *Proposition 3.* The participants in a personal dispute can generally make better decisions about their own lives than can an outside authority such as an arbitrator.
- *Proposition 4.* The participants to an agreement are more likely to abide by its terms if they feel some responsibility for the outcome and develop a commitment to the process used to reach agreement.
- *Proposition 5.* In mediation the past history of the participants is only important in relation to the present or as a basis for predicting future needs, intentions, abilities, and reactions to decisions.
- *Proposition 6.* The more accurately a mediated agreement reflects the needs, intentions, and abilities of the participants, the more likely it is to last.
- *Proposition 7.* Since the participants' needs, intentions, and abilities will probably change, the process should include a way of modifying the agreement in the future. Thus change is seen as a constructive and viable part of the agreement and must be considered in the mediation process.
- *Proposition 8.* The mediation process is substantially the same for all participants and all situations, but techniques, scheduling, and tasks to be accomplished must vary to match the circumstances, the participants, and the uniqueness of the mediator.

Acceptance of these propositions, or similar principles, is essential to the development of mediation as a process and a profession. While these propositions are quite basic, they are useful as a starting point for further development. (For a list of forty--eight other propositions and their references, see Mack and Snyder, 1973.)

Although these eight propositions are thought to be universal, other basic assumptions need to be confirmed by the participants in each case. It is normally true, for example, that both participants in a mediation session wish for the conflicts between them to be resolved. This is particularly true when the mediation process is voluntary, but it may or may not be true in court-mandated mediation services. A further assumption that should be confirmed with the participants is that they must, to some degree, change their perceptions, feelings, beliefs, priorities, thoughts, or actions in order to bring about a resolution of the conflict.

Another assumption is that the participants are accepting the mediator as a guide to lead them through the mediation process. In private practice, this assumption should be double-checked and formalized into an employment agreement or agreement to mediate (see Chapter Three and Resource A). Still another assumption is that the mediator's attitudes and conduct provide a model for the mediation process. The participants will expect the mediator to follow the same rules and offer structure and techniques they can use during the course of the mediation session. While this modeling may not be overtly discussed, the mediator must present a clear example of good communication skills and involvement in the process in order to elicit the same from the participants.

Most mediators who have gained expertise in the mediation process share one further assumption. Trained mediators can assist the process better than ad hoc mediators who have not had the benefit of specific education and experience, particularly when the issues have substantial impact. Thus disputes regarding use of natural resources, business mergers, or divorce and custody should be brought to trained mediators rather than well-intentioned but untrained friends or volunteers.

Recommended Reading

Historical and Cultural Roots

Beyond the Courtroom. B. Alper and L. Nichols. Lexington, Mass.:
   Heath, 1981.
        Describes various programs in community justice and con-
flict resolution focused on diverting cases from criminal courts. Includes a chapter on mediation and profiles several ethnic and
cultural models for resolving disputes.

Disputes and Negotiations: A Cross-Cultural Perspective. P. H.
   Gulliver. New York: Academic Press, 1979.
        An anthropological examination of models of dispute nego-
tiation with a chapter devoted to mediation and its role.

"Divorce and Family Mediation: History, Review, Future Directions." D. Brown. *Conciliation Courts Review,* December 1982,
   20, 1-37.
        Comprehensive treatment of the divorce mediation move-
ment—its history, players, procedures, and issues.

Law in Culture and Society. L. Nader (Ed.). Chicago: Aldine, 1969.
        An informative collection of essays, each examining law and
dispute resolution processes in different cultural settings from
American Indian practices to African moots.

The Litigious Society. J. K. Lieberman. New York: Basic Books,
   1981.
        Traces the growth of litigation and the reasons why it has
become this nation's "secular religion."

The Politics of Informal Justice. R. Abel (Ed.). 2 vols. New York:
   Academic Press, 1982.
        Diverse chapters analyze informal mechanisms for dispute
resolution in the United States and other social contexts with an
emphasis on power relationships and political analysis.

Rationale

"Bargaining in the Shadow of the Law: The Case of Divorce."
R. Mnookin and L. Kornhauser. *Yale Law Journal*, 1979, *88*,
950–997.

A provocative discussion of the role of law in private settlement of disputes and the advantages of "private ordering" over
adjudication.

"Mediation—Its Forms and Functions." L. Fuller. *Southern California Law Review*, 1971, *44*, 305–339.

This often cited law review article examines the functions
and limitations of mediation.

"Varieties of Dispute Processing." F. Sander. *Federal Rules Decisions*, 1976, *70*, 111–133.

In this paper, delivered at the Pound Conference on the
Causes of Popular Dissatisfaction with the Administration of Jus-
tice, Professor Sander envisions a multifaceted Dispute Resolution
Center, three models of which are now being established by the
American Bar Association.

2

❈ ❈ ❈ ❈ ❈

Nature of Conflict and Dispute Resolution Processes

The study of conflict and conflict resolution in whatever setting may be the most significant and rewarding study of the decade.—Jandt (1973, p. 5)

Mediation is a process that can be used to resolve many different conflict situations because of the universal nature of conflict. Mediation is only one of several acceptable conflict resolution methods, however; persuasion, problem solving, consensus building, voting, negotiation, arbitration, and litigation are other ways people settle their differences. Each process has different steps, and some are more effective or desirable than others for a particular conflict. Mediators should understand other methods of resolving conflict and may at times need to refer to them or use them. To be an effective mediator, one should have a conceptual understanding of conflict.

The Nature of Conflict

Psychologists, sociologists, lawyers, diplomats, public servants—all deal in their work with conflict. Conflict, whether between individuals, groups, or nations, has certain basic features.

Each discipline and profession has contributed to a better understanding of conflict in specific terms, yet few works have been aimed at understanding conflict as an entity. Fewer still have provided common concepts for those outside of academic circles.

Conflict can be divided into two categories: intrapersonal and interpersonal. The causes and effects of *intrapersonal* conflict, or conflict within the individual, are described in Chapter Four. Mediation is primarily concerned with *interpersonal* conflict—situations that arise between individuals or groups of individuals. The issues discussed during mediation may trigger internal conflict for participants, however, so it is necessary to recognize both kinds of conflict, interpersonal and intrapersonal, and to distinguish between them. We should also note the distinction between conflicts and disputes, though the literature often uses the two terms interchangeably. A *dispute* is an interpersonal conflict that is communicated or manifested. A conflict may not become a dispute if it is not communicated to someone in the form of a perceived incompatibility or a contested claim (Abel, 1973).

Although conflict is not necessarily bad, wrong, or intolerable, our society often views conflict negatively because it is equated with win/lose situations. Conflict can function in important and positive ways: It can help set group boundaries by strengthening group cohesion; it reduces incipient tension by making issues manifest; it clarifies objectives; and it helps establish group norms. (See Coser, 1956, and Mack and Snyder, 1973, for further discussion and references.) Conflict can generate creative energy and improve situations. As Jandt (1973, p. 3) puts it: "Conflict is desirable from at least two standpoints. It has been demonstrated that through conflict man is creative. Further, a relationship in conflict *is* a relationship—not the absence of one. Such a relationship may result in creativity because of its intensity."

Conflict is commonly viewed by the participants as a crisis. A crisis mentality lends itself to destructive processes because people will often rush to use anything they believe will relieve the conflict. Intervention techniques have been developed to help create constructive outcomes from crises, which may result from intrapersonal conflicts. By controlling the perception of what is at stake in a conflict, a mediator can prevent destructive outcomes. This ability to defuse conflict, reframe the issues, and realistically analyze outcomes is an important skill in mediation and is further discussed in many other chapters. Crisis intervention techniques are summarized well by Okun (1982) and are discussed later in the context of crisis mediation.

Kenneth Boulding, in his excellent and seminal work (1962, p. 5), has defined conflict as "a situation of competition in which the parties are *aware* of the incompatibility of potential future positions and in which each party *wishes* to occupy a position which is incompatible with the wishes of the other." Boulding differentiates between static models of conflict and the dynamic or reaction processes of conflict in which the movement of party *A* affects the subsequent movement of party *B*, which in turn affects the action of party *A*, and so on. While others had developed similar dynamic theories using differential equations from physics (Richardson, 1960), Boulding notes that these dynamic processes apply to *all* spheres of human interaction: conflicts between husband and wife, union and management, nation and nation. He views conflict as divisible into three levels: simple conflicts (persons acting for themselves), group conflicts (unorganized subpopulations), and organizational conflicts (representatives).

Boulding believes that conflicts have their own "life cycle" (p. 307). According to his theory, conflicts are spawned, exist for a time, and eventually cease because of their own inherent tendencies, without conflict resolution interventions such as mediation. It may take a long time for unaided conflict to cease, however, as evidenced by the continuation of national and religious feuds spanning decades and even centuries. Boulding's concepts regarding conflict resolution will be discussed later.

Work done by the researchers Dollard and Miller (see the excellent summary of their work by Patterson, 1973) has helped conceptualize three categories of conflicts: approach/approach, approach/avoidance, avoidance/avoidance. While Boulding concentrates on the attributes of the parties in conflict, Dollard and Miller focus on the options for resolution. *Approach/approach* refers to a conflict in which both options for resolving a situation are equally attractive but mutually exclusive—the person can have only one but wants both. *Approach/avoidance* refers to conflicts in which the person desires an option but must not have it for equally strong reasons. Dollard and Miller think this type of conflict is inherent in cases of neurotic repression. The conflict is created by wanting something yet needing to avoid the topic because it is frightening; this conflict leads to repression, a particular type of distortion of reality. (See Chapter Four.) *Avoidance/avoidance* conflicts are caused by disliking both of two options yet having to select one of them—as when an employee is told he must either take a 15 percent pay cut or be moved to a less desirable position in an undesirable part of the country.

A comprehensive analysis of conflict is offered by Rummel (1976), who views it as "the clash of power in the striving of all things to be manifest" or as a set of social behavior, an event, or a process. He further defines conflict as "the process of powers meeting and balancing" (p. 238). This definition seems the most universal and applies equally to human and natural sciences. Since mediators work with people, we shall focus on this definition's implications for interpersonal problems.

Rummel differentiates between latent conflict and actual conflict by devising three levels: (1) potentialities, (2) dispositions and powers, and (3) manifestations. He refines the second category even further by making three subcategories. He defines a *conflict structure* as interests that have a tendency to oppose each other; a *conflict situation* refers to opposing interests, attitudes, or powers that are activated. The third level, *manifest conflict,* is the set of specific behavior or actions—demands, threats, assassinations, terrorism, armed aggression, wars—that signal and comprise the conflict. They are the actions that communicate the conflict, thus making it a dispute by our earlier definition.

An illustration of this tripartite system is in divorce, which is inherently a conflict structure insofar as both persons are headed in opposite directions toward separate goals. Divorce may or may not become a conflict situation by Rummel's definition—in other words, a situation where conflict is activated. There are amicable divorces. If conflict is activated, such actions as a threat to withold custody or one spouse's withdrawal of all the money from the joint savings account would become the manifest conflict in Rummel's terminology.

The life cycle of a conflict can be divided into five phases according to Rummel: (1) the latent conflict, (2) the initiation of conflict, (3) the balancing of power, (4) the balance of power, and (5) the disruption of equilibrium. This five-phase cycle is illustrated in the following example. In environmental issues the interests of the timber industry often diverge from those of conservationists and therefore form a conflict structure (phase 1). This conflict structure may remain latent for many years before a conflict situation emerges, such as the sale of extensive timber rights adjoining a wilderness area (phase 2). After a trigger event, such as a lumber company sending crews to the most sensitive ecological areas for clearcutting, the conservationists and that company are then in a manifest conflict. This uncertain situation requires each opposing interest to prepare for action. These interests must be balanced through coercive means, such as injunction and adjudication, or through noncoercive methods of conflict resolution, such as mediation (phase 3). The disputants must make accommodations through one of these methods in order to resolve the conflict. After a balance point is reached through a conflict resolution process (phase 4), conditions change over time and the balance of power and equilibrium that had been established will also change. Timber markets may decrease or conservationists may change their view about how much damage clearcutting does to the adjoining wilderness (phase 5).

Rummel sees these phases as a continuing spiral, a helix, that is set into motion by change but is shaped by the type of power or society (exchange, authoritative, or coercive) in which it is manifested. When the issue has gone through these five phases, it has completed one turn of the helix. These changes in values and norms can affect the sociocultural structure and these changes in turn may produce new latent conflicts (phase 1) or directly create a manifest conflict (phase 2) by serving as a new trigger event, thus repeating the cycle. Empirical studies have shown some validity to his assertion that there are three kinds of manifest conflicts, each a result of the prevailing power system.

Mediation is therefore one of the processes of balancing power in noncoercive ways that will achieve accommodations and result in agreement. The mediation process can be used at two different times in this conflict cycle. It can be started after a trigger

event or action has pushed the conflict into the realm of manifestation. Or it can be instituted when the people involved are aware of a
conflict structure or conflict situation, thus detouring the usual escalating progression and eliminating the uncertainty and subsequent need for manifested conflict behavior such as threats, denial of
rights, or physical violence. In effect, the mediation process can be
used to prevent the outbreak of manifest conflict behavior.

Rummel's insightful work sets the conceptual stage for conflict resolution processes such as mediation, while at the same time
explaining the scope of conflict within or between societies and
nations. Although Rummel's work is more abstract than others cited
in this chapter, it provides a conceptual framework for the universal
nature of conflict. He points out that the wish to eliminate all three
levels of conflict is a desire for a state of unchanging, homeostatic
balance, a frozen and fixed reality, which is rare indeed in the natural world and perhaps not even desirable. It is well for mediators to
remind themselves and the participants of this observation. In most
cases, mediators only attempt to eliminate the manifest conflict behavior and influence the conflict situation. Conflict structure is
generally dealt with through political, social, and psychological
means that are beyond the scope of the mediation process.

Morton Deutsch (1973) has analyzed the nature of conflict
and offers a conceptualization that can be particularly useful in
mediation. In Deutsch's terminology, the *manifest conflict* is overt or
expressed whereas the *underlying conflict* is implicit, hidden, or
denied. The manifest conflict often involves symbolic components
of the underlying conflict but is felt to be "safer." Thus the manifest
conflict between father and son over the keys to the car seems safer to
dispute than the underlying conflict of who is more powerful. Indian tribes may actively dispute government fishing quotas, while
the underlying conflict involves the more fundamental conflict of
the white man's control and exploitation of Native American traditions. Others have called this dichotomy between the overt dispute
and the hidden conflict the *presenting problem* and the *hidden
agenda,* respectively.

Mediators must sort out which issues are manifest and which
are underlying in order to develop effective options and outcomes. If
the agreements reached in mediation are based only on the manifest
conflicts, they are unlikely to last (see Proposition 6 in Chapter

One). It is important to remember, however, that dealing with the underlying conflicts may be emotionally painful and can stimulate internal conflict and defensive behavior (see Chapter Four) unless dealt with skillfully.

The constructive and destructive outcomes of conflict have been categorized by Deutsch (1973): mutual loss (lose/lose); gain for one and loss for the other (lose/win); mutual gain (win/win). Walton and McKersie (1965) add two other outcomes: stalemate and compromise. Mediation has a distinct advantage over some other methods of conflict resolution in obtaining constructive outcomes because it promotes resolution of the conflict in the mutual gain or win/win mode.

To summarize the preceding definitions, we find it helpful to regard *conflict* as a set of divergent aims, methods, or behavior. The degree of divergence determines the severity and duration of the conflict and affects the likelihood of successful conflict resolution. Conflicts can be subdivided into various types. We believe Rummel's (1976) description of the conflict process to be the most universal, while Deutsch's definitions of manifested and underlying conflicts appear particularly useful for the mediation process.

We define the opposite of conflict as *convergence:* the aims, processes, methods, or behavior that create order, stability, and unity of direction. An analogy from the natural sciences may be helpful in understanding the nature of conflict and convergence.

Nuclear fission is the ultimate in conflict and divergence; fusion, a merging of diverse elements that produces great energy, is the ultimate in convergence. These two forces—divergence or conflict and convergence or unity—can be visualized as intertwining double helixes (Figure 1).

In effect, then, Rummel's scheme of the conflict process can also be used to describe the opposite of conflict: convergence. Like conflict, convergence can be seen as having an inherent tendency (convergence structure), actualized unity of interests, attitudes, or powers (convergence situation), and specific actions that comprise convergence (manifested convergence). While much attention has been given to conflict, this formulation of its opposite, convergence, has been hampered by simplistic notions that convergence is peace and that peace is the absence of conflict. Delineation of the "life

Figure 1. The Double Helix.

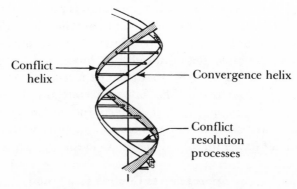

Conflict helix → ← Convergence helix

Conflict resolution processes

cycle" of convergence is a natural outgrowth of the study of conflict and requires further thought. An understanding of the place of conflict and the processes that promote convergence—the mediation process is one—is essential for mediators.

Conflict Resolution and Conflict Management

What is the difference between conflict resolution and conflict management? This question should be answered before we discuss different methods and processes. If conflict is a set of divergent aims, methods, or behavior, then conflict resolution and conflict management are both processes designed to realign those aims, methods, or behavior.

Conflict resolution creates a state of uniformity or convergence of purpose or means; *conflict management* only realigns the divergence enough to render the opposing forces less diametrically opposite or damaging to each other. Conflict management does not demand an identical aim, method, or process, as does conflict resolution, but simply one that is sufficiently aligned to allow unobstructed progress for the separate entities. Using the analogy of the double helix, both conflict resolution and conflict management direct movement from the conflict helix to the convergence helix, the former to a greater degree. In fact, one could say that the term *conflict resolution* is a misnomer since it is named for the condition one is trying to avoid (conflict) rather than its goal. Perhaps it will eventually be known as *convergence promotion*.

Boulding (1962, pp. 308–309) points out that the most commonly used method of conflict resolution is avoidance but the most extreme method is by one side conquering the other, which puts an end to the conflict by coercion or force. If neither method is appropriate or desirable, the third category, procedural resolution, must be used. Our subsequent use of the terms *conflict resolution* and *conflict management* will fall under this category of procedural resolution. To summarize, then, both conflict resolution and conflict management are general terms for specific processes that achieve a balance of power through noncoercive means.

Approaches to Conflict Resolution

Table 1 shows the traditional conflict resolution and management models used in our social, business, institutional, legal, and interpersonal relations. Adjudication and arbitration involve the least control by participants. The other approaches offer varying degrees of participant control depending on the methodology, the setting, and the nature of the conflict.

Adjudication and arbitration are the most rigid and often the least satisfactory methods of conflict resolution for the participants. These processes operate on the following logical principles:

1.   Person 1 wants A.
2.   Person 2 wants B.
3. A and B are mutually exclusive.
4.   Either A or B must be selected.
5.   There are no other options.

The conflicting parties tell their viewpoints and present their evidence, and the judge or arbitrator makes a decision based on criteria that have been predetermined by the parties themselves or by a higher authority (legislation, case precedent, custom, and practice). Howard (1969) points out that these processes are but one form of conflict resolution. However, litigation has been used so extensively in our society that it has become the norm. The chief justice of the United States Supreme Court has urged reform and the development of alternative methods of resolving disputes (Burger, 1977); many

Table 1. Conflict Resolution Processes.

Process	Provider (or Decider)	Process Sequence
Adjudication and arbitration	Judge or arbitrator; higher authority	1. Listens to each side's presentation. 2. Decides option based on predetermined criteria (legislation, precedent, fairness, etc.).
Counseling	Counselor or therapist; manager	1. Gains rapport. 2. Assesses the real problems. 3. Applies intervention strategy.
Negotiation[a]	Lawyer or agent; parties themselves	1. Orientation and positioning. 2. Argumentation. 3. Crises. 4. Agreement or final breakdown.
Problem solving[b]	Individual or delegated official of an organization	1. Identifies the problem. 2. Communicates with appropriate people. 3. Develops alternatives. 4. Decides on alternative. 5. Carries out action. 6. Monitors to ensure completion. 7. Evaluates effectiveness.
Mediation	Mediator; selected third-party facilitator	1. Introduces, structures, gains rapport. 2. Finds out facts, isolates issues. 3. Helps create alternatives. 4. Guides negotiation and decision making. 5. Clarifies/writes an agreement or plan. 6. Provides for legal review and processing. 7. Available for follow-up, review, revision.

[a]Williams' (1983) legal negotiation process.
[b]McMaster model (Epstein, Bishop, and Baldwin, 1982).

others (Curran, 1977; Felstiner and Drew, 1978; Sarat and Grossman, 1975) have pointed to the legal and social problems created by using this form of conflict resolution as a first resort.

Litigation, adjudication, and arbitration have been used successfully where hierarchical systems demand an acceptance of higher authority, but they seem less suited as a first choice for conflict resolution in a society where great value is placed on individual choice and freedom, where structures are more collective and egalitarian, and where few persons or institutions are universally accepted as worthy of having the necessary authority to impose decisions. Moreover, the criteria used to make the decision are often themselves in as much dispute as the ability of the arbitrator or judge to evaluate the information. As Deutsch (1973) points out, if the parties have no faith in the criteria or the arbitrator but are bound by the power vested in them, the issue will resurface in further conflicts and disputes.

Counseling can be used as a conflict management or conflict resolution process primarily for intrapersonal conflicts, although some therapies apply counseling to interpersonal conflicts as well. Counseling has three basic steps: (1) gaining rapport, (2) exploring and assessing the problems, and (3) applying the appropriate intervention. The counselor must gain rapport and project trustworthiness and competence so that the client feels able to divulge painful conflicts and discuss behavior that has become self-defeating, uncomfortable, or socially unacceptable. The counselor must then assess, or help the client assess, the difference between the presenting problem and the real emotional issues. Finally, when the problems have been identified, the counselor applies intervention strategies in order to relieve the client's conflict and help the client change behavior.

This three-step process is valid for all therapies, despite philosophical differences over who should assess problems, what kind of intervention should be applied, and what the goal or outcome should be. Table 2 reduces this often confusing terminology into a simple formula showing the three-step process inherent in each counseling approach. The following sentence plots the course: "The (current situation/problem), when given appropriate (intervention/ therapy/treatment), leads to the desired (goal/outcome/response)."

Table 2. Basic Counseling Models.

Counseling Model	Current situation/ Problem	Intervention/ Therapy/ Treatment	Goal/Outcome Response
Medical	Diagnosis	Treatment	Cure/stabilization
Behavior modification	Behavior to be promoted or stopped	Reinforcement/ extinction plan	Behavior change
Conflict theories	Conflict	Problem solving	Conflict resolution
(Neo) Freudian	Id Control	Psychoanalysis	Ego Control
Transactional analysis	Child/parent reaction	Awareness	Adult reaction
Phenomeno- logical	Discontinuity	Environment	Self-actualization
Perceptual	Improper perception	Learning/cues	Proper perception
Social work	Maladjustment	Services	Social order

Counseling is traditionally used when the presenting problems have their origin in intrapersonal conflict. Adaptations of the counseling model for use with interpersonal conflict have, however, been introduced to the profession in such works as *Conjoint Family Therapy* (Satir, 1967). Conjoint family therapy is now commonly employed to address problems that originate primarily between people. Whether it is used for conflict management or for conflict resolution depends on the counselor's orientation and goal.

Many books on business management, personnel development, and administration use essentially this same model for preventing, eliminating, or managing interpersonal conflict in the work setting. Managers "counsel" their subordinates by implementing the three-stage process (rapport, assessment, and application). In that context, counseling is seen as a better management tool than imposed decisions, because it directly involves the conflicting parties in seeking understanding of their problems.

Negotiation is the most pervasive and diverse approach to dispute resolution. Negotiation of disputes need not follow an established framework, although some have systematically studied the process (Williams, 1983). It is often pursued through the use of designated representatives such as attorneys. Most writers equate negotiation with bargaining—that is, the exchange of one thing for another (Bellow and Moulton, 1981).

Williams (1983) has observed that negotiations between legal representatives predictably follow the four-stage pattern set forth in Table 1. Above all, negotiation involves the formulation of opposing positions, and fulfilling one negotiator's position necessarily defeats fulfillment of the other's. Negotiating to achieve one position at the expense of another is a function of perceived power, bargaining tactics, and a crisis orientation. Viewing negotiation as a competitive, adversarial zero-sum game, which requires considerable game playing and manipulative skills, has been the hallmark of professional texts (Illich, 1973) as well as popular "Me Decade" books telling how to get what you want by bullying your way through any conflict in life.

More recently, both popular and professional books on negotiation have emphasized the cooperative model that seeks mutual gain through constructive settlement of disputes. These books echo Deutsch's win/win analysis. The most helpful and concise of the new works on win/win negotiating flows from the experience of the Harvard Negotiation Project. Roger Fisher and William Ury, in their national bestseller, *Getting to Yes* (1983), urge negotiators not to bargain over positions. The method they offer for successful negotiation provides a four-part approach based on these simple statements:

- Separate the people from the problem.
- Focus on interests, not positions.
- Invent options for mutual gain.
- Insist on objective criteria.

Stating these four maxims is, of course, easier than implementing them in a dispute. One role of a mediator is to help the parties avoid positional bargaining and guide negotiations toward a resolution of mutual gain for which power alone is not the criterion. In the next chapter we shall have more to say about the use of win/win negotiation methods as a phase of the mediation process.

Problem solving is a process that can be used alone or with other conflict resolution methods. The McMaster model of family functioning (Epstein, Bishop, and Baldwin, 1982) explains how families can engage in group problem solving to keep functioning. The McMaster model defines two categories of problems and formulates a sequence for solving them. This sequence is not limited to family functioning; it applies to all problem-solving situations. *Instrumental* problems are related to "mechanical" issues involving provision of necessary materials such as food, money, time, and the like. *Affective* problems deal with feelings. Effective problem solving is seen as a sequence of seven steps that can be applied to both categories of problems (Epstein, Bishop, and Baldwin, 1982, pp. 119-122):

1. Identifying the problem
2. Communicating with appropriate people about the problem
3. Developing a set of alternative solutions
4. Deciding on one of the alternatives
5. Carrying out the action
6. Monitoring to ensure that the action is carried out
7. Evaluating the effectiveness of the problem-solving process

This model is similar to the mediation process, but it can be used by individuals or groups to solve problems without outside facilitators or helpers. Not every person or group is able to use the problem-solving process outlined above, however. Mediation incorporates many of the same stages, but it has the advantage of being facilitated by a neutral third party who is not a member of the group and thus can direct the entire process.

Hayes (1981) has further analyzed the problem-solving process and found that it contains four general methods: (1) trial and error methods, (2) proximity methods, (3) fractionalization methods, and (4) knowledge-based methods. *Trial and error* methods can be either blind or systematic, but both approaches are unsatisfactory for some problems. *Proximity* methods are based on the question,

"What step can I take that will bring me closer to the goal?" Hayes describes two proximity methods, *hill-climbing* and *means-end* analysis, both of which lend themselves to computer programs or subroutines for problem solving.

Fractionalization methods involve subgoals to guide the problem solver around detours. This tactic can often be used by mediators to facilitate problem solving with their participants. The idea is to take a complex situation, such as an environmental dispute or a divorce, and break it down into subgoals that lead the participants closer to the overall goal. Thus if a couple's overall goal is to part amicably and fairly, each issue of child custody, visitation, division of property, and financial planning can be related to the "fair and friendly" criterion. If the overall goal is to preserve the splendor of an area such as the Columbia River Gorge, decisions about each issue—fishing rights, tourism, housing developments and zoning, recreational use, navigational rights—should all be tied to the original criterion: preservation of a unique scenic area. *Knowledge-based* methods of problem solving have been further classified into four areas: learning, searching for related problems, pattern matching, and search algorithms (routine procedures leading to correct solutions—long division, for example).

The final process discussed here, *mediation,* is approached in this book as a seven-stage conflict resolution process:

1. Introduction—creating trust and structure
2. Fact finding and isolation of issues
3. Creation of options and alternatives
4. Negotiation and decision making
5. Clarification and writing a plan
6. Legal review and processing
7. Implementation, review, and revision

Our seven-stage model is intended as a "megaprocess" that can form the basis of mediation in all situations. Each stage is composed of separate tasks, but not all stages will be completed in every case. Other authors portray a similar mediation process but divide the stages differently or use different labels. In the next chapter we illustrate our seven-stage process and suggest specific techniques and roles for the mediator. Other conflict resolution processes—such as avoidance, legislation, marketplace supply and demand, boycotts, violence, coercion, dictatorial fiat, civil disobedience, and peace-winning or peace-keeping strategies—are tangential and important but beyond the scope of this book.

Comparing the Alternatives

It will be helpful here to compare the seven-stage mediation process we have outlined with the counseling/therapy process and the process of adjudication. Table 3 compares these three approaches to conflict resolution—traditional legal services, mediation, and counseling/therapy. Mediation does not have the same goal as counseling and therapy. The primary goal of mediation is to create a set of agreements that will guide future actions and consequences between the participants. Its other goal is to reduce the negative effects of the conflict by improving communication and enhancing negotiation skills. The goal of counseling and therapy is to change certain behavior or perceptions. While some counseling approaches may involve "behavioral contracting," it is usually not a written contract and certainly is not legally binding upon the client, as a signed agreement or mediated plan may be.

Sheila Kessler (1979) has suggested that counselors are becoming mediators, yet many counselors are unaware of the mediation process and how it differs from counseling. Many counselors and therapists do not work with interpersonal problems but see their role as dealing only with the "cause" of the problems: the underlying intrapersonal conflicts. Although the majority of counselors do not work with clients simultaneously, whereas mediation requires at least two participants, counselors can use mediation as the second of their three-step process if they are trained in mediation techniques.

The basic assumption of counseling could be stated as follows: *If* the counselor and client have developed a sufficient relationship of trust, and *if* the counselor has accurately assessed the real problem, and *if* the client's problems match the style of the counselor, and *if* the counselor applies the intervention correctly, the client's problems can be resolved. These assumptions put the responsibility for success or failure primarily on the counselor; in the

Table 3. Comparison of Three Conflict Resolution Services.

	Legal Services	Mediation	Counseling/Therapy
Basic Assumption	Justice and individual interests are best served via the adversarial process in which legal representatives negotiate or substantiate the validity of their client's interests before a judge or hearings officer with power to decide.	Equity and joint interests are best served through cooperative techniques of conflict resolution and guided negotiation resulting in the maximum degree of individualization and self-determination.	The welfare of client, individual, or group is best served through diagnosis and treatment by a therapeutic professional; variations of the medical model are used in this diagnosis and treatment.
Clients served	Individual or group with no conflicting interests.	All parties in conflict.	Spouses, parents and children, extended family members, small groups. Determined by diagnosis of the therapist, theory, and the availability of clients.
Customary objectives	Maximizing and protection of client's interests.	Creation and selection of client options, continuing cooperation, and independence from professional help.	Rehabilitation and conciliation of individuals and family or group relationships.
Strategies	Development of negotiation strategies so that client realizes maximum gains, minimum losses. Also involves legal information, advice on certain areas of finance, referral of clients to other professionals as needed.	Development of interpersonal communication between clients; balancing the interests and needs of all parties; suggesting alternatives; developing a balance of power and legitimacy between parties; assuring minimal losses to all parties; referral of clients to other professionals as needed.	Development of treatment modalities such as individual therapy, group therapy, family therapy; referral of clients to other professionals as needed.

Source: Adapted from Koopman and Hunt (1982).

mediation process, by way of contrast, success or failure rests primarily with the participants.

Mediation furthers the policy of minimum state intervention in interpersonal conflicts. The argument for minimum state intervention is founded not only on economic considerations but also on the value placed on personal autonomy. If litigation or other adversarial proceedings can be avoided, the savings to the public and the parties can be considerable. Mediation is most often conducted in private so that private matters may be freely discussed without concern that the discussion is part of a public record, as in adjudication. Mediation is also usually speedier than adjudication. The principal advantage of mediation compared to adjudication is not economy or speed, however. The primary benefit is self-determination.

Disputants should be presumed to have the capacity, authority, and responsibility to determine consensually what is best for themselves through the process of mediation. People are encouraged in mediation to assess and meet their own needs and resolve their conflicts responsibly without professional paternalism or state interference.

One of the most noble functions of law is to serve as a model of what is expected. Adjudicatory procedures, instead of providing models, are too often used coercively to supplant self-determination with no evidence that the disputants have been encouraged and helped to resolve their differences. The law should be premised on the expectation that people will not abdicate to a lawyer or a judge the responsibility of deciding what is fair. Using mediation to facilitate conflict resolution and encourage self-determination thus strengthens democratic values and enhances the dignity of those in conflict.

The legal system is not able to supervise the fragile and complex interpersonal relationships between family members, parents and teachers, landlord and tenants, neighbors and others that may continue after their immediate dispute is resolved. Once lawyers and judges intrude into the decision-making role between those in conflict, the disputants are less likely to function independently in the future—thus promoting further professional involvement and individual noncooperation with imposed orders. By definition, a consensual agreement, whether reached through mediation or negotiation, reflects the parties' own preferences and will be more acceptable and durable than one imposed by a court. Since the participants in mediation formulate their own agreement and invest emotionally in its success, they are more likely to adhere to its terms than one negotiated or ordered by others. Mediation is particularly advantageous for conflicts between those who must have continued contact together, such as people involved in family disputes and divorce. Continuing contact on unresolved conflicts may produce postdivorce skirmishes in court that exceed the intensity of the initial dispute.

Mediators can facilitate private ordering, or negotiated outcomes, between disputants by helping them get information on applicable legal norms and principles, as well as the probable outcome in court if the case is litigated. Mnookin and Kornhauser (1979), in developing the theme of private ordering, pointed out that a rational client will want an accurate assessment of the costs of alternative modes of dispute settlement. A mutual assessment of the alternatives during the mediation process helps assure a fair and rational outcome. Mediation can also educate the participants about each other's needs and provide a personalized model for dispute resolution both now and in the future. In such situations, mediation can teach the participants to work together, isolate the crucial issues, and realize that cooperation can be to their mutual advantage.

Recommended Reading

The Nature of Conflict

Conflict and Conflict Management. J. S. Himes. Athens: University of Georgia Press, 1980.
    Delineates the meaning of conflict management.

Conflict Resolution Through Communication. F. Jandt (Ed.). New York: Harper & Row, 1973.
    An excellent collection of readings spanning the nature of conflict and the scope and application of conflict resolution methods.

The Resolution of Conflict. M. Deutsch. New Haven: Yale University Press, 1973.

A succinct and insightful analysis of conflict and the principles necessary for the constructive resolution of disputes. This work should be required reading.

Understanding Conflict and War. Vols. 1 and 2. R. J. Rummel. New York: Wiley, 1976.

A scholarly yet lucid treatise covering all aspects of conflict and its manifestation in the three basic types of society.

Approaches to Conflict Resolution

The Complete Problem Solver. J. Hayes. Philadelphia: Franklin Institute Press, 1981.

A compendium of the different categories of problem solving.

Fundamentals of Negotiating. G. I. Nierenberg. New York: Hawthorn Books, 1973.

An overview of the skills and assumptions needed for negotiating; offers many applications.

Getting to Yes. R. Fisher and W. Ury. New York: Penguin Books, 1983.

A straightforward, step-by-step strategy for constructive negotiation based on studies at the Harvard Negotiation Project.

The Process Is the Punishment: Handling Cases in a Lower Criminal Court. M. M. Feeley. New York: Russell Sage Foundation, 1979.

A persuasive argument revealing the inadequacies of the litigation/adjudication process of conflict resolution.

Theories of Counseling and Psychotherapy. (2nd ed.) C. H. Patterson. New York: Harper & Row, 1973.

A concise but complete description of the major counseling and therapy models in current use.

3

※ ※ ※ ※ ※

Stages in the
Mediation Process

In Chapter Two we described mediation as having seven stages. In this chapter we discuss each stage with respect to its goals and tasks, the methodology we have found most helpful to accomplish these tasks, and the general role of the mediator during each phase. While we consider the tasks for each stage to be part of a generic process of mediation, we know that completion of every stage may not be feasible or appropriate in every situation. The suggestions about the mediator's role and methodology reflect our own collective experiences in providing mediation services. The methodology and steps we present constitute *our* style of mediation. While we recommend this approach as a starting point, we encourage mediators to develop personal styles compatible with their own unique backgrounds, personalities, and training.

Stage 1: Introduction—Creating Structure and Trust

Stage 1, the introduction, is vital to the establishment of a relationship that will facilitate the rest of the mediation process. The mediator must provide initial structuring, gain the participants' trust and cooperation, and elicit their active participation in the process.

Mediators enter a dispute by referral or by direct choice of the participants. Some participants may accept mediation only to avoid negative consequences, such as litigation, and may respond to stage one with resistance. How the mediation process is initiated determines how much effort must be exerted by the mediator to create both understanding and acceptance of mediation. An important task of stage one is to assess the participants' attitudes about mediation and their readiness for the process.

Beyond introductions and reviewing guidelines, this stage is used to gather relevant information about the participants' perceptions of the conflict, their goals and expectations, and the conflict situation. Essential information should be gathered during this stage:

- The participants' motivation to use mediation
- The immediate background and precipitating events of the conflict
- The interactional and communication styles of the participants
- The present emotional state of the participants
- Arrangements for legal processes and the involvement of other participants
- The presenting problem as opposed to the hidden agenda
- Immediate safety and security concerns for each participant and their dependents.

The sequence shown in Table 4 helps elicit this information and serves as a guide to the mediator for facilitating the introductory session. Not all the steps presented here will be followed in every case. The order of the steps in all stages must remain flexible to fit the dynamics of each case. Each case is different and the mediation process must not be rigid. The process must be adapted as needed. It should be noted that guidelines, employment agreements, and worksheets are optional tools that may or may not be needed in mediation settings. These, as well as the confirmation of case data (step 3), are contingent on the content and context of mediation.

In our *introductions* (step 1), we prefer to avoid small talk. We allow the participants to determine where they sit in individual chairs or couches arranged in a semicircle or other conversation area; at the apex, near a small table or desk, is the mediator's chair. The seating chosen by the participants can be a helpful nonverbal

Table 4. The Eight Steps of Stage 1.

Step	Data Obtained
1. Brief introductions and seating	Nonverbal impressions
2. Preparatory statement by mediator (repeated if one participant is late)	Present emotional state of participants; legal processes
3. Confirm case data	Immediate background and precipitating events; involvement of attorneys, advocates; safety concerns
4. Handover discussion to participant	Interactional and communication styles; emotional stages
5. Discuss expectations	The presenting problem vs. hidden agendas or conflicts
6. Review guidelines	Interactional styles; emotional states
7. Review and sign employment agreement and pay fees	Participants' motivation
8. Discuss worksheets	Immediate security concerns

clue about their relationships and attitudes. The positioning of the mediator's chair and the distance between the mediator and each participant can be used to indicate the mediator's neutral stance. Three aspects must be considered in all physical settings for mediation: comfort, communication, and control (Neighborhood Justice Center of Atlanta, 1982). Additional parties, such as spouses, friends, lawyers, advocates, interpreters, and related professionals, may have to attend mediation sessions for convenience in decision making or because of legal requirements. These participants must be dealt with immediately—before the actual session begins, if possible. Mediators should develop policies concerning additional persons in the sessions (see Chapter Six).

The second step begins with a *preparatory statement* (see Chapter Five) that outlines the roles of both mediator and participants and rewards the participants for having made the risky decision of coming to the session. If one participant arrives later than the other, we summarize all that has been said to the other participant, no matter how redundant it may be for those who arrived earlier. For those who were on time, this summary recapitulates material that may have been missed because of anxiety; it also confirms, by behavior, the scrupulous neutrality the mediator must maintain. It shows that what is said to one participant will be said to all.

The next step is to *confirm case data*—whatever the mediator knows about the participants and their situation—in the presence of all. (See Chapter Five for a discussion of techniques.) This review serves the same purpose as the repetition for latecomers: It confirms by action that the mediator is not keeping secrets. The information should be the same as that gathered on the contact sheet and will then become part of the case file. (See Chapter Five for further discussion of data management.)

The next step is the *handover* to the participant—a definitive signal from the mediator, usually verbal, that indicates the need for the person to become an active part of the communication. For example: "It must be hard to open up after all the problems, but please try to tell us your perspective." We often find it best to encourage the more passive participant or the one who is more upset. The more passive is thereby urged to become a true participant; the more upset is allowed a legitimate way to vent feelings of anger, anxiety, hopelessness, and vindictiveness. The handover shows the mediator's willingness to openly confront the major emotional tendencies and displays a truthful picture of the interactions. It is important not only to encourage such involvement but also to reward it verbally, since to express deep personal feelings is risky and threatening to the participants. Such phrases as "Thanks for sharing some important points of concern for you" will provide the reward. We believe this openness reduces any tendencies toward passive-aggressive behavior, which can undermine later negotiations.

Another technique that may be helpful in certain cases is to have a protocol. The complainant (the one who has brought the issues to mediation, the one who is seeking resolution, or simply the one who first contacted you) goes first in all dealings as a general policy, followed by the respondent (Neighborhood Justice Center of

Atlanta, 1982). The terms *complainant* and *respondent* stem from
the adversarial legal perspective and are more appropriate in some
settings than others. However, the terminology does help remind the
mediator that participants have often entered mediation from such
adversarial positions. It also reminds mediators that the concerns of
the person who has brought the case to mediation should be addressed by the end of the mediation process.

The *discussion of expectations or positions* tends to expose
hidden agendas or "icebergs"—conflicts that are only barely acknowledged by the participants. By using open questions and silence, the mediator can facilitate discussion while maintaining
control and providing recognition and encouragement by means of
interpretations and summary. The participants should be doing
most of the talking and will often become incensed at each other's
perceptions. At this point the emotional level of the session often
begins to rise. The mediator can let each participant "tell their side
of things" while the other participant and the mediator listen in
silence, or each participant can explain the situation to the mediator, who can ask pertinent questions. Allowing uninterrupted story-
telling is best when participants are openly angry, verbally abusive,
or even explosive. Interrupting is best when both participants are
controlled. Both styles allow participants to hear the other's views of
the issues.

The next step, *reviewing the mediation guidelines*, helps
calm the tension—partly because it is a break in the sequence, partly
because it once again reminds the participants that they will not be
allowed to get out of control despite their strong emotions. It sets up
explicit expectations. Participants can take an emotional time-out
from their initial anxiety while the mediator is busy explaining the
structure. Some mediators use separate mediation guidelines; others
incorporate guidelines into the employment contract. Either method
is acceptable provided the mediator reviews the guidelines with the
participants to verify that they are understood and acceptable. We
find it important at this time to emphasize the natural inclination
of the participants to become discouraged or disinterested in continuing the mediation at critical points in the process. During the
review of the guidelines, we legitimize this natural tendency to
defend against pain but point out that such defenses have negative
consequences and are avoidable. Here are some examples of spe-

cially contracted consequences: Serious lateness is given a financial penalty; withdrawal from mediation requires a written statement; noncompliance with a guideline will result in an *impasse* and termination of the session by the mediator.

The guidelines or the employment contract should address the question of whether the participants will be allowed to talk separately with the mediator. Separate sessions are a common practice in environmental, labor, commercial, and crisis mediation but are less frequent in family mediation. Separate caucusing may be an effective mediation technique, but it does raise significant ethical considerations, as discussed in Chapter Six. Participants are encouraged by some mediators to talk to them separately if they are feeling discouraged or want to end mediation. This gives the mediator a chance to discuss concerns privately, get a better understanding of the underlying conflicts, and encourage without embarrassment. It must be established in the guidelines, however, that an acknowledgment of the separate conversation and its general contents will be conveyed to the other participant in the next mediation session.

Other issues that fall in the category of setting guidelines should be discussed at this step: (1) disclosure of information within mediation (discovery), (2) confidentiality, (3) fees and payment, (4) length of sessions, (5) how the mediator will function should the participants be unable to make a decision later in the process, (6) provision for legal input and processing, (7) review and revision, and (8) termination. A sample set of mediation guidelines is presented in Resource B at the back of the book.

The next step, *signing the employment agreement,* is an overt method of gaining cognitive, if not emotional, commitment to mediation on the part of the participants; it is also a legal necessity for the mediator. If the mediator has been skillful up to this point, the participants will have enough information about the process (and emotional relief) to feel good about mediation. Many, nonetheless, express their doubts and fears at this time ("I'll sign it, but I'm not sure it will work for us"), and the mediator should acknowledge expressed ambivalence and the reversibility of this commitment should mediation not work. Consider the following hypothetical divorce mediation case, which follows the process sequence we have outlined.

When the wife called the mediation service for information,
she said she wanted to avoid an ugly courtroom scene that could
involve the two children, aged ten and seven, in more disruption,
but she was not sure her husband was willing to go through mediation. She felt he did not really understand mediation, but the concept had been explained to her and she had been referred by a counselor. She did think her husband would appreciate the lower cost of
mediation, since they were feeling the financial crunch of starting
two households on the same income and would have to dip into
their savings to hire a lawyer and complete the divorce proceeding.
She set an appointment for the first mediation session one week after
her phone call to the mediator. She stated that the husband wanted
sole custody of their children, but she anticipated a struggle around
this issue, since she was not willing to allow him sole custody.

At the first session, the participants arrived in separate cars,
the wife a little early and the husband a little late. The wife's affect
seemed very social, her tone of voice business-as-usual. The man
arrived, barely said anything by way of introduction, and seated
himself in the chair in a slumped and withdrawn manner. Resentment and anger seemed to emanate from him.

The mediator, a woman in this example, had her work cut
out for her, since the man was obviously defensive and did not play
an active part in arranging for mediation. His tacit acceptance be-
lied his true feelings of anger, hurt, and frustration. He may automatically have assumed that the mediator was going to align herself
with the wife's interests, either because of their common gender or
because the two of them had arranged the meeting. Consider the
following dialogue:

Introduction

Mediator: . . . . Ah, here he is now. Hello, Joe. Please come in and
have a seat. [Points to a chair.] While we were waiting
for you, I got your mailing addresses and home phone
numbers from Charlene, and we were just discussing a
few things which I think everyone in mediation needs
to know. [*Repeats preparatory statement.*]

Confirmation of Data

I want to verify some of the information I got from Charlene when she called to set this appointment. [*Turns and addresses Joe.*] I understand that you have two children, boys, who are seven and ten years old and that you are living separately in an apartment. [*Silence.*]

Joe: Yes, that's right. The boys have been with me up until this week when they went to stay with their mother.

Mediator: Can you tell me, Joe, how long you've been living apart?

Joe: Well, I think it's been, well, about [*looks briefly at Charlene*] . . . I'd say nearly two months.

[*Charlene nods slightly, head down and eyes averted.*]

Mediator: Have you had the boys most of that time?

Joe: Yes.

Mediator: Charlene tells me she's been seeing a counselor at Metropolitan to try and help her through this stressful period, and that's how she heard about mediation and decided to give it a try. I'm assuming you've only briefly talked about this together. [*Looks at both to get nonverbal confirmation.*] Charlene [*turns to her*], can you tell me what you know about mediation and why you want to give it a try?

Charlene: Well, I just think we're, you know, low on money right now, and that maybe this will be less expensive than fighting it out in court, having to pay two lawyers and all. . . .

Mediator: Yes, that's what you told me on the phone, and also that you'd like to avoid disruption and additional tension for the children.

Charlene: Yeah, that's right. [*Looks down.*]

Handover (Directive Statement)

Mediator: How about you, Joe? Tell me what you hope will
              come from mediation.

Joe: I'm not hoping for anything. She told me that if I
              didn't come, she'd fight me for sole custody of the kids.
              So I figured we'd give it a try this way. But I'm pre-
              pared to go to court, to hire lawyers, to do what I have
              to do to make sure I get custody. I'm not going to lose
              my kids just because *she* wants out of the marriage!
              I've talked to a lawyer and he tells me I have a pretty
              good chance of winning custody if we don't get it
              straightened out here, so I feel pretty confident.

Charlene: [*Squirming in seat, showing other signs of increasing
              stress and anger.*] You *know* that would hurt them!
              They shouldn't have to go through that!

Intervention to Relieve Tension

Mediator: Well, I can see that custody of the children is a big
              issue and I think mediation can help. Joe, you don't
              want to become just a weekend father, and Charlene,
              you don't want the kids hurt by a nasty custody battle.
              Is that a fair statement? [*Looks back and forth until a
              nonverbal or verbal acknowledgment is made by
              each.*]

Reassurance (Gives Time to Calm Emotions)

              Well, I think I understand now what you both
              want, and I think the mediation process can help you
              with this and any other conflicts you have. One of the
              strengths of mediation is that if you both *actively*
              [*looks at Joe*] cooperate with the process, you can *all*
              win. You can work out plans that help to meet not
              only your needs but those of your children as you re-
              structure your family.

Reframing into Nonadversarial Terms

              Because that's what you're going to be doing
              now—changing your family into something that every-

body can readily live with. [*Looks to both to detect emotional state.*]

Review of Rules

And for you to do that, you have to be part of this process. We know a lot now about what people have to do to resolve their conflicts, and these guidelines [*hands them out*] will help us make mediation work. Let's start with number one. . . . [*Explains each guideline, getting nonverbal acceptance after each one.*]

Some mediators do not hand out printed copies of the guidelines but prefer instead to cover them verbally. This is a question of style that should be based on the mediator's preference and the ability of the participants to comprehend. It should be noted that in stage 1 the mediator is at once acting, speaking, and presenting while at the same time receiving and evaluating the participants' responses.

Stage 2: Fact Finding and Isolation of Issues

Before good decisions can be reached, both participants must have equal information and both must fully understand what the issues are. Stage 2 of mediation is used to find out all the relevant facts and isolate the true issues for the participants. The mediator must help the participants fully understand their areas of agreement and conflict. Often some idea of the manifest and the underlying conflicts has already been gained in the first stage.

During stage 2 the mediator must determine the nature of the participants' underlying and manifest conflicts by using the following evaluative criteria: immediacy of the conflict, duration of the conflict, intensity of feelings about the conflict, and rigidity of positions. In the divorce example used earlier, the custody issue is perhaps the most immediate question and the duration of the conflict has been short but acute in the last two months. It is obvious from the dialogue that both participants have strong personal involvement in the conflict, and both seem rigid in their position on

custody. Each participant may be experiencing internal conflict as
well. The woman may have this as her emotional issue: "What kind
of mother would abandon her children?" The man may be dealing
with another emotional issue: "It's not fair!"

The real issues, then, are both interactive and intrapersonal.
As explained in Chapter Two, conflicts can only be resolved if they
can be acknowledged. The participants in this example are acknowledging the interactive issue—the manifest conflict—but not
their personal underlying conflicts. It is the task of this stage in
mediation to provide a place where defenses can be set aside and the
underlying issues can surface.

This stage of mediation requires delineation of *all* the issues.
In complex conflicts, such as environmental and divorce cases, there
are usually several issues that must be addressed. By using a worksheet, the mediator helps the participants cover all the areas of dispute and interrelated issues they must discuss to produce the desired
outcome: a plan they can live with. The mediator acts as a tour
guide, showing what is important to examine. The mediator also
acts as a scribe, recording data and determining which areas are
closed (or already resolved) and which are open for discussion.
Remember that not all items on the worksheet will be issues of
conflict; some simply need to be discussed and have a decision
acknowledged.

The mediator can best accomplish this complex role by using
the skills described in Chapter Five. Use of open-ended questions
helps explore the perceptual worlds and value structures of the participants. By organizing, summarizing, and setting priorities, the
mediator is able to translate gigantic concerns into smaller items
that can be decided one at a time.

In the hypothetical divorce case in our example, the participants had not discussed property settlement or financial distribution
of resources prior to mediation. The mediator handed out a financial worksheet at the end of the first session, asking each participant
to fill it out based on current and ideal custody situations. Joe did
not complete his worksheet; Charlene had some questions but seriously attempted to complete hers. Haynes (1981, p. 62) suggests,
for the situation outlined here, that the mediator help the participant complete the form during the session, thus learning "whether

the inactivity is due to an unwillingness, a lack of knowledge, or a strategy." We have found that insistence on completing a form may bring out more resistance by the participant who did not complete it and frustration for the one who did, especially when any of Haynes's three criteria are present. (See Chapter Thirteen for a discussion of resistance.) We usually try to assess and even document nonparticipation because such behavior can be one reason for declaring an impasse.

This stage comes to a close when the mediator knows where the disagreements and conflicts lie, what the underlying conflicts are, and what each participant wants and will not under any circumstances accept. It may take several sessions to complete this stage, depending on the number of underlying conflicts that are related to the participants' self-concept. Moore (1983b) has suggested that this stage includes not only data collection and data verification, but also identification of interests and needs, determination of mutually exclusive positions, and the ordering of all issues into an agenda. This addition to stage 2 would be particularly useful in the more complex labor/management, environmental, commercial and international cases.

At this point the mediator, along with the participants, must determine a case-specific set of goals, objectives, and strategies that incorporate the participants' values and intentions. It is the participants who must determine whether they seek resolution of all issues or only some, while identifying and managing those that remain.

A decision to suspend the mediation due to a declared impasse could be made at this time. (See Resource B: Mediation Guidelines.) Allowing the mediation to continue if one participant remains obstructive is a waste of the participants' time and money, frustrating for the one who is active, and unproductive from the mediator's standpoint.

Stage 3: Creation of Options and Alternatives

Stage 3 asks the basic question: "How can you do what you want to do in the most effective way?" Both participants must be involved in finding the answer. After going over the worksheet or notes, the mediator needs to review the issues of conflict. Sometimes the answer to the question for a dozen issues rests on the answer to the most basic question or issue of highest priority. This is often the case in child custody cases. This domino effect can be maximized by a skillful mediator who brings the participants to an awareness of *which* issue is the crucial stumbling block.

After reviewing the issues, the mediator should list any options that have been mentioned and then make a statement reminding the participants of the criteria to be used in evaluating those options. We suggest the following criteria for developing alternatives:

- Needs of the participants and others who will be affected by the decision
- Projections of the past onto the future (likely predictions)
- General economic and social forecasts that may affect an option
- Legal and financial norms, roadblocks, and limitations
- New people and situations that are anticipated
- Predictable changes in any of these criteria

More specific criteria may need to be suggested by the mediator for the situation being mediated.

Looking at this list of criteria for creation of options from a perspective of environmental mediation (Chapter Eight), the needs of the larger population must be taken into account, along with the needs of the participants who often represent narrower interests. Past errors in environmental planning should be considered so that mistakes are not repeated. If allowing higher stream temperatures from power plants without cooling towers killed fish and wildlife in the past, that option should be ruled out during this stage in mediation. Social forecasts, such as increased popular knowledge and attention to ecological concerns, as well as general economic trends should eliminate options that may not be supported by citizens who must pay for the outcome of mediation. New or proposed legislation that limits deficit financing by a power company may limit the construction of a cooling tower. A new Secretary of Energy or new federal regulations may indicate changes that directly affect the practicality of some options.

There are two main tasks of this stage: (1) to help the participants articulate the options they know or want and (2) to develop
new options that may be more satisfactory than previous ones. The
mediator's role must reflect this duality, for the mediator must be a
facilitator for the first task and an originator or synthesizer for the
second. It is important not to let the latter role overshadow the
former, since a mediator who is offering too many new options too
fast will inhibit the participants' own expression and views. To
reduce this risk, some mediators find it helpful to list all the options
that come to the participants' minds before offering additional
options.

Getting the participants to "brainstorm," either during the
mediation session together or as homework, can be a useful tool for
accomplishing the first task. If the underlying conflict has come to
light through the mediation process, it is expensive to use the mediator to create options because the participants often have not
thought about options. Moreover, a participant who does not come
back with at least two options from a homework assignment probably has unresolved internal conflict that can be confronted very
easily by pointing out the resistance (see Chapter Thirteen) and then
probing further with direct questions (see Chapter Five).

We find that using a form for writing each option for a given
issue on forms adapted from Janis and Mann (1977) saves time in the
subsequent stages and prevents options from being mentioned but
passed over for consideration. One way of making sure that the
participants have truly listed all the options they can think of is for
the mediator to set up imaginary scenarios for the future and then
ask the question: "What if . . . ?" The scenarios should be based on
the evaluation criteria mentioned earlier.

The following example illustrates this technique. The participants in a custody dispute during a divorce have realized that the
main issue is the child's need for private education as opposed to
public school attendance. Both make a case for sole custody based
primarily on this disagreement, and both regard their own interest
as the only legitimate option. The girl, a sixth-grade student, has
been acting up in class and receiving low marks in the past year.
The parents see the following as options:

Mom	*Both*	*Dad*
1. Only private school will do.	3. Try public school one more year, then decide. 4. Try public school with additional tutoring. 5. Switch to private school for one year, then decide. 6. Mediator suggests: Get an evaluation with a recommendation.	2. Public school is fine.

Because the mediator is outside the conflict, he or she can see some options the participants have missed. In this example, the mediator suggests another option: getting an educational evaluation by professionals in the community and then basing the decision as to schooling on the recommendation. At the same time, the mediator may want to extricate the decison about schooling from the larger issue of custody by focusing on each parent's ability to care for the children. Furthermore, the underlying conflicts regarding each parent's view of the child's needs must be explored more fully.

If the participants have sufficiently dealt with their emotional and psychological tasks, another method that can be suggested during this stage of mediation is a *trial period*. In this way, an option can be used as an experiment before it is selected and both participants are able to experience the consequences of their options. This method is particularly effective when one participant has rejected an option in the belief that it will not work while the other is convinced that it will. By participating in a trial period for a specified time with the understanding that the option must be reviewed before a final decision on its suitability is made, the participants will learn for themselves whether the option is appropriate. A manager who finds two employees in violent conflict over the proper way to fill out an insurance form might mediate the situation by calling both into the office, ensuring that there is no underlying conflict, and having the employees propose two options and then each select one for a trial period. After the specified time (unless an irate call from the home office suspends the trial), the method can be reviewed and an appropriate decision made.

This stage of mediation is perhaps the most creative part. Mediators must think associatively as well as linearly in order to develop options that connect bits of information expressed earlier in mediation. This role is vastly different from the nondirective role espoused by many counselors and the highly authoritarian role taken by those who function as arbitrators. The mediator needs to be a resource person: an expert who can suggest new options based on extensive knowledge of the subject in conflict. The mediator must offer new options in such a way that the participants can either accept or reject them. The participants should not feel pressured to consider an option nor accept a trial period they do not think will be beneficial. As facilitator and developer, the mediator often feels a strong urge at this point to rush to completion and closure. But if mediators have staked their egos on the selection of a particular option, they will be unable to function as neutral facilitators of the process. Coercion, favoritism, and bias must not be allowed. Mediators should be especially aware of the ethical responsibilities of their role while providing new insights and guiding the participants.

Stage 4: Negotiation and Decision Making

Cooperation of the participants is the major task of stage 4 in mediation, along with an outcome that has been mutually agreed to by the participants. Both participants must be urged to compromise on some of the smaller items in order to accomplish this task. For each major issue, participants must choose the option they can live with, even if it is not what they originally wanted. Participants should be encouraged to take the risky step and *decide*.

Having several options in front of the participants does not necessarily help them to make choices. Often, developing many options during stage 3 seems to confuse the participants. Most people can mentally manipulate only a small number of variables at a time. One way the participants can approach a decision is by using simple forms of negotiation. This bargaining can take the form of "horse-trading" or "this-for-that," simple exchanges of desirable features or options, similar to what a person does in economic bargaining. The basic messages conveyed are: I'll give you what *you* want most if you will me what *I* want most" or "What is it worth to you to have *x*?"

This style of negotiation is not the calculated approach discussed in Chapter Two. Most people in mediation, when confronted with a range of options, need to reduce them to a smaller number. They often do not have a predetermined opening position, fallback, and bottom line as they would if they were involved in traditional negotiation. However, they often rule out certain options immediately, based on their perception of what is necessary or what is impractical. They are then left with options that cannot be ruled out and must be negotiated.

As an example, the participants in our earlier custody dispute, who have already developed options, might first try to horse-trade in order to select an option. Mom might offer to take a smaller cash settlement, something less than had already been decided, if Dad will agree to the option of private school for the daughter. He counters with a similar horse trade: If Mom will let the daughter stay in public school just as she is now, he can afford to let Mom stay in the house or have more spousal support. As is often the case, neither Mom nor Dad wishes to accept these trades; because they felt good about the earlier financial agreements, they do not want to disrupt earlier decisions, and they still see acceptance of each other's options, even with added incentives, as "giving in to the other person's wishes." In their personal cost/benefit analysis, they feel the costs are too high to trade.

The participants might then try to eliminate each other's favored options altogether, since they realize that neither will ever agree to those conditions. That leaves the couple in this example with the four options developed during stage 3. By using the same evaluation criteria that they used to develop the options, they could try to eliminate some. Perhaps option 6 could be eliminated because neither parent, under the terms of the prior financial settlement, can affort the tuition and auxiliary costs of the local private school now or in the predictable future.

The negotiation and decision-making stage is a time when participants examine the reality and consequences of the options they have developed. The mediator's task is to reframe this bargaining to ask the question: "Which option will best meet everyone's needs?" Mediators should move the participants from competitive negotiation to cooperative problem solving while encouraging interaction between them.

During this stage, conversation patterns switch. Originally the mediator initiated communication to each of the participants separately; now the participants interact primarily between themselves. (See Figure 2.) To accomplish this conversational switch, the mediator can introduce specific suggestions to the participants to help them evaluate the options. The mediator can clarify the goal (in this example, finding the most appropriate education for their daughter) and remind the participants of the procedures they can follow to get to that goal or mention the methods and problem-solving techniques described by Hayes (1981). The mediator supplies the technique, but the participants should be doing the talking.

The mediator is an agent of reality, someone who makes the participants doubt the assumptions and firmness of their original positions while they are negotiating: "I wonder if your daughter will like this." Instead of undermining or preventing this vital talking-out, the mediator amplifies what the participants are doing through reflection, clarification, and simple questions (see Chapter Five). As listener, the mediator is a process observer and monitor who should periodically intervene in the exchange in order to question the practicality or advisability of the option, as well as to prevent coercion. During this stage, mediators must be aware of the content being discussed *and* the process being used by the participants to arrive at a decision. The mediator should help the participants by drawing them back to their underlying conflicts and implicit expectations.

The mediator's role during this stage is to start the interchange between participants and then monitor it so that each person is given a chance to talk, make offers, and consider them without undue pressure. Both participants must have the opportunity to understand the other's perspective and feel that their own viewpoint

Figure 2. Communication Patterns in Mediation.

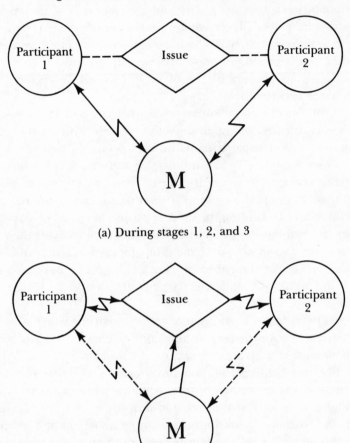

(a) During stages 1, 2, and 3

(b) During stage 4

is understood. Mediators can use directive and bridging statements, or they can clarify and summarize, to keep control while allowing the participants to explore for themselves which options are really viable. Mediators can stop negative remarks or gestures by reminding the participants of the guidelines discussed in the first stage. Mediators can also reflect earlier statements about the true interests of the participants: "You both want your daughter to have the most appropriate education to meet *her* unique talent and needs."

To help the participants carry on principled negotiation, the mediator must direct them away from bargaining over positions and encourage them to develop objective criteria for decisions (Fisher and Ury, 1983). If objective criteria can be agreed upon, the mediator can then focus their negotiations on considering options and making decisions with these criteria in mind. Conflict may dissipate and fears may be quelled if a common objective of applying a nonthreatening criterion is reached. In a breach of contract dispute, for example, rather than bargaining over what each side wants, the mediator can help the participants agree, with advice from their attorneys, on an objective criterion—such as restoring both participants to the economic positions they had *before* the contract or having the breaching party pay the out-of-pocket expenses of the other. This strategy establishes a fair standard, as Fisher and Ury (1983) suggest, for reaching a mutually acceptable agreement without a loser. Fisher and Ury (p. 89) also suggest that if a fair standard of decision cannot be reached, a fair procedure for resolving the conflicting interests or deciding on an option can still produce an outcome independent of sheer willpower. For example, deciding to take the average of two independent appraisals to fix the value of the disputed price of goods is a principled way of reaching a decision in a commercial dispute—compared to arguing over what the price should be. Gains to be made for both participants by agreeing on a fair standard or procedure should be pointed out, and the consequences of delay in decision making should be stated.

Maintaining some sort of equality in communication is important so that a verbose participant does not stifle the opinion of a quiet or passive one. In this way, decision making is protected from self-defeating and manipulative communication styles, and decisions are made out of active cognition rather than reactions such as guilt, fear, or shame. The mediator may want to use directive statements ("Tell us what you think, Jim") or reflections ("Elaine, you've said all along how happy you'd feel if you could find a way out of this problem"). Verbal rewards for having reached this stage of the process are also helpful.

Reflecting the doubts and fears of each participant can highlight their objections to an option while acknowledging their underlying conflicts. Another technique—having the participants start decision making with the least costly or lowest-priority items—can help build confidence in the process and produce tangible outcomes that encourage further decisions.

Direct confrontation by the mediator is sometimes necessary to activate decisions. The mediator can acknowledge the block and then give his or her own view of the resistance to decision. Confrontation must be done in such a way that the participant clearly understands it to be directed at the lack of progress in the mediation process, not a personal attack. Guilt and shame should seldom be used to motivate movement in a session; realistic assessment of resistance and consequences is a more productive approach.

Another technique that sometimes works to motivate decision making is to withdraw power arbitrarily from the resistant participant. The mediator can deny access to a decision by declaring an impasse or suggesting that the matter go to arbitration since the participants cannot decide. Since the mediation process provides great empowerment of the participants, they will often jump to recover their right to choose for themselves if they fear their loss of choice. Another variation is to acknowledge their right to block decision making. When the mediator legitimizes their right to be where they are, to remain ambivalent, some participants voluntarily make a move toward choice. This paradoxical intervention should be used cautiously, however, and only as a last resort.

Throwing the responsibility of making decisions back on the participants can temporarily block progress even if they are willing to make a choice. Yet it is important to reconfirm that it is *they*, the participants, who must not only make, but live with, the choices. A way of softening this often overwhelming responsibility is to remind the participants that they have already decided a process for future conflicts should their current decisions not work. They can change their arguments when they are no longer useful. Asking the participants to make their decisions true for themselves at this point in time, yet to remember that they can be changed, contributes to a healthy climate for decision making. (Some exceptions to this rule are discussed in Chapter Seven.)

Often participants ask the mediator's advice on which option to select. This is a difficult moment for a mediator. While mediators should not make decisions for participants, they can remind them of the sociological and statistical data or likely patterns surrounding their choice. Traditionally mediators have reminded disputants of community norms or values; however, this must be done in a non-judgmental manner. The response "I'm sorry, I can't advise you on this, you must make your own choice" tends to break down rapport with the participants and should be avoided. Mentioning earlier remarks and making generalized recommendations based on strong psychological or normative principles is often helpful to the participants.

Participants who are afraid to decide often want to defer the choice to an outside party or the mediator. The mediator should not suddenly become an arbitrator at this point unless the participants have already specified that this role is acceptable. If the mediator is so empowered, the role distinction should be clearly made in a preliminary statement.

The three categories of conflict called approach/avoidance, avoidance/avoidance, and approach/approach (see Chapter Two) are useful for mediators to remember during this stage. Not only do these categories describe the type of internal conflict participants may have regarding the cases of the manifest conflict, but they also speak to the problems participants may have in the decision-making stage. Options often fall into the approach/approach or the avoidance/avoidance categories. The participant wants both options but can only have one, or wants neither option but must choose the lesser of two evils. The approach/avoidance category could be said to include choices that the participant wants but does not want, thus creating ambivalence and a stalling of the mediation process until the conflict is resolved by additional information or a change in perception.

If mediators can determine which type of conflict a participant is experiencing, they can help facilitate a choice. For *approach/ approach conflicts*, the mediator can verbally reward the participant for having developed, or for being willing to consider, two options but then encourage the participant to make an arbitrary choice between them, reassured by the fact that he or she can switch to the other alternative later through further mediation. For *approach/ avoidance conflicts*, the participant can be encouraged to try a trial period of the ambivalent option to see if it works. For *avoidance/*

avoidance conflicts, the mediator can discuss how a choice must be made and try to help the participant feel better about being in the dilemma. Another technique is to offer to go back to the earlier stage of developing options. Perhaps there is another option free of this avoidance/avoidance conflict. Sometimes the mere mention of retrenchment will spur a decision, because the participant knows that stage 3 was thorough and that there are no other options. Participants recognize that the task is to accept this conflict and make a choice that will, in turn, free them from the stress of the conflict.

Readiness for decision is a personal matter. Sometimes it requires a change in perception, sometimes just another item of information, or even just time to create a change in individual development and maturation (see Chapters Four and Seven). Mediators should become skilled at evaluating each participant's readiness before proceeding with this stage and should know how to deal with participants who are not yet ready.

Stage 5: Clarification and Writing a Plan

Most participants will be able to make choices among options during stage 4. The function of stage 5 of mediation is to produce a document that outlines clearly the participants' intentions, their decisions, and their future behavior. This agreement, or plan of action, should be written in a form the participants can read easily and review later if the issues resurface. It should be written concisely, yet completely, with language the participants understand, and in a clear format. The participants should understand it to be a working document that can be modified after legal review or by subsequent written amendments to reflect the reality of the moment.

The mediator should be the primary person involved in recording, organizing, and accurately reflecting the decisions that have been reached. The participants, either separately or jointly, may need to write their own wording of an option to ensure that it reflects their idea of the agreement and submit it to the mediator for inclusion in the mediated plan. The mediator can supply a model on which they can base their version. This technique is useful when there has been a lot of controversy over the option, when the participants are highly motivated and literate, and when the mediator feels that active participation in this manner will forestall passive-aggressive behavior and many revisions. However, it may not be appropriate for participants who want to "wrap it up quickly" as a way of ending their internal tension and conflicts. Nor is it appropriate to request this type of cooperation when the participants lack the skills or when the power dynamics between them would simply lead to competition over whose version is accepted as written.

The mediated plan should include not only some provision, mutually agreed upon, for legal review and processing but also a statement regarding the revision policy and procedures that can be used when future changes necessitate rewording of the agreement. The Resources at the end of the book include a mediated plan for a custody dispute as an example of contingency planning (see Resource C).

Copies of the proposed plan should be given to the participants to think about and review with others before the next session. If there are underlying conflicts that have not been resolved during earlier mediation stages, they will surface at this time—often in the form of a manifest conflict over the wording of a section that addresses the underlying conflict. Suppose a landlord reviews a proposed plan that states: "The landlord is aware of noncompliance with certain fire and safety codes and agrees to install an approved fire escape from the second floor back window within sixty days." He may refuse to sign the plan, not because he refused to install the fire escape but because of the underlying conflict of his earlier responsibility according to the codes. Getting the participants to articulate their objection to the wording—and at the same time determining the underlying conflict (in this case, an ambivalent approach/avoidance conflict brought about by the landlord's familiarity with codes yet reassurance from the prior owner of its rentability)—is very hard work requiring great skill in reflection, summary, open questions, and other techniques.

It is difficult for the mediator to resist the urge for closure, yet this is precisely what the mediator must do. Mediators must not take on the responsibility for producing the final synthesis that each participant can accept. The participants must see that the mediator has no interest in the outcome beyond a professional duty to facilitate the sessions as expertly as possible.

Most participants feel relieved at this stage and need reassurance that the process they have undergone has helped them produce a document that is as accurate and true for them as it can be. Most participants, or their attorneys, need to make one or two word changes. Be prepared to revise the document immediately upon their review, or have the proposed agreement retyped and ready for signing within a day or two of the session when it is discussed.

The signing of this mediated plan is a symbolic act that should be marked by special behavior. After signatures have been added and personal copies distributed, small glasses of champagne with a toast to the hard work and success of the participants may be appropriate in some cases. Even a handshake after signing can help the participants start working together on a positive note. If one of the participants is still involved in the process of grief and loss (see Chapter Four), the plan should be treated positively but less joyfully and an appropriate referral for support made if necessary (see Chapter Twelve). The signing of a document reflecting the agreements made and the plan for the future is itself a symbol of cooperation and closure.

When the mediated plan is signed by both participants, it may become a legally binding contract (depending on the subject matter and the formalities) enforceable in the civil courts under private contract law. While each document should reflect unique wording for the participants' situation and understanding, the sequence of agreements within the mediated plan should flow in an organized, logical manner so that participants can easily refer to its stipulations. This format becomes more important as the complexity increases. The suggested worksheets can ease the mediator's problem of remembering and reproducing the agreements in an organized form. Mediators should guard against becoming a "mediation shop," as Crouch (1982) has put it, grinding out identical mediated agreements. The very nature of mediation is to allow for customized outcomes, even when they take more time and thought. The scrivener aspect of the mediation process is perhaps the least dramatic but one of the most important roles the mediator plays.

Stage 6: Legal Review/Processing

Stage 6, legal review and processing, is necessary when the conflicts being mediated must be connected to society at large. This stage and the next are the two phases of mediation that are contingent upon forces outside the mediation process itself. In these stages the power, control, and responsibility are no longer entirely in the hands of the participants and mediator. For this reason stages 6 and 7 are less universal than the preceding stages and depend on the subject of mediation as well as the setting of mediation services. They are perhaps more suited to the areas where individuals are mediating for themselves, rather than when representatives knowledgeable in relevant laws and systems are the mediation participants. We therefore are prescribing the inclusion of these two stages for educational, workplace, and family disputes.

Legal review and processing serves as a watchdog to earlier stages by passing the agreements through socially accepted processes that check and legitimize what has been done. This ratification leads the participants to a perception of closure and commitment and, in turn, helps to bring about a greater sense of ownership in the mediated agreements. It also allows a brief respite from the stressful tasks of developing options and making choices. It gives participants a chance to gain useful information from others who are qualified to judge the agreement's completeness and feasibility, as well as time to rest and reassess the agreement's durability and long-term benefits.

Mediation cases involving divorce or custody must be processed through the courts and pass legal review by a judge; an important preliminary stage is to submit the mediated plan to legal counsel before submitting it to the court. (See Chapters Seven and Ten for more information on mechanisms and implications of legal review.) Cases involving environmental disputes may need to be processed and ratified by a government agency or official.

The mediated plan must often be submitted to superiors, committees, boards of directors, executives, or other authorities for final ratification, especially if the agreements include transfers of time, money, or power as in workplace or educational disputes. If this is the case, the mediator should determine who should be notified and suggest a convenient way of submitting the mediated plan to them. Since it is often impractical to have representatives come to the mediation sessions, participants should be informed as early as possible what mechanisms are necessary to provide ratification. If the participants are not empowered to sign agreements regarding certain items, this constraint should be recognized at the outset and pointed out when they are considering options. The legal processing or ratification should also be clearly noted in the written plan.

Mediated plans can be a waste of time and money if they are not supported by institutional policies and attitudes or the participants are not the true decision makers or representatives for the factions in conflict. One way to circumvent this problem is for mediators to notify the president, director, or other leaders of the institution about the intention of the participants to mediate certain issues and to request a written statement concerning the ratification processes that must be used and the empowerment of the participants.

This need to submit the mediated plan to the participants' superiors in the organizational hierarchy is illustrated in the following example. A large city hospital has been troubled by staff problems that are interfering with patient care. The administrators are anxious to resolve this conflict quickly. While they have tried to be helpful by using a counseling process, the conflict remains. They themselves cannot be effective mediators because they are seen by the staff as biased. A mediator has been called in by the head of nursing and told that the problems are due to an informal group of married nurses who refuse to work any shifts except the eight to four o'clock shift, despite the hospital's dire need for "graveyard" slots to be filled between midnight and eight in the morning. The single nurses resent this refusal by the married nurses and, in turn, have refused to work the graveyard shift. Their rationale for refusing is that for the past two years they have felt pressured to fill the vacancies. The single nurses feel that all nurses should do their share. The manifest conflict between these groups is what requirements should be made of nurses to fill the time slots. The underlying conflicts are fractionalization of the nurses by marital status and the judgments being made by all nurses regarding professional responsibility to patients.

The mediator should immediately attempt to get confirmation from each group that the persons whose names were given to the mediator by the head of nursing do in fact represent the married and single nurse factions, respectively, and that their decisions will be honored by all members of their respective groups. Other matters must be confirmed also: whether participation in mediation is truly voluntary, whether the administration will cooperate with any scheduling changes that may arise from mediation, whether these changes must be ratified by the hospital's attorneys and board of directors, what happens if they refuse to ratify the mediated agreement, and whether mediation will be an in-house affair or be publicized by the media from the outset.

Such questions should be answered in writing or by investigation by the mediator prior to starting the mediation process with the participants. In this example, the attorney who is on retainer by the hospital may be able to function as an advisory attorney at certain points of the mediation process, advising the participants on the legal requirements and consequences of options (such as regulations prohibiting discrimination on the basis of marital status). Coogler (1978) has delineated the role and function of impartial advisory attorneys in divorce mediation, but their use remains controversial (see Chapter Six). If the hospital's board of directors has a policy of ratifying agreements made in mediation (unless they violate other hospital policies, civil law, or ethical constraints), mediation will be the preferred means of conflict resolution for this situation. In this way, both legal review (via the attorney) and legal processing (via the board of directors) will be accomplished.

Stage 7: Implementation, Review, and Revision

In stage 7 the participants in mediation are trying to implement the terms of the mediated agreement they have produced. This stage, similar to stage 6, takes place outside the confines of the mediation setting and does not demand the active, continuous involvement of the mediator. Although this stage does not appear to coincide with the others in that it really relies on the participants, there is in fact a dynamic role for the mediator, though an indirect one in many types of disputes—family, educational, some neighborhood and workplace conflicts that involve relationships that must continue after the resolution of the dispute. Stage 7 is similar to stage 6 in that it is not universally applicable to all mediated situations. During this stage the important process of follow-up is begun either by the mediator or by the participants who may need further help.

During the first few weeks and months following the signing of the mediated plan, the participants are trying to actualize what was only conjectured before. It is a difficult time at best. While they may intend to follow the agreement as written, the participants' ability to match their intentions may have suddenly and drastically been altered. Unforeseen problems may arise, stemming either from the fluidity of the situational context that was mediated or from the introduction of new factors beyond their control—a sudden job layoff, a death in the family, the outbreak of war, unexpected technological or environmental changes, and so on. If underlying conflicts were not fully resolved during mediation, or if the participants' internal conflicts are not being resolved by counseling or therapy, the successful implementation of the mediated plan is threatened.

Let us pose an example of the use of follow-up during the implementation phase (stage 7). A couple agreed to mediation to resolve a protracted and bitter custody dispute. They now have a signed plan to provide approximately equal custody of their only child. Several months later, the mother phones the mediator. She is frustrated with the refusal of the father's new live-in fiancée to talk with the mother concerning the child's behavior. She presents this manifest conflict, asking the mediator whether it is a violation of the terms of the plan. One of the underlying conflicts, however, is the mother's heightened perception of her loss of complete control over her child. Another is the internal conflict caused by the fiancée's judgmental attitude toward the mother, symbolized by the subsequent lack of acknowledgment. The mother's self-identity is involved with her liberated sexual behavior, one cause of the marriage's breakdown. She would like to pass on her liberated values to her daughter, yet she realizes that the fiancée, who actively looks after the child during the father's custodial time, is very conservative, perhaps even reactionary and judgmental against the mother's values and sexual identity.

The participant's deeper understanding of the internal, underlying conflicts, as well as her better appreciation of the implications of the option selected in mediation, can only come about by living within the terms of the mediated agreement. Disillusionment, frustration, and confusion, common feelings experienced during this stage, can cloud the benefits of the options that were selected. Such uncomfortable feelings can also bring about new awareness, however, if there is someone available to put the new feelings and perceptions into a useful framework for the participant.

In the preceding example, the mother needs to see that her new role as a joint-custody parent can only influence the child during her custodial time. She also needs to see that expecting the fiancée to change her attitude toward the mother, let alone the fiancée's view of appropriate sexual expression in general, is unrealistic. This mother also must see the child's increasing need to affiliate and live within the family system the father and fiancée will create. This leaves the mother with an important task—practicing toleration of the fiancée's views. She must show the child that there is an alternative to the code of behavior that will be demanded in the father's reconstructed family *without* undermining the structures and beliefs under which the child must live. Unless these realizations are reached, the joint-custody arrangement will be at risk.

Mediators should make themselves available to discuss the first clash during the implementation phase and either reframe it or refer the participant to someone who can provide ongoing help with the underlying, unresolved, intrapersonal conflicts. If good rapport and trust in the mediator were developed during earlier stages, the participant is likely to bring a concern to the mediator before going to others, particularly if the mediator's training involved counseling skills. Mediators should be willing to refer participants to community-based services that can help them deal with the emotional underpinnings, however, while the mediator deals with the content of the agreement itself (see Chapter Twelve). A nonjudgmental and pragmatic approach to the implementation stage can help participants keep most of the mediated agreements while working on the difficulties.

To prevent certain predictable problems, the mediator can give the participants printed handouts concerning difficulties in implementation; this information can be given before the plan is written and signed or later during its implementation. Handouts concerning the difficulties of divorce agreements are an obvious example, and similar materials can be prepared to explain common experiences subsequent to mediation of other types of conflicts.

Because of time, money, or emotional constraints, the mediator is the only professional many participants will see concerning the issues raised in mediation. Many prefer to begin with the mediator rather than starting over with another helping professional should problems arise during implementation. It is important to convey a conceptual framework for reducing the participants' internal conflict or simple reward, approval, and support for maintaining the agreements.

Routine follow-up at specific intervals, initiated by the mediator, can put out brushfires of discontent and provide positive reinforcement. These phone calls, letters, or personal contacts initiated by the mediator can encourage the participant to clarify the meaning and reality of the plan as time goes on. However, enough time must elapse during this implementation stage to make the follow-up useful. Mediators should start the follow-up no sooner than one month after the plan has been signed unless the plan lists an earlier date that is of crucial importance to its continuation. In a divorce case, the mediator might have to contact the participant who agreed to accomplish a physical separation from the former spouse three weeks following the signing; in environmental disputes, the critical date might be completion of an environmental impact statement. The next follow-up could be at six months, and again at the one-year anniversary of the signing. The follow-up not only gives the participant a chance to ventilate feelings and receive support but also provides mediators with useful information regarding the effectiveness of certain options.

A follow-up sheet with open-ended questions and multiple-choice answers not only organizes the follow-up contact but also the subsequent statistical evaluation of mediation. Whether the follow-up is scheduled or initiated because of a participant's contact, the contact should be handled with warmth and reassurance. If the problems are many or very involved, or if the participant's contacts are frequent, the participant should be invited to come back for additional services.

Not all disputes lend themselves to this follow-up system. If the implementation has gone well and the mediation process was followed completely, there may be no need for follow-up or review. People who agree to mediation but need not relate to each other further may find follow-up calls annoying at best. Mediators must judge for themselves the utility of the process for their cases.

Things change, children grow, new situations are encountered, institutions revise their procedures, new alliances are formed. As discussed in Chapter Two, mediation is unique among conflict resolution processes in that it can build into the mediated plan a process for review and revision of the agreement. Mediators can either include a short review session into their scheduling and fee structures or can make it clear that review sessions will be provided only upon request of one of the participants and payment of additional fees. Whichever model is selected, it should be made clear whether the mediator will contact the other participant and whether noncooperation or nonattendance at a review session requested by one participant invalidates the clause of the mediation plan that specified the review. A refusal to meet again or to follow the terms of the review process outlined in the plan may hold other negative consequences as well, such as invalidation of the entire document as a breach of contract through subsequent litigation. It may be a good idea to include one review session in the employment agreement for family mediation cases, because the participants are more likely to avail themselves of it when needed. If the review session has not been held prior to the one-year anniversary of the signing of the plan, the mediator may want to suggest such a session when contacting the participants for follow-ups. In any case, initiation and payment for a review is a matter for the mediator's judgment.

Unlike the follow-up contact, which is usually made over the phone or in person, a review session is a mini-version of the earlier mediation process and usually attends to the first six stages in one session. Both participants are present at a joint session. The mediator invites exploration of current or impending issues; options are discussed; choices are made. These choices can then be written up by the mediator, reviewed by the participants, signed, and made part of the plan as an amendment; signed copies can be attached to the participants' copies, as well as the mediator's. In the case of mediated agreements that have been included in legal proceedings, such as divorce decrees, a copy of amendments must be submitted to the court to be made a matter of record. Since the participants have been through the mediation process, this truncated version of the seven-stage process is usually easily and quickly done. If review of the original mediated plan reveals major conflicts or desired revisions that require considerable reworking of the intent of the original agreement, additional sessions for this stage may need to be provided.

In summary, then, follow-up is a process of eliciting feedback from the participants at certain intervals during the implementation stage. Such contacts may lead to the mediator's suggestion to hold a review and revision session at which the terms of the mediated plan can be looked over and changed. While follow-up contacts are most often initiated by the mediator, a review and revision session, which usually includes stages 1 through 6 in a shortened time span, is usually initiated by the participants because of impending changes that affect the plan or problems in keeping the agreements during the implementation phase. The flowchart in Figure 3 shows the progression of mediation stages and the simplified questions that must be asked in order to move to the next stage.

As we shall see in Chapter Eleven, the mediation process can be scheduled as a periodic set of sessions, each lasting a specific amount of time, or it can be provided in a single session that lasts until all necessary stages (usually stages 1 through 5) are completed. We call these single sessions *marathon* mediation. Crisis mediation is similar to marathon mediation in that it is held in a single session; however, crisis mediation does not require completing of one stage before progression to the next for all conflicted issues, only the issue that is a crisis. The three types of scheduling are:

- *Periodic:* Sessions are held at regular intervals.
- *Marathon:* A single session lasts until the plan is clarified and written; it can take many hours.
- *Crisis:* A single session of short duration deals only with crisis issues.

Figure 3. The Mediation Process.

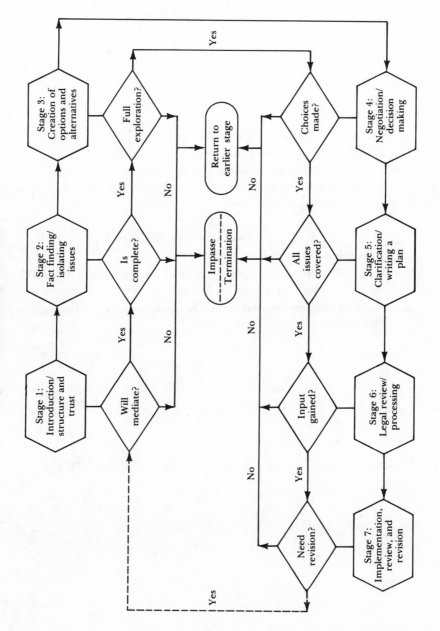

Recommended Reading

Decision Making: A Psychological Analysis of Conflict, Choice, and Commitment. I. L. Janis and L. Mann. New York: Free Press, 1977.

    Relevant as background for all conflict resolution.

Divorce Mediation: A Practical Guide for Therapists and Counselors. J. M. Haynes. New York: Springer, 1981.

    A landmark book by the nation's most celebrated divorce mediator. Offers practical suggestions for negotiating during mediation and presents case studies.

Structured Mediation in Divorce Settlements. O. J. Coogler. Lexington, Mass.: Heath, 1978.

    The first text offering a model for mediation. Although the model has been criticized for being too structured, the book offers helpful insights into the mediation process and specific suggestions of techniques.

4

Counseling Concepts for Developing Mediation Skills

Because mediation is a fusion of concepts from the disciplines of psychology, counseling, law, and other human services, we believe it is necessary to have a common vocabulary and understanding about people, change, and processes. The ideas expressed in this chapter represent the basic constructs and viewpoints that we think are necessary for working with participants in mediation.

We ask those who have studied these topics in depth, such as psychologists, social workers, counselors, and therapists, to review or simply skim the chapter, keeping in mind that it is impossible to discuss every theory here. Those who have not been trained in psychological theory or counseling, such as many attorneys, police officers, clergy, and parents, will need to read carefully and augment this chapter by referring to the recommended readings.

Motivation

Mediation has not emerged out of thin air but is connected theoretically with many schools of psychology and constructs of human behavior. Here we present some of the most useful theories that can serve as a mediator's methodological background when working with people's feelings and behavior. Unlike Coogler (1978), who used transactional analysis solely, we believe that an eclectic approach has benefits for mediators and that no psychological view, no matter how acclaimed or popular, should be used exclusively for the presentation of mediation. Each has its own explanation of human behavior that enriches a mediator's work with participants. Each can become an additional tool for the mediator to use. We have, though, for the sake of brevity and clarity, selected the concepts that we believe are the most relevant and useful to the development of mediation.

Why do people do what they do? And why do people change? These simple questions of motivation have been asked and answered for centuries by the widely diverse disciplines of religion, behavioral sciences, and philosophy, but it is still important to answer them personally before attempting to work directly with mediation participants. What follows is a synthesis of the most germane and useful concepts for mediators regarding these two questions.

Concepts of motivation were integrated into Freud's general theory of behavior. Freud posited that people did what they did because of innate needs and desires that reside in the *id*. These needs surface under the varying control of the censorlike *superego*, which contains rules and behavior first learned from the parents and then from society at large (Patterson, 1973, pp. 98–99). It is the function of the *ego* to moderate and integrate the demands of both the id and superego. An excellent summary of Freudian and other psychodynamic theory has been made for attorneys by Freeman (1964).

This Freudian tripartite system has been reshaped by Erik Berne (1947, 1964), who described a conceptual framework called transactional analysis. Transactional analysis is primarily concerned with ego states. An analogy may be made between Berne's and Freud's views of the personality as follows:

Berne's Terminology*	Freud's Terminology
1. *Parent:* controlling, critical, or nurturing "Don't . . ." "Shut up!"	1. *Superego:* learned rules and values; censorship of id impulses that are contradictory ("morality")

Berne's Terminology*	Freud's Terminology
"You ought to . . ." or "I'll help you . . ." "Take care of yourself."	
2. *Adult:* data processing "I think . . ." "The facts are . . ." "When or where?"	2. *Ego:* the moderator caught in the conflict between desires (id) and prohibition (super-ego); must find compromises
3. *Child:* rebellious, adapted, free and natural "I can't." "I wish . . ." "I don't know . . ." or "Wow" "I love you."	3. *Id:* The instinctual self that desires pleasure and self-ful-fillment without regard to others or conventions (amoral)

*Based on Hallett (1974, p. 12).

While they represent important contributions, we find that neither Freudian theory nor transactional analysis is essential to the practice of mediation. Mastering Freudian and transactional concepts requires extensive study and experience beyond the scope of training necessary for mediators and well beyond what can be explained to participants in mediation. Such books as *A Guide for Single Parents: Transactional Analysis for People in Crisis* (Hallett, 1974) can, however, be useful reading for participants who need a cognitive approach to their intrapersonal conflicts.

Other concepts of motivation and personality are more immediately useful to the mediator and more readily mastered. The view that people are motivated by internal needs has been refined by Maslow (1954) and more recently by Glasser (1965, 1981). We find their constructs to be more helpful in understanding human motivation than other psychological approaches.

Maslow (1954) proposed that people's needs fall into a hierarchy. Basic biological survival needs, such as food and water, form the base of the pyramid while psychological needs, such as the need to love, form an upper level. A person who is meeting all possible needs simultaneously is termed *self-actualized* (see Figure 4). Maslow further proposed that a person who has not met basic physical and security needs cannot achieve the higher state: These lower needs demand the person's attention before the fulfillment of any higher needs.

Figure 4. Maslow's Hierarchy of Needs.

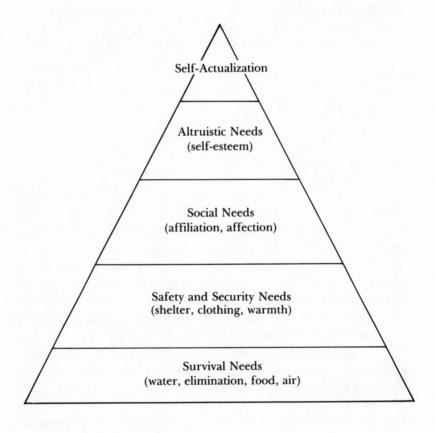

Self-Actualization

Altruistic Needs
(self-esteem)

Social Needs
(affiliation, affection)

Safety and Security Needs
(shelter, clothing, warmth)

Survival Needs
(water, elimination, food, air)

This concept of a hierarchy of needs is particularly relevant to mediators since most clients come to mediators because of the threatened loss of their basic needs. Most participants in mediation are concerned that their private lives, security, or well-being may be shattered by a divorce, a custody dispute, loss of a job, an accusation, or other legal or personal threats. These threats force people to seek professional help as they mobilize their attention toward this stress. Their standing on the pyramid has been lowered. The inarticulated goal of participants in mediation is often to regain or improve their standing on the pyramid and thereby better meet their needs. With this in mind, it is important to remember how difficult it is to get two participants to pay attention to altruistic concerns or long-range consequences of decisions while their attention is focused on the higher priority of immediate safety and security. Participants involved in family disputes find that their self-esteem as well as their social needs are severely threatened (see Chapter Seven).

Glasser (1965, 1981) proposes that *all* behavior is an attempt to meet certain basic needs: a need to love, for belonging, self-worth, recognition, fun, and freedom, as well as the biological needs of the organism. Glasser disagrees with Maslow's emphasis on the primacy of survival needs to the individual and cites suicide as an example. The suicide often feels worthless, unloved, left out, or hopelessly trapped and, in total contradiction to biological survival needs, chooses extinction of the physical self. Others, such as Victor Frankl (1963), have pointed out that the organism's physical needs are not the only factors for survival; attitude, perception, and other psychological factors are at least as important. In his article "Why We Should Abandon Maslow's Need Hierarchy Theory," William Fox (1982) points out that Maslow's theory is inconsistent with observed behavior and is not supported by research findings.

Glasser (1981) explains how monitoring and controlling of basic physiological needs is done by the "old brain," the neural brainstem, which sends its message of needs for water, food, oxygen, elimination, and so forth to the "new brain," or cerebral cortex, which is responsible for developing and implementing effective behavior to meet those needs. When there is a *difference* between our internal perception (what we want) and what is presented to us by the world (what we think we have), we experience a "perceptual error" that motivates us to produce behavior from the categories of feeling, thinking, and doing. This behavior is designed to have an impact on the world and thereby reduce "error" by meeting our need and consequently reducing the frustration and high arousal state, or stress, caused by the internal conflict. In the following chapters we shall have more to say about stress and its effect on thinking, feeling, and doing.

Following Glasser's line of thinking, if needs are being met there is no internal conflict or perceptual error and also no behavior that is being produced; the system is at rest (homeostatic) until there is an unmet need. If there *is* behavior, whether it is thought, feeling, or action, it is due to internal conflict, according to Glasser. The greater the conflict, and therefore perceptual error, the greater the frustration and the more intense the motivation to alleviate it and reestablish a calm internal state.

Using a workplace setting to illustrate this point, suppose an employee is doing well on the job. Her needs are being met and no behavior, other than job performance, is being produced. Then the efficiency consultants who are brought in suggest a faster rate for completion of her task, with the result that she will have to stay at her desk through the usual lunch hour. This change brings about a great internal conflict, because the employee looked forward to socializing with other workers and friends as a break in her otherwise monotonous day. She wants to be a good employee and obey the rules, but she also wants to meet her social needs at lunch (an approach/approach conflict).

As time progresses under the new regime, she begins to interrupt the nearest worker, seeking to meet her internal need to belong, to feel good about herself, to communicate. She starts to smoke and fetch coffee to her desk. The quality and volume of her work decline to the point where her supervisor admonishes her for slacking off and gives her an ultimatum to produce on time. She responds to the threat, but now her work is less accurate and another employee must double-check it before proceeding. Her frustration and stress grow, and unless she finds a positive way to meet her unfulfilled needs, she will quit to find a better situation, the supervisor will fire her, or she will attempt to unionize the clerical workers in her office to gain control over such issues as lunch schedules and coffee breaks.

Which behavior a person chooses is determined, in Glasser's view, by its anticipated consequences. If the behavior has worked effectively before to meet needs and the person has not suffered drastic consequences, the person is likely to try it again. Most people have a repertoire of action they use for certain situations, seemingly without thinking. As we have noted, however, the choice of behavior a person makes to fulfill perceived needs is a highly complex series of thoughts carried out in the cerebral cortex in fractions of seconds. If the goal is to meet their needs, people's repertoires of action can be changed by learning more effective behavior. Therefore all actions, thoughts, and feelings are intricately involved in the process of choice.

To summarize Glasser, people do what they do because they are attempting to meet their needs as they perceive them. The implication for mediators is that, first, they will often be working with people who are *not* currently meeting their needs and, second, it is very difficult to predict how people will choose from a range of alternatives unless you know their perceptual and learned world. Therefore it is essential to understand the participant's perceptual world in order to realign it to reframe issues and resolve conflicts, a necessary requirement of the mediator's role.

Participants may be willing to change one set of behavior for another if they are made to see that one option holds more of a threat to their needs or will maintain an internal conflict. In other words, if the behavior continues to meet the person's needs for fun, freedom, affection, and belonging, it is likely to continue until a truly negative consequence results from it. Dissatisfaction with the present condition, either naturally occurring or created by skillful professional intervention, must occur before a person is ready for change (Jung, 1978). In Glasser's view, a person must experience an internal conflict produced by unmet needs before he or she will be motivated to do something about it.

Other approaches to counseling, however, see Glasser's concepts as simplistic. They argue that behavior is motivated not just by unmet needs but by the following variables: genetic predisposition, past history of learning, present physiological state, current environment, and cognitive beliefs. Psychological theory developed by Festinger (1964) proposes that intrapersonal conflicts are the result

of a state of cognitive dissonance, or a difference between perceptions and thoughts. According to this line of thought, behavior
is motivated and personal change is made when the individual
tries behavior to reduce the dissonance (internal conflict). While
Festinger's theory is a major contribution to the field of psychology,
his ideas are hard to apply to interpersonal conflicts, the issues of
primary relevance in mediation.

Learning theorists and behavior therapists contend that behavior is based on a complex equation of the following components
(Patterson, 1973, p. 181):

S = prior stimulation
O = biological state of the organism
R = response repertoire
K = contingency relationship
C = consequence

These components interact to make up what we see as observable,
measurable behavior. Accordingly, controlling any one of them will
bring about a change in the behavior. Behavior modification is
therefore the use of different techniques to influence one or more of
these components. Among the techniques that have been used are
desensitization, aversive stimuli, aversive consequences (punishment), selective reinforcement, contingency management, and behavioral contracting.

Bandura (1969) found that social learning, through the modeling of appropriate behavior, is a successful technique for changing behavior. Having the client see someone else demonstrate the
desired behavior in a certain situation increases the likelihood that
the client will exhibit the same behavior when placed in the same
situation. This technique has direct implications for the role of the
mediator, who should therefore model the appropriate behavior the
participants are to learn.

Another psychological approach with which mediators
should familiarize themselves is the rational-emotive therapy (RET)
of Albert Ellis (1962; Ellis and Harper, 1975). This theory is based on
the works of many ancient and modern philosophers, but the concepts are characterized by the assumptions that (1) humans are

primarily rational beings and (2) emotional disturbance is the result of learned and biologically predisposed irrational thoughts that must be reordered into rational thoughts; by doing so, the person can change self-defeating emotions and behavior (Patterson, 1973, pp. 51–52). By helping clients abandon their misperceptions and irrational thoughts and see the world differently in rational terms, the rational-emotive therapist helps them change their behavior.

Ellis (1962, p. 61) lists the following statements of values that are inculcated by Western culture but are irrational and lead to neurosis if not reframed:

1. It is essential that one be loved or approved by virtually everyone in his community.
2. One must be perfectly competent, adequate, and achieving to consider oneself worthwhile.
3. Some people are bad, wicked, or villainous and therefore should be blamed and punished.
4. It is a terrible catastrophe when things are not as one wants them to be.
5. Unhappiness is caused by outside circumstances, and the individual has no control over it.
6. Dangerous or fearsome things are causes for great concern, and their possibility must be continually dwelt upon.
7. It is easier to avoid certain difficulties and self-responsibilities than to face them.
8. One should be dependent on others and must have someone stronger on whom to rely.
9. Past experiences and events are the determiners of present behavior; the influence of the past cannot be eradicated.
10. One should be quite upset over other people's problems and disturbances.
11. There is always a right or perfect solution to every problem, and it must be found or the results will be catastrophic.

Certainly many participants in mediation express these notions as their implicit message while seeming to talk about the issue at hand. Mediators, as a group, might be tempted to fall into wrong thinking themselves (especially number 11) if they are not also observing their own belief systems.

While mediators cannot vigorously attack such wrong thinking in head-on confrontation as Ellis does in therapy, they can note
the implicit message and act as an agent of reality, getting the participant at least to question the validity of such thoughts. Some mediators may find it useful to hand out a list of these irrational beliefs at
the introductory stage or when such beliefs are interfering in stages 3
or 4 of the mediation process (see Chapter Three). Mediators can
promote change in their participants' thoughts and behavior by
noting and questioning them.

Now that we have examined some of the most useful answers
to the questions about motivation and change posed at the beginning of this chapter, what are some of the practical blocks to choice
and change during mediation sessions? How does this abstract information relate to the practical problems of participants?

In addition to the internal conflicts described earlier, there are
social and interactive problems that can reduce a participant's motivation and ability to communicate effectively. If the mediator's style
prevents the participants from speaking freely in sessions, it will be
that much harder for them to reach their goal, which is the im-
provement of their status in the needs hierarchy described earlier *and*
the reduction or elimination of the conflicts, both interpersonal and
intrapersonal, that they are experiencing.

Seven factors that can inhibit the motivation of a participant
to talk during a mediation session have been outlined in another
context by Binder and Price (1977, pp. 9–14):

- *Ego threat:* defined as information withheld by the client because of fears about its damage to the client's self-esteem
- *Case threat:* information withheld because of fears of its potential damage to the case
- *Role expectations:* learned deference and subordination to the
  higher authority and status of the mediator
- *The etiquette barrier:* things that cannot be told to members of
  certain groups by members of other groups
- *Trauma:* a past event so painful to remember that the client
  blocks out the memory
- *Perceived irrelevancy:* information withheld because the client
  does not understand its relevance and importance

- *Greater need:* similar to Maslow's "lower" needs overshadowing "higher" ones

Generally, the interpersonal blocks of a participant's motivation can be forestalled or allayed by use of the techniques described in subsequent chapters. Mediators who learn these skills and practice them will be better equipped to discover and meet the participants' needs.

Affect, Behavior, and Cognition

Now that we have discussed motivation, we must consider behavior. We need to look not only at what mediation participants do but also what the world does to them. Every event that happens to the participants has a reaction that contains three components: affect, behavior, and cognition, or "A-B-C's." Affect is the client's *feeling* or emotional reaction before, during, and after the event. Behavior is the client's *action* before, during, and after. Cognition is the client's *thought* before, during, and after.

Glasser (1981) would say all three, including affect and cognition, are behavior, and we separate them here only for elaborative purposes. Ellis (1962) would say that cognition is the most important and that a change in cognition affects emotion and action. Some psychological theorists, such as Skinner (1938, 1953), contend that thoughts and feelings are not behavior in the same way that observable action is because they are not directly observable or measurable but are side effects or past learning.

To neglect the other two components, feelings and thoughts, is to ignore the real truth for the individual, since a person's response to a given event probably includes all three components. These three components are often hard for participants to delineate after the event has happened, but they can be separated by skillful questioning, as any trial lawyer is aware. The more mediators can help participants separate these elements, the more promise there is for building agreements on cognition rather than reaction or feelings left over from the past.

Later in the book we suggest a sequence for conducting the process of mediation that requires the mediator to listen to the participants' views and positions uninterrupted by questions. During that listening phase, and later when questions are being asked, it is vital that the mediator focus on all three aspects since they can lead to a complete understanding of the participants' world view and situation.

The following example illustrates the usefulness of the "A-B-C" method—affect, behavior, cognition—for understanding the participants' perspective and thus eliciting and organizing the information the mediator needs. In this example a divorcing couple coming for mediation both work in separate professions that require transfers and moving across the country for advancement within their respective fields. During the last move from Texas to California, the wife felt that she gave up a major career opportunity by following her husband, and she decided she would never again place his career over hers. The couple has one daughter who is now three years old. The dispute facing the couple, who want to plan a joint-custody schedule involving a one-week parenting cycle, concerns what should happen if the woman wants to advance in her career by relocating. The man is currently weighing a lucrative job offer in Oregon; he would like to take the job but is worried that the woman will not move to Oregon if he does, since the only job she could get within her company structure would, in effect, be a demotion.

Using the A-B-C method, the mediator can first isolate the events in the past, present, and future and then apply the A-B-C's to it. Table 5 presents a diagram of this situation. Note that the woman's behavior for the present situation is not helpful to resolution of the issue, nor is the man's. Moreover, the future concerns that are being discussed represent an inversion of the present issue. If the mediator is skillful, he or she will reopen the present issue first, deferring future concerns until the present issue is resolved. The mediator will also reframe the issue so that both parents focus on the real needs of the child and reconcile their attitudes toward those needs as a way of changing their behavior. The mediator tries to align both sides in their cognition ("C") in order to get a mutually agreeable behavior ("B") from both; this behavior then constitutes the terms of the settlement.

In this case, by reopening the cognition component for the present issue and stopping the current behavior that is destructive to agreement, both the man and the woman focus on parenting issues for the future and stop bringing in A's, B's, and C's from the past.

Table 5. The A-B-C Matrix.

Event	Woman	Man
Past: the move from Texas to California	A: Resentful, grudging. B: She followed the man to a new state. C: She told herself that next time she would give her own career the highest priority.	A: Pleased, excited. B: He made the decision. C: He assumed she would follow him to a new state because that is what a wife does.
Present: job offer for the man in Oregon	A: Angry, weary. B: She tells mediator about the past issue; says her present position is the same as past cognition—that is, she will do what is best for her own career this time. C: She does not think Oregon will meet the child's needs because of loss of contact with relatives.	A: Indecisive, fears isolation in a new state. B: He changes the focus of discussion in order to force the woman to make a decision that will determine his choices. C: He believes he will serve child best by making more money at the new job.
Future: what if the woman wants a job in another state?	A: Conflicting. B: Not yet made (open issue). C: She believes that the child needs two active parents (via joint custody) until at least age five.	A: He fears loss of his child through a move. B: He negotiates to have the woman commit herself to the move and then stay in his locale. C: He thinks the woman will capitulate in order to promote joint custody.

A = affect; B = behavior (response); C = cognition.

After discussing a new issue—what the child *really* needs—both parents decide that their child's best interests can be served by maintaining cooperative parenting no matter how much money they make, in what state they reside, or whether relatives are close enough for frequent visits. This decision unlocks both participants' posi-

tions by reaching cognitive consensus and points the way to appropriate behavior for both sides.

The man can then determine that he will take the job only if
it will not interfere with whatever joint-custody arrangement meets
the child's needs; the woman can make concessions to the joint-
custody schedule so that custody could last two weeks, until the
child attends school. This accommodation leads the woman to
make a similar commitment to joint custody, rather than to her own
job advancement and relocation, for at least two more years until the
child is five and ready for school. At that time, the parents must
renegotiate the joint-custody arrangement. Table 6 shows the revision on an A-B-C matrix.

It is not practical to prepare a detailed diagram of the
participants' positions *during* a mediation session because it would
break down rapport, but this schematic analysis of the participants'
feelings, actions, and plans and thoughts can be done by the mediator after a particularly complex session or when an impasse has been

Table 6. The A-B-C Matrix Revised.

Event	*Woman*	*Man*
Present: a job offer in Oregon for the man	A: Relieved. B: She will postpone job advancement if necessary to maintain joint custody. C: She believes the child is best served by joint custody.	A: Decisive. B: He will only take the job if it will not jeopardize joint custody. C: He believes the child is best served by joint custody.
Future: what if the woman wants a job in another state?	A: Calmly acceptant, trusting. B: She will postpone her decision until the child is five or more; or she will allow broadening of the joint-custody schedule to enable a move to a nearby state.	A: More secure. B: He will continue joint custody and allow broadening of the joint-custody schedule to enable the woman to move to a nearby state.

A = affect; B = behavior (response); C = cognition.

reached. The matrix will show the mediator exactly what is happening and the next session's goals. It can also be used to resolve an impasse by showing the participants how the past is interfering with the present and the future. More will be said in later chapters about the use of pictorial representations, the maintenance of rapport, and the selection of the mediator's goals.

Feelings and Empathy

Since the law tends to emphasize the action part of events, people who work with issues such as divorce, that must be adjudicated or negotiated and legally processed, often focus on the factual data and become masters at manipulating this information in useful ways. This mastery is advantageous from the standpoint of the work traditionally done by an attorney, but it does not necessarily help in understanding and developing rapport with mediation participants. Since gaining and maintaining that rapport allows for better isolation of issues and alternatives, it is essential for a mediator to become attuned to feelings and skilled at empathizing with the participants. Lawyers, too, and other helping professionals who wish to function as mediators should develop skills in creating and conveying empathy.

An important task in becoming a mediator is to evaluate your own empathic level and become sensitized to feelings in yourself and others. Whole courses have been developed to provide people with empathy training. To test your ability in regard to empathic statements, you must evaluate two areas: frequency of empathic responses and skill in their use for facilitating communication of the participants. Tape record yourself in a mock mediation session. Then count the number of feeling words you use in the first five minutes and again at the end of the session. To evaluate the effectiveness of your empathic responses, it is necessary to review both your verbal and nonverbal behavior. Ask an experienced professional to observe you at work or practice and evaluate your timing, phrasing, and use of the response.

It is useful to review the following list of feeling words (adapted from Wood, 1974) before your first few mediation sessions as a way of sensitizing yourself to the affective messages you may send and receive. This list, of course, is far from complete.

Accepted	Hurt
Affectionate	Inferior
Afraid	Jealous
Angry	Joyful
Anxious	Lonely
Attracted	Loving
Bored	Rejected
Community (connected)	Repulsed
Competitive	Respect
Confused	Sad
Defensive	Satisfied
Disappointed	Shy
Free	Superior
Frustrated	Suspicious
Guilty	Trusting
Hopeful	Unworthy

Another helpful way to deal with affective content is to categorize the participant's words into basic emotional states. Cormier and Cormier (1979, p. 69) present a chart that is useful for this kind of review.

Feelings often come in conglomerates and have distinctions that are generalizable. Bullmer (1975) states that fear, joy, and anger are linked by the fact that all three relate to goal attainment, whereas guilt, shame, pride, success, and failure relate to a person's self-perception along a good–bad continuum. Another category of feelings he proposes includes envy, love, hate, and jealousy, all of which correlate with a person's perceptions regarding relations with others. It is often important to differentiate envy, a desire to possess what another has, from jealousy, a desire to protect a relationship from a perceived threat. Both feelings are commonly seen in mediation, particularly in family mediation cases, and both are socially unacceptable, therefore creating an increase in defensive behavior.

With these definitions, the skillful mediator can build trust and rapport by reflecting and clarifying a hidden feeling for the participant prior to the participant's expression of that feeling during the session. This shows the participant that the mediator understands exactly what he or she is feeling and does not think badly of him or her for feeling it. Most participants want the mediator's acceptance, if not approval, and this is one way of showing acceptance. The mediator must not be obvious in providing this empathy, however, since many participants do not expect to be dealing with their feelings at all in mediation. Many people react negatively and resist enthusiastic empathic responses. Judiciousness is the key to successful use of empathy in mediation, and this quality can be learned through experience and training.

Anger in our society is hard to acknowledge and even harder to show in socially acceptable ways. Often the participants in mediation deemphasize their anger by calling it frustration. Moreover, many men will not openly acknowledge to others, as well as to themselves, that they are afraid, unless they are given permission to do so. By using precise terms for the feelings, and perhaps even setting the stage by normalizing the feelings, the mediator can create an atmosphere of greater openness and comfort for the participants, as well as get useful information for later sessions.

To summarize, then, empathy is a dynamic process of accurately perceiving another person's emotional state and that person's perception of its meaning. It is a process that can be learned and taught. And when used in conjunction with precise definitions of feelings, empathy can help explain consequent behavior, facilitate communication, and establish rapport and trust in the mediation session.

Blocks to Communication

We have just presented a view of empathy as a process of sharing interpersonal perceptions between mediator and participant. There are two basic types of problems that can occur with interpersonal communication: The sender can be ineffective by sending a vague, incomplete, or incomprehensible message, or the receiver can interpret the message incompletely or incorrectly.

The term *defensive reaction* refers to the incomplete reception of a message or the sending of a message in oblique and contradictory ways. The purpose of all defensive reactions is to reduce the internal conflict felt by the person who is experiencing a perceptual error. That person is attempting to distort reality to minimize frustration and anxiety. There are several classification systems for grouping these defensive reactions. According to Bullmer (1975, p. 64), *instrumental* responses "reduce anxiety by the elimination of the causative conflict or frustration" and *noninstrumental* responses "reduce anxiety without resulting in any change in the causative conflict or frustration by operating to deny, falsify, or distort reality."

Rationalization is the term for attributing acceptable motives to one's behavior that could be viewed as unacceptable. A former spouse who is threatening a lawsuit over the rights to the family heirlooms may justify the action by rationalizing that the suit is helping to preserve the family heritage, when in fact the action is creating complete family disruption and discord.

Compensation is the term used for the acceptance of a substitute for the original goal that only partially meets the person's needs. When a prospective student accepts the offer of dental college because he or she was denied admission to medical school, that student is compensating. The student may be convinced that being a dentist is as good as being a physician; if this is the case, then compensation is operating to defend against a perception of inadequacy or failure. Not all such choices are defensive adjustments, however. The choice to accept dental school in place of medical school may be a realistic evaluation of one's best interests. Compensation can often be distinguished from a cognitive choice by the intensity of feeling involved in the adoption of the compensatory choice.

Identification is a method of ascribing another's attributes to oneself. Wives may affiliate with their husbands' occupations and interests so strongly that they become "Mrs. Lawyer," "Mrs. Banker," or "Mrs. Ph.D." Religious-minded people try to "become one with" their ideal, teacher, or concept as a way of identifying strongly with their beliefs. People generally identify only with favorable attributes. *Projection*, on the other hand, is displacing one's own negative qualities onto other persons. Both mechanisms are attempts to feel better about oneself and to meet the inner needs for self-worth, belonging, and affiliation described earlier.

The term *reaction formation* is used to describe a person's defensive reaction of behaving the opposite of their true feelings and desires. Because of social conventions, all of us have experienced having to smile or be polite to people we really dislike. This is an example of a reaction formation. The smiling helps us hide from the fact that we do not like the person, since not liking that person, yet having to interact with him, throws us into perceptual error and internal conflict. Anxiety and internal conflict are lessened or averted by all these defenses and distortions of reality. They help change perceptions of oneself that would be unacceptable to our conscious awareness. The only problem with these defenses is that they require vast amounts of energy to maintain and never completely eliminate the unwanted perceptions.

Being able to listen to a participant's story and recognize these defenses will speed the mediator's understanding and subsequent handling of the case, since the unacceptable motives can be discovered without having to force the participant into a fully defended position, or what is called *resistance*. By calmly accepting and reflecting the unacceptable perception or the real goal (in the case of rationalization and compensation), the mediator can normalize and relax the defense system of participants and elicit their help and cooperation. This skill can be perfected by practice. Further suggestions for specific techniques are given in Chapter Thirteen.

Remember that defenses are usually there for a reason—be cautious in attacking them or removing them violently, thus leaving your participants vulnerable. If a participant is hostile, realize that the participant *needs* the anger and defensive reactions until he or she is ready to try instructions for new behavior, or until the perceptual error and resulting anxiety are reduced.

Stress, Anger, and Anxiety

Mediators see people when they are in stressful situations. Either their personal goals are being blocked by someone or something and they are angry, or they perceive a known threat and feel fear, or they perceive a generalized threat and feel anxious. Fear, anger, and anxiety act on the body in the same way—they create a stress reaction that involves strong physical arousal. According to Woolfolk and Richardson (1978, p. 9): "Stress is a perception of threat or expectation of future discomfort that arouses, alerts, or otherwise activates the organism."

When the person perceives the block or the threat, the brain starts the autonomic nervous system functioning at a higher, aroused level. The outward signs of this arousal are dilated pupils, faster or more shallow breathing, a flushed face, an increased pulse, general bodily tension, and perhaps even a loss of sphincter control, vomiting, sweating, or loss of consciousness. This archaic fight-or-flight mechanism was once useful for survival. Now, paradoxically, it is literally killing people; if they experience unrelieved stress for long periods of time, the high arousal level will create a physical breakdown. The result is a type of disease created by dis-ease.

When a person under stress is angry, that anger manifests itself as a set of behaviors that attempts to make the world change in order to stop the internal conflict. According to Woolfolk and Richardson (1978), anger happens most often if there is a perception of infringement, if there is frustration, or if there is a perception of wrongfulness or intentionality. A good example of this is found during divorce, when one party, say the man, becomes incensed if he feels that an adulterous act was done intentionally to hurt him, or in environmental disputes, when a group feels that certain actions infringe upon their rights or territory.

Studies have been done to discover which life events are the most stressful. The following list (Woolfolk and Richardson, 1978, pp. 26–27) shows the events that ranked highest in the social readjustment scale, a research tool developed in 1967 by Holmes and Rahe at the University of Washington Medical School. The scale can be used to predict the onset of serious illness by adding points for each life stress encountered by an individual.

1. Death of spouse
2. Divorce
3. Marital separation
4. Jail term
5. Death of a close family member

6. Personal injury or illness
7. Marriage
8. Being fired from a job
9. Marital reconciliation
10. Retirement
11. Change in health of a family member
12. Pregnancy
13. Sex difficulties
14. Addition of a new family member
15. Business readjustments
16. Change in financial state
17. Death of a close friend
18. Change to a different line of work
19. Change in the number of arguments with spouse
20. A large mortgage
21. Foreclosure of mortgage or loan
22. Change in responsibilities at work
23. Son or daughter leaving home
24. Trouble with in-laws
25. Outstanding personal achievements
26. Wife begins or stops work
27. Beginning or ending school
28. Change in living conditions
29. Revision of personal habits
30. Trouble with boss
31. Change in work hours or conditions
32. Change in residence
33. Change in school
34. Change in recreation
35. Change in church activities
36. Change in social activities
37. Mortgage or loan less than $10,000
38. Change in sleeping habits
39. Change in number of family get-togethers
40. Change in eating habits
41. Vacation
42. Christmas
43. Minor violations of the law

Most of these stressful events lend themselves to mediation and involve many of the issues that mediators must deal with. Divorce and marital separation, for example, are the second and third highest stressors encountered by people in our society. Because of this, the mediator must understand the mechanisms of stress and help the participants reduce their stress level during the mediation sessions and afterward as a way of promoting better decisions and better life habits.

Certain experiences are likely to promote stress, which can then turn into distress. Schafer (1978, pp. 69–83) lists these general categories: overload, understimulation, absence of meaning, role conflict, role ambiguity, transition, loss, unfinished business, banal lifescripts, and perceived gaps between ideals and reality. For some clients participating in divorce mediation, several of these categories may contribute to their level of distress. Consider a fifty-five-year-old woman whose husband has just announced his desire to divorce her after twenty-five years of marriage and whose twenty-year-old son, one of two grown children who continues to live at home, has reacted to this news by crashing the car into an abutment and hospitalizing himself with a bad leg fracture. This woman must not only deal with the stress of a huge life transition; she must also deal with a conflict in her role between caretaking mother and woman who needs to spend time on, and for, herself. She is caught in a role ambiguity as a wife, since she does not know how to act around her husband, who has not been able to leave the residence and will not be able to do so for more than a month because of financial reasons. She is upset at the tragic lifescript her son's actions have created for himself and her. She has much unfinished business to discuss with her husband, and she is suffering from loss of self-worth because of things her husband has said to her. She also fears the possible loss of a comfortable home and a secure retirement.

Obviously this woman is overloaded. As she tries to carry on with the household routines of shopping, laundry, cleaning, cooking, and social responsibilities, she goes from the initial alarm reaction of stress to a state of resistance and then to the exhaustion phase; this is the three-part process of human reaction to stress called the *general adaptation syndrome* (Schafer, 1978, p. 40).

There are really only three ways to reduce stress. First you can try to eliminate the stressor from your environment, but often this cannot be done conveniently or without additional stress. If your spouse is the stressor, for example, you can start divorce proceedings, but divorce itself brings even higher levels of stress, at least temporarily. Most people favor eliminating the stressor, since it is really an attempt to get the world to change to meet your needs. Eliminating the stressor requires an action by the person experiencing the stress. In the A-B-C model, this is an attempt to change the "B." If you are successful and the world does change, it will reduce your conflict and perceptual error, thus lowering your arousal level and removing the general adaptation syndrome you may be experiencing.

The second method is to try to change your thoughts and perceptions (the "C" of the A-B-C model) about the stressor. (See the reference to Ellis, 1962, earlier in this chapter.) While this option works well with some stressors, it is not effective in reducing stress from biological or lower-order needs. Nevertheless, this reshaping of the problem as a cure is often successful as the client begins to see that there really is no recourse and the stressor will have to be coped with for a period of time.

The third option is to work on altering your emotional and physical reaction to stress, thus reducing the arousal state. This is often done by drinking, taking drugs, meditating or praying, progressive relaxation or other relaxation techniques, self-hypnosis, and other therapies. This third option as well as the second is probably needed when the stressor is simply unavoidable. Consider the woman who must commute but undergoes great stress and anger in traffic jams. She could learn to relax her bodily tension progressively during a traffic jam as a way of altering her physical and emotional reactions to the stressing condition.

To summarize, stress is the state of physical arousal that accompanies prolonged emotional reactions to unpleasant situations. Stress can be considered acute when it causes a temporary high arousal level; when it is chronic and prolonged, it is called distress. Stress relief is provided by eliminating or changing the stressor, by eliminating or changing one's physical and emotional reaction to the stressor, or by changing one's thoughts about the stressor. (Another way to alleviate stress is by denying that the stressor exists. See earlier parts of this chapter for more information on denial and distortion of reality.)

Again we emphasize: The mediator's clients are often in acute stress or distress situations. They may often need professional help from doctors, counselors, and the clergy, as well as mediation services, to help them cope with this temporary stress as well as to learn to deal with chronic stress in their lives. We feel strongly that mediators must take an active role in helping their clients acknowledge and deal effectively with their stress, both during the sessions and after.

Grief and Loss

Most participants come to mediation with a perception that they have lost, or may lose, something of importance to them. Divorce cases involve the loss of the intimate relationship and often a loss of self-esteem, financial security, identity, and familiar surroundings. Mediators who work with corporate and business disputes find that these cases may involve a loss of corporate image, job security, benefits, and self-esteem, as well as financial losses. Tenant/landlord cases often involve a loss of expectations, time, energy, security, privacy, and money. All disputes involve potential loss.

Loss does not have to be actual in order to elicit what we shall term the grief/loss process. Just anticipating the loss of an expected inheritance, profit, tax advantage, or desired opportunity can make people sad. The intensity of their grief is usually equal to the intensity of their self-involvement in the person, object, feeling, or concept at stake. The finality of the loss and the uniqueness of the item are also involved in this factoring, since that which is irreplaceable—a parent or one's childhood—elicits a far greater grief response than an everyday object.

Several researchers have studied their subjects' reaction to loss. Kübler-Ross (1975) proposes that people who are experiencing a loss, such as death, undergo a five-stage process: anger, denial, bargaining, withdrawal, acceptance. Colgrove, Bloomfield, and

McWilliams (1976) propose a three-stage process for loss. The first stage is shock/denial; the second stage is anger/depression; the third stage is understanding/acceptance. Schafer (1978, p. 79) describes the process as outcry, denial, intrusion, working through, and completion.

No matter which description the mediator finds most helpful, the important thing is to reassure grieving clients that what they are experiencing is not uncommon and will change in time, even if no active intervention, such as therapy, is sought. The importance of these schemes for the mediator is to remember that someone still in the denial, depression, or withdrawal stage will not be *emotionally* ready to negotiate a mediated settlement, even if he or she demands that the settlement be completed quickly. While an understanding of the dynamics of loss will not totally mitigate the mediator's frustration with changing demands and settlement agreements, it may serve as a guide to a skillful evaluation and appropriate action. Thus a mediator who has assessed a participant as still "actively bleeding" should bring that fact to the parties' attention in a divorce mediation and, if necessary, forestall review or execution of the mediated settlement until the client is emotionally ready to accept that action as the true ending of the marital relationship. The mediation guidelines discussed in Chapter Three allow for this possibility by declaring an impasse and halting the resulting actions and consequences for those who are not ready to continue mediation because of emotional loss.

The connection of grief to depression is explained succinctly by Jackson (1957), who says that both involve disorganization of functioning and feelings of hopelessness about the future, but grief, unlike depression, does not involve a loss of self-worth. Participants who are experiencing intense grief at the time they see a mediator may need to be referred for professional therapy or counseling. In Chapters Twelve and Thirteen, we discuss both depression and referral more thoroughly, but we feel it is important for the reader to be sensitized to the issue of loss and grief early in our writing, since this process dominates many of the interactions between participants. It is in the mediator's own interest to perceive the differences between grief and true depression accurately so that appropriate interventions and referrals can be offered.

Recommended Reading

General

Effective Helping: Interviewing and Counseling Techniques (2nd
ed.) B. F. Okun. Monterey: Brooks/Cole, 1982.
   Comprehensive text with glossary.

The Helping Relationship: Process and Skills. L. M. Brammer. Englewood Cliffs, N.J.: Prentice-Hall, 1973.
   Sums up the basic skills.

Helping Relationships: Basic Concepts for the Helping Professions.
A. W. Combs, D. L. Avilia, and W. W. Purkey. Boston: Allyn &
Bacon, 1971.
   Good overview of the process of helping.

Intangibles in Counseling. C. G. Kemp. Boston: Houghton Mifflin,
1967.
   Presents a philosophical basis for understanding people.

Feelings and Empathy

*The Art of Empathy: A Manual for Improving Accuracy of
Inter-Personal Perception.* K. Bullmer, New York: Human Sciences Press, 1975.
   Programmed learning text format that provides quick review
and reinforcement on the subject of feelings.

The Helping Interview. (2nd ed.) A. Benjamin. Boston: Houghton
Mifflin, 1974.
   Provides a view of the helping role based on empathic
listening.

Stress, Anger, and Anxiety

Positive Addiction. W. Glasser. New York: Harper & Row, 1976.
   Outlines the needs and outlets for altered states that become
fulfilling.

Stress, Distress, and Growth. W. Schafer. Davis, Calif.: Responsible
   Action, 1978.
      A basic text on stress.

Stress, Sanity and Survival. R. L. Woolfolk and F. C. Richardson.
   New York: Monarch, 1978.
      Easily read book by practicing clinicians.

Grief and Loss

*How to Survive the Loss of a Love: 58 Things to Do When There is
   Nothing to Be Done.* M. Colgrove, H. H. Bloomfield, and P.
   McWilliams. New York: Bantam Books, 1976.
      A short book that uses poetry to amplify feelings. Makes
practical suggestions and would be useful for grieving clients.

5

✳ ✳ ✳ ✳ ✳

Methods for Enhancing Communication

Now that we have provided a basic theoretical picture of how people act, think, and feel and have suggested definitions for common emotional processes and feeling states, we present a basic set of skills that can become tools for mediating. Most mediation work, and most of what this text has to offer, is in the realm of verbal exchanges, although many useful techniques involve nonverbal skills. The more aware you are of your own style, reactions, and abilities, the better able you will be to serve participants as an effective mediator.

The major consideration for the use of these skills is the development of rapport between mediator and participant in order to gain essential information. Such information is not only behavioral but also affective and cognitive. After this information has been gathered, it then becomes the mediator's job to organize it, verify it, evaluate it, and use it to the participants' advantage. For this reason, the mediator will need all the skills we describe to provide a complete mediation service. Such skills require both verbal and nonverbal behavior by the mediator.

Preparatory Structuring

Establishing a relationship conducive to the flow of information depends largely upon how the initial mediation session begins. The mediator should not aggravate the participants' anxiety by keeping them waiting for long periods of time in a reception room. The setting of the waiting area and the attitude of the office staff are important factors shaping the participants' willingness to confide in the mediator (see Chapter Eleven).

Meeting the participants in the reception room and escorting them to the mediation setting, after greeting them by name in a friendly but professional style, should help put them at ease. However, spending more than a short time on greetings and introductions may lead the participants to conclude that the mediator is either insensitive to their reason for being there or has time to waste at their expense. We find that it is often awkward to offer a cup of coffee in the waiting area that must be carried, juggled, and then disposed of at the end of the mediation session.

The sessions should be conducted without interruption by phone calls, secretaries, or associates. The mediator's attention should be singularly directed to the participants. Some mediators like to instruct their receptionist, in front of the participants, to hold any calls that come in during the mediation session. This step informs the clients that the mediator is fairly busy, that this period of time belongs solely to the participants, and that there is a limit on the amount of time the mediator can spend with them.

Once the participants have been greeted and have taken a seat, an *initial preparatory statement* by the mediator helps to structure the session. This statement usually includes information on the following: privacy, confidentiality, time allotment for the session, the scope of mediation, fees for this and following sessions, discussion of the participants' and mediators' roles, and rules to be used during the sessions. The Neighborhood Justice Center of Atlanta suggests that these opening remarks should clarify whether to use first or last names, notify the participants of the mediator's qualifications, state the mediator's authority to settle the issues (capability or mandate as an arbitrator), acknowledge any acquaintance with any of the participants, and reconfirm the mediator's neutrality (Neighborhood Justice Center of Atlanta, 1982, p. 62). All of these items, which are discussed further below, should be considered in formulating the structuring statements.

Just as therapists are advised by Bandler, Grinder, and Satir (1976) to start from the basic assumptions for their field, so mediators should include the basic propositions underlying mediation (see Chapter One) in their preparatory statement. Eventually there needs to be a handover phrase, the verbal cue that will start the participants actively communicating about the situation (see Chapter Three). It is also important at the outset to clarify whether all statements will be held in confidence and whether the participants may speak freely, uninhibited by the fear of unauthorized revelation. For more discussion of confidentiality and privilege see Chapter Ten.

The following preparatory statement can be adapted to begin nearly any type of mediation session; it is based on the example given by Bandler, Grinder, and Satir (1976, pp. 13–22):

Structuring

Mediator: Well, I'm glad both of you have decided to try mediation to resolve the conflicts between you and avoid a battle. We have two hours today to go over the mediation process, to discuss my fees, to have you sign an agreement to mediate if you want to proceed, and to talk more about the issues between you that you want mediated.

Assumptions

I don't know whether the process you went through in deciding to come here was easy or difficult for you, but I do know that just by coming here you are taking the first step in making changes that are acceptable to both of you. You're both making a choice for [*remaining effective and caring parents after divorce, trying to become better neighbors, and so forth*].

Handover

I'm wondering if you, John [*the participant with whom the mediator has not had contact*], can tell me what you know about mediation and what you are hoping for? What is it you would like mediation to help you do?

You may want to amplify your description of the mediator's role before the handover phase, as in the following example that can be altered to fit most mediation situations:

Stages of Mediation

Mediator: I see it as my role to help couples sort out the business of reaching an agreement by helping them know *what* they have to decide and then helping them decide *how* to go about resolving those issues. Then I have a worksheet that helps me make sure that everything that needs to be discussed is talked about. When you make decisions together, I write down what was decided for use later on in the settlement agreement.

Responsibility

It's not my role to tell you what you should do. I really believe that both of you can make better decisions than anyone else about your situation. But most people need help in getting started, staying on track, and developing options.

Outcome

I also believe that this process helps people make better decisions and clear away the emotional obstacles so that agreements will last longer and everybody can feel better about the situation and each other.

This longer preamble allows the participants more time to allay any anxiety while making no demands on them. If there is great stress on the participants, the preliminary statement allows time for them to really start listening to the content of your message instead of noting all the unfamiliar stimuli in the mediation setting. It also conveys a nonverbal message that the mediator is friendly and easy to talk to. It shows that the mediator is in control of the session and has explicit expectations of the participants.

If the mediator still notes nonverbal signs of stress and anxiety, it may be a good idea to mention such cues directly to the participants and ask them what is going on. A statement such as "You appear very tense right now; there must be something that's really bothering you" can acknowledge the nonverbal cue and give the participant a chance to express concern. You cannot assume that all participant anxiety is related to the subject of the mediation itself. Often participants enter the office preoccupied by concerns such as child care, lateness and parking meters, or the arrangement for the payment of fees. After the participant has expressed the concern verbally, the mediator can give reassurance. By verbally acknowledging the tension you may notice, the participants will know that you are concerned, interested in listening, and observant.

Mediation may be a new process to many, and most participants will have but one case to be mediated in a lifetime. They are generally unfamiliar with both mediation and legal processes. To the extent that many do have an image of what they will be experiencing, it is formulated by overstated television dramas and understated journalistic articles. They fear being cross-examined and judged by the mediator as well as by the other participants. The participants' anxiety about the mediation process, and perhaps about you in particular as a mediator, will cause them to want to present the facts in the most favorable light possible.

Since all participants want the mediator to sympathize with their position and judge them favorably, they tend to state the facts in a manner calculated to obtain the mediator's favor, or at least to avoid disapproval. This may result in omitting some facts and exaggerating others, all to the irritation of the other participant. Often participants relate information from the past that is not relevant, but they offer it anyway to validate their perceptions and actions. The structuring statement tends to reduce initial anxiety and avoid irrelevancies, but it is also important for the mediator to use other techniques to reduce anxiety and redirect the session should it continue.

Preparatory statements can be used at other times besides the initial contact with the participants. They are helpful structuring tools prior to a major switch in the topic and are also useful as a preliminary to each session. Make sure that the preparatory statement contains at least the following: the reason for the change; the process that will be followed; the basic terms that will be used during the session. An example from an educational dispute involving a child's need for special services for learning disabilities shows the use of these three components:

Preliminary Statement at Start of Later Session

Mediator: Last session we talked a lot about the school's evaluation of Johnny on standardized inventories and that has given us some good baseline data. I think it's time to change to another topic—the specific goals and expectations for Johnny in regard to math and reading. I'd suggest that we hear first from his parents, then from his teacher, about what they think is a useful and achievable goal. By discussing what you hope and expect for him, we'll probably be able to understand any differences and similarities between home and school. Maybe you are both in agreement. But before we begin on expectations, let's review the term "learning disabled." My understanding is that a learning-disabled person is unable to receive and use information. Is this correct?

Teacher: No, that's not quite right.

Mediator: Well, could you tell us your understanding of the term?

Bridging and Directive Statements

Bridging statements are shorter versions of preliminary statements in that they contain information to the participant about the upcoming process or about what is important to know. But they are different in that they are used during the mediation session to control, explain, and redirect. As the participant gives you information, you must often go from subject to subject in order to develop the factual or emotional material. More will be said in a later chapter about how and when to do this. A bridging statement is the tool for returning to earlier material or finding a new direction. This example highlights the use of a bridging statement:

Mediator: Bob, you expressed an interest in joint custody at our
                first session. Joint custody requires strong commit-
                ment by both of you to work together in scheduling
                and to allow the other person freedom to do what they
                want to do with the children when they have them. I'm
                wondering if your position, not letting your daughters
                visit their maternal relatives in Seattle, contradicts the
                spirit of joint custody that you see as an option.
                [*Silence.*]

This statement is an indirect request to explain an incon-
sistency of position between Bob's stance on extended family visits
and joint custody. Bob needs to understand that he cannot have an
effective joint-custody arrangement unless he is willing to share
control and major decisions regarding the children. However, the
spouse may be willing to agree to a stipulation that bars visits to her
mother longer than three days. She is more likely to do so if she
hears him express concerns that seem reasonable to her as well as to
him. He can respond in many ways to this bridging statement, and
the mediator has directed the conversation into a path that can be
used either to confront a paradoxical or arbitrary position or to
facilitate discussion about concerns for the children that may be
mutual.

The following type of directive statement is more abrupt and
harsher, but it is just as effective in redirecting the conversation:

Bob: I just don't want her bringing any old guy she picks up
                at a bar into the house and sleeping with him in front
                of Amy, like she did back in Texas. Who knows what
                they might do to the girls? I mean, from what I hear
                from Suzie, the guy in Texas didn't leave until ten
                o'clock the next morning. And he was a pretty tough
                sort of guy too. I'll be damned if that kind of stuff is
                going to go on around my daughters . . . .

Rhonda: Who told you this garbage? Suzie? I can't believe that
                you'd believe . . .

Acknowledgment

Mediator: All right, we've got a touchy issue here for both of you.

Reflection

Bob, I hear that you are interested in protecting your daughters from strangers. I'm glad you shared this concern with us, because now we can see what kind of safeguards can be built into your agreement to protect your daughters. [*Turns to Rhonda.*]

Cognitive Compliance

Rhonda, whether or not an incident like this happens, do you share a belief that your daughters ought to be protected from strangers?

Rhonda: Of course, but . . .

Mediator: Are you willing to talk more about what kind of safeguards to build into this joint-custody arrangement for your daughters?

Rhonda: I guess so.

Mediator: All right, then, let's start off on this issue by having Bob tell us how long you need to know someone before that person is no longer a stranger. [*Turns to Bob.*]

Explanatory Statements

You know, Bob, that Rhonda is going to be trying to fill her needs for company and affection by meeting other people after the divorce is final. That's part of her job of building a new life for herself. You'll probably do that, too. [*Pause.*]

Directive Demand

So think for a minute and tell me what you consider a fair amount of time for her to get to know somebody. How long does it take you to know whether a person is harmful or safe?

It should be understood that this dialogue is only an excerpt from an attempt by the mediator to reframe the issues in conflict. Ultimately the mediator is attempting to allow Bob to experience the futility of trying to control Rhonda by having him first set up criteria regarding strangers. The next step would be to examine the enforceability of such criteria.

Here it took a series of statements and requests for compliance before a directive demand was given to produce a reasonable negotiable alternative. Here is another bridging statement that shows reward and redirection:

Mediator: Your description is very good, Bob, and I'll want to ask you more questions about that in a minute. But right now I want to get back to something you said earlier, something about "this whole thing being unfair because of one mistake in the past." It's important to check out and understand the real reasons why parents disagree about who should have custody. Did some incident happen in the past that you think Rhonda holds against you?

Bob: Yeah, I think she thinks I'm a terrible parent just because I once left Jimmy in the tub and he scalded himself with the hot water.

Rhonda: That's not true! I've never blamed him for that. I know that was an accident. I don't think he's abusive. I just think I can provide Jimmy a better home life because I don't have to work past three o'clock.

In this example, the mediator is accepting and rewarding the participant while at the same time redirecting the line of discussion from an account of behavior information into the affective content. This is done by explaining the need for more information in a personalized way ("I want to get back to . . ."). This statement would serve to gain more rapport, because the rather long-winded, emotionally stirred client who was telling "objective" information about the couple's past would be relieved that the mediator was turning attention from inconsequential items to material that the participants know must be resolved. By using a bridging statement to pick up emotionally laden components that were only vaguely expressed, the mediator demonstrates true listening and empathy.

Directive statements are similar. They too can redirect the conversation and demonstrate control, but they are usually more blunt, often taking the form of a command, and do not explain as much to the participant about the change of direction. Moreover, they do not necessarily involve earlier contents. The simplest example of a directive statement is, "Tell me more about. . . ." This statement can keep the participants actively communicating if they are reticent, or it can be used to stop a loquacious speaker and shift the conversation to another topic. Another example does use earlier material, but not in the same way as bridging statements: "Earlier you said you had considered kidnapping your child to end the visitation problem once and for all. . . ." (Silence.) The real redirectional force of this statement is its use of silence, which pressures the participant to fill up the spaces and explain.

Another form of directive statement is more explicit. For example: "Mrs. Lewis, I don't need to know what you're telling me now, but I do need more information regarding your future job plans." While sometimes interpreted by the participants as blunt or rude, this type of statement will bring an immediate change of direction in the interview and remind the participants who controls the session.

Because bridging statements are often better received and contribute to rapport, whereas many directive statements do not, the former are better used early in the session. Some mediators develop a personal style that dictates the use of the bridging statements almost entirely. As with any tool, proficiency can only be mastered by practice.

Types of Questions

Perhaps the most overused tools in the novice mediator's repertoire are the questions used to gain information. If questions are used to the exclusion of other techniques, the conversation will cease to be an exchange and will become an unsatisfactory form of verbal ping-pong or interrogation. With this caution in mind, it is necessary to know the different types of questions in order to have them serve their proper function.

Open questions allow the respondent to answer in any way; *closed questions* limit the flexibility and scope of the answer and often lead the respondent in a particular direction. Examples of open questions are "What have you done since the physical separation?" or "Can you tell me your thoughts at the time of the announcement?" The following closed questions ask for the same information but leave the respondent with less flexibility in the answer: "Did you go to your parent's home?" or "Did you think he was joking?"

Obviously, open questions can be so undirected that they fail to produce the needed information, while closed questions can stifle the true answer by intimidating the client into believing that the only acceptable answer is the one proposed in the question. Because of these hazards, it is best to start each subject or event with open-ended questions and let the answers suggest closed questions.

Starting with open questions also avoids the uncomfortable and often unproductive verbal ping-pong mentioned earlier, where the mediator asks closed questions and the participant answers them in short phrases or one word. Since that pattern sounds interrogative, it breaks down rapport and makes the mediator work especially hard for every bit of information. By using either an open question or a short directive statement, such as "Tell me more about . . .," the mediator can keep the participant actively supplying information and use closed questions later to pinpoint specific information.

The way a question is worded, whether because of naive artlessness or deliberate tactics, is likely to affect the answer. Leading questions, as the law has long recognized, encourage error because of their suggestiveness. Generally, leading questions should be avoided in the early mediation sessions. After the participant has given a statement of expectations, however, the mediator may wish to employ leading questions in order to test the participant's story. This is particularly true if there are inconsistencies or suspicious omissions of factual material.

One style of question to avoid is the either/or format. Some examples are:

- "Do you dislike your mother *or* your father?"
- "Did you go to the police *or* to the hospital?"

- "When he jumped out at you, did you think to scream *or* to run?"
- "Do you want to pursue your case in court *or* mediate it?"

As you can see from the examples, it can be awkward for a participant to explain that neither choice is accurate or satisfactory. Either/or questions rule out many creative options and can connote shame or negative behavior if one's answer does not fit the choices offered. This sort of question can distort the information that comes back in the answer and can produce hostility in the respondent, especially when common sense rules out one choice offered by the question, as in the following examples:

- "Are you a good mother or a neglectful and abusive one?"
- "Did you stay to assist the other passengers, Mr. Jones, or did you decide to run for help?"

Most either/or questions can be changed into effective open questions. We can convert the previous examples into questions that are more open:

- "How do you provide care for your children?"
- "What did you think was the most effective way to help the others?"

When the mediator assumes the more positive of the either/or options, the participant is apt to choose examples that support the positive view of self and lessen the internal conflict and perceptual error created in the either/or format. The same questions could also be changed to directive statements by broadening their scope:

- "Tell me some examples that show how you operate as an effective mother."
- "Tell me how you assessed the situation you saw the remaining passengers in."

Another type of closed question used too often is the yes/no format. While the answer will tell you what you asked, its effect on the direction, flow, and ease of conversation can be devastating, as in the following example:

- "Tell me yes or no, Mr. Grief, are you being fair?"
- "Can you say, yes or no, whether you plan to marry again soon?"

This type of question is best used with a participant who is skirting an issue, but it will seriously damage rapport with your participants if you force them to acknowledge a threatening point by using only a yes or no. Reflective statements, discussed later, can acknowledge the same information with less pain.

A usual sequence of questioning, in the first session, after the participant has expressed his or her concerns on issues, is to start with open questions to get the broad outlines of the story, then use closed questions to seek specifics in each area, and then add some open questions or bridging statements to establish connections. Asking closed questions before the full picture is learned will distort the direction of further questioning.

The style of question you should use depends on the specific goal you have in mind at any particular point in time. After deciding on the goal based on the information and the situation, the mediator can generally anticipate a specific reaction to a specific type of question as illustrated in Table 7.

Reflection, Summary, and Clarification

These three skills—reflection, summary, and clarification—will probably be the least comfortable to use at first, but they will become invaluable for maintaining rapport and satisfying your needs as a mediator. While these three skills all share a similar outcome, their uses are different. *Reflection* is the term used when the mediator supplies the unspoken feeling or missing content behind the participant's words. *Summary* is when the mediator or participant lists what has gone before; it helps to synthesize events or ideas, thereby concentrating meaning into a few words. *Clarification* is a request for confirmation of what has been said.

Reflections are useful for allowing the participant to release the tension of a perceptual error by acknowledging feelings directly,

Table 7. Matching the Question with The Goal.

Goal	Type of Question	Best Time To Use It	Reaction by Respondent
Keep a reticent client talking	Open	Beginning of session, when participants are silent	Will usually comply
Establish parameters of situation	Open	During early questioning	Will feel empowered
Pinpoint specific information	Closed	Later fact finding; during review of agreement	Can stop easy flow of conversation as client waits for next question
Get an acknowledgment	Yes/no	During review of agreement	The issue is sensitive, anger, nervousness, or withdrawal
Emphasize the negative judgment	Either/or	During neogtiations concerning options	A distorted answer
Frustrate, embarrass, or discredit	Either/or	As a paradoxical intervention during fact finding	Anger; silence
Redirect conversation	Open (preceded by directive statement)	Middle of interview	May produce startled reaction, but will change conversation pattern

especially feelings that are usually thought to be unacceptable. The mediator can provide this reflection by stating it as a statement or as an interpretation:

- Statement: "You are angry and ashamed that you have been accused of not paying your debts."
- Interpretation: "It seems you're feeling pretty angry and embarassed about this."

Another way of eliciting the participant's acknowledgment of a hidden feeling or motive is to show that it is acceptable by saying, "Many people in your situation feel angry and embarrassed when they are accused of not paying their debts. Are you feeling this way, too?" This indirect reflection is more risky and fraught with pressure for the participant because it requires a yes/no answer or explanation and thus must be used cautiously. The major uses of reflection during a mediation session are to establish the affective content, to contribute to rapport, and to reduce tension for the participants. A good reflection can often take the session further, faster, than a dozen closed questions.

Summary is particularly useful as a way of regaining control of the session after a long statement by a participant or as a way of organizing the information being given. It gives the mediator time to figure out where to go next and can often bring out the importance of a bit of information that otherwise might get lost. We recommend its use immediately after the participant's uninterrupted story of expectations and position. Summaries can be used as a bridge into a reflection or an open question. Summary is not only useful for beginnings; it can be used effectively before any transition. Before the mediator goes into the discussion of options and consequences (see Chapter Three), it is good to sum up what was discussed. As a preliminary to closing, summary can help solidify what has been accomplished, thereby rewarding participants for their hard work.

Clarification, while it does list and sum up, also has the effect of binding together or throwing out conflicting information. It is helpful to clarify intentions or wishes by the participants and get explicit confirmation of what they mean. An example of clarification would be:

Mediator: Earlier, Dave, you said that you think you should receive some spousal support from Mary while you are going through this master's program. Now I hear you refusing to discuss it. Can you tell us what has changed for you?

The use of reflection, summary, and clarification is not limited to the session where you are seeking information. They are useful skills during all phases of mediation, especially when you help the participants evaluate options and make choices. All three techniques can be used to stall for time as you simultaneously think about a specific point, look for resource material, or need to slow the session in order to evaluate where you are and what the goal for the session should be. Used too often, however, these tactics will cause participants to grow resistive and impatient. Too many reflections may seem to be off the point or uncovering painful feelings; too many clarifications may suggest that you have not been listening carefully. Used too early in a session, they can reduce rapport for the same reason. Interspersed with effective questions and directive statements, all three contribute to an encounter that meets the participant's, as well as the mediator's, need for clear positions and negotiable options.

Catch Phrases and Clichés

Language can be used to obfuscate as well as to clarify meanings, particularly when the true meaning would put the speaker or the listener into an internal conflict or perceptual error called variously "little white lies," "being polite," or "evasion." Depending on the circumstances, words are often chosen to convey a sufficiently acceptable response while not totally lying.

Most conversations can be reduced to well-worn catch phrases. Their use is to help the speaker evade the real issue or distort it in an acceptable way. These catch phrases can also be warning signals to the good listener, however, and can be used in reverse by the well-organized speaker. In their book *Meta-Talk: The Guide to Hidden Meanings in Conversation,* Nierenberg and Calero (1980) divide these short phrases into groups according to their intended purpose. The first group they term *hiding the halo*: phrases used to disguise arrogance and false modesty. Examples in this category include the "royal We" ("We are not amused") and other overdone phrases of self-deprecation, such as "in my humble opinion" or "after all, I'm *only* your mother." One-upmanship is the true intent of these phrases.

Softeners—for example, "it goes without saying" or "just off the top of my head"—are used to cushion a statement that is predicted to be disliked by the listener. *Foreboders* are defined as an attempt to create a negative effect on the listener—such as "it really doesn't matter" or "nothing is wrong."

Continuers are phrases designed to keep the other person talking. Rewarding ("that's very good") and incensing remarks ("what else is new?") are two forms of continuers. *Interesters* are phrases to do just that—interest the listener ("guess what happened?" or "I could say something about that"). *Downers* are either acknowledgments of being a winner in the verbal contest—"that put him in *his* place"—or they are intended to make the other become defensive or subordinate—such as "don't make me laugh" or "now are you happy?"

Convincers are phrases that try to persuade the listener to trust and believe. Such comments as "I think we all agree that . . ." or "that's the only option there can be" try to persuade a cognitive consensus. *Strokers* are attempts to use the other person's needs and values to manipulate the situation. When one participant says "you win" to another, the implication is that a win/lose game has been played and the one who is accused of being the winner started the game. While such an accusation is in some ways a positive stroke, it is also a slap in the face in a mediation setting, considering the nonadversarial approach promoted in mediation.

Pleaders are attempts to deal with emotions that are seen as negative, such as envy and self-interest, or incompetence and failure. They begin with a positive assertion followed by a "but" that leads into a negative or doubling phrase. Here are some phrases that predict what they deny:

What Is Said	What Is Meant
"I'll do my best."	"My best is not too good."
"I'll try, but . . ."	"I'm not sure if I can do it."

These tip-off phrases are useful in assessing the affective and cognitive parts of a participant's perceptions and can be used effectively when changed to reflective statements. In keeping with the earlier premise that mediators must model appropriate behavior, they should not use these catch phrases during a session unless they want the participants to do the same.

Nonverbal Cues

The previous sections of this chapter have dealt with the basic verbal skills needed to conduct the mediation session, skills that minimize perceptual errors by the participants and maximize your rapport with them. This section deals with the nonverbal skills that mediators must use in order to detect the participants' affective information and enhance their own verbal strategy. As Goffman (1963, p. 35) has said, "Although an individual may stop talking, he cannot stop communicating through body idioms; he must say either the right thing or the wrong thing. He cannot say nothing." Mediators must not only *read* the nonverbal behavior of participants but must also *send* effective messages. It is also important to be aware that your own style transmits nonverbal cues to participants. Skillful manipulation of your nonverbal cues can be an effective tool in your mediation repertoire.

Studies have found that people in the helping professions often misinterpret the nonverbal messages that are implicit in a series of photographs, whereas untrained people immediately see the meanings and relationships implied in the pictures by the subject's stance, closeness, touching, and eye contact. Those coming to the field of mediation from legal or business backgrounds, in particular, are often trained to listen more than to look, and if they do look, they often have no vocabulary for assessing what they see. As members of a different professional group, they also may have been socialized to include and exclude certain nonverbal cues from their repertoire. Touching a client may not be seen as a legitimate nonverbal cue and is generally discouraged because of its doubtful appropriateness or unintended sexual implications. The range of feelings regarded as acceptable behavior in the office by most lawyers and other professionals is unduly narrowed by fear and uncertainty, as well as lack of skill in dealing with affective states.

Many popular books are available on the subject of nonverbal skills. We recommend Nierenberg and Calero's *How to Read a Person Like a Book* (1973), a well-illustrated volume that was written by an attorney and a business executive to show the reader the meaning of nonverbal signs, and *Body Language* by Julius Fast (1970). Another excellent resource book for those desiring additional reading in this area is *Unmasking the Face: A Guide to Recognizing Emotions from Facial Clues* by Ekman and Friesen (1975).

Nonverbal cues can be divided into several categories: facial expression, tone and inflection of voice, somatic characteristics, hand gestures, body stance and pose, speed of movement and speech, and clothing cues. Caution must be exercised in not overreading a single cue, however. The nonverbal items discussed here form a constellation of information. One cue must be checked against another, realizing that one or two cues observed out of context may be misread or lead to a false impression. Cormier and Cormier (1979) have an excellent inventory of nonverbal cues and their meanings based on the categories of kinesics, paralinguistics, and proxemics. All these factors can be used by a perceptive mediator and pieced together to augment and provide a check on information about the participants already gained through conversation. Each of these categories deserves study by aspiring mediators in regard to the information they themselves are giving back to the participants in nonverbal signals. Mediators too often forget that the participants are looking at them and searching for nonverbal cues that everyone seems to think they have a unique and extraordinary ability to interpret.

Most people consider their *face* to be their "self." How directly you look into another's eyes often says a lot: "The eyes are the windows to the soul." And, as mentioned earlier, involuntary arousal states such as fear, stress, and relaxation show up often as changes in the dilation of the pupil and the movement of the eyes. Some participants have difficulty facing one another or talking directly to each other. They may fear what their face reveals or prefer not to look at the anger or anguish displayed in the other's face.

Common linguistic idioms reflect this facial importance. Participants will be evaluating each other as well as *you* based on whether you "look them square in the eye" and "tell them face to face" some of the difficult things that need to be said. Some participants fear they may not be able "to face it" if the other participant brings up past indiscretions or old feelings. Japanese culture has always acknowledged this possibility of "losing face," and a skillful mediator must remember this concept when a participant needs to change a hard-fought position on an issue. The importance of the face as manifestation of the self is reflected in many levels in our culture and is even made ironic or funny as a way of reducing society's anxiety about it. The decorative harlequin mask popular in interior design and illustrations implies that what is shown "on the face of things" is not always the reality. Even the cartoon character Charlie Brown walks around with a brown paper bag over his face until his problems have been talked over with Lucy, his "psychiatrist."

Facial appurtenances such as glasses, cosmetics, beards and mustaches, earrings, and, of course, hairstyles are clues to the person's externally manifested values. "Punk" haircuts and elaborate costuming are an attempt to establish a sense of personal power by creating an immediate emotional reaction in observers. Designer's initials on glass frames or scarves are an attempt to add distinction and remind the observer of one's status by identifying with a particular designer's image.

Beyond these external characteristics of the face, the mediator must note the ephemeral expressions of tension, stress reaction, confusion, and disagreement that can show on a person's face as he or she is talking. As mentioned earlier, dilation of the pupils, blushing, and faster respiration or even nausea and incontinence in some acute cases can be signs of the fight-or-flight arousal system being activated. A participant who is showing these signs may be hearing only one word in five or ten and then is most likely to be selectively hearing only the emotionally charged words, words that can be interpreted as positive or negative according to the listener's perceptual world. A much more subtle expression is the participant's mental or emotional withdrawal, usually detected as a glazing of the eyes or removal of eye contact. In effect, the participant wants to change the subject but feels that it would be unacceptable to interrupt. The participant is probably experiencing perceptual error and has resulting tension. Meanwhile the participant is keeping up the facade of attention while mentally churning things over or planning the next question or response.

Another facial expression the mediator should learn to recognize requires looking behind the social mask. When participants are shocked by a proposed alternative or the other participant's position on an issue, they often feel they dare not express their amazement and must accept what is happening. To express shock or dismay would destroy their carefully managed image of detachment from the situation. This reaction often registers as a flaring of the nostrils or a flickering expansion of the eyes; in older men, the motion of the eyebrows downward and together may indicate the same condition. It may or may not be accompanied by other body cues. If you suspect this might be happening, it is best to normalize the reaction as described earlier in the discussion of reflection, clarification, and summary. Bellack and Baker (1981) have developed a system of reading faces for personality cues based on the hypothesis that right and left hemispheres of the brain control different processes. Their "split-face analysis" is presented as an easy method to obtain information about a person.

Voice tone and inflection mean everything in current American English. Typed transcripts of trials and mediation sessions often lose this dimension, a reason why some lawyers and mediators have encouraged the use of videotape or other sound/picture technology. Compare the following dialogues, which use the simple phrase of agreement "Yeah, sure."

No Big Deal

Mediator: Have you ever left the children alone?

Mary: *Yeah, sure.*

Dave: See what I mean? She doesn't think that's a problem. *That's* why I want sole custody . . .

Casual Agreement

Mediator: Do you like to have fun, Dave?

Dave: *Yeah, sure.*

Wary, Concerned

Mediator: Do you spend money to have fun?

Dave: *Yeah, sure.*

Where's the Trap?

Mediator: Do you think most people spend money in order to have fun?

Dave: *Yeah, sure.* Why?

Mediator: Well, I think that is probably true. Most people do have to spend some money in order to have fun. So one of the things you both need to allow each other in your financial planning is some "discretionary money," money that could be used either for overages in other areas or that could be used for fun things. Let's look at these budgets you've made up to see if there's any leeway for this.

Disgust

Mary: So you want it all. You don't care about Billy at all.

Dave: *Yeah, sure.* [In other words, "Yes, I do but you won't believe me.]

Mediator: Wait a minute, here. Mary, you're accusing Dave of being selfish, and that accusation has just turned him off. Let's look at this again. What do you think is a fair settlement? How much money do you think you should get? And how much do you think should be set aside for Billy from the savings account?

Being able to interpret the true meaning behind the statements and the tone is the first step toward helpful reflection. It is a skill that should be practiced. The videotapes and exercises now on the market will provide you with a standardized practice tool for mastery in this area, something a paper and pen discourse cannot.

Somatic characteristics, another nonverbal category to be watched, include basic body type as well as life events that have indelibly left their mark on the person's physical structure. Even though psychologists and researchers have not determined that people of the same body type have similar personality factors, the general public still has stereotypes and beliefs about the three somatotypes: the endomorph, a soft, round, fat body; the mesomorph, a bony, muscular, athletic body; and the ectomorph, a tall, thin, fragile-looking body (Knapp, 1972).

There is often a fine line between the somatic characteristics of those who are mentally retarded and those who have an ongoing disease such as cerebral palsy and multiple sclerosis, or still others who have a grave psychological problem. Many of us have had the experience of meeting a person who has some obvious handicap but not being able to assess the specific problem. To overlook a missing body part, a wheelchair, a lisp or stutter, an enlargement, or a disfiguration in order to show your sophistication and acceptance of the handicapped is to lose valuable information about the person in front of you. It is important to take these factors into consideration even in the preliminary stages of the session.

Hand gestures are perhaps the most easily observed of all nonverbal cues and are subject to misinterpretation. Again hand gestures and all other nonverbal cues are but clues that must not be viewed in isolation but pieced together with other clues to provide helpful information. If the hands are clenched, gripping the chair, or the arms are crossed over the chest, participants may be literally holding on for dear life, clinging to their position or beliefs. This posture can also denote anger ("I'd like to punch this mediator!") or impatience ("I can't stand it!"). Drumming the fingers may send the same message with a hint of boredom thrown in. Hands neatly folded in the lap show contrite penitance, submission, or just being a good boy or girl by following all the rules. Grooming the nails denotes scorn and an "I don't care" attitude that belies the true feelings of hurt. Nailbiting and destructive picking at a sore spot is a regression to earlier childhood behavior that is used to control anxiety by sheer repetitiveness.

Fumbling around with a purse, smoking materials, or a cup of coffee can be a nonverbal gesture used to avoid, stall, or break away from something the participant feels is too intense. Fingering a paper clip or rubber band, however, may indicate a restless mind. Hands stroking a beard, chin, upper lips, or earlobes indicate again a regressive, learned behavior that is used to calm anxiety during the session. A woman patting her hair and a man smoothing his tie between two fingers are equivalent gestures. A woman twirling a lock of hair around her finger may indicate an attempt at sexual seduction or manipulation, but brushing a lock over her shoulder may be meant to show sophisticated languor and therefore identity with a certain social standing. A man's casual glide over his pants zipper may be an attempt to maintain composure and avoid embarrassment (is anything showing?), as is a woman's fingers at her décolletage or her quick look to her side hem to see if her slip is showing. The examples are too numerous to include in this book, but a helping professional needs to be aware of these unconscious but meaningful gestures.

Body stance and pose can indicate how people feel about themselves and others. While there are vast differences between subcultures (see Hall, 1969), closeness and leaning the upper body toward another can indicate an attempt to affiliate. Family and corporate group pictures often indicate the ones who are literally "sticking their necks out" to avoid each other. Pose can indicate attention to that which is happening—according to Carkhuff (1973) the best way to elicit conversation is to sit facing the other party with one ankle on the other knee, the back curving forward, with hands folded either resting on the chin or one hand holding the chin as its elbow rests on the extended knee and the other dropped into the lap. Having tried this position, we can say that we find it extremely difficult to maintain for longer than ten minutes at a time, and it is often inappropriate for women, whether they are wearing slacks or a skirt.

Most of what you can detect from this category of nonverbal behavior would be termed general impressions. Is the person upright, slinking around, rigid, smooth, or disconnected? The same is true about speed of *movement and speech*. It can be used as a guideline for determining the pace of presenting material or the length of time it may take the other party to respond to questions or decisions.

So much has been written about *clothing clues* that to repeat much here would be inappropriate. *Dress for Success* (Molloy, 1976) has become a popular manual for those who want to influence people in this regard, and *The Official Preppy Handbook* (Birnbach, 1980), although an overstated parody, does point out the type of clues you might expect from someone trying to establish an identity as a person with high status. These books also evidence the growing public awareness of how certain nonverbal messages can be manipulated for individual purposes.

It is well for mediators to remember that nonverbal responses are often a better choice for their own responses during mediation sessions than are verbal responses, simply because they seem more real and provide greater emphasis for the point. They can allow for "subtle, inoffensive repetition that promotes clarity" (Thompson, 1975, p. 184) and can also promote a similar response in the observer. The mediator's nonverbal cues can also create participant reactions and responses that may not be desired. The questions posed in the following quote by Thomas Schaffer, former dean of the University of Notre Dame Law School and advocate for the blending of psychological skills with the traditional legal education system, are perhaps the best checklists that mediators could use to evaluate themselves in regard to nonverbal skills. Reviewing such skills with a competent adviser via a videotape recording session would be perhaps the best indicator of a mediator's ability to understand the nonverbal signals of participants and his or her own competence in this area. Schaffer (1976, p. 76) poses the following questions:

> What is my client's physical attitude towards me? Does he act as if he were here to see a doctor? An undertaker? A principal in school? His father? His friend? Someone he would like to be his friend? . . . What am I seeing, for instance, when I put the client on one side of the desk and myself on the other, with all the apparatus of lawyering and mastery on *my* side of the desk or, at best, an ashtray on his? What am I *feeling* when I keep my hands writing and my notes in front of me and my eyes down most of the time? How would it feel, and what would it say, to move around to the other side of the desk? Or to take off my coat? Or to throw the yellow pad away? What would happen if I interviewed my client in *his* place instead of in mine?

More will be said in a later chapter about how to set up an environment for mediation that is conducive to face saving and other nonverbal communication, both by the mediator and the participants.

Eliciting and Organizing Data

Once you are using these auditory, verbal, and nonverbal skills, you will elicit a vast amount of information. Another necessary skill for mediators is to collect and organize this information in such a way that it enhances the mediation process and can easily be retrieved when you need to review it. In this section we suggest a starting point for building your skills in this regard.

We have found that in contrast to traditional legal interviews, chronological ordering of events is not as universally necessary or helpful in the mediation process. Chronological ordering can be useful as part of the background material you gather in the first phone contact with the participants or in the first mediation session. Since mediation deals primarily with the present and the future, however, events and facts that have a direct bearing on the issues at hand are most important. Information needed to identify the participants, contact them, and provide the mediator with a ready reminder of the nature of the case for quick reference should be listed at the top of a case folder on some type of contact sheet. The contact sheet should contain all the biographical and demographic information you will need for statistical purposes and later contact of the participants for many mediation uses. Haynes (1981) and Coogler (1978) suggest versions of the contact form that are worth reviewing.

The matrix format for describing the A-B-C material (Tables 5 and 6 in Chapter Four) is another organizational method for storing and retrieving data about the feelings, actions, and beliefs held by both participants for one or more issues. Its best use is after the sessions as a summarization for case planning.

Some cases contain facts or concepts that can be expressed in terms of a diagram or chart. This is particularly true in cases involving neighborhood or organizational relationships, spatial relationships, or family structures, which may include extended family members or remarriage. The mediator should encourage the participants to draw a diagram outlining the essential facts, physical scene, or relationships as a prelude to going over the information with the participants during the mediation session. (In some cases the mediator may wish to draw it and then seek confirmation.) The diagram will help the participants put relationships or distances in perspective and assure the mediator that both the participants and the mediator are perceiving the same set of circumstances. It may be useful to show the participant a pictorial representation when trying to explain legal processes that may be experienced as an adjunct of mediation.

Two charts we find helpful when participants feel confused about options are the decision sheet and the decision balance sheet suggested in Janis and Mann's book, *Decision Making: A Psychological Analysis of Conflict, Choice, and Commitment* (1977). When discussing the nature of restructuring the participant's family, we find that Virginia Satir's (1972) style of diagramming the nuclear family, first as it is currently constituted and then as it may turn out to be, is helpful as a descriptive tool.

A checklist such as a Divorce Mediation Worksheet can be used both as a notetaking format during the session and as a reminder of what issues must be covered and subsequently written into the settlement agreement. This worksheet can be modified to meet the demands of any regularly encountered problem in mediation. Other sets of mediation issues such as those in tenant/landlord situations can be reduced to a worksheet that then assures the mediator of full coverage of all the potential issues. Notes jotted during the session by the mediator can be color coded or labeled to indicate open or closed issues, wording changes that may be tried out, or the specific session when an issue was resolved. Because it is a worksheet, the categories can be used as components and modified to meet the participants' situation.

Leslie Ellen Shear, in her article "Developing Parental Responsibility Schedules" (1982), shows a daily responsibility schedule she uses in planning and illustrating joint-custody scheduling. Her "Holiday-Vacation-Special Days" chart allows full planning of the exact terms of visitation possibilities for what otherwise might be awkward times. Such graphic representation is ideal during the decision-making stage of mediation. It contributes to the readability and participant "ownership" of the settlement agreement since it can be posted in a conspicuous place for all mediation participants to review should there be continuing questions. Other schedules are recommended by Galper (1980). Any diagram or chart that the mediator finds useful should be adopted and refined through use.

It is important that the actions and decisions obtained in the sessions be preserved in some form other than the mediator's memory. Notetaking can hinder the development of mediator/participant rapport if not appropriately timed and explained, however. There are many different theories about the advantages and disadvantages of extensive notetaking, written narratives, shorthand transcriptions, electronic recordings, and videotaping. There are several points to consider with each of these methods.

Everything the mediator does or allows to be done in the mediation session influences the way the participants reveal information. Notetaking may distract the participants, impede the flow of communication, and break down the rapport you are trying to establish. If a mediator at a certain point picks up a pencil and starts to write, participants may get the impression that what they are saying is especially significant and may tend to enlarge on that aspect until it looms larger than truth. Conversely, if the mediator should stop taking notes during certain periods, it may give participants the impression that what they are saying is not important enough to note and should thus be cut short.

Most people are nervous about having their voice or image recorded. Particularly since Watergate, we all tend to be suspicious of the use that might be made of confidential recordings. The uncertain effects of electronic recording on a participant's story argues against recording the initial session until a trusting relationship has been established and the participants are comfortable with the process.

When notetaking or recording in the presence of the participants is desirable, it can best be done after they have provided the initial presentation of their story or their individual positions on certain issues. The mediator can then explain that it is important that the facts or the reasoning or the decisions be accurately taken down in their presence. In the process, the facts or other information can be arranged in a more orderly manner and the notes or recording will likely be of greater value. It is usually a good idea to go over your notes or recordings with the participants before the end of the session. This step allows the participants to correct obvious errors and puts them at ease with what was accomplished. It can also serve as a reward to them for having discussed difficult material and arriving at mutual decisions on certain points.

Setting aside some time immediately after the mediation session for jotting down or dictating full notes, or revising the wording of a proposed agreement to reflect the participants' wishes more accurately, often saves the necessity of taking extensive notes later or revising the mediated plan. This procedure allows you to compose your notes carefully and perhaps editorialize. Your notes should include your observations about what seems to be of most concern to the participants and your first impressions of the participants' appearance, their level of sophistication with mediation, their personality traits and communication style, their sincerity, and their verbal abilities. While your perception may change during the course of the mediation, your initial impressions may be valuable for later evaluation. They will also reveal the emotional changes that have taken place during the course of the mediation process.

Recommended Reading

General

"Client Interviewing and Counseling." H. J. Folberg and A. Y. Taylor. *Civil Litigation Manual.* Vol. 1. Portland: Oregon Continuing Legal Education (CLE), Oregon State Bar, 1982.

The Lawyer in the Interviewing and Counseling Process. A. S. Watson. Indianapolis: Bobbs-Merrill, 1976.
    Excellent work describing listening skills directly applicable to mediation.

Legal Interviewing and Counseling: A Client-Centered Approach. D. A. Binder and S. C. Price. St. Paul: West, 1977.
    A helpful basic text that describes the use of preliminary statements, active listening and advising skills, and techniques for special interviews pertaining to legal counseling and similarly to mediation.

Listening Behavior. L. Barker. Englewood Cliffs, N.J.: Prentice-Hall, 1971.

Contains suggestions for improving listening skills, plus a section on biased communication.

Nonverbal Cues

Body Language. J. Fast. New York: M. Evans, 1970.

Popular book explaining nonverbal cues with many entertaining examples.

Body Politics. N. Henley. Englewood Cliffs, N.J.: Prentice-Hall, 1979.

Perhaps the best book regarding nonverbal communication and power.

The Hidden Dimension. E. T. Hall. New York: Doubleday, 1969.

Seminal work on spatial needs in interaction.

How to Read a Person Like a Book. G. I. Nierenberg and H. H. Calero. New York: Pocket Books, 1973.

Easy reading with pictures showing nonverbal poses and their meaning.

Nonverbal Communication in Human Interaction. M. L. Knapp. New York: Holt, Rinehart and Winston, 1972.

A readable yet scholarly work covering all aspects of this chapter.

6

Diverse Styles and Approaches to Mediating Conflict

The approach used to mediate a dispute depends on the nature of the conflict, its setting, the experience and resources of the disputants, and the background and training of the mediator. The shuttle mediation utilized by an American diplomat to resolve a conflict between nations would not be the likely approach taken by a therapist to mediate an inheritance dispute over a family heirloom. The private nature of the inheritance dispute, the relative ease of face-to-face meetings of the would-be heirs, the likely inexperience of the heirs in matters of probate, the relatively small stake involved, the psychotherapeutic background and training of the mediator—all are in contrast to the public conflict between nations whose representatives are experienced political leaders dealing with the possibility of armed conflict and working with a mediator who has international diplomatic experience.

The variables that shape mediation are so numerous that it is more helpful to view the possible approaches to mediation as a matter of style dependent on a number of intersecting continuums, each with many shadings, rather than attempting to define specific mediation models. The first continuum or set of variables depicts an array of conflicts from the most private disagreement between siblings over an heirloom to global conflicts between nations on the brink of war. This scale has gradations relating to the severity of the conflict. Other continuums would show the immediacy of the conflict's consequences, its private or public setting, and the extent of public interest in the outcome.

Another mediation continuum has gradations relating to the experience and background of the disputants as well as the training, orientation, and authority of the mediator. At one end is a scrivener recording and clarifying points of agreement; at the other end is a judge asking litigants if they wish to agree voluntarily to a suggested resolution or have it imposed on them.

Still another continuum arranges mediation according to the extent of procedural rules or the lack of a structured format. At one end is a personal dispute among parties, such as neighbors, who have no history of conflict resolution between themselves and who are using a mediator, perhaps a mutual friend, with no prescribed format or rules. At the other end of the scale are disputants with a tradition of resolving the inevitable conflicts between them in a systematic fashion, such as General Motors and the United Auto Workers, who turn to the Federal Mediation and Conciliation Service with its refined set of procedures and regulatory parameters.

Intersecting points between these continuums and other variables that could be imagined may at times appear to represent a mediation model. Closer examination would show that the nature of the conflict, the setting, the resources and experience of the disputants, and the background and training of the mediator are so diverse that the models are illusory. What are often described as mediation models could more appropriately be viewed as variations or styles of practice. The styles and variations enumerated below are like caricatures—exaggerating some characteristics and minimizing common factors in order to distinguish one style of mediation from another. In reality the distinctions are not always clear, styles are blended, and the same mediator may attempt several different variations in the development of a hybrid personal style. The unique demands of the controversy being mediated may require an eclectic approach.

Labor Mediation

Labor mediation is the most often referred to "model" of third-party dispute intervention. The private and public expense of

unresolved labor/management conflict led to early efforts to implement alternatives to the strike and lockout. Like litigation, a strike
or lockout exacerbates differences and makes future cooperation difficult, and both tactics are costly.

The distinguishing elements of labor mediation include a
professional mediator; experienced representatives as participants
mediating behalf of others; separate caucusing or meetings between
the mediator and each side to explore minimum settlement positions, procedural traditions, precedents, and regulations; and
frequent requirement of ratification or approval of the mediated
agreement. There is a body of literature describing and critiquing
the use of mediation in labor disputes (Maggiolo, 1972; Simkin,
1971). Many of the early writings and proposals for alternative
dispute settlement techniques drew heavily from labor mediation
experience and literature (Fuller, 1971). The mediation process outlined in Chapter Three can be adapted to work well with the labor
mediation approach.

Therapeutic Mediation

Both therapeutic mediation and legal mediation, the next
approach considered, are more a function of the training and experience of the mediator than any other factor. Mediators with a psychotherapeutic or mental health background are trained to recognize the underlying conflict and deal with its causes rather than
simply settle the manifest dispute or the presenting problem (see
Chapter Two). A therapist is accustomed to helping people understand why they are in a position of conflict and helping them move
through the psychological layers that may inhibit their openness
and ability to communicate. A therapist serving as mediator is likely
to emphasize the emotional dimensions of the dispute and to help
the parties deal with them. The goal of this approach is not only the
cessation of manifest conflict behavior but also the participants' understanding and resolution of the internal conflicts that promoted
the dispute. This emphasis on understanding the underlying conflict, resolving or changing its emotional aspects, and psychologi-
cally accepting its resolution tends to prolong the mediation process.

The therapist's sensitivity to the underlying emotional context of the dispute and concern for the mental well-being of both

participants may result in individual sessions with them. The emphasis will be on the emotional needs of the parties, their understanding of the causes of the conflict, and their acceptance of the situation, rather than on their legal rights and responsibilities. This approach may be most effective for disputes that are more emotional than legal, such as child custody, juvenile issues, teenage pregnancies, and other family conflicts (Haynes, 1981).

Mediation is not the same as therapy, though mediation may have a therapeutic effect (Chapter Two outlines the differences; see also Kelly, 1983). Therapeutically trained mediators have unique skills that may help shape a style of mediation. Therapists should not be uncomfortable in applying this style to the mediation process, provided they are aware of the distinctions between mediation and therapy. They must be on guard to offer either mediation or therapy in accord with the wishes and contractual expectations of the participants. When offering mediation they must not neglect the legal review and processing stage set forth in Chapter Three.

If therapists offer mediation services as part of their professional mental health practice, the mediation model will probably reflect their therapeutic practice. The mediation sessions will tend to be for fixed periods of time, what we have termed periodic scheduling, and may have less structure than would be found at mediation centers or court-connected services (Bienenfeld, 1983). Private mediation, like private therapy, is often individualized to the unique needs and wishes of the participants who are paying for the service as well as the unique orientation and training of the provider.

Lawyer Mediation

Like therapists who offer mediation services, lawyers serving as mediators tend to draw from their professional training and orientation. The lawyer mediation approach is likely to focus more on the manifest dispute and less on the underlying conflict. Many lawyers who undertake mediation share with the participants their knowledge of legal parameters or inform them of resolution options and the alternatives that might be imposed by a court should the participants proceed to litigation. A lawyer serving as a mediator is also able to advise the parties about tax considerations, if they are relevant to the settlement options, and address questions of enforce-ability. The lawyer practicing mediation may draft a proposed settlement agreement containing the terms discussed by the partici-pants and subject to independent review by their respective lawyers.

A lawyer-mediator has to be particularly sensitive to avoid advocating the interest of one disputant over the other or even ap-pearing to favor one party's interest. Therefore the lawyer mediation style is likely to preclude individual caucusing with the partici-pants, except in the most unusual of circumstances where the partici-pants knowingly agree to such individual sessions in order to over-come a mediation impasse. The lawyer-mediator, like the therapist who integrates mediation services into a private practice, tends to follow a less structured approach and the mediation services gener-ally reflect law office procedures and scheduling (Elson, 1982).

Not all attorneys who mediate choose to follow this style. Some attorneys (Massengill, 1982) purposely avoid any appearance of practicing law when mediating in order to assure that neither participant feels he or she is being individually represented or that his or her legal interests are protected by the mediator. An attorney offering a lawyer mediation approach must take precautions that only impartial legal information is given. Neither participant should have any reason to believe his or her individual interests, as compared to joint interests, are advocated or protected. Each partici-pant should realize the importance of independent legal advice and review.

Supervisory Mediation

This is one form of meditation that most of us have expe-rienced personally. Informal, authority-based mediation occurs in many hierarchical situations when perceived self-interests among subordinates come into conflict. Parents intervene in squabbles or bickering between siblings. Teachers, residence hall managers, de-partment supervisors, bosses, coaches, and others with some degree of authority and a personal interest or responsibility for the outcome employ an approach to mediation that uses their position to compel an examination of the conflict and workable options for its resolu-tion. Implicit in supervisory mediation is the realization that if the disputants cannot come to their own settlement, the mediator may use authority to decide for them and the privilege of self-determination will be lost.

The supervisory approach is recognizable by its informality, the private nature of the conflicts, the authority or respect afforded the mediator, the mediator's personal interest in the outcome, and the speed of the process. This style, with all its variations, is the most commonly practiced form of mediation. It is usually used when continuing relationships must be preserved after the dispute has been resolved. Despite the informal nature of such common conflict situations, as well as the element of compulsion in supervisory mediation, the principles described in this book apply also to those in supervisory or managerial roles.

Muscle Mediation

The term *muscle mediator* denotes a style of mediation that should be separately recognized and generally avoided (Milne, 1981). In muscle mediation the mediator, sometimes resembling a "closet arbitrator," tells the parties what is fair and appropriate. Muscle mediators apply the supervisory mediation approach inappropriately when no subordinate or parent/child relationship exists and where they have no personal interest in the outcome or responsibility for it. They inform the disputants of the best "voluntary" resolution or narrow the options to preclude effective choices.

Unlike supervisory situations the muscle mediator does not have to live with the settlement and cannot monitor the results. The authority of a muscle mediator is imposed by the mediator rather than sought or contracted by the disputants. Agreements may be frequently and quickly reached by this approach, but serious questions will persist about compliance and the long-term effect of the mediation. Attorneys, court-connected staff, and others, who may be viewed by the disputants as figures of authority or experts on the subject in dispute, must be particularly sensitive to balance the authority and expertise they bring to the mediation with the understanding that muscle mediation is more akin to arbitration. It is unlikely to produce a resolution that will work effectively for the parties in the long run.

Scrivener Mediation

A scrivener is one who writes down the thoughts and ideas expressed by others so that they can be reported in proper form. Some mediators, at the opposite end of the spectrum from muscle mediators, view their role as little more than recording in appropriate form the points of agreement and disagreement expressed by the participants; they emphasize stage 5 of the mediation process: clarification/writing a plan.

In some cases the issues are clear, the disputants have excellent negotiation skills, and the balance of power is relatively equal; here the scrivener role may be an appropriate approach for the mediator. In other cases, however, this passive style may allow mediation to proceed without isolation of the issues, without discovery of all the facts, without development of an array of options, and without any benefit of a third party to help balance the power or serve as an agent of reality. The fact that the scrivener approach to mediation exists attests to the ability of some disputants to resolve their conflicts with no intervention other than the provision of a safe and peaceful setting, an expectation of reasonableness, and someone present to clarify and record their agreement.

Structured Mediation

Perhaps the only true models of mediation are those that set forth detailed rules of procedure. James Coogler (1978), for example, developed rules that divorcing couples must pledge to follow in order to use the services of the Family Mediation Association. These rules encompass a step-by-step process and specify who may attend the sessions, the goals of each session, the role of the mediator, the length of each session, the ordering of the issues, the consequences of not meeting the stated goals, the times when outside attorneys or consultants can be contacted, permissible conduct between sessions, and how the final agreement will be formalized and implemented.

This structured approach provides a sense of security for the participants and for the mediator, as well as a common set of procedural expectations and a degree of predictability. The more structured the approach, however, the less flexibility there is for contingencies and the unique concerns of the disputants. There is particular danger that the rules, in being explicit about what the participants may or may not do during the mediation, may circumvent legal rights such as choice or use of independent legal counsel. The structured approach should be balanced with some degree of flexibility to accommodate not only the uniqueness of each dispute and each set of participants but also unforeseen contingencies. Many different mediation approaches may include early negotiation and agreement on the procedures to be followed in order to ensure an element of structure (see Resource B: Mediation Guidelines).

Court-Connected Mediation

Litigation is, perhaps unfortunately, the acceptable norm for resolving many disputes and for which alternatives such as mediation exist. Court-connected mediation programs have developed an appproach distinguishable from other forms of mediation. The appropriate subjects for court-connected mediation are limited to disputes that would be litigated if not otherwise resolved. As the threshold before litigation, court mediation may be a last-ditch effort following unsuccessful efforts to resolve the dispute. The issues in the dispute have often been refined or pinpointed by pleadings, discovery, and other court procedures. The mediation must proceed on a timetable compatible with court scheduling and dockets. The mediation service is usually without direct charge to the participants and may be voluntary or compelled. The mediator is most often a professional employee of the court or serves under contract to the court. The participants are often represented by attorneys, who are usually not present during the mediation sessions. The mediated settlement is subject to court approval and generally enforceable by the court (McIsaac, 1981).

Court-connected mediation was initially developed for the resolution of divorce and custody issues. Its success in those areas has resulted in selected expansion by some courts into the areas of support enforcement, juvenile delinquency and dependency cases, the diversion of minor criminal matters, and resolution of civil disputes involving a fixed dollar amount or limited subject matter (Vorenberg, 1982). Court-connected mediation may be less distin-

guishable as a style and more reflective of a particular setting or
format for mediation in the public rather than private sector. The
seven-step mediation process discussed in Chapter Three is based in
large part on experiences and information gained from court-
connected mediation, which provides a laboratory for mediation
techniques.

Community Mediation

Community mediation employs an approach that most closely parallels the dispute resolution process observed by anthropologists studying small societies and kin groups (see Chapter One).
Community boards, neighborhood justice centers, and other com-
munity-focused dispute resolution programs have drawn upon this
method of keeping peace within groups of people (Shonholtz, 1981).
The mediator is usually a nonprofessional drawn from the community who shares the same social or cultural experience as the
disputants. The mediator may, however, have special nonacademic
training for this role. The disputants, who are usually inexperienced
in mediation, are themselves the participants, though groups of
disputants may be represented by one or more of their number serving as mediation participants. The mediation service is without cost
to the disputants and is offered in the neighborhood setting by a
public agency or private nonprofit organization. Since the agreements reached are often unenforceable through normal legal procedures, implementation must depend on personal acceptance of the
settlement terms, the goodwill of the disputants, and community or
subgroup expectations. Again, the seven-step process set forth in
Chapter Three is well suited to this community-based approach to
mediation.

Shuttle Mediation

Shuttle mediation is closely identified with the resolution of
international disputes in which leaders of the disputing nations
agree to confer separately with a mediator from a neutral country or
international organization. The separate caucusing to narrow the
issues and explore minimum positions, the representative capacity
of those in mediation, the experience of the mediator and the

parties, the need for ratification of the mediation agreement—all these elements parallel many aspects of labor mediation. However, the geographical distance between the parties, the public attention to the process, and the stakes involved distinguish it from most labor mediation (Fisher, 1978).

Because of the public attention focused on international shuttle mediation, it has become a familiar approach that may be adapted to other public and private disputes where it is difficult to get the parties together and the stakes justify the cost and time required in shuttling. The seven-step process is applicable to shuttle mediation as well as other approaches. Telecommunications, video transmissions, and computer modems could facilitate agreement on the details of the settlement, even when participants cannot meet in person.

Crisis Mediation

Mediation can be effective in a crisis situation if all the disputants recognize the crisis and have a mutual appreciation for the adversity that will follow if it is not resolved. Crisis mediation is extraordinarily demanding on the disputants and the mediator, so there must be a high degree of motivation in order to complete the mediation and extinguish the crisis. Crisis mediation lends itself least to firm procedural rules or structure and is usually marked by marathon sessions.

Crisis mediation differs from other types of mediation because of the demands created by the crisis. The most urgent issues must be isolated from those that can wait so that the limited mediation time can be spent on diffusing the crisis-creating issues. The mediator's goal is not necessarily to resolve the dispute but to defer its resolution to a less critical time. Crisis mediation requires an active role for the mediator, including a willingness to suggest separate caucusing to find out what each side is willing to concede in order to end the crisis.

Techniques to calm the participants and help them focus on a temporary truce are particularly important. Police and medical personnel are often required to offer crisis mediation (Schreiber, 1979). In some crisis situations, such as prison disturbances, riots, boycotts, or strikes, the mediation approach must include some assurance that those in mediation in fact represent the disputants who are not present and have some control over them. Though the step-by-step boundaries in crisis mediation may not be precise, the seven stages set out in Chapter Three can provide the process needed for effective crisis mediation.

Celebrity Mediation

This style of mediation, which may be most effective in conjunction with crisis mediation involving great public interest, can help in expediting the first step: gaining trust. The novelty of a celebrity or public figure as mediator may help move the parties from recalcitrance to a willingness to participate. Particularly if the dispute is public in nature, the popularity and publicity skills of a celebrity or high public official may help to marshal public opinion to bear upon a speedy resolution. Elected public officials, for example, have effectively mediated environmental disputes (Burgess, 1980).

Few disputants wish to appear unreasonable in the spotlight of public attention or recalcitrant in the shadow of a noted public figure. The celebrity serves as a catalyst to allow the disputants to unlock an impasse and as a representative of public concern and sentiment. A dramatic example of a failed effort at celebrity mediation occurred in the Attica prison riots (Wicker, 1975). Even if the celebrity is not a skilled mediator, he or she may bring some order to the conflict and some progress toward its resolution by following the basic seven-step procedure outlined earlier.

Team Mediation

Most of the conflicts subject to mediation are multidimensional. They have an emotional side and a legal or technical side. Divorce, for example, is a matter of the heart and the law (Gold, 1982, p. 45). Environmental disputes usually combine all three aspects. Individual mediators rarely have the interdisciplinary training, experience, or expertise to address fully the combined emotional, legal, and technical aspects present in some cases.

Mediation presents a unique opportunity for the combining of services from different disciplines and the merging of expertise by use of a team or co-mediation approach. Integration of professional services through the context of mediation allows professionals to avoid overstepping the limits of their knowledge and training, while providing a unique opportunity for disputants to receive comprehensive help with their conflict. Mediation should promote cooperation among professionals, as well as between clients.

There are many advantages to co-mediation, as well as certain disadvantages. The most obvious advantage of team mediation is the opportunity to combine different skills to provide a better service. This combination is not limited to attorneys and therapists. Accountants, engineers, educators, psychologists, scientists, physicians, nurses, managers, and other specialists may be combined together or paired with nonprofessionally trained people who have a unique understanding of the dispute or its subject.

A single mediator can, of course, call in others to confer with the disputants during the process of mediation. The mediator or the parties may also consult independently with an expert for background and technical information that can be of assistance in conveying information for consideration in mediation or in creating more options. Co-mediation, however, provides much more than combined knowledge and expertise.

Co-mediation enhances the *process* of mediation. One mediator can concentrate on the factual content of the dispute while the other helps the parties deal with communication barriers and the emotional content of the dispute. While one mediator is talking with the parties, the other might be observing communication patterns and nonverbal clues that will be helpful in facilitating the mediation and overcoming resistance to settlement.

Some mediation teams may choose to divide these process/content functions in accord with their different professional training or background. A therapist/lawyer team, for example, would probably assign the therapist the process role and the lawyer the responsibility for dealing with factual content. The therapist's skills in facilitating communication and unblocking emotional obstacles, coupled with the lawyer's assessment skills and informational resources, enhance the likelihood of a comprehensive negotiated settlement. However, the team may opt for a division of labor by which roles are alternated in order to allow each mediator to step back from active conflict management for purposes of observation and considering strategy.

The benefits of combining the talents and energies of mediators are not limited to cross-disciplinary pairings. Mediators from the same discipline can complement one another's efforts by assuming different mediation postures or by juxtaposing strategies to see what works most effectively in a particular case. One mediator may play the skeptic while the other is accepting; one mediator may be harsh while the other is kind; one may joke while the other is serious; one may be practical while the other is visionary. The ingenuity required for successful mediation can be enhanced, and more settlement alternatives can be developed, through the combined efforts of two mediators.

Mediation can be hard work that exhausts the mediator's energy and control during a session. Having another mediator ready to pick up and continue the momentum can be of great value. Since there are always at least two participants in mediation, the involvement of two mediators allows a better matching of energy and a symmetry of effort.

The complexity of issues in some disputes, particularly if the mediator is not an expert on the subject in dispute, can become overwhelming for the mediator, as in environmental mediation. It may be hard to limit the participants' discussion to one issue at a time. The job of the mediator in helping to sort out all the facts, the elements of each issue, the points of agreement and disagreement, the options available for each issue, and the details of that which has been agreed to, all while managing the conflict, may be too much for one person to handle. Using a pair of mediators in such complex cases allows each mediator to take responsibility for a set of issues and an opportunity to note what has transpired without bringing the mediation to a temporary standstill. One mediator can keep the process going while the other reflects on where it has been. If the participants shift gears from one issue to another during the course of a session, two mediators stand a better chance than one of following them without getting lost. One may be assigned to fulfill the primary role of one stage while the other prepares for the next.

The interaction between two mediators can also serve as an immediate model of constructive dialogue for the participants. The participants will note how the mediators go about developing and considering the possible advantages and disadvantages of each option. At times the mediators may take opposing sides to let the disputants hear one another's position calmly debated by others.

Mediators, like therapists and lawyers, can sometimes overcome resistance to settlement by trying techniques that carry a risk of failing or damaging their rapport with participants. Confrontive tactics or the expression of unspoken premises, for example, may be highly effective in some cases and disastrous in others. The mediator can never be sure of the result and may choose not to try a potentially effective technique without a backup. A team approach allows each mediator to take some risks to move the mediation along, knowing that if the technique fails the other mediator is there to begin another approach or divert the mediation from a dead end.

In contrast, if a single mediator fails to identify premises, or misinterprets feelings, or tries to articulate an argument on one side, it could easily lead to a sense of triangling. One of the disputants may feel an identity with the mediator and the other may think the mediator is unsympathetic or has taken the other side. This perception of bias can be particularly difficult if the dispute is between two people of different sexes. In a divorce case, for example, the husband may assume that the male mediator will be sympathetic to his wife while the wife may feel that the same mediator will naturally side with her husband. A dispute involving alleged gender discrimination or between two groups with traditional gender identity—physicians and nurses, for example—may be most difficult to mediate unless both sexes are represented on the mediation team. Even if the participants are all of the same sex, some may have prejudicial notions that a male or a female mediator would see the issue in some stereotypical fashion that will be disadvantageous. In the heat of a dispute, fear and irrationality may create a perception of triangling or bias that would not otherwise exist.

A team consisting of a male and female mediator can provide a balance that counteracts actual or perceived triangling or bias. Two mediators, particularly if they are male and female, can help one another recognize and counteract their own bias or gender-limited vision. Moreover, the disputants may be less inclined to employ sexually manipulative tactics and may be more cordial because of the presence of both a man and a woman together. There will be less opportunity for gender-based transference or rejection.

It is important after a mediation session to think about what happened and to plan the agenda, strategy, and techniques to be used in the next session. Two mediators can share perceptions about what occurred and why, and together they can plan the next meeting. Collegial support and evaluation are important by-products of co-mediation. A built-in peer review and mutual check helps avoid error and promotes professional growth.

Training, as discussed in the next section, can be elusive, and the interdisciplinary nature of mediation makes effective training difficult. Co-mediation provides an opportunity for peer training and sharing of mediation techniques. Experienced mediators may offer to work with the less experienced in order to provide a training opportunity. If the co-mediators are from different academic or professional backgrounds, they will find that working with one another affords a unique opportunity to learn the skills and dynamics of the other discipline in a way that no amount of reading or formal instruction can provide.

Co-mediation is not without its drawbacks. Two mediators may double the cost of the service. In order to reduce the expense to participants, the mediators may choose not to charge the same hourly amount as for their individual services because of the rewards they derive from working as a team. They may be employed by an agency or public office that does not pass on the full expense to the mediation participants. Even so, the resources involved in co-mediation are greater and represent an added cost, regardless of how it is paid or absorbed.

Mediation, unlike most office or clinical practices, usually requires that the participants come together at the same time. Scheduling a mutually acceptable time with a single mediator can be troublesome. Scheduling an acceptable time for a multiplicity of participants *and* a team of mediators can be a tremendous problem, particularly if the mediators do not normally work together or do not have offices nearby.

Mediators not accustomed to working with one another may at first find the team approach awkward. Politeness or deference may create a hesitancy to intercede or to cover a point that appears to be in the other mediator's territory. Important points may slip through the mediation team like a tennis ball landing between new doubles partners. One mediator may fail to read the other's clues. The other, failing to see where the discussion is heading, may interrupt or divert the mediation from a productive course.

Some co-mediators may have difficulty working as a team because they are not accustomed to performing in front of peers or those from other disciplines. For example, both therapy and law are normally practiced in private and without critique. The very risk taking that may be enhanced by the resouces of a team may also be inhibited by fear of peer scrutiny or disapproval from someone of different training or educational background.

Any team effort requires coordination, timing, and practice. Before actually working together as a team, mediators should take the time necessary to understand one another's philosophy, strengths, weaknesses, approaches, and techniques. This preparation, though immensely beneficial, takes time that cannot be charged to participants and might not be available without considerable sacrifice. Time spent after a mediation session in comparing notes and perceptions is also unlikely to be compensated for in private practice and may shortchange other clients or responsibilities in an agency setting where resources are limited and waiting times are already long. This is another expense of team mediation that must be considered before it is undertaken.

The participants may be confused by the roles of the co-mediators or may not understand the division of labor. They may feel manipulated by co-mediation tactics or may question the need and cost for two mediators. If the subject or dynamics of a mediation session falls heavily upon one mediator while the other sits silently through most of the session, the parties may question the need for both to be present. These questions, if unspoken, may hinder the progress of mediation.

Each benefit of co-mediation can be matched with a corresponding cost or risk. A team approach does offer distinct advantages in some situations that more than merit its use. Each situation is different and each must be separately evaluated to determine what will work best. Complex cases or those with important elements calling for the expertise or skills of different disciplines appear to justify co-mediation.

Once undertaken, the co-mediation approach should be evaluated continuously during the case to determine if it is working and satisfying the needs of the participants. It may be mutually agreed that one mediator should bow out or that the mediators should alternate, depending on the task and subject of a particular session. If the principal purpose of co-mediation is training, that purpose should be made clear to the participants. They will rarely object, provided they are not expected to pay for someone's training.

Recommended Reading

The following titles discuss the dynamics and benefits of interdisciplinary team mediation in divorce and family conflicts. Each reflects a different approach to the role differentiation within the team.

"Divorce Mediation: An Emerging Field." J. Kelly, C. Zlatchin, and J. Shawn. In C. Ewing (Ed.), *Psychology, Psychiatry and the Law: A Clinical and Forensic Handbook*. Sarasota: Professional Resource Exchange, 1984.

"A Lawyer/Therapist Team Approach to Divorce." M. Black and W. Joffee. *Conciliation Courts Review*, 1978, *16* (1), 1–5.

"Lawyer-Therapist Team as Mediator in a Marital Crisis." J. Wiseman and J. Fiske. *Social Work*, 1980, *25*, 442–450.

"The Psychological Context of the Interdisciplinary Co-Mediator Team Model in Marital Dissolution." L. Gold. *Conciliation Courts Review*, 1982, *20* (2), 45–53.

7

✖ ✖ ✖ ✖ ✖

Family and Divorce Mediation

Mediators working with divorce or other family-related issues, such as unwanted teenage pregnancies, parent/child controversies, contested wills, or juvenile delinquency issues, should have a solid background of knowledge about normal family interaction, patterns, and systems. It is also important to be sensitive to diversity of lifestyles, as well as the choices and crises that most people face as individuals and family members, whether or not their families are restructured through a divorce, death, or other crisis. Only by having this kind of larger picture will the mediator be able to communicate the inevitability of change, one of the basic principles discussed earlier. This chapter is intended to illuminate the processes and structures that are influenced by divorce.

Even those whose education has provided theory and practice in working with families to effect positive change are encouraged to review this chapter. For mediators who come from law, business, and other fields, in-depth study of the first part of this chapter and the recommended readings would be particularly helpful before offering family mediation.

The second part of the chapter outlines the custody and financial aspects of divorce, or marital dissolution as it is referred to in the law of some states. This chapter can do no more than provide the basics of the financial and custody issues that must be resolved upon divorce and some of the legal considerations that may affect the decisions to be made. The latter sections will appear rudimentary to attorneys and should not be considered a legal trainer for nonlawyers. It is no more than a guided tour that can only bring into view the landmarks and legal points of interest in divorce. It provides an itinerary for mediation of divorces, not a detailed map by which others can be advised on how to get there.

Normal Family Structures and Processes

What is "normal" for a family? Is divorce necessarily an abnormal event? The answer to the latter question depends on the definition used in the former. Walsh (1982, pp. 4–5) has categorized the references to "normal" most often found in the literature as the following: normality as health, normality as utopia, normality as average, normality as process.

Following these points of reference, then, divorce may or may not be a healthy action for the individuals within the family; it is usually regarded as less than utopian as a solution to family conflicts and is most often perceived as antithetical to ideal family life by some of the participants in mediation, as well as society in general. Divorce is fast becoming a statistically average condition for even the normative distribution among the population; it is creating a new set of transactional systems and processes via shared parenting, single adulthood, remarriage, and blended family units.

Structural family theory (Minuchin, 1974) has treated families as complex organizations that must deal with problems presented by those within the structure as well as problems brought to bear by the outside world. In this conceptual framework, the absence or number of problems alone is not a reliable criterion for judging a family's normality. As Walsh (1982) points out, structural family theory stresses that each family is a complex tapestry of interwoven functional demands that organize the way each person interacts with another. All families have either explicit or implicit rules regarding power and expectations for each others' behavior. These rules persist due to habit, usefulness, and mutual need. Families resist change in these structures, yet a healthy, functioning family must respond effectively to both change brought about by the individual development of members and change from without. In this respect, all families can be seen as social systems that are transforming and evolving. Often these demands require major reconstruction of the system. Such changes in the basic structure naturally bring about anxiety and stress for the members, but these feelings should not be mislabeled as pathology.

Another useful set of constructs about families is the paradigm developed by Haley (1976) and others: the *strategic model* or strategic problem-solving approach. According to this model, the family members' behavior is motivated by a desire to be helpful. They do what they do either because they believe it is right or because it is the only way they know. The role of the professional, according to this model, is to interrupt behavior that is not effective by using various strategies and then to help the family members develop new, more effective behavior.

In this view, if problems exist it is because the family as a group has been unable to adjust to life cycle transitions and family members are unwilling or unable to meet the demands of the situation by changing their own behavior. As Walsh (1982, p. 17) has noted, "Haley ultimately sides with Minuchin in defining a healthy family as a functional system that accomplishes its task." A functional family must provide economic and emotional support to its members, must care for the children, and must protect its members from external pressures and threats. It must help each member progress toward self-actualization on Maslow's pyramid while being responsible as defined by Glasser (1981)—that is, meeting individual needs without infringing on the needs of others (see Chapter Four).

The couples coming to divorce mediation often relate to this conceptual framework. The relationship has broken down so that tasks, such as cooperative parenting or supportive services that facilitate the role of the economic provider, are incomplete or nonexistent and individual growth has been stopped. Because of this breakdown, it may be hard to get such a group of participants to perform the tasks necessary for divorce. By using the mediation process and the techniques described in this book, the mediator can show the participants a way to do the business they must do together and reestablish at least minimal ability to negotiate and solve problems.

The systems view of families has at least four assumptions. These principles relate to the work of the divorce mediator and are a subset of the propositions we have described in Chapter One. According to Beavers (1982, p. 47):

1.   An individual needs a group, a human system, for identity and satisfaction.
2.   Causes and effects are interchangeable.
3.   Any human behavior is the result of many variables rather than one "cause"; therefore simplistic solutions are questioned.
4.   Human beings are limited and finite. No one is absolutely helpless or absolutely powerful in a relationship.

⅄   The first assumption repeats the concept of need and self-fulfillment explained in Chapter Four. It also explains why people fear divorce as a breakup of their personal system and why support groups serve such a useful function as a stopgap substitute that provides a temporary sense of belonging and personal worth.

¯ The second point, that causes and effects are interchangeable, is perhaps more philosophical but can be discussed with mediation participants indirectly. If the feelings that dominate the creation of an option are anger or revenge, the feelings that follow the selection of an option are likely to be the same. This is one reason why so many couples have to return to court to resolve continuing problems— the adversarial process does not encourage consideration of the emotional foundations of the decisions that must be made. The more the mediator is able to get the couple to acknowledge their feelings about the conflicts, the less likely they are to be repeated.

¯ The third assumption implies a suggestion for the role of the mediator. When a mediator sees participants in a session who are choosing an option based on a single variable, it is the mediator's duty to point out the simplistic nature of the solution being considered and to keep the issue open and the discussion focused until another solution can be found that considers more variables.

Suppose we pursue this concept further with an example. If a man believes that the only reason the marriage failed was because of the wife's mother's overinvolvement, physically and financially, he

might ca tailing all contact between the children and
grandm this step would relieve his anger and hurt, it is
a simp n that denies the reality of the very enmeshment
on w ased. Artificially eliminating postdivorce contact
wi s mother will not be helpful to the man's understand-
i wn role within the restructured family system; nor will it
p the woman's growth as a separate individual. It may also have a
negative impact on the children's sense of connectedness and their
postdivorce adjustment. While the mediator should not choose for
the client, it is important to bring this whole system to light and
focus the discussion on how the wife can become separate, without
destroying relationships, after the husband leaves. A session in a
custody dispute where this interaction is developed might sound
something like the following:

Open Question

Mediator: What about the issue of grandparents and extended family visits?

Bill: Your mother was always poking around in our business, and I want it to stop. In fact, I don't think it's good for the kids, so I want to make sure that she doesn't bug the children and load them down with too many toys. She's always tried to buy their affection. I only want her to visit with them for a short time on Christmas and each of their birthdays and to give each child only one gift.

Mary: [*Clearly disturbed, she turns away from Bill, clenches her fists, and softly mutters an unintelligible expletive.*]

Letting the Client Fully Express the Emotion

Mediator: So you're angry at her mother for being too involved with your family.

Bill: You better believe I am!

Mediator: Are you angry with Mary for letting her butt in too much?

Bill:	Yeah.
Mediator:	How about yourself, for allowing it to happen?
Bill:	Yeah, I guess. . . . [*Pause.*]

Legitimizing and Conceptualizing

Mediator:	It's only natural that you feel that way. You think that's what caused your marriage to fall apart.
Bill:	Yeah, I do.

Questioning a Simplistic Assumption

Mediator:	Mary, is this what you think happened?
Mary:	No, I don't. I'll admit that Mom helped us out a lot, but that's not the whole reason.
Mediator:	Do you think it hurts the kids to have grandma over so much, bringing too many things, like Bill said?
Mary:	It's not like she visits every day or anything.

Gaining Data for Evaluation

Mediator:	How often does she visit?
Mary:	Well, she lives pretty far away, but she usually comes up and stays a week or two every couple of months.
Bill:	What do you mean? She stayed the whole month of December!
Mary:	Well, she just wanted to help out with the holidays and see the kids at Christmas.

Isolating and Acknowledging the Issue

Mediator:	Well, there is an issue here of how often she ought to be a part of things. Bill, your solution is to have her time with the children severely limited.

Acting as an Agent of Reality

More and more, the courts have been recognizing the rights of grandparents to visit their grandchildren after divorce. I understand that you wish Mary would stop letting Grandma take over, but maybe she's not ready or able to restrict her own mother. And it sounds like you had a difficult time too, Bill.

Reframing the Issue to Operationalize a Plan

I think there is a larger issue here, and that is how you want your children to relate to their grandmother. I think you both agree that some contact, even *some* goodies and presents, are okay. Can you both think for a minute about how often the kids should be able to visit their grandmother? Can you come up with an option that puts both Mary and you back in control, even though you will be living separately?

− This example also illustrates the fourth assumption of a systems orientation. Neither Mary nor her mother will necessarily be the one calling all the shots. Even with the impending divorce, Bill and Mary must find an accommodation that acknowledges each other's rights in the parental relationship that must continue beyond the divorce. If the grandmother issue is not resolved independent of who has custody, Bill and Mary may each fight for custody.

Beavers (1982) points out that families can be rated on a continuum from healthy to severely dysfunctional. Healthy families possess clear boundaries, contextual clarity, relatively equal power and the process of intimacy, the encouragement of autonomy, joy and comfort in relating, skilled negotiation, and significant transcendent values. Severely dysfunctional families, on the other hand, have poor communication patterns and negotiation skills, an unclear power and decision-making system, and a pervasive tone of depression and cynicism.

It may be a surprise to say that mediators deal with divorcing families from all parts of this continuum, since divorce can often be an uncomfortable expression of all that is positive about a family, as well as that which is dysfunctional. Some families make the choice to restructure in order to allow for further personal growth, a step up on Maslow's hierarchy. Mediators must not presume that all the cases they will see are dysfunctional in every respect. However, when the participants in front of the mediator are unable to negotiate or carry on constructive communication patterns, extra work must be done to reestablish at least those two elements. Mediation should help reestablish these constructive communication and negotiation patterns by setting reasonable expectations for both parties. The guidelines for mediation (see Resource B) might require that the participants attempt to reestablish and utilize skills that will help them in subsequent relationships.

Normative patterns of families that have been disrupted by divorce, as discussed by Montalvo (1982), are helpful in understanding the dynamics that may be going on in a mediation session. Montalvo's analysis is germane for the visitation, custody, or support problems that come to mediation following the finalization of a divorce. Montalvo's categories—System with Only One Compass, The Crippled Executive, The Uneven Race, and The Abdication Contest—can help form the basis for development of specific mediation techniques that address the concealed emotional context and thereby promote complete emotional dissolution. (See Table 8.) Depending on the participants, the most predictable of these four scenarios for their postdivorce adjustment may need to be discussed, based on the interactions shown in mediation, at the signing of the mediated plan or memorandum of agreement.

Goldsmith (1982, p. 301) emphasizes that members of a postdivorce family system may continue to be interdependent "in such a way that a change in one will cause a change in all of them and the total system." She reviews the subsystem of relationships that exist after divorce and after subsequent remarriage and reminds us that while the custodial parent/child subsystem (usually called a "single-parent family") has been given most of the attention in the literature, other relationships are equally important. Other authors (McGoldrick and Carter, 1980) have further described these reconstituted family units.

Individual and Family Development

✳ Individual life cycles and "pivot points" are joined through family life into family stages. It is necessary for mediators to understand the developmental stages of both in order to interpret the perceptual world of the participants in divorce mediation.

Table 8. Four Interpersonal Arrangements Among Divorcing Families.

Triangular Arrangement	Child's Problem (Example)	What is Concealed?	What is Confusing?	Usual Divorce Locus	Dysfunctional Extreme
System with Only One Compass Mother uses child as compass to find out where she is in uncharted new relationships. Child's comments and behavior are used to slow down or accelerate the relationship's progress. Child modulates the sense of dislocation experienced during the transition to becoming a new threesome. Child is not free to comment by word or deed; mother is mostly conscious only of child's "intrusiveness," not the "help" child is offering.	Child is hyperalert, feels mother is bringing new person into her life too quickly, demanding a betrayal or abandonment of father. Child handles dislocation experiences for self and mother—for example, mother's backrub to new boyfriend gets "You are getting too personal now . . . you are on Daddy's turf. Can I slow you down?" Child feels occasional fear when mother cannot make up her mind about new relationships.	Mother ostensibly sees child as "intrusive" but conceals that she feels rudderless and needs it as a cue. Child conceals that it is not just anxiety over betraying Dad that bothers. It is mother's looking helpless without child's orientation. Mother's front: "It isn't me who is unsure of the new linkage. It's my daughter." In some cases mother unconsciously demands: "Go as fast as I go," denying child's independence.	Looks like a problem of an intrusive child that will yield to behavior modification. Mother appears to control pace of her relationship. "It's just that my child is in my business." Blocking the child as critic, pacemaker, or commentator reveals that Mom becomes less organized without child's comments.	Divorced as spouses, but not as parents; caretaking problematic but not endangered.	Mother lost, disoriented, dependent without child's comments and choice. Child enmeshes further and becomes phobic to protect mother. Erratic choice of new partners; possibilities of another divorce.
The Crippled Executive Wife becomes helpless as mother to ensure husband's participation; child	Child screams and cannot be stopped; wants to sleep in mother's bed all the	Mother ostensibly wants child to stop screaming and go to sleep in its own bed.	Change will be offered in many areas but withheld in others. Mother stops	Divorced as spouses, but not as parents; caretaking problematic but not en-	Mother cannot recover effectiveness in childrearing unless husband parti-

Table 8. Four Interpersonal Arrangements Among Divorcing Families, Cont'd.

Triangular Arrangement	Child's Problem (Example)	What is Concealed?	What is Confusing?	Usual Divorce Locus	Dysfunctional Extreme
becomes unmanageable, straining mother's executive capacities. Husband adopts a remote control executive stance that fails to resolve the cycle of defeat, ensuring that he will be called in again.	time; resists attempts to get her out. Child overestimates mother's power over mother, which is based on coalition with grandmother and father.	Mother conceals that she really wants child's company to mitigate loneliness, to replace husband's presence, and to avoid facing her own social restoration tasks.	the child's screaming, develops her own interests, asserts herself with grandmother's relatives, resists husband's help, but allows child to stay in bed. Mother retains one area unchanged in order to prove independent control.	dangered.	pates and disrupts his life; allows the children to regress; restricts her own interpersonal field; stagnates. Mother jumps into another marriage pushed by relatives who support her helplessness; remains tied to grandmother and other helpful relatives.
The Uneven Race Mother behaves perfectly in keeping with caretaking and visitation routines; she fulfills all duties carefully. Picks up child and returns punctually, calls child regularly and predictably. The child detects something wrong, tense, but cannot pinpoint it. Father is polite and cooperative as he "watches" mother for failure in visitation and caretaking routines. A subtle tug of war.	Child uncertain, overalert, happy facade. By being good the child feels it will keep intact whatever remains of the couple. Child's happiness front eventually breaks into delayed psychosomatic expressions of chronic stress: losing hair, skin rashes, problems in school.	Wife who left presents herself as strong, unwilling to give in or forfeit her rights. Wife conceals that "only if I give in to what he wants will I be allowed visitation as I want it." She fears she cannot catch up with his advantaged supervisory position. She conceals her fear that she may not buy enough time to "redeem" herself fast enough. At first husband looks reas-	Initially they look like a balanced seesaw, a fair contest of evenly matched antagonists. The asymmetry in the arrangement, and the accompanying feeling of dislocation experienced by both (particularly the wife), is not projected clearly. Sexual reencounters are difficult to judge. Are they using each other to get what they want? Can they honestly reconcile? Therapist hesitates	Divorced as spouses, but not as parents; caretaking problematic but not endangered.	Sexual blackmail. Child develops chronic severe psychosomatic illness. Wife feels she cannot escape husband unless she links to a strong protector who will pluck her from the husband's domination. Double dealing, dangerous jealousy triangle, violence possible unless she is helped to move from one relationship to another, going first through a nonrelationship stage. High

	onable, benevolent, ready to negotiate. He conceals fears that he cannot deal with her as an equal and must dominate her into returning or else be rejected.	and the conflict and tension are prolonged.			risk for parental kidnapping.

The Abdication Contest

Husband about to respond to his ex-wife's call and act as father but does not carry through. She acts as if she will pick up as mother, but really drops it for him to pick up. A repeating cycle in which child continues acting out and parents continue ineffectual until outside help steps in: courts, police, hospitals, and so forth.	Child constantly elicits and yet sabotages feeble executive moves. Multiple and exculpating acting out, anarchy, stealing, confrontation, and intimidation of parents. Parental child emerges to console mother in her sadness. Child conceals a fear that if it acts responsibly it will be let down once more. And conceals that it is out to protect its own freedom at parental expense.	Father: "I must pretend I'm out to stop them and socialize them, but what I really want is my kid's approval and consolation. I want it to take my side." Mother conceals from herself and others that "he may be leaving me because he does not love me." She protects self-esteem. "He is leaving me because of something wrong in him"—for example, he is homosexual.	Looks as if husband is going to take over, but doesn't quite do it. Investigative and supervisory moments that look encouraging turn out to be whitewash. Mother's depression is not capable of keeping husband. Difficulty in determining which are the most influential relationships—coalition with youngsters, with new partner, with ex-wife—in motivating new parental efforts to modify acting out.	Divorced as spouses and parents; caretaking is endangered.	Anarchy, delinquency, psychosis. High risk for joining religious cults.

Source: Adapted from Montalvo (1982, pp. 292–294). Reprinted by permission.

Erikson (1968, 1978) has proposed an eight-stage process of personal development; the task of each stage is to deal with a certain issue, the outcome of which can be fixed along a continuum between extremes in attitude (see Table 9).

Even the popularized works *Passages* (Sheehy, 1978) and *Pathfinders* (Sheehy, 1981), as well as more professionally oriented descriptions such as *Seasons of a Man's Life* (Levinson and others, 1978), delineate the predictable points in adult life where certain values and activities take on new meaning. The "thirties crisis" or "male menopause" are really individual developmental crises. People in such crises often need to reassess their family structures to determine how adequately they meet their personal needs. Many divorces are spurred by the sudden crisis in a developmental stage by one member of the couple or by the growth process involved when one member of the couple starts to deal more adequately with the issues of an earlier age. It is a two-way street: Individual developmental crises can precipitate a decision to divorce; the decision to divorce can bring on a series of developmental crises for an individual. Based on the second proposition discussed earlier—that causes and effects are interchangeable—it is safe to say that divorce creates or affects a developmental crisis for *all* members of the family. For this reason, mediators who work with divorce must be aware of these developmental stages and help normalize them for the participants.

A divorce mediator who has not gained sufficient background in family and personal development may want to suggest or even require concurrent individual therapy or family counseling so that the participants can explore their individual or collective developmental crises in depth. Mediators who have the expertise to perform counseling functions must clearly define the differences in role and not allow the mediation to become individual counseling or family therapy sessions. The pragmatic and ethical issues raised in this potential role conflict are discussed further in other chapters.

Just as individuals have developmental cycles and consequent issues, so do families as structural entities. Erikson (1968, 1978) proposes several major transition points for families. According to Patterson (1973, p. 219): "The child's leaving the family to enter school, the onset of puberty, becoming economically independent, marriage, parenthood, and retirement with the prospect of

Table 9. Stages of Human Growth and Development.

Age	Issue	Responsibility	Attitude	Strength
Maturity (60+)	Meaning	↑ Self-responsible	Value or despair	Wisdom
Adult (30–60)	Teaching		Giving or stagnation	Care
Young adult (18–30)	Responsiveness		Intimacy or self-absorption	Love
Adolescence (12–18)	Identity		Self-awareness or role confusion	Fidelity (loyalty)
Preadolescence (6–12)	Skill mastery		Adequacy or inadequacy	Competence
Childhood (3–6)	Initiative	Dependent ↓	Outgoing or guilty	Purpose
Babyhood (1–3)	Authority		Acceptance or rebellion	Will
Infancy (0–1)	Dependency		Trust or mistrust	Hope

Source: Based on Erikson (1968); chart developed by *Creative Initiative*, Palo Alto.

death may become a crisis." Each one of these events indelibly marks the individual *and* the family. The insightful work of McGoldrick and Carter (1982) and others provides an excellent background from which mediators can view their own cases.

Virginia Satir (1967) notes that a helping professional cannot presume to know the stage of family life or the relationship of the parents and children to the parents' families unless a family life chronology is constructed. A family chronology may also assist in mediation. While not all the information gathered from such a chronology may be germane to the topic of mediation, it may help the mediator to understand the perceptual world of the participants and availability of resources such as time, transportation, money, food, shelter, or caregiving within the extended families of both parents. If a man or woman comes to custody mediation demanding sole custody of a preschool child while working sixty hours a week, the mediator may want to know before the first session the willingness of relatives to look after the child. In addition to the biographical data on the contact sheet (see Chapter Five), the mediator may want each participant to fill out a family life chronology.

Statistically predictable stages of middle-class American families in the last quarter of the twentieth century are described by McGoldrick and Carter (1982, p. 176) as follows: (1) between families: the unattached young adult; (2) the joining of families through marriage: the newly married couple; (3) the family with young children; (4) the family with adolescents; (5) launching children and moving on; (6) the family in later life. Each stage has characteristic emotional processes and tasks that must be done to proceed developmentally. Divorce is seen by these authors as the largest single variation from the standard pattern, and they cite the points of highest family tension (1982, p. 189):

1. At the time of the *decision* to separate or divorce
2. When this decision is announced to family and friends
3. When money and custody visitation arrangements are discussed
4. When the physical separation takes place
5. When the actual legal divorce takes place

6. When separated spouses or ex-spouses have contact about money or children and at life cycle transition points of all family members
7. As each spouse is making the initial adjustments to rebuilding a new life

They and other researchers further predict that it takes a minimum of two years for a family to readjust to its new structure and proceed to the next developmental stage; unresolved anger or revenge can block step-family integration for years or even permanently. Mediators can do much to reduce the time by helping participants acknowledge such negative feelings and move on.

McGoldrick and Carter (1982) outline the developmental issues for a divorced family in a comprehensive chart that mediation participants may find helpful. These developmental issues are juncture points similar to growth rings along a reed—the areas just above and just below are the most likely to bend when pressured. So, too, families are likely to make a decision to change their structure right around these times, since they add stress to a system that may be only marginally meeting the needs of the members. The mother whose child has just entered school may be thrust into an internal role conflict because her justification for staying home, and the meaning she derived, is no longer sufficient in her own as well as society's eyes.

Families change in predictable ways even if they try to remain the same—children grow up and leave, parents age. Divorce can be a deliberate way to create change in a family, or it can be an unconscious response to a change that has already taken place.

Divorce Disputes and Decisions

Most couples are glad to have a less combative and more emotionally complete way of making important decisions about restructuring their family than is usually provided in adversarial proceedings. Mediation can be useful at many points in the divorce process. It can be initiated by referral from attorneys when litigation or negotiation has not been effective, by court order or rule, or as an alternative to such traditional processes before attorneys are retained. Mediation can also be provided later to help resolve questions relating to modifications or noncompliance to previous court orders. Divorce and custody mediation involves the participant's perception of self-worth and competence, particularly with respect to sexuality, role enactment, and parenting ability. A majority of divorce mediation cases involve the needs and rights of others not present in the session, since a majority of couples have children or other dependents. Mediation of divorce disputes also affects the individual and family development covered earlier in this chapter. It is helpful to understand such dynamics and know what techniques to use when they arise.

Most couples coming for divorce or custody mediation do not present serious roadblocks to the skillful use of the mediation process outlined in Chapter Three. They are usually scheduled for weekly sessions (see Chapter Eleven). Some divorce situations, however, such as an imminent move to another state, urgent financial need, pending parental responsibilities or decisions, a docketed court hearing date, or even pragmatic concerns such as distance from mediation services, may indicate use of the crisis or marathon style of mediation. This style, which often requires the use of individual caucuses, may break down trust between the couple, heighten fears of inequality or preferential treatment, or lessen the effectiveness of the mediation process to reestablish communication between the two participants. The use of individual sessions as a routine part of divorce mediation has been advocated by some authors (Haynes, 1981) as part of a periodic or scheduled mediation, but their use may need to be reviewed in light of further experience. Haynes (1983) has subsequently questioned the use of caucusing in family cases because it may align the mediator with the secret agenda of each participant. Marathon sessions and individual caucuses should be used only when required by court schedules or when unique circumstances dictate an absolute need. Their use should be decided prior to the start of mediation and should never be allowed to reflect a participant's manipulative move for power within a session. The rest of this chapter is premised on the assumption of weekly joint sessions.

In this era of "no-fault" divorce actions, a recalcitrant spouse often displaces his or her anger and resentment against the divorce action itself into the questions of child custody, visitation, and financial arrangements. A spouse who does not want to be divorced can slow the progress of the divorce by resisting attempts to settle issues amicably. The spouse's resistive theme is often unrealistic, simplistic, and mechanistic: "Okay, divorce me, but I'm not going to lose the [car/house/children] along with the marriage."

The underlying conflict for such people has to do with unacceptable perceptions of self. They fear that they will see themselves or be seen by others as losers, as weak and ineffectual bargainers. To guard against this perception, and in a desperate bid to maintain the relationship, however temporarily or futilely, such participants can create roadblocks to the necessary division of property or the appropriate parenting of the children. This resistive behavior will continue until the person has been given enough information to understand the self-defeating and ineffective nature of that behavior *and* is ready at last to accept the inevitability of change and move through the painful loss process (see Chapters Four and Thirteen). Education alone will probably not be sufficient to move the individual toward a less bitter process.

To start with the least emotionally threatening technique, mediators must first clarify for the participants exactly what they stand to gain and lose from continuing the conflict. The participant involved in a custody or financial dispute must understand rationally that noncooperation with the divorce and mediation process may result in lowered esteem from the former spouse and often the children, as well as additional high costs paid to professionals such as lawyers and mediators, funds that could be better used to rebuild lives. The mediator can give such information as part of the preliminary statement during the first stage of mediation (see Chapters Three and Five) but must often continue to remind the recalcitrant spouse of such facts. Rational facts alone are not necessarily enough to change perceptions and behavior.

One of the most effective techniques that can be used in a conflicted custody case is to have the mediator request the "divorcer" to declare to the "divorcee" the equivalent of one or more of these phrases:

- There is nothing you can do that will stop me from divorcing you.

- There is nothing you can do that will bring us back together as we were.
- I am a parent to our children forever. Nothing you do will change that fact.

Such statements, said with calmness, conviction, and full eye contact from the other participant, when used at the proper time in mediation, can bring about the emotional recognition of powerlessness for the recalcitrant spouse—such a declaration is often accompanied by tears and collapse of the defenses. This technique is only to be used with great sensitivity, since it leaves the participant vulnerable. Because it is such an emotional moment, the mediator must control its misuse by the other participant and not allow the other to press for concessions immediately, just as the referee in a boxing ring does not allow another hit after a knockout until the boxer is up again and capable of defense. This technique is best used in the decision-making stage of mediation when progress seems blocked by underlying conflicts. It requires the mediator to become very directive and active. It should not be used toward the end of a session—techniques urging emotional acceptance in such confrontational ways often take more time than expected, since they can be the first small opening in the participant's emotional dam.

The article "A Typology of Divorcing Couples: Implications for Mediation and the Divorce Process" (Kressel and others, 1980) sets out four basic patterns found in couples who are divorcing: enmeshed, autistic, direct conflict, and disengaged conflict. These four categories, based on the couple's degree of ambivalence, their communication style, and the level of overtness of actual manifest conflict, can serve as the basis for further study, development, and discussion of techniques, since each requires a different intervention by the mediator.

The first two categories, enmeshed and autistic, represent direct opposites in communication and overt conflict. The enmeshed pattern is characterized by high levels of both conflict and communication, whereas the autistic shows little evidence of either and is characterized by avoidance, physically and emotionally. Both the enmeshed and the autistic patterns have proved to be the most difficult to mediate.

In the *enmeshed* pattern, the mediator needs to control and redirect the communication constantly—to point out that the source of the resistance and constant self-defeating squabbling over petty items is the underlying fear of ending the relationship. Basically, enmeshed patterns are approach/avoidance conflicts: The couple wants and does not want the end of the intimate relationship. In enmeshed relationships, the skills that would be most effective include the technique mentioned earlier (having one participant make a definitive ending statement) plus some normalizing and education done through the techniques of reflection and interpretation. Referral for auxiliary services should also be considered. Often the resistance is manifested by sexual acting out, such as renewed courting and coupling between the participants, or grudging, passive participation during mediation. Mediators can intervene by seeking agreement that both types of behavior will be prohibited and by calling an impasse if they continue (with the stipulation that mediation can continue when they end).

In the *autistic* pattern, it is essential to recognize the underlying personal conflicts despite the noncommunication and conflict-avoidance behavior. True negotiation and problem solving are often absent. Unilateral, often explosive or vehement demands are accepted by the participants out of fear that to discuss them further will "open a can of worms" or let out the suppressed affective content. If they are not discussed, however, the accepted conditions may soon become intolerable and the subject of future conflict and possible postdivorce litigation. A referral for counseling or therapy for the couple or for each individual is often appropriate when the autistic pattern is evident.

Mediators working with such couples should allow the defensive behavior of remoteness, but they should also explain their skepticism that such unilateral decision making will provide a truly mutual and lasting agreement. Another thing a mediator can do for couples caught in this pattern is to force them to imagine *new* options. By requiring them to go to the bother of outlining other options besides a unilateral pronouncement, tension is diffused and the parties may recognize that the former acquiescence is based on something other than reason. The mediator need not confront the defensive acquiescence but rather may act as an agent of reality, creating doubt that the option demanded and accepted is necessarily the best and most fair. The following dialogue shows how this is done:

Husband: Of course, I'll have the house.

Wife: Of course.

Husband: And I'll pay $200 per month child support. And you'd better not let me hear you complaining about it, or telling Billy that his father didn't provide well for him, because if it weren't for *you*, he'd still have a house with both parents in it.

Wife: Okay. Whatever you say.

Acting as an Agent of Reality

Mediator: I've heard some discussion about the house and child support, but I'd like to make sure all the options have been explored before you make a final agreement. Let's take them in stages. First about the house. I'm wondering if a judge would see your keeping the house as fair, George. [*Looks at husband.*]

Husband: Well, I think so.

Mediator: Susan, what do you think is fair? Are there any other options that would make more sense to you?

Wife: No, not really. I had thought I would stay in the house, but I really don't care.

Mediator: The house is the biggest asset you have. Some people, looking at this, would see it as an unbalanced distribution. I'd like you to think about this, Susan and George, and wait until next week to come to any conclusion on this.

Leaving Room for Changes and Urging Legal Advice

You need to discuss this with your separate lawyers to better understand the legal consequences of your decisions and whether they would be acceptable to the court.

Supplying New Options

Once you decide who should have the house, it will be important to decide how the decision of equity should be handled. Your lawyers can discuss with you the possibilities of creating a lien or deferring the transfer of title. After you've had a chance to obtain more information and think about it, we'll talk again about the house at the next session. Now let's go on to the child support issue . . . .

The third category, the *direct-conflict* pattern, is categorized by manifest conflict and prior discussion about divorce. However, this category has less intensity of negative emotions and behavior than the enmeshed pattern. Couples in the direct-conflict pattern do not deny the reality of marital breakdown or the disputes they are having; they often seek joint marriage counseling, individual counseling, or both. They show a lessening of ambivalence about whether or not to divorce, and they negotiate the business aspects of parting in mutual, but often uncomfortable, problem solving. Again the mediator dealing with couples in this category should try to keep them searching for alternatives and considering the details of options while giving them some verbal reward for staying with the mediation process.

The final category, the *disengaged-conflict* pattern, is constituted by couples who have little emotion, interest, or communication with each other. Like the autistic group, these couples have little manifest conflict. Unlike those in the autistic group, however, they truly are disinterested, not merely anxious or suppressing their underlying conflicts. Often these couples strongly approve of the concept of mediation and seek out a nonadversarial approach because of a shared desire to minimize conflict. Some see mediation as a simple way to go about the business of parting. Since they have already changed their interactions from an intimate to a working relationship, they are efficient at making essential decisions. Since there is no underlying conflict, the sessions do not have a lot of affective content.

This system of categorizing cases and these few suggestions about techniques are but the start of a compilation of mediation

skills based on common patterns of behavior. There is a continuing
need for divorce mediators to develop specific techniques for specific
issues that arise in these categories of divorce mediation cases.

Mediating Financial Decisions

Most divorces involving contested issues of child custody or
visitation also present unresolved financial disputes. Any attempt to
separate the process of deciding child-related issues from the process
used to resolve disputes regarding support and the division of property is bound to be artificial. These interrelated aspects of marital
conflict should be resolved *together* through the process of mediation resulting in a comprehensive settlement plan. The mediation of
financial issues and property division upon divorce remains controversial, however. In particular, the legal profession is concerned
about the potential for unfair and incomplete agreements resulting
from mediation, the unauthorized practice of law by nonlawyer mediators, and ethical conflicts for lawyers who offer mediation. Many
lawyers are also alarmed by the absence of formal discovery or production of financial data for each participant and the lack of any
imposed legal criteria for settlement beyond what the participants
impose on themselves. Some attorneys believe that, regardless of the
validity or invalidity of the participants' financial and legal positions, mediation is but a process of compromise.

These issues are addressed in Chapter Ten. It should be
noted here, though, that mediation of economic issues does depend
on voluntary disclosure of financial information by the participants
with the guidance of the mediator. Therefore the mediator must
explain the importance of full disclosure of all financial information if an ultimate agreement is to be fair and enforceable. Required
documents for production should be listed for the participants and
may include income tax returns, payroll records, pension plan
summaries, business records, checkbooks, and so on. In complex
cases an accountant or actuary may have to be consulted to aid in the
discovery and interpretation of necessary financial information.

Mediation need not prevent formal legal discovery when attorneys are representing the participants. In divorce cases involving
large assets, the participants should strongly be urged to retain sep-

arate attorneys during the mediation process to assure full disclosure of assets and liabilities and to consult on the tax considerations. Mediation can promote cooperative financial and tax planning upon divorce that can save both participants tax dollars and enlarge the financial assets available for division in mediation. Extensive legal discovery and technical information can be integrated in the mediation session to enhance stage 2, fact finding, as well as increase the alternatives available for consideration in stages 3 and 4. The adversarial tone of depositions, interrogatories, and subpoenas to produce documents may create tension that will have to be recognized and dealt with in mediation in order to retain the important element of trust. Mediation is not incompatible, however, with attorney-assisted divorce proceedings.

The financial issues to be resolved upon divorce include division of property, spousal support, and, in the case of minor children, child support. Each of these three financial decisions can involve questions of taxation and present problems of documentation, drafting, and conveyancing.

Child Support. The duty of parents to support their children is generally established by state statutes, though the statutes rarely provide detailed guidelines for determining the exact amount and proportionate contribution of each parent upon divorce. There are three basic approaches to the determination of child support: the case-by-case method, schedules or percentage tables, and the formula method. Each of these approaches allows a degree of flexibility in the decision between parents and comparable discretion on the part of a judge who must decide child support should the parents themselves be unable to decide.

In the *case-by-case method,* the unique facts of each case must be considered. The following factors for consideration are drawn from section 15(e) of the Uniform Parentage Act:

1. The needs of the child
2. The standard of living and circumstances of the parents
3. The relative financial means of the parents
4. The earning ability of the parents
5. The need and capacity of the child for education (including higher education)

6. The age of the child
7. The financial resources and earning ability of the child
8. The responsibility of the parents for the support of others
9. The value of services contributed by the custodial parent

The second approach for establishing child support is the *schedule or percentage method*. This method relies on preestablished schedules or percentages applied against the noncustodial parent's net income, depending on the number of children to be supported. These schedules and percentages can be adjusted to include a contribution by the custodial parent or to recognize the joint obligations of parents sharing custody. This method has been used primarily to establish the amount of child support in cases of welfare reimbursement and temporary support orders. The use of a schedule for percentage is the quickest and least complex method of determining child support.

The *formula method* of determining support has been adopted in a few states and has attracted renewed interest lately. The formula method is an equation that sets the amount of support obligation for each parent as a proportion of their combined incomes measured against the child's needs. The equation is basically as follows:

$$\text{Obligation of } N = \frac{\text{income of } N}{\text{income of } N + \text{income of } C} \times (\text{needs of children})$$

where N is the noncustodial parent and C is the custodial parent. More specifically, if we assume that in a hypothetical family the noncustodial parent earns \$20,000 per year, the custodial parent earns \$10,000 per year, and the child's needs are \$3,000 per year, then the formula would look like this:

$$\begin{aligned} \text{Obligation of } N &= \frac{\$20,000}{\$20,000 + \$10,000} \times \$3,000 \\ &= \frac{2}{3} \times \$3,000 \\ &= \$2,000 \end{aligned}$$

This simple equation can be altered to take into account the number of days the child spends with each parent. Credit can be given to the noncustodial or joint-custody parent for such expenditures as food, housing, fixed expenses, and other expenditures incurred by both parents in cases of joint or shared custody (Folberg, 1984).

The formula method was proposed by Maurice Franks (1981) in an article illustrating all the variables that can be factored into the mathematical equation. One such factor to consider is the inequality of requiring both parents to pay the same proportionate amount of their income for child support if the incomes are significantly disproportionate. In other words, if a mother earned $10,000 a year and a father earned $40,000, with a child's needs fixed at $2,000 a year, the basic formula would require the mother to pay one fifth of the child's needs, or $400 a year, and the father to pay four fifths or $1,600 per year. Assuming that it requires all of the mother's $10,000 per year to meet her minimal needs, she has no excess dollars to pay child support. If, on the other hand, the father similarly requires $10,000 to meet his basic needs, he has $30,000 spendable money over his basic necessities. The father's payment of $1,600 for child support would then represent less of a sacrifice for him than the mother's $400 payment. This difference can be factored into the formula approach by subtracting from each parent's salary the minimal amount required for the necessities of their own lives.

Although the formula sounds neat and mathematically straightforward, it assumes that the child's economic needs can be easily determined and plugged into the formula. In fact, a child's exact economic needs are most difficult to determine. Consideration of the child's economic needs, as well as the actual needs and ability of each parent to pay, can best be done by the parents through the process of mediation. Mediation concentrates on an assessment of each family member's needs and the balancing of those needs within the reorganized postdivorce family. Litigation, on the other hand, promotes the advocacy of exaggerated positions and the likely use by the court of formulistic or categorical figures that may not relate to the unique needs and abilities of the participants. It would be better for the parents to agree upon their child's financial need and their respective abilities to meet that need than for a court to decree it, regardless of which of the three approaches the court applies.

Child support, whether fixed by agreement of the parents or set by a court, can be prospectively modified by a court at any time on petition of either parent or, in some states, by the child. The petitioner seeking an increase must show a significant change in the child's economic needs and a corresponding ability on the part of the paying parent to meet a higher need. Conversely, a paying parent may seek a modification of child support if the child's needs significantly decrease or the paying parent is unable to meet the previously set obligation.

The payment and receipt of child support is generally a nontaxable event. Payment of child support cannot be deducted from the income of the paying parent and is not added to the income of the receiving parent for purposes of calculating income tax obligations.

The collective disregard for court-ordered child support payments constitutes one of the strongest statements of civil disobedience in our society (Krause, 1981; Chambers, 1982). Mediation of child support amounts and arrangements for payment stand a much better chance of voluntary compliance because mediators can help the parents look at the pragmatic aspects of support in order to minimize frustration by both the payer and the payee. Mediation can help to foster a sense of individuality and control, as well as the ability to respond cooperatively to changed circumstances. The consensual nature of mediation, as previously discussed, should lessen the incidence of child support noncompliance and nonsupport.

Spousal Support. Spousal support includes what is still referred to in some states as alimony. Some states impose an obligation of spousal support in appropriate circumstances following divorce; others do not allow it at all or sanction it only if the court finds one spouse to be physically and mentally incapacitated such that he or she is not self-supporting. Most states allow some form of spousal support or alimony if the particular facts require it as a matter of equity and justice. Spousal support is considered by those courts as a substitute upon divorce of the obligation of marital partners to support one another. In states allowing spousal support, the obligation for payment must be set as part of the initial divorce proceeding. Spousal support cannot be added as an enforceable obligation after the divorce if it was not included in the original divorce decree (Krause, 1977).

Spousal support usually takes the form of periodic payments over an indefinite or fixed period of time, although lump sum payments of support are sometimes agreed to or ordered by courts. Unlike child support, the payment and receipt of alimony is usually a taxable event. It is generally deducted from the income of the paying party and added to the income of the recipient for purposes of calculating income taxes. IRS regulations and rulings do, however, allow some flexibility in the tax treatment of such payments, depending on the technical rules relating to how the payments are designated and structured.

Court determinations of the amount and duration of spousal support are hard to predict because of the great discretion allowed judges in most states. A few states still require, or allow, the judge to consider matters of "fault" in deciding questions of alimony. In the more progressive "no-fault" states, the goal is to provide each divorcing spouse of a long-term marriage with enough of a share of the collective income so that each can maintain a standard of living as close as possible to their former standard. This standard must, of course, be shaped by the realities and costs of maintaining two separate households.

A theme emerging from the statutes and court decisions of some states is that spousal support should serve the purpose of rehabilitation of the lesser-earning spouse as an independent economic unit capable of generating enough income to maintain a separate household. Spousal support is then viewed as a subsidy allowing the lesser-earning spouse to acquire the economic skills, training, education, or experience needed to earn an adequate income independent from the former spouse or from government payments. Spouses receiving such temporary rehabilitative support are generally required to make reasonable efforts to become self-supporting within a specified period of time which, in some states, is set by statute.

Another factor that may be taken into consideration in setting spousal support in some states is the original expectations of the spouses at the time they marry. Generational differences and social norms may affect these expectations. Many women marrying in the first half of this century were only expected to work or bring home income in emergency family situations, and they had every reason to expect their marriages to last until they died. Couples marrying more recently may have very different concepts about outside work, economic independence, and marital longevity.

The Uniform Marriage and Divorce Act (1979) has been adopted in a substantial number of states and typifies the legislative approach to spousal support in most states. Section 308 of the act provides the following guidance in setting the amount of spousal support:

> a. . . . the court may grant a maintenance order for either spouse, only if it finds that the spouse seeking maintenance:
> 1. Lacks sufficient property to provide for his reasonable needs; and
> 2. Is unable to support himself through appropriate employment or is the custodian of a child whose condition or circumstances make it appropriate that the custodian not be required to seek employment outside the home.
>
> b. The maintenance order shall be in amounts and for periods of time the court deems just, without regard to marital misconduct, and after considering all relevant factors including:
> 1. The financial resources of the party seeking maintenance, including marital property apportioned to him, his ability to meet his needs independently, and the extent to which a provision for support of a child living with the party as custodian;
> 2. The time necessary to acquire sufficient education or training to enable the party seeking maintenance to find appropriate employment;
> 3. The standard of living established during the marriage;
> 4. The duration of the marriage;
> 5. The age and the physical and emotional condition of the spouse seeking maintenance; and
> 6. The ability of the spouse from whom maintenance is sought to meet his needs while meeting those of the spouse seeking maintenance.

Although these guidelines may be helpful to a court in determining the appropriateness and amount of spousal support, the ultimate determination is based on the standard of what is fair in the circumstances. What is fair for any set of people must depend on too broad and nebulous a set of facts, including emotional attitudes and feelings, to be determined in a formal court hearing. Mediation ideally lends itself to a participant-centered determination of what is fair and just, as well as workable for them.

Economic circumstances are seldom static. What is fair and just today, in terms of fixed support obligations, may not be fair or just tomorrow. Spousal support, like child support, can be modified by the courts upon a significant change of circumstances affecting either the economic need of the receiving spouse or the economic ability of the paying spouse. Infinite variables such as health, change of jobs, fluctuations in the economy, and inflation can require modifications of support obligations if they are to remain fair and just. Appropriately modifying support is even more of a problem than setting a fair amount to begin with. No one better knows their economic needs and abilities and the impact of changing circumstances than do the participants themselves. Mediation provides an approach to conflict resolution that allows the couple to consider cooperatively the full mix of economic variables relevant to support. Mediation should encourage a realistic review and modification of the support amount, pursuant to stage 7 of the mediation process, without the necessity to return to court (except as may be required to record the modification).

Creativity can be used in stage 3 of the mediation process in drafting support provisions that either anticipate changed circumstances or provide a mechanism for adjusting support when certain variables change. For example, "escalator" provisions might be incorporated that adjust the amount of support in accordance with indexes of inflation or changes in actual income. Any provision attempting to balance changing economic factors for purposes of setting support must take into account both the needs of the recipient and the ability of the payer to meet the imposed obligation. In other words, inflation may be an economic hardship on both parties and some incomes tend not to change as rapidly as do standard economic indicators such as the cost-of-living index. For this reason, the courts of some states have disallowed enforcement of escalator provisions or the use of incomplete economic formulas intended to adjust support automatically.

Property Division. Property division following divorce is also guided by the statutes and appellate court decisions of the state in which the divorce occurs. There are three basic systems of marital property law and a total of fifty variations. The most simple and archaic approach to property division is the *title* approach. Under this system, in effect now in Mississippi, South Carolina, West Virginia, and several other states, a judge must apply the objective standard of whose name was put on the title or other ownership papers. Upon divorce the property remains in the ownership of the person holding title. This system has generally favored the husband in families where the traditional sexual division of labor has allowed the man to arrange the economic affairs of his family.

At least eight states follow the *community property* approach to the division of marital assets: Arizona, California, Idaho, Louisiana, Nevada, New Mexico, Texas, and Washington. In these states, the family is viewed as an economic partnership. All assets acquired during the course of the marriage are considered community property belonging equally to both spouses, with a couple of noted exceptions regarding separately held property brought into the marriage and not intermingled and gifts and inheritances from third parties. Each partner is therefore entitled to one half of the community property should the marital relationship be dissolved. In some states this equal division approach is rigid despite any disproportionate need by either spouse. The rules for the division of the community property do, however, vary among the community property states. Several states have recently provided by statute for common ownership of marital property on commencement of a dissolution proceeding in order to achieve for their residents the same tax treatment as afforded by the federal government for the division of marital assets in community property states. These states have not adopted all the aspects of the community property system and it is not clear how either the courts or the taxing authorities will treat these statutes.

The most prevalent system of marital property distribution, to which New York, New Jersey, Missouri, and Oregon subscribe, along with a majority of other states, is referred to as *equitable distribution*. Equitable distribution lacks the rigidity of both the title and community property approaches and thus makes it all the more difficult to predict how the courts in those states will divide the marital property if the spouses are unable to agree on their own distribution plan. In helping the spouses determine what is fair for themselves and to consider all alternatives, mediation has obvious benefits.

Most, but not all, states have statutory criteria for the equitable distribution of marital property (Freed, 1983). The factors to be considered have frequently been amended or changed by court decisions to conform to changing social values and concerns. Rebuttable presumptions and guidelines have been added to direct the courts toward what is considered a fair approach for property division. Many states now have a rebuttable presumption that each spouse has contributed equally to the acquisition of the marital property, for example, and the recognition of a spouse's contribution as a homemaker is now explicitly legislated in several states. The Uniform Marriage and Divorce Act (1979), Section 307(a) establishes the following criteria for property division:

> The court, without regard to marital misconduct, shall, and in a proceeding for legal separation may, finally equitably apportion between the parties the property and assets belonging to either or both however and whenever acquired, and whether the title thereto is in the name of the husband or wife or both. In making apportionment the court shall consider the duration of the marriage, and prior marriage of either party, antenuptial agreement of the parties, the age, health, station, occupation, amount and sources of income, vocational skills, employability, estate, liabilities, and needs of each of the parties, custodial provisions, whether the appointment is in lieu of or in addition to maintenance, and the opportunity of each for future acquisition of capital assets and income. The court shall also consider the contribution or dissipation of each party in the acquisition, preservation, depreciation, or appreciation in value of the respective estates, and the contribution of a spouse as a homemaker or to the family unit.

One of the more challenging issues confronting divorcing couples, mediators, judges, and lawyers regarding the fair division of marital property is the threshhold question of what should be included in the marital property. Some items that may be hard to evaluate are, nonetheless, valuable assets in which both marital partners may have an interest. For example, pensions, annuities, and deferred income not yet in the hands of either party are now generally considered part of the marital kitty. The dollar value of professional degrees and business or professional goodwill are also now considered in some states to be marital property. The legal uncertainty, the difficulty of accurate financial assessment, and the personal nature of these items engender intense emotional conflicts better managed and resolved in mediation than in the courtroom.

The complexities, legal subtleties, tax considerations, and evolving criteria for the division of marital property at divorce are compounded by the legal doctrine making marital settlement agreements absolute and nonmodifiable following a divorce. The couple might agree to adjust their settlement plan later, but neither can go back to court to demand modification (absent fraud or nondisclosure of requested information relevant to the decision on property division). This doctrine of finality underscores the importance of complete financial disclosure at the outset and the need to know what is relevant for consideration. That is why attorneys are nervous about mediation of financial issues surrounding divorce and the absence of formal "discovery" of all financial data. This rule of finality of property division makes it all the more important that participants not be asked to sign a settlement agreement until they have had an opportunity to think it over and consult with independent attorneys or trusted financial advisers. Nonlawyer mediators are, again, well advised to prepare only a "memorandum of decisions" or a "mediated plan" that is given to the participants to be put into proper form by their attorneys following legal review.

To help the mediator work with the participants on financial needs and division of marital property, as well as spousal and child support issues, a method of collecting data is necessary in addition to the production of financial documents previously discussed. Several forms and worksheets are suggested in the literature (Coogler, 1978; Haynes, 1981) for gathering financial information to facilitate distribution of marital property, child support, and spousal support decisions. Various law publishers also market financial information interview forms for use by attorneys. We advise mediators to select a worksheet that matches the participants' financial sophistication, since it is often given out as homework. In this respect, we find Haynes' (1981) form a simple but concise model that is excellent in its visual presentation for participants who are not well versed in financial analysis.

We often find that families coming for divorce mediation have never before tried, either separately or together, to categorize their assets and liabilities and prepare a budget. Having a simple but complete and well-formatted sheet helps the participants and minimizes confusion and intimidation. Seeing their joint financial picture in black and white (or red) may help dispel the myth that one or the other participant will be gaining financially from the divorce action. It helps put the expectations at a more realistic level. Many men whose spouses have started the divorce action feel particularly punished financially, especially if spousal support is desired by the former wife. Exploration of what is economically needed and possible and then bargaining on what is fair can begin when *both* participants see line by line on the worksheet the burdens each one must undertake in order to maintain two separate households and support the children.

Children, Custody, and Visitation

Mediation is particularly well suited to help resolve parental conflict over issues of child custody and visitation and to facilitate joint decisions about children. We shall not attempt here to duplicate or summarize the helpful volumes about children of divorce and custody mediation that have been published for both professionals and participants. (See Recommended Reading at the end of this chapter.) One message that emerges from many of these works is that no matter what the final disposition of custody and visitation, it is important that children be left with two functioning parents and a method of intimate communication with them. Mediation promotes cooperative parenting following divorce and, in any case, facilitates continuing communication between parent and child.

The involvement of children in the mediation process is an unsettled issue for mediators. Dorothy Huntington (1982) considers the developmental needs of the child and contests the position that has been taken by Haynes (1981) and Coogler (1978) that children should not be part of the decisions made during mediation. She contends that children need to feel they are part of the decision making about their own future. She also believes that children need to know that the terms their parents agree to can be changed—"that if people need to come back and remediate, it's not only because something has gone wrong, but that it's because something has gone very right, and that parents have become aware of the changing developmental needs of their children" (p. 35).

Huntington also advocates that decisions regarding children should be based on the child's basic temperament—that is, the child's ease in adapting from one thing to another—as well as the child's attachments to places and people such as caregivers, teachers, neighbors, and organizations. Another important dimension in fashioning a custody arrangement is the child's coping style. When asked skillfully, most parents can tell the mediator the child's style of coping and the child's familiarity with his own negative feelings of anger, anxiety, and depression. Another important factor in determining a custody plan is the child's ability to understand, cognitively, what will be happening. If the child cannot understand the calendar or sequence of days, then the routine of switching care in joint-custody cases or predicting visitation becomes a frightening blur. To minimize the fear of abandonment, parents should try to make their separation from the child no longer than the child's ability to project into the future. All these factors should be weighed by the parents when making decisions and should be brought to their attention by the mediator if they are not discussing them spontaneously.

Table 10 is based on the work of Wallerstein and Kelly (1980), who separate children into four age categories for the purpose of elaborating their differences developmentally and showing the implications for divorce and custody decisions. According to Wallerstein and Kelly's views, parents may choose to involve children who are in middle or adolescent stages during the mediation process— particularly at stage 4, the decision-making point, or even sooner, in stage 3, when viable options are being developed. However, this must be done in a way that does not further burden the child with the weight of decisions that rightfully belong to the parents.

Table 10. Children's Developmental Stages and Divorce Implications.

Age Groups	Basic Issues	Children's Fears	Where Parents Can Help
Preschool (birth to 5+)	• Confusion • Fantasy explanations • Regressive behavior	• Abandonment • Lack of food, physical care • Parental violence • Going to sleep, going other places • Loss of both parents	• Ensuring understanding of new structures • Telling the child in advance what and when • Ensuring physical closeness and comfort
Early school (5½ to 8½)	• Reactive depression • Intense missing of absent parent • Loss of academic progress • Acting out against friends, support systems • Loyalty conflict	• Who is taking care of the absent parent? • Will I be replaced?	• Dealing with anger and loneliness • "You don't have to choose between parents" • Reassuring child about the other parent's care and the permanence of their affection
Middle (8½ to 12)	• Good vs. bad parent • Actions against "bad" parent • Great unabated anger • Reliance on religious or ethical teachings	• Being asked whom they want to live with • Being totally excluded from decisions	• Avoiding a good/bad dichotomy • Listening but remaining in control
Adolescence (12½ to 18)	• Lack of concentration at school • Understanding marriage and divorce cognitively	• Having to maintain adult responsibilities, caring for parent • Loss of parental con-	• Helping the child stick to its own developmental need to prepare for independence • Not asking age-

Table 10. Children's Developmental Stages and Divorce Implications.

Age Groups	Basic Issues	Children's Fears	Where Parents Can Help
	• Inappropriate adult behavior	trol over be-havior • What will happen to me? • How can I ever have a lasting rela-tionship?	inappropriate behavior from the child • Clarifying the child's own values concern-ing marriage and divorce in general

Whether or not children should be involved in the other stages of mediation, such as stage 3, the creation of alternatives, should be determined not only on the procedures of the mediation service but also the realities of the family in question. Children can undermine the best-laid plans of parents very quickly, but they can also help the parents keep to their intentions and decisions. Children need to understand their new role within the family and the new family structure. To try to impose an irritating structure or impossible agreement on a child is useless.

One way to involve children in the process without undue pressure is to cast them in the role of an advisory panel, with the parents or mediator soliciting their reactions prior to a final decision or the signing of the mediation plan. The parents are then acting as agents of reality, and the children's review and comment bring about a sense of involvement and sharing while still asserting the parents' obligation to make the decisions. Often this discussion takes place informally at home. The mediator may want to suggest to parents that such discussions should be done calmly and with all members present, including both parents, to avoid coercion and misinterpretation.

If the mediator thinks that the parents are unwilling or incapable of providing this setting (as are most enmeshed and autistic couples), the mediator may recommend that the work be done during the mediation session itself, probably the session when options are discussed. During this session young children should be under the care of another trusted adult, who can shepherd them into the mediation session when the parents are ready and care for them during the remainder of the session while the parents discuss the children's remarks.

Some mediators believe that children should be present for at least the symbolic signing of the mediation plan or memorandum of agreement, so that both parents can provide emotional closure to the children by taking that opportunity to restate the lack of blame and the finality of the decision. This suggestion is especially valuable for families in enmeshed patterns. This simple step, it is thought, might save children the personally defeating job of acting out at home or school in a futile attempt to bring the parents together. If, for example, the parents can say at the signing of the mediated plan that they will never be back with one another the way it was before, and that they look forward to seeking a new life, the children will see them as strong and will not, therefore, have to function as their helpers or as good excuses for any later difficulties in their new lives.

In autistic-patterned families, the children are often left in a limbo of vagueness and suppressed conflict. Inviting them to watch the signing of the document can help them feel less burdened by their inevitable guilt and confusion and also give them something concrete to hold onto. In direct-conflict families, the lessening of the hostilities, negotiations, and trial periods brings great relief to the children who have been on an emotional rollercoaster and living in ambiguity. In disengaged families, the signing is an outward marker of an internal reality the children already understand. While their attendance is not as necessary for their emotional relief, they may react to it as they would a commencement exercise—social validation of a change that has already taken place.

Some custody mediation cases revolve around the suspected abuse of children. In many states mediators may be required to notify authorities. This consideration may override confidentiality (see Chapter Ten); but it also destroys trust in the mediator who must report a participant to the authorities for investigation. Mediators who handle custody or divorce mediation as a primary source of their practice may ask prospective participants to sign a document notifying them of the consequences of divulging child abuse information. In this way, the participants themselves can make an informed choice whether or not to bring the subject to the mediator's attention. Moreover, since the consequences have been clearly indicated, the mediator need not feel uncomfortable about turning the information over to the authorities. Because this critical area affects mediator ethics and liability, we urge all mediators to familiarize themselves with their state's child abuse and reporting laws.

The rapid acceptance of joint or shared custody in many states has created an even greater need for the availability of mediation services to help parents decide on a joint-custody plan and resolve conflicts arising from the attempt to share custody following divorce. Mediation is a useful decision-making forum that provides structure and help for parents to review all the options and determine the most appropriate plan to make shared parenting work successfully. State laws vary so much that mediators should become familiar with their own states' statutes and cases concerning the following issues: a policy of continuing contact; the differentiation between joint legal and joint physical custody; the award of joint custody upon the request of one parent; the court's preference for joint custody; a presumption of joint custody; and the process if joint custody is denied. Note that some state statutes and court rules require a joint-custody plan before custody will be awarded and provide court-connected mediation services for this purpose (Folberg, 1984).

Unequal Power Situations

Divorce and custody disputes are conflict situations that often highlight the issue of how mediators should deal with unequal power between participants. (See discussion of fairness in Chapter Ten.) Participants in divorce come to mediation with long-standing patterns of dominance and submission, deference and competition, dependence and competence. Virginia Satir (1972) has analyzed the basic patterns of personal power into the simplified roles of placater, blamer, computer, or distracter. When decisions need to be made, these long-standing communication patterns emerge as each participant attempts to gain a sense of personal power. These roles are used as defense mechanisms (see Chapter Four) against the threat implied by the demand for equality inherent in the mediation process. Mediation participants can be expected to resort to their most comfortable power pattern while negotiating and making decisions.

Inequalities of power brought about by lack of information regarding family finances, the legal process, typical postdivorce reactions, or the developmental needs of children can be countered by the educational function of the mediator. The financial worksheets described earlier can provide a crash course in home finance and may bring about equality in facts and information when they are reviewed in joint sessions. Preliminary statements (see Chapter Five) and explanations or comments by the mediator will create a common base of information from which both participants can work. We often find it helpful to suggest that the participants read from resource books, many of which have been used in preparing this volume and which have been suggested in the Recommended Readings, in order to augment their information and perceptions.

It is a crucial function of the mediator to distinguish unequal power ploys that can be changed from those that cannot be addressed during mediation. If the inequality is based on a negotiating or decision-making style, or on a lack of information, the mediator should intervene to remind the participants of the need for equality in decision making. This can be done by use of reflection, clarification, redirective statements, supplying information, and other techniques described in Chapter Five, as well as individual caucusing with each participant to discuss his or her behavior.

The mediator may decide that the inequality is a permanent condition or one that cannot be effectively dealt with in mediation—such as physical abuse or intimidation, a total disparity in financial sophistication, significantly lower intelligence of one participant, a language or physical handicap, or a long-standing behavior or mental problem. In such cases the mediator has an ethical responsibility to notify both participants of the evaluation, suspend the mediation process, and refer them to lawyers, psychologists, or other helpers outside of mediation. This ethical position should not become a professional escape clause, however—a way of hiding a mediator's lack of skill by reframing it as the participant's problem. In divorce it is important to realize that the basic inequality between the spouses has often led to the decision to part. Mediators are not charged with the responsibility of balancing all relationships. They must ensure, however, that participants are not railroaded into choices that are unconscionable (see Chapter Ten).

Divorce and other family mediation situations may be the most challenging for the mediator in the development of skills for the equilization of power. Jay Haley (1976), in his description of strategic family therapy, has provided considerable information for understanding the basis of power struggles and inequalities within the family. These insights (p. 163) can be applied to other mediation situations:

> When the status positions in a hierarchy are confused, or unclear, there will be a struggle that an observer would characterize as a power struggle. If the observer has a theory of innate aggression or of a need for power, he may say the participants are satisfying an inner drive by struggling for power. Yet it would seem more useful to characterize such a struggle as an effort to clarify, or work out, the positions in the hierarchy of an organization.

From Haley's viewpoint the mediator's function is to help the participants in divorce, custody, or other family mediation clarify their roles and functions with each other and, by doing so, eliminate the conflict or power struggle. The reader is referred to Chapter Two, where the nature of conflict as powers meeting and balancing is discussed more fully, as well as Chapter Thirteen, where resistance is explored.

In summary, then, mediation during or after divorce is an intervention in the structure and function of not only the couple but the family as a whole. Mediators should be prepared to facilitate the mediation process, but they should also be prepared to reflect and intepret the reality of the current situation and the future alternatives. Allowing the family the freedom to explore and choose, while at times holding them fast to explicit expectations and behavior, requires some wisdom on the part of the mediator. No simple rulebook can be developed to direct mediators working with families: "If this, then do that." But the preceding chapters should give mediators some perspectives on what happens to families in mediation and the role of a family mediator.

Recommended Reading

General

Conjoint Family Therapy. (Rev. ed.) V. Satir. Palo Alto: Science and
 Behavior Books, 1967.
  A comprehensive yet concise professional text incorporating
substantial techniques for working with more than one person
simultaneously.

Peoplemaking. V. Satir. Palo Alto: Science and Behavior Books,
 1972.
  A primer about family life and communication that is ideal
reading for mediation participants.

Problem-Solving Therapy. J. Haley. San Francisco: Jossey-Bass,
 1976.
  Contains the fundamental concepts of strategic problem-
solving family theory, plus many helpful suggestions for interviewing and determining the issues within a family.

Normal Family Structures and Processes

The Family Life Cycle: A Framework for Family Therapy. E. Carter
 and M. McGoldrick (Eds.). New York: Gardner Press, 1980.
  A helpful collection spotlighting the developmental stages of
families as a unit.

Normal Family Processes. F. Walsh (Ed.). New York: Guilford
 Press, 1982.
  Excellent short articles provide a complete overview of the
newest theories and techniques involving normal family processes.

Individual and Family Development

Family Breakup. M. Little. San Francisco: Jossey-Bass, 1982.
  Overview of reasons why families separate, typical categories,
and the current legal processes and services available.

Divorce Disputes and Decisions

Divorce Mediation: Theory and Practice. J. Folberg and A. Milne (Eds.). New York: Guilford Press, in press.
Comprehensive treatment of divorce mediation with chapters by the most notable names in the field.

Living and Loving After Divorce. C. Napolitane and V. Pelligrino. New York: Rawson, Wade, 1977.
Popularized book, written from a woman's view, that describes the eight stages of emotional divorce which mediation participants may be experiencing.

"A Typology of Divorcing Couples: Implications for Mediation and the Divorce Process." K. Kressel and others. *Family Process,* 1980, *19* (2), 101–116.
Categories of divorcing couples that can help mediators identify and use different techniques.

Mediating Financial Decisions

Child Support in America. H. D. Krause. Charlottesville, Va.: Michie, 1981.
Surveys the entire field of child support—from methods of fixing the amount to how it can be collected.

Domestic Relations: Law and Skills. W. Slatsky. St. Paul: West, 1978.
A textbook written for paralegals. Provides the legal and practical information needed by nonlawyers to assist with domestic relations cases; contains case decisions, practice assignments, and forms.

Family Law in a Nutshell. H. D. Krause. St. Paul: West, 1977.
Law-in-a-nutshell paperback offering comprehensive coverage of the law relating to the family. Provides an excellent overview and refers the reader to many case citations.

Children, Custody, and Visitation

Child Custody Mediation: Techniques for Counselors, Attorneys and Parents. F. Bienenfeld. Palo Alto: Science and Behavior Books, 1983.

A text for the mediation of custody and visitation disputes. Shares the wisdom and techniques of an experienced court-connected custody mediator with many anecdotal examples.

Joint Custody and Shared Parenting: A Handbook for Judges, Lawyers and Counselors. J. Folberg (Ed.). Washington, D.C.: Bureau of National Affairs, 1984.

An extensive collection of articles on the pros and cons of joint custody as well as research findings, the law, and the literature on joint custody. Also contains joint-custody agreement forms.

Mediating Child Custody Disputes: A Systematic Guide for Family Therapists, Court Counselors, Attorneys, and Judges. D. Saposnek. San Francisco: Jossey-Bass, 1983.

A book for professionals on how to resolve custody disputes efficiently and effectively. Explains each step in the mediation process and includes case studies and other practical examples.

The following books present helpful information on joint custody and shared parenting. Practical information and helpful guides are provided in each:

The Custody Handbook. P. Woolley. New York: Summit Books, 1979.

Joint Custody and Co-Parenting. M. Galper. Philadelphia: Running Press, 1980.

Mom's House, Dad's House: Making Shared Custody Work. I. Ricci. New York: Macmillan, 1980.

Sharing Parenthood After Divorce: An Enlightened Custody Guide for Mothers, Fathers, and Kids. C. Ware. New York: Viking Press, 1982.

8

✻ ✻ ✻ ✻ ✻

Applications
to Various
Conflict Situations

Mediation is a process that can be applied to diverse conflicts and disputes. The purpose of this chapter is to acquaint the reader with the diversity of application and point out some mediation techniques unique to certain dispute categories. Some are categories of conflict in which mediation has worked well. Others represent new or expanded uses of mediation into dispute categories that have traditionally been resolved by other conflict resolution methods.

This chapter can provide no more than an overview of the application of mediation to the types of conflict discussed. To those working in these areas our discussion may seem cursory. It is intended to be but a brisk survey of the variety of uses for mediation. Each topic could be treated more extensively. Three areas of conflict are so comprehensive and the potential use of mediation so pervasive in each that we have not attempted a summary treatment of them in this book. Although labor/management conflicts, commercial disputes, and international conflicts certainly lend themselves to the concepts and techniques presented here, a thorough exploration of these topics would require three separate books.

Many other areas of potential dispute could be categorized as special subtopics for the application of the mediation concepts and techniques we have discussed. Health care and hospital issues, consumer disputes, sports-related conflicts, boundary questions, intragovernmental and agency differences, construction industry disagreements, and banking problems all present unique considerations or require a particular sensitivity or expertise that could merit separate treatment. The reader will, no doubt, think of other areas that might benefit from the application of mediation techniques. If the concepts and approaches developed in this book ring true, they should form a solid foundation for all these specialties. The similarities for each application should be greater than the differences. The uses of mediation as a participatory, problem-solving approach are infinite. What follows is but a sampling.

Housing and Neighborhood Mediation

A large part of the American population in 1980 lived in housing owned by someone other than themselves (Bureau of the Census figures, 1982–1983, item 1349, p. 751), and renter-occupied housing may climb as more families are started and individual ownership of houses is lost to unemployment and inflation. Ownership of rental property is often a sizable part of a total economic investment picture for a landlord, yet to the tenant an apartment is not just another tax loss or gain but home, a place that should respond to the tenant's need for privacy, safety, and security. Because disruptions in this home environment threaten the basic needs described by Maslow (see Chapter Four), the tenant is often extremely agitated. Often the property owner is less than sensitive to this dimension when dealing with the tenant, thus provoking still greater anxiety, frustration, and fears that produce concomitant defensive behavior. This escalation can be reduced by mediating, rather than arbitrating or litigating, such landlord/tenant disputes. For this reason, and because students must learn how to become cooperative yet assertive as tenants, many large universities that have thousands of students living in rental units promote the mediation of disputes by having student service staff available to act as mediators. City housing authorities and neighborhood justice centers have also promoted mediation as a way of settling housing conflicts.

Mediators serving clients with housing disputes can find themselves switching between the role of mediator, as defined earlier, and the roles of educator and advocate. Although each role is a necessary part of the total service needed to help people with housing conflicts, it is necessary to differentiate the role of advocate from that of mediator, especially if one person is expected to handle a case requiring both functions.

Let us take an example that shows the difference between the mediation and advocacy function. Three young men, aged nineteen, rented a house that was the home of a young executive whose job required him to stay at a subsidiary in England for one year. All furnishings and typical household goods were made available for the use of the tenants except for the stereo and certain other personal items locked in a closet. The tenants had promised not to smoke in the house. All three had signed a lease to that effect. When the owner returned, he discovered a sizable burn hole in the wall-to-wall carpeting, a bed and its linen in disrepair, a stereo that did not work and appeared to be in a different place in the closet, and only two of the original tenants, the third having moved out a month early without paying his share of the rent. A security deposit had been paid by each tenant, but its total would not cover the loss of rent as well as the damages. The landlord needed to fly to Houston in two weeks to oversee his company's interests there, and he could not find the whereabouts of the missing tenant. He therefore turned the matter over to a community housing officer authorized to offer free mediation.

Because the landlord and tenants would not have a continuing relationship after the damages were settled, and for pragmatic scheduling reasons, the housing mediator decided that much of the work could be handled by telephone and individual caucus, meetings with only the landlord or only the tenants. At those private sessions, much of the educational function mentioned earlier was done by the mediator. The landlord was informed about his legal rights and the usual procedures regarding the use of the security deposit, as well as the possible consequences of pursuing his rights in court. The landlord decided to try to settle the dispute through formal mediation. The mediator then telephoned the two former tenants and set up an individual caucus, urging them to bring the missing tenant, since they could be held liable for any damages he had created.

All three tenants arrived at that meeting, but the one who had moved out was surly and uncooperative. The mediator started by informing them of the seriousness of the situation and their potential liabilities should they not be able to mediate the situation. In this individual caucus, the tenants aired their grievances against each other and arrived at a decision regarding an acceptable level of repayment and an equitable division of costs among themselves. The mediator then telephoned the landlord, who had presented a full cost analysis to the mediator in an earlier caucus; the analysis showed the cost of replacing or repairing the damaged items and listed the items not yet found.

The agreement of the tenants did not match the demands of the landlord, so a joint mediation session was scheduled (stage 3 of the mediation process: creating new options). At that joint session, several new plans and amounts were looked at, taking into account the tenants' actual ability to pay. A mutually agreeable plan of repayment was worked out after much active negotiation requiring considerable direction and facilitation by the mediator to prevent angry walkouts. A mediated plan reflecting the agreements was subsequently drawn up by the mediator, and a brief session was held with both the tenants and the landlord to sign and distribute the document. In addition, the mediator explained the role that the housing officer would take should the terms of the agreement not be upheld during implementation. They agreed that the legal review and processing stage would be unnecessary if they all kept their agreements, so this stage was deferred. However, one of the tenants said his father, a high corporate official, had told him to bring the document home so his company lawyer could review it.

All went well with the implementation stage for about a month, at which time one former tenant, whose father's lawyer had reviewed the mediated plan, stopped paying his weekly amount. When notified of this by the landlord who was still in Houston, the mediator sent notices of violation of the mediated agreement to all the former tenants, along with a statement that his role had changed from mediator to advocate for the landlord. He then advised the landlord how to pursue his rights to the remaining damage repayments in small claims court and how to get a writ for garnishment of wages from the former tenant who had defaulted the small claims

action. The change from neutral mediator to advocate for the landlord was based on the violation of the mediated agreement and was
permitted by the housing officer's job description and the participants' prior agreement. If the mediator had not been authorized to
take on this role, he could have referred the case to others.

Housing officers for cities, housing projects, or other institutions such as colleges and universities may be called upon to educate
roommates about their liability on leases, help mitigate tenants'
damages by facilitating subleasing, or warn landlords of dangerous,
unlawful, or unethical practices. Moreover, violations of housing
and building codes could be brought to their attention for a mediated resolution.

Mediation provides an excellent format for ventilation of
negative feelings. It allows the participants to learn what is responsible action and what negative consequences can be avoided by
agreement. It allows for decisions based on fairness rather than only
the letter of the law. While cleaning is not considered a damage and
is not a deductible item from a security deposit under many state
laws, any landlord who has had to clean up a filthy apartment
knows it takes time and money and is often more than just normal
wear and tear. One option that can be considered during mediation
(but perhaps not in litigation) is having the tenants return to clean
the place themselves.

Mediation can help the landlord prevent costly and time-
consuming evictions and summary judgments by providing an opportunity to discuss the underlying as well as the manifest issues. A
case that comes to mind involved a single mother living on ADFC
who was a fine tenant in all other respects but who continually paid
her rent at least two weeks late. The landlord, having been told to
keep good records, spent time filling out and mailing Notices to
Quit each month for eight months. He was tired of the situation.
Rather than evicting her, another option was developed through
mediation. The woman could not pay until she got the ADFC check,
even though the rent was due on the fifteenth. A prorate was set up
for twenty days so that next month the rent was due on the fifth,
giving her several days grace in case the check was late. In another
case the landlord said he would send a thirty-day notice to two
tenants if they could not mediate their constant friction about the

loudness of the stereo and controlling the cat. By using a legitimate and natural consequence to motivate the tenants to work out their differences through mediation, the landlord kept two renters.

All the points mentioned in earlier chapters pertain to the use of mediation in tenant/landlord and other housing conflicts. Styles that are effective with certain minority or cultural groups will not work as well with others. Depending on the circumstances and the urgency of the problem, sessions can be held as private caucuses, joint mediation sessions, or public sessions viewed by other neighborhood members (Merry, 1982). In conflicts involving people who want to (or must) remain in a relationship, it is probably best to hold all sessions as joint sessions with all participants. As noted by Merry (1982, p. 35): "The willingness of a tenant to compromise with his landlord may be far greater when he plans to stay in his apartment for another ten years than that of a tenant who has been there ten years but is planning to move the following week." Thus mediators should not only look at the past relationship but consider the expected future relationship of the participants to understand their motivation to settle differences or, conversely, to win and leave.

When owners have hired managers or intermediaries, such as subcontractors, it is wise to have everyone present for at least the signing of the agreement, if not the creation of options and decision-making phases. It is also important to make all dates and processes clear, specific, and achievable, as well as to specify who will monitor the implementation of the plan. Having well-written, complete handbooks about the basic laws and procedures will facilitate the educational function, and many conflicts can be averted through this educational function before they become disputes that must be mediated.

Like the agencies and designated officials described earlier, neighborhood associations can provide not only information but also training and nonprofessional mediation services to their members. An outstanding example of such a program is the Community Board Program (Shonholtz, 1981), which involves community leaders and neighborhood representatives in the San Francisco area. Such programs are not limited to housing disputes. They can mediate conflicts about parking, animal control, security, waste disposal, use of block grant money, and other issues that can disrupt the life of a neighborhood. These neighborhood mediation services can turn such disputes into positive community values and promote individual and community responsibility. By resolving individual conflicts, they prevent a buildup of frustration and criminal conduct. Some neighborhood conflict centers hold their sessions in full view of the neighborhood so all will know the outcome and thereby prevent further agitation. Preventing problems from escalating is perhaps the most cogent reason for instituting mediation in housing disputes and other neighborhood conflicts.

Educational Disputes

Parents and teachers are often caught in conflict over what they believe to be the most appropriate plan of instruction for a child's educational needs. Although almost every parent experiences such disputes concerning children, even in regular education classrooms, the identification, evaluation, and placement of handicapped children in appropriate programs has created a number of special education disputes. Clearly, in so vital an aspect of parenting and societal responsibility, systems and procedures need to be developed to reduce these educational conflicts, as well as to provide advocacy services to those who are intimidated by the educational system.

In an attempt to provide parents of handicapped children requiring special education with an opportunity for redress and empowerment, the Congress passed Public Law 94-142 in 1975 as a funding statute to help states develop special education services. A federal agency developed precise but complex federal regulations to implement it. In those regulations, parents were given detailed rights: to be part of developing an Individual Education Plan (IEP), to receive prior notification of changes in their child's educational plan or placement, and to be given notification and access to all school meetings regarding their child. The goal of this legislation was to require the provision of a "free appropriate public education" in the least restrictive environment possible.

The language of educators and the procedural steps required under this law, such as the IEP meeting, are very intimidating to parents. In most IEP meetings the parents are usually outnumbered by educational specialists and evaluators by three or four to one. Further, the full range of options available to assist their handicapped child is often unknown to the parent or fairly limited in scope. This shortcoming sets the stage for conflict between parents and school officials unless they recognize the factors involved in their disagreement. Once parents and the school district reach a point of impasse—that is, when the use of local procedures is viewed by both parents and school district as unproductive and futile—then educational mediation should be considered. Mediation can help resolve the issues in disputes by providing a neutral third party who can uncover the underlying issues as well as ensure that parents and educators are communicating in the language of mediation: movement toward an agreement.

When conflicts arise concerning rights or obligations regarding handicapped children, parents and school districts are given rights to a due process hearing under PL 94-142, where information, testimony, and witnesses may speak to the disputed issues in front of a hearings officer, an arbitrator who then decides what should be done. Due process hearings, while less strict and formal than regular court proceedings, are still adversarial in nature. Moreover, they are so complex, time consuming (usually sixty to ninety days), and expensive a way of resolving these educational conflicts that they usually require specially trained advocates, or lawyers, to present the separate views of parents and schools according to proper procedure (Bateman, 1980). For this reason, they have often been avoided as a conflict resolution method. Informal negotiation processes have been tried, but often they do not recognize the unequal power situation or are less than effective in resolving the conflicts.

An example of a special education dispute may clarify the need for mediation programs. A mother of a trainably mentally retarded (TMR) twelve-year-old girl wanted the school district to provide three hours a day of academic instruction in reading, language, mathematics, and spelling. The school district refused, arguing that although there was an available program in the school she attended, it was not the policy of the district to enroll handicapped children in two separate programs. This dispute was successfully mediated, and the girl was provided one hour per day of academic instruction.

Other examples of education disputes that can be mediated are:

1. The parents want more one-to-one tutoring than the school wants to give.
2. The child has been determined eligible to receive special education services because of serious emotional impairment, but the school has no services.
3. The school has not provided related services such as transportation and social work.
4. Parents want a resource room placement for their learning-disabled child but the district feels it is too restrictive for a full-day placement.
5. Parents do not agree with the school's diagnosis of the child's educational problem.
6. The school wants to expel a certified special education student.
7. Parents want a private placement out of state because there are no comparable public placements in the state, but the district refuses to pay for such placement.
8. The district refuses to designate a child as having more than one special education eligibility (learning disabled and emotionally impaired).

There are many legal provisions pertaining to conflicts in special education. Section 504 of the Rehabilitation Act of 1973 (29 U.S.C. §706) is a civil rights statute that prohibits discrimination against handicapped individuals in any program receiving federal money, which includes most schools (Neighborhood Justice Center of Atlanta, 1982, p. 17). While this provision is not limited to education, it has a strong impact on it, including the "barrier-free" right of physical access to buildings. Case law, which is composed of decisions by state and federal courts interpreting Section 504 and applicable state and local statutes and ordinances, also has an impact on special education disputes. Due process and equal protection rights assured by the Constitution in the Fifth and Fourteenth Amendments have also served as a legal basis for special education disputes (Neighborhood Justice Center of Atlanta, 1982, p. 19).

Twelve states and the Washington, D.C., school district currently have special education mediation programs: Connecticut, Colorado, Florida, Georgia, Iowa, Michigan, New Jersey, New York, North Carolina, Oregon, Texas, and Wyoming. These mediation programs augment the existing conflict resolution process by providing another alternative to a due process hearing. Mediation can be concurrent with a due process hearing or can be used as a first step to resolve disputes, without waiving the parents' or districts' rights to request a due process hearing later if the mediation does not result in a set of agreements (Gallant, 1982, pp. vii-viii). Such mediati n programs and networks are to a large part based on the thinking of and training by the Division of Personnel Preparation, Office of Special Education, U.S. Office of Education, and the National Association of Social Workers (NASW).

In most of these mediation programs, parents, even when they have requested a due process hearing under PL 94-142, can mediate their concerns at any point before a final verdict has been reached by a hearing officer or after a due process hearing has failed to resolve the continuing issues. In most programs, the district pays the costs, a motivating factor for parents to use the program. The typical due process hearing costs several thousands of dollars; it usually costs $2,000 to $3,000 just to set up a hearing and the figure can go as high as $15,000 to $20,000, which is prohibitive for most school districts. By contrast, state-certified mediators usually cost the district between $100 to $500 per day. Considering the advantages of mediation in terms of lower expenditures of time, money, staff involvement, and stress for all participants, mediation is certainly a preferable alternative and deserves a recognized position in the flow of disputes from local schools up to the state departments of education.

Both Gallant (1982) and the Neighborhood Justice Center of Atlanta (NJCA, 1982) have developed training models specifically for special education disputes. Both emphasize learning by experiencing role playing in each of the three basic roles: mediator, parent, and school representative (teacher, administrator, or both). Both can be fit into the universal seven-stage process outlined in Chapter Three.

The NJCA model emphasizes the use of individual caucuses after the disputants have had an opportunity to explain their perceptions of the problem and their positions uninterrupted by either the mediator or other participants. The mediator's goal is to get a signed agreement (which may only be a statement of intention to have further meetings) within a one-day marathon session. Private caucuses are used to diffuse tension, keep control, and create and weigh new options (stage 3 of the mediation process). The acceptable options are reviewed by the mediator in a positional bargaining framework in joint sessions. The mediator must have great skill in knowing when to allow the participants to bargain and discuss by themselves and when to intervene during stage 4. The mediator's role in this model is to act as facilitator and agent of reality, continually asking the participants to doubt the absoluteness of their own perceptions and positions and to find convergence. In this model mediators also write the mediated plan at the end of the session for the participants to sign.

The state department of education, or other designated agency, is usually responsible for providing stage 6: legal review and processing. The department does this by making sure that the mediation system itself is in compliance with federal, state, and other legal precedents. It can also function as the higher authority to oversee the implementation of the written agreement by the school personnel and, moreover, often sets up and provides follow-up to participants, as well as evaluations of the mediation process and the mediators. The department of education, which is usually the party contacted should the mediated agreement break down, can again send out a mediator for more mediation (stage 7: review and revision).

Special education is not the only area where mediation applies to education. Parents attempting to advocate for a person's unique needs within an educational bureaucracy may find mediation to be the best way to resolve a conflict. Gallant (1982) believes that students should be given coursework to build their mediation skills and prepare them for life's conflicts.

Curricula (K-12) are currently being developed to provide students with the skills to mediate their own conflicts in the classroom and outside the school. Fellers' plan of action (1982, p. 58) requires the intervenor, usually the teacher, to act as mediator and take the children through the mediation process outlined in Chapter Three by asking them to go to a "conflict corner," where they follow a five-step sequence in only a few minutes:

1. Each student relates his or her view of the problem uninterrupted.
2. The teacher paraphrases and clarifies.
3. Students and teacher decide on a solution.
4. The teacher helps evaluate behavior to minimize its reoccurrence.
5. Students give each other a sign of reconciliation.

   School districts are currently being put into financial squeezes that require choices unfavorable to the interests of even large segments of their students—a case in point is a decision regarding which school building to close. Instead of trying to arbitrate the inevitable conflict between groups that are created by such a closure, school boards could hire a person to function as a mediator to the situation while they themselves serve as advisers brought into the mediation process during the second stage (fact finding and isolation of issues) as informed consultants about the realities of the financial picture. They would then step out of the controversy while representatives of the factions developed options and alternatives and made selections.

   In this model, the school board would resume its usual role as higher authority when the plan, agreed to by the representatives during mediation, is submitted to the board for its ratification (stage 6: legal review and processing). If the plan met all legal requirements, the board would adopt it and then become responsible for its monitoring and periodic review or subsequent change (stage 7). In this way, school boards could effectively discharge their civic and legal responsibilities while allowing a flexible system of representation. The affected constituencies themselves would be empowered to make decisions in mediation. Competing factions would feel included in the decision-making process without having to pressure or lobby individual school board members. Because they, too, would be privy to the full information and allowed to weigh the pros and cons of each possible option, the factions would be more likely to live with the decision.

As issues such as desegregation face the schools, new means must be found to alleviate tension and find effective ways of fulfilling constitutional and statutory mandates without violence. An excellent description of successful mediation within a public secondary school that averted racial conflict is described by William F. Lincoln (1981). By effectively using shuttle mediation techniques between the black student leaders, the white student leaders, and the principal, he was able to mediate a settlement to the issues and avert violence. Certainly mediation can help not only in future planning but in an immediate crisis too by using shuttle techniques (Chapter Six).

As noted earlier, a distinction must be drawn between persons performing mediation and those performing an advocacy function. Our experience has taught us that it is difficult to maintain credibility in either role when they are performed sequentially or simultaneously by one person. Therefore, agencies and programs mandated to provide both types of service in educational settings would be well advised to designate specific persons or teams for each function.

The mediation process can provide a format for full exploration of the issues, options, and consequences—from the parent suddenly confronted with an arbitrary age cutoff for admission to kindergarten that ignores the child's developmental abilities to the school district forced to drop either the band or the football team due to financial pressure. Rather than allowing halfway measures or temporary solutions, which can force the underlying issues still deeper, creating more stress and interfering with a child's or a school's progress, mediation can bring about the much-needed closure of the conflict by looking to a future that is mutually desired. It empowers the individual (or the group) to make appropriate choices while leaving designated entities such as principals and superintendents the ultimate responsibility for ratifying the plan according to predetermined criteria. These administrators can continue to be responsible for development of policies, or the "larger perspective," but can allow mediation to settle most of the lesser decisions. Mediation does not undermine authority; it enhances it by putting it in the proper sequence.

School counselors and school psychologists, as well as administrators, should receive training in mediation skills so that districts and students can use the mediation process without having to pay an outsider. Many school counselors currently provide informal mediation when disputes are brought to them, such as fights between students or personality clashes between students and teachers. This would require that departments of education, as well as departments of counseling or psychology, create curricula that would give graduate students a chance to *experience* mediation in educational disputes. We hope that states with mediation programs will also provide training in mediation for those currently employed in these positions in secondary education.

Curricula are being developed in higher education as well as on the grade school and high school levels to teach students conflict resolution skills such as mediation. Universities currently offer graduate programs designed to provide professional training for prospective mediators as mentioned in Chapter Six. Undergraduate programs, however, are also being developed to provide students with core concepts about the nature of interpersonal, community, and international conflict and the selection of appropriate conflict resolution processes. Such curricula fit well with the spirit of interdisciplinary liberal arts colleges that emphasize leadership skills training for their students.

From preschool through college the trend will be to maximize the wisdom of the disputants by allowing them to work out creative solutions rather than imposing traditional answers to modern problems. If educational systems use mediation, they will be promoting two of the most respected principles of education: experiential learning and correct modeling.

Police and Crisis Mediation

Mediation is a useful adjunct to other strategies for crisis intervention and conflict resolution now provided by the police and other services. Some training programs for police officers include work with mediation. We believe this training should be expanded, and the curriculum should stress the role of officer as mediator of the many disputes police encounter.

Police are called in to prevent escalation of violence and other criminal behavior. Often there is no criminal or civil statute upon which an officer can detain or arrest a party in a dispute, yet others have seen the problem as severe enough to warrant calling in a third party, often with only a vague expectation that the officer "*do* something, do *anything*, just stop them." Society has mandated that police become the enforcers of the peace—the authority to deal with manifested conflicts that could affect the safety of the parties themselves or others. They have been cast in the role of mediator, the one in between the factions, the one who must educate them as to the rules and the processes, as well as enforce those rules, in order to bring about conflict resolution or conflict management. Many officers have functioned for years as effective mediators without ever identifying their role as such. While conflict resolution and conflict management skills are inherent in most of an officer's training, the mediation process and role may not have been clearly defined.

The role of the officer who is functioning as a mediator is the same as the role for all mediators—to help the people in conflict find a safe and workable way out of the conflict, a way that saves face and meets their needs better than any illegal action such as violence. The seven-stage process we have outlined in Chapter Three is still the basis of mediation, but it must be adapted to the urgent circumstances; most mediation done by police officers is crisis or marathon mediation.

Most police officers may not have the luxury or need to spend much time in the first stage of mediation: creating structure and trust. Either the parties are respectful and somewhat chagrined by the officer's presence or else they are openly hostile. In the former case, the officer can use the deference and authority to enhance decision making; in the latter, it makes no difference—society has ordered the officer to be there. The disputants' disrespect will not stop the officer from functioning effectively as a mediator. The second stage of mediation, fact finding and isolating the issues, is something police officers are well trained to do. The amount that needs to be done in mediation depends on the officer's assessment of the situation. Stage 3, developing new options, is a set of skills that has always been a stock technique. How often has an officer had to inform the disputants of their behavioral options and the consequences they entail? How often has an officer told a brawler: "You hit him and you're arrested. You hit *me* and I'll see you in jail. Why don't you go home and sleep it off?"

Sometimes officers have to help the disputants make decisions. One police sergeant related a case where mediation was used and can serve as an example. The officer was called by a wife whose husband had found a possum in the garage. The husband wanted to kill the animal with his .22 deer rifle, but the wife had been screaming that she wanted the officer to stop the husband before he, or someone else, got hurt. The conflict was between the husband and wife, but the *real* issue was how to get the possum out of the garage, something the couple had forgotten in their commotion. The officer had to come in between the spouses as a neutral third party to reestablish effective communication and help them develop more options than Shoot versus Don't Shoot.

The officer did some fact finding with the couple to discover what had been done so far and who had been contacted. He then reintroduced the issue ("Your yelling isn't getting the possum out of here. Let's see what *can.*") and helped them locate the nearest animal control unit that had trained personnel with nets who could remove the animal without harming it. This was an option the couple had overlooked while they argued. Another way the officer helped them during mediation was by educating the husband about the laws surrounding the discharge of firearms within the city. In this situation, because of the officer's work as a mediator, the issue was effectively and safely dealt with, the disputants were calmed and reconciled, and the animal survived unhurt.

Perhaps the most common instance when police use the mediation process and its skills, sometimes without even having a conceptual framework for its use, is the area of domestic disputes. Police are called in by onlookers who are disturbed by the noise and threat of physical violence, or they are often called in for the same reasons by the disputants themselves. They often arrive on the scene with little information about the source of the conflict. In this case mediation is the most reliable and useful means of dispute resolution. Someone must calm the disputants and reestablish sufficient order to assure the safety of all members of the family. The officer knows that, as a crisis mediator, he or she cannot offer therapy. Yet someone must help these people stop fighting. This peacekeeping function of the police officer is enhanced by the inherent authority to enforce the rules and become an arbitrator. Mediation is a process and role well suited to these domestic conflicts. When one party has locked the other out or disposed of his or her possessions illegally, the mediation process is far more expedient than are litigation and court-ordered arbitration.

When police officers are called to the scene of domestic disputes, the first determination that must be made is whether there has been physical abuse. When there is evidence to suspect physical abuse, some states take the discretion out of the hands of the officer: The officer *must* take one or more parties into custody to prevent further abuse. Because of the risk of continuing abuse after the police have left, mediation is not necessarily the preferred technique for officers in such domestic disputes. Manuals such as Schreiber's (1979) can provide officers with calming techniques for crisis situations in general, as well as for domestic disputes. It may take legal consequences unmitigated by mediation to impress on the abuser the unacceptability of such behavior. This crime certainly needs a greater commitment of our resources and more research. Several worthwhile articles on the subject of domestic violence mediation are collected in *Alternative Means of Family Dispute Resolution* (Davidson, Ray, and Horowitz, 1982).

When children must be cared for but both spouses have been taken in for custody, the designated personnel, such as the recognizance officer, can usually release one or both of the spouses for twenty-four hours or over the weekend to enable them to make arrangements for the children, with the stipulation that the parties shall not meet. Often the officer must use mediation or other conflict management skills to orchestrate this release of the spouses and their need to go in and out of the home or share transportation.

There are other situations where skillful use of mediation is advised for police and crisis workers: drunken brawls, fights or threats with knives or guns, and disputes arising from cultural, racial, ethnic, or religious differences. In these disputes, mediation allows for a more timely and satisfactory resolution of differences than does the arrest/incarceration/adjudication sequence. Certainly it is a lot less costly to the disputants; also, taxpayers need not expend funds for court-appointed lawyers for the defense, county prosecutors, and the scarce resource of judges' time, as well as the costs to feed and house the offenders in jail. While we are not advocating a cessation of arrests for serious crimes, we are suggesting that de-escalation of hostilities by mediation can save time and money for all.

Another type of call where police are often asked or required to serve as mediators is in kidnapping, hostage, and suicide threats. Although threats of violence may not be appropriate subjects for mediation, the officer can act as the agent of reality and facilitator of communication between the persons threatening the act and the people with whom they must bargain. In hostage or kidnapping cases, the FBI or a tactical negotiation team can be the authority while the local police officer outlines the mediation process. If negotiations between the authority and the offender proceed through mediation by the local police, a plan can be worked out that is preferable to a shoot-out, although we are not of course advocating the compromise of violence or threats (see Chapter Ten). In suicide cases, the police officer may need to be mediator between the person making the suicide threat and the people toward whom the threatener has strong feelings of anger, remorse, or dependency.

Another application of mediation with which police and crisis workers should become familiar is its use for minor criminal cases (Salius, 1983), status offenses, and other juvenile offenses (Vorenberg, 1982). Many communities are investigating mediator services such as the Near West Side of Cleveland's Community-Youth Mediation Program (Kavalec, 1983). Some juvenile mediation/diversion programs are based on the Scottish Children's Hearing System that was instituted in Scotland by an Act of Parliament ten years ago (Children's Hearing Project, 1982). Many projects across the nation use mediation, as well as counseling and social work services, to act as a diversion program for those who meet certain criteria (first offense, no prior record, and so forth). It is ideal for shoplifting, vandalism, and minor personal property charges, because it allows the victim a chance to negotiate proper restitution. Mediation in these court-mandated or court-connected programs provides the judges the option of settling conflicts engendered by the offenses without expensive and time-consuming litigation. Police officers whose arrests end up in these programs may not have to testify in court proceedings, thus freeing them to do their job of law enforcement without entering into the judicial machine.

Workplace Mediation

Much of the early literature on the theory and techniques of mediation was developed in regard to labor disputes. Because of the richness of material and history in the area of labor mediation, we shall not review the resources and procedures available on this subject. However, there are many disputes in the workplace that are not mediated because they are not directly connected to collective bargaining. It is the application of mediation to this type of workplace dispute that we want to discuss here.

The experience of personnel managers, supervisors, and executives all support the same conclusion—unresolved conflicts between workers, or between workers and management, result in loss of productivity. People of all occupations will tell you that the most uncomfortable, stress-producing parts of their jobs are the interpersonal conflicts they experience on a daily basis between themselves and co-workers or supervisors. There has been a regrettable absence of effective mechanisms to reduce, manage, or eliminate conflicts in the workplace. Most adults spend the largest part of their waking life engaged in work within organizations. If conflict is inevitable (see Chapter Two), organizations must plan for it and develop conflict resolution strategies.

Many people lack the personal negotiation and communication skills required to successfully confront the other disputant with their perceptions of the issues, elicit useful discussion, look at options, and negotiate a bargain. They are often unable to do anything more than politely ask for changes, having no authority to produce the changes they are seeking. People in workplace disputes have two options: they can remain in their jobs or they can leave. If they stay, they often try to relieve the stress by pretending the conflict does not exist or by manipulating other people into actions they hope will reduce the conflict. If these two approaches to dealing with the conflict fail, the last recourse is to leave the job altogether—a risk few people can take in troubled economic times. Condemned to an unresponsive situation, people's energies are subverted into negative approaches such as withdrawal, noncompliance, and other obstructionist or undermining behavior that gives temporary satisfaction but often leads to nonvoluntary dismissal or other undesirable consequences.

To break this negative cycle, a worker's conflicts must be allowed to surface at appropriate times and should be acknowledged by a supervisor with empathy and support. Instead of being personally judged as wrong or bad for having the conflict ("Oh, he's just a troublemaker"), the supervisor should help the person specify the conflict and attempt to separate the manifest conflict from any underlying or internal issues. A little mediation effort can go a long way toward peace and productivity in the workplace.

This rather abstract discussion can be illustrated by the following example. A counselor was an employee of a large nonprofit organization with several branches, one of which was designed to help teenage alcoholics. He was concerned about the clients' right to confidentiality and his personal liability pursuant to strict federal guidelines when he reported the information required on a state-required accountability form. Because the federal guidelines imposed a $5,000 personal penalty for its violation, the counselor discussed it with his immediate superior, a man recently transferred to his present position from another branch. This coordinator was unaware of the dimensions of the conflicting legal and ethical situation and was unable or unwilling to become more involved. Rather than approving the counselor's behavior in bringing the issue to his attention, he saw it as a threat to his fledgling authority and labeled the counselor as a troublemaker in private meetings between himself and other program coordinators. Insensitive to the ethical dilemma, he halted progress on the resolution of the issue and left the counselor and other direct-service workers with the requirement to report to the state.

Since the coordinator was seen as impervious, the counselor informed others about the issue and tried to reach the attention of the executive director. Feeling caught in the dilemma of having to acknowledge his coordinator's lack of expertise in a basic matter, the executive director attempted to avoid the conflict by revising the staffing pattern in such a way as to eliminate the counselor's position on the pretext of agency budget problems. The counselor was given a choice of switching to another position (not covered by the federal regulation) or be laid off. The manifest conflict—how to protect the clients' rights ethically while still complying with state rules—was never resolved. The conflict was distorted by the explanation that the lateral move was due to budget and "personality problems" between the two men; if this had not been true originally, it was certainly the case by the end. General employee morale was adversely affected and staff performance decreased, resulting in actual budget cuts.

In this case, mediation of the manifest conflict would have avoided the subsequent distortions and agency losses brought about by suppression of the conflict. If the nonprofit organization had had access to mediation services—either provided in-house by the executive director or other high-ranked official or provided by a contract employment dispute resolution service on a consultant basis—the coordinator would not have felt so threatened by his own lack of knowledge, the counselor would not have been put in the position of having to go over the head of his coordinator, and the executive director would not have had to cover up and create Machiavellian changes in the system.

Other examples of workplace disputes, which can distract attention from the primary purpose of the business, point to the need for managers and supervisors to become effective mediators for their employees. A business manager in a medical clinic may need to be able to mediate a dispute between doctors on how to distribute the assets of the professional corporation, as well as conflicts between nurses on which supplies to order, as well as conflicts between the office staff on the way to bill insurance companies or schedule vacations. Any one of these conflicts left unresolved could diminish the effectiveness of the team of professionals and support staff—and therefore the staff's ability to provide patients with smoothly run medical care. Any one of these conflicts left unresolved would bring about conditions conducive to the loss of well-trained employees, particularly if the conflicts hardened into rigid patterns.

Employment disputes often fall into the categories depicted in Figure 5. According to these categories, a conflict could develop between a supervisor and employee with regard to the employee's

Figure 5. Common Areas of Employment Conflicts.

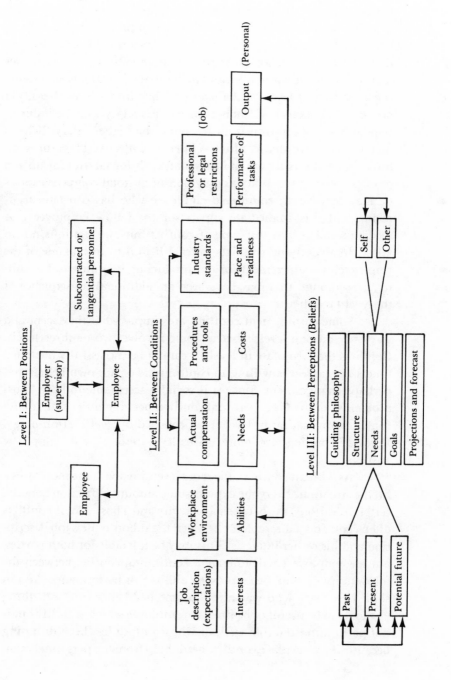

perceived financial needs, actual compensation, and industry standards for compensation that relates to that employee's past and present view of financial needs. If the employee in the past believed
that he needed a $20,000 salary to live the good life but now believes
that the good life cannot be bought for that salary, he is experiencing a conflict in level III that can translate into a level II conflict
between those perceived financial needs, his salary, and the industry
standards that keep him from receiving the higher salary. If he is
unable to resolve that conflict—either by collective bargaining efforts aimed at raising the industry standards for salaries for his job
or by perceiving his salary as only part of his total compensation—
he may become an embittered employee who has constant arguments with his immediate supervisor (or fellow employees). A
mediator called into this type of conflict must be cautious not to
allow the underlying conflicts in level II to turn into blame of the
employee by management for not producing according to his ability, even though that may have been an additional consequence of
the level I conflict.

     Some employment conflicts are simply what they seem and
stay only on one level, whereas some involve two or three levels.
Conflicts that originate in level III cannot be successfully mediated
unless the person is willing to confront his or her own beliefs and
perhaps change them. Since it is socially acceptable to have "boss
problems" or to expect personal conflicts between office staff, many
conflicts originating in level II are couched in level I terminology.
Level II conflicts are more difficult to resolve with simplistic
answers.

     As with all conflicts, the more levels involved, the more stress-
ful the situation. Everyone expects some amount of friction between
certain positions, say between a secretary and a boss. These conflicts
often center on a discrepancy between the subordinate's job description and his or her interests. This may be tolerable for both parties,
but few employers will tolerate a continuing conflict between the
job description and the employee's abilities or performance. An un-
skilled secretary who was hired to type had better find something
else to do to be useful or be fired. An employee who has ability but is
not performing the role well, or whose output has been dropping
because of a workplace conflict, needs help from the personnel man-

ager and should not be fired until the conflict has been acknowledged and the employer has tried to change or eliminate the problems promoting the conflict.

Employees who are hampered in the performance of their tasks by restrictions should be able to appeal to their supervisors for help in changing the restrictions. Employees who feel they are paying too high an emotional, physical, financial, or personal cost in order to keep working will quit. Even higher compensation will not hold them. Likewise, employees whose goals are different from the present or future aims of the company will probably leave, particularly after they become aware of their powerlessness to change the beliefs of the other employees or managers.

Where does mediation fit into this conceptual framework? Mediators can be useful facilitators for conflict resolution in employment disputes that fall into positional or conditional conflicts (levels I and II). They can mediate conflicts between two individuals or between groups. They can mediate a far wider range of disputes than just the collective bargaining disputes for which arbitrators and mediators have traditionally been used. By mediating across job conditions, or between person and job conditions, they can speedily resolve conflicts that, untended, result in disruption, delay, loss of productivity, and payment of additional expenses of sick leave and medical costs for employees under stress. Mediators can prevent costly and time-consuming retraining of personnel because of employee turnover. Ultimately all these factors result in increased job satisfaction as well as better efficiency.

In order for mediators to promote such conflict resolution, businesses should install effective mediation programs and systems that can help resolve management-level conflicts and also be used by even the least sophisticated employee. Personnel managers and their associates could provide mediation for employees after adequate training in the mediation process. A new management position could be created so that a professional mediator could be retained to serve, as do industrial safety consultants and nurses, when needed. Smaller corporations could retain a mediator or contract for mediation services as needed. Mediation services should be provided to businesses in ways that relate to their present and future structures. It is compatible with the advocacy provided to workers by unions.

Mediation could even be offered as part of a modern fringe benefit package: a form of "conflict insurance."

The future of business and employment will be changed for the better by the inclusion of mediation for resolving conflicts between employees as well as conflicts between employees and supervisors or corporate entities. Employees might be relieved of their high stress levels, and the cost of providing mediation can be cost-effective because of the reduced sicktime and higher productivity of employees who are able to work free of resolvable conflicts.

Minority Relations Mediation

Our society has legislated that minority groups, such as blacks, American Indians, Spanish-speaking persons, and the disabled, should be guaranteed equal treatment under the law. Additional legislation and social energy have been focused on preventing discrimination against people on the basis of age, religion, sexual preference, place of national origin, or beliefs. While some of this legislation has also designated a mechanism for resolving conflicts engendered by its application, most members of minority or other designated groups who feel aggrieved must pursue their rights to equal treatment through the litigation/arbitration conflict resolution process provided by the judicial system. As many victims of discrimination have discovered, that system often makes them a victim a second time by forcing them to prove the discrimination according to strict guidelines. The wheels of such conflict resolution systems grind slowly and produce additional stress and expense for those who often can least afford either (Sander, 1977). As Malcolm Feeley (1979) has observed, the process is the punishment for those who least of all should be castigated. While some states, such as Colorado, have institutionalized mediation for age discrimination and civil rights cases, mediation is not yet available through grievance mechanisms in all states.

One alternative for minority groups is to develop mediation services within their own community, where not only problems between members could be resolved but conflicts between members of that subgroup and nonmembers could be submitted. Communities and minority groups could also train their own people to serve in a voluntary mediation service to which conflicts of any member could be brought as a first step before starting the litigation process. Neighborhood and alternative justice centers, described earlier, could be used for this purpose. New mediation services could also be developed by local, state, or federal agencies. No matter what delivery system is developed, mediation, with its accent on nonadversarial problem solving, would help to create a positive climate between minority members and others—the original intention and thrust of the legislation.

Let us take, for example, the case of blacks concerned about potential discrimination against them by a high-tech corporation that is building a factory and starting to hire. To litigate there must be provable discriminatory acts, not suspicions or possible neglect of the minority groups during hiring. In order to resolve this issue of access to employment, the black community must wait until all hiring has been completed; but by then it is too late to obtain jobs if there has in fact been discrimination. Even if the complicated, time-consuming litigation is done, all that is likely to result is promotion of negative feelings and, at best, the right to have blacks considered first when new jobs become available. If the turnover or expansion rate is low in that industry, blacks may end up waiting five or more years before they see any real progress.

This need not be the case if mediation is started by voluntary agreement between black community leaders and the corporation even before hiring begins. The blacks' motivation to agree to mediate is obvious, but the company may need help from pressure groups to see the advantages in agreeing to mediate. Certainly the corporate image can be improved by mediation rather than hindered; moreover, the nonminority workers will feel less animosity, threat, and stress and will therefore be more productive if racial tensions decrease; finally, the physical plant and personnel will not be endangered by acts of violence or vandalism caused by persistent tensions.

There are other examples of conflicts in a minority group that threaten the stability and effectiveness of all members in the pursuit of their rights within society as a whole. Suppose a religious group, such as the Pentacostal churches, is factionalized in its reaction to new legislation regarding the designation, zoning, and taxation of small residential area churches. Unless these factions can resolve their differences effectively, they will not be able to make a unified impact on legislators and the voting public. As a minority group, their collective voice is already small, but it will become even smaller if they are divided still further. They need a process, such as mediation can offer, to help them reduce their conflicting viewpoints to a few convergent reactions. Mediation could be provided to this group either by people within their own group who have been trained to provide this function or by contracting with professional mediators.

Still another example is based on the need for individuals within a minority group to have effective help in resolving interpersonal conflicts that are unique or particularly germane to their group identity. Gay couples who have been emotionally, if not legally, married find that they need the same help in parting as do straight husband and wife couples; they may also need help determining custody of children they have adopted jointly or who remain in their custody from earlier marriages. They are finding, however, that counselors and lawyers who are not gay themselves often do not understand the roles they have played for each other, the underlying conflicts, or the options available within the gay life-style. Mediators need not belong to the same minority groups nor must they champion the same issues as the participants in order to provide the seven-stage mediation process we have outlined. Self-help organizations within the gay (or other minority) community can train persons who have special sensitivities and understanding to be effective mediators. (See Chapter Thirteen for more information regarding mediation and minorities.)

To summarize, then, minority members will always be likely to have conflicts with the rest of society simply by being part of a subgroup rather than the mainstream of society. Indeed, some theorists think that recent trends indicate there *is* no mainstream, no predictable bell-shaped curve of norms and deviation. We are all members of subgroups, whether by choice or by nonvoluntary attribution, as Boulding (1962, pp. 105–109) has pointed out. We illustrate from his work in the following list:

Involuntary Groups	*Voluntary Groups*
1. Sex	1. Religious groups
2. Age	2. Social groups
3. Race and physical type	3. Political parties
4. Family position	4. Class groups
5. Kinship	5. Civil status
	6. Economic categories: occupation, consumer, and so on

All such groups have conflicts among themselves and also between themselves and the interests of other groups pulling in diverse directions. Mediation, whether provided by members within each group or by contract services or larger social entities to each group, can promise a more constructive resolution or management of conflicts and should be tried before adversarial litigation processes are imposed.

Environmental Disputes

As one very wise observer put it, "Good planets are hard to find." Many of the decisions we face and disputes we are encountering as a nation and as a planet have long-term, irreversible consequences for all of us as well as short-term impacts on specific societies, subpopulations, or surroundings. Examples of this are the use, storage, and disposal of nuclear materials, whether used in power stations, warheads, medical aids, or submarines, and the degradation of our water systems. The use and disposal of toxic substances such as PBB, PCB, Agent Orange, and dioxin pose a potential threat to many aspects of our local and global environment. These environmental issues require us to look at our basic values, assumptions, and belief systems about humanity's "rights" to create and destroy, the nature of progress, the relative worth and priorities given to the needs of various groups, and the processes and mechanisms by which such decisions should be made.

The following discussion can only attempt to give the reader a brief summary of the relevant definitions, issues, parameters, and perspectives that form the basis of environmental mediation. We shall attempt to integrate information from this field with the mediation process outlined in Chapter Three. This section is but a summary of this emerging use of mediation, a use that becomes more essential daily. We have concentrated here on the issues for the field, rather than specific techniques, and must refer readers to earlier chapters for general descriptions of roles and tasks. It is also suggested that the reader review the books we recommend at the end of the chapter.

While the larger picture of environmental concerns is important, a shift of focus to our own individual spheres of awareness and influence is also helpful in understanding the very real environmental issues we all face. We have only to open a local newspaper, listen to a radio or television news report, or just look around at the immediate surroundings to discover how pervasive, perhaps even intrusive, environmental issues and conflicts are in the human fabric. Many of these environmental conflicts could be mediated. In the northwestern United States, for example, there are many disputes and unresolved environmental conflicts: the needs of the forestry and logging industry versus the need for wilderness; the needs of American Indian tribes versus those of sport fishermen and the fishing industry; the need for people to cut and burn wood as fuel for woodstoves to conserve petrochemical energy versus the need for urban environments to reduce particulate pollution from such burning; the need for people to drive conveniently to work and play sites from their suburban enclaves versus the needs of homeowners and shopkeepers to prevent the disruption of their neighborhoods and marketplaces by massive highways. These and other conflicts affecting our environment must be more effectively managed than in the past.

The piece of legislation that set the stage for the development of environmental mediation in the United States was the National Environmental Policy Act of 1969, usually referred to by its acronym, NEPA. NEPA governs the actions of the executive branch and its federal agencies and calls for the development of the Council for Environmental Quality (CEQ) to advise and assist the President in carrying out the act. All federal agencies must abide by NEPA and the regulations, standards, and interpretations set pursuant to NEPA by the CEQ. The CEQ prepares reports for Congress and recommends needed legislation, but it does not itself regulate government agencies. The Environmental Protection Agency (EPA) is the federal regulatory agency with the primary responsibility for monitoring and protecting the environment. It reviews all environmental impact statements required by NEPA. The EPA is also charged with implementing the following environmental legislation: the Clean Air Act; the Clean Water Act; the Safe Drinking Water Act; the Resource, Conservation, and Recovery Act; the Toxic Substances Control Act; the Federal Insecticide, Fungicide, and Rodenticide Act; the Marine Protection, Research and Sanctuaries Act; the Noise Control Act; and the Energy Supply and Environmental Coordination Act.

While it did not specify mediation as a conflict resolution method, NEPA contains language allowing the use or development of mediation by its expressed requirement of the exploration of alternatives and citizen involvement. In its role as enforcer of this legislation, the EPA has begun to recognize the need for negotiation, if not mediation, for resolving disputes related to the violation of its standards (Harter, 1983).

Federal environmental regulations are preeminent over state regulations, but there is considerable state activity in regulating and monitoring environmental matters. State and local environmental agencies responsible for state regulation, development, and planning—for example, the Department of Environmental Quality (DEQ) in Oregon—may allow some discretion to their executives to reduce penalties when good faith efforts are shown. While these executives may negotiate penalties, they generally do not mediate the disputes. Some do not see the latter as part of their role, since they consider it the mandate of their agencies to keep control and decision-making functions.

The EPA's actions are closely watched by special-interest groups such as the National Resources Defense Council (NRDC), the Sierra Club, and others, that represent the often mutually antagonistic interests of industry and environmentalists. When these groups believe that the EPA, or similar state or local agencies, have made decisions contradictory to their interests or their interpretation of statutory intent, they have initiated litigation of such disputes, thus delaying the EPA's efforts. The EPA finds its defense of such disputes costly in terms of the timetables for compliance by affected parties, as well as costly to its own internal financial and staff resources. By litigating these disputes, the special-interest groups sometimes are able to hamper the effectiveness of the public agencies and move important policy decisions into an adjudicatory forum.

Adjudication casts well-meaning participants in an adversarial posture and is generally considered unsatisfactory (Golten, 1980). Litigation is an awkward and confined way of shaping environmental policy and determining long-term environmental effects. Litigation puts policy interpretation and implementation beyond the control of the disputing factions and in the hands of a judge. The resulting decisions may not be to anyone's liking. It is a slow and expensive way to resolve questions of specific application of environmental policy.

Mediation can provide conflict management and conflict resolution (see Chapter Two) for environmental disputes far less expensively, in terms of time and money, than can litigation. Moreover, it can provide all participants a greater sense of satisfaction because of their active role. It allows the participants to maintain a degree of control. It allows the consideration of more creative environmental options than does litigation. Most important, mediation promotes cooperation, which is the missing element in the solution to most environmental problems. It also allows consideration of a more comprehensive range of expertise and technical data affecting environmental decisions than does litigation. Environmental mediation is an attempt to manage resources and make decisions that incorporate as many relevant factors and consequences as possible. As Mernitz (1980, p. 42) describes it, environmental mediation is one of a continuum of interventions that has the unique characteristics of being voluntary, informal, and assistive rather than a process that forces settlement.

Mediation offers a process for decision making in environmental and resource conflicts. It provides a positive response to the two most negative "earth-centered perspectives" (the convinced neo-Malthusian and the guarded pessimist) summarized by Kahn, Brown, and Martel (1976, pp. 10–16): Mediation is an attempt to cooperatively create a positive impact on (1) the rapidity of change and growing complexity and (2) the increasing number of conflicting interests we are experiencing. Mediation promotes more effective management of resources, control of pollution, and resolution of social conflicts than does traditional legislation, litigation, arbitration, and other social mechanisms, some legitimate, some not.

Mediation also allows for the constructive use of expertise and technical data rather than the adversarial posturing and obstructionism commonly displayed by experts hired to testify in heated court proceedings. As summarized by Mernitz (1980), mediation has the following advantages over the time-honored tradition of the American judicial system:

1. It can be as speedy as the participants want it to be.
2. It is less expensive than litigation.
3. It provides for flexibility and directness because it is not hampered by the restrictions of legal procedure.
4. Because it is voluntary, it is often more lasting, leading to better enforcement.

Although mediation is not currently used as much as it could be, there should be a larger role for the process in settling conflicts involving public agency standards and regulatory disputes. Mediation could reduce the time necessary to resolve such disputes while not upsetting the healthy check-and-balance system surrounding public agencies. Private environmental mediation organizations could be used to provide neutral facilitation on a contractual basis, or a federal or state environmental mediation service could be developed to provide mediation for public agency-related disputes. The present system of litigating disputes between public agencies and private interest groups might then be used only when mediation, as the method of first resort, has failed.

The term *environment* is rather all-inclusive. Historically the "environmental movement" originated in disputes over the destruction or degradation of wilderness and special ecological areas. Contested environmental issues now include matters involving water sources and uses, solid waste and sewage, toxic waste and hazardous substances, and noise. Mining, drilling, and the exploitation and allocation of all natural resources are also broadly classified as environmental issues. Still other issues involving land use, recycling of materials, agriculture, and the use of pesticides and radioactive materials fall under the general heading of environmental issues and conflicts.

While the list grows larger with our increasing perception of natural systems and ecologies, the categories of environmental issues that have been, or could be, mediated appear to be unlimited. All the following issues could be considered legitimate categories for the use of mediation: pollution control; land use decisions and disputes; conservation of natural resources; governmental or industrial planning of transportation and site developments; setting industry standards or regulations to preserve or restore the environment; development and revision of regulatory mechanisms themselves; power source development and utilization; remedies to technological crises or mistakes affecting the environment; and factors, such as overutilization, that affect the quality of urban "social environments." And with the opening of outer space to use by spacecraft and satellites, space itself should no doubt be included under the heading of "world environment" for the purposes of cooperative decision making, conflict management, and mediation.

Some environmental mediators believe the mediation process can be used before an environmental conflict has become a recognized dispute (that is, a conflict that has been communicated). They call this use of mediation *conflict anticipation* (Bellman and others, 1981). For example, if a state highway commission has documented a need for a road to be widened in order to handle current and projected traffic more safely and efficiently, it is likely that this change will conflict with the interests of several community groups. The current process of citizen's advisory committee, public hearings, and environmental impact statements—a sequence outlined by federal regulations in accordance with NEPA—provides only for group or individual input rather than decision making. NEPA does, however, provide for a process called *scoping*, discussed later in this section, that has certain similarities to conflict anticipation. Mediation, in addition to or in place of the typical notice and hearing sequence, can provide a more active participatory and powerful role for community groups affected by the outcome of decision making. According to Bellman and others (1981, p. 4): "Potential areas of dispute can be identified, information and viewpoints can be shared, and questions can be answered early enough in the project planning that the proposed design itself can reflect mutually acceptable solutions."

There are many similarities between labor mediation and environmental mediation because of the multiple participants, statutory and regulatory frameworks, and continuing contacts or relationships between participants. However, the need to clarify the empowered representative of a constituency or interest group in environmental conflicts contrasts with the well-defined parties to a labor dispute. Moreover, environmental disputes usually concern complex issues rather than the well-defined and narrow concerns of labor disputes. While some of its background is linked to the mediation of labor disputes, environmental mediation as such developed much later, in the late 1960s and early 1970s, when conventional social processes threatened to break under the strain of new environmental conflicts and awareness. As these environmental conflicts exploded in the courts, the shortcomings of litigation became apparent.

Mediation can work for environmental issues when there is a range of options, solutions, or processes; it is useless when there is no room for negotiation. An excellent example of the either/or conflict is the one given by Charles Warren (1978, pp. 10–11), former chairman of the Council for Environmental Quality, concerning the breeder reactor, whose opponents flatly refuse to consider any arguments for its use. Cormick (1981, p. 9) concludes: "Thus, mediation can best be seen as a process for *settling* disputes, not for *resolving* basic differences."

Deutsch's (1973) differentiation between underlying and manifest conflicts, summarized in Chapter Two, brings clarity to this point. Environmental mediation can help make necessary decisions and resolve the immediate manifest conflicts, but it may not be able to resolve the underlying philosophical or technological conflicts. Seen in this way, mediation may not eliminate all environmental conflict, but it can be an effective process for resolving or managing certain disputes. The goal of environmental mediation is most often to realign the divergent positions enough to create a balance point that allows all participants to escape harm from each other. It is conflict management more than conflict resolution.

Many prestigious organizations have supported the development of mediation as an effective instrument for resolving environmental issues. The Ford Foundation has directed funds for the development of dispute resolution programs to resolve not only environmental and natural resources disputes but other social, institutional, community, and interpersonal disputes as well. The Conservation Foundation, established in 1977, as well as the Atlantic Richfield Foundation, the William and Flora Hewlett Foundation, the Andrew W. Mellon Foundation, the Rockefeller Foundation, and other private sources, have funded many early programs for the use of mediation in environmental disputes. The Kettering Foundation has developed a method termed the *negotiated investment strategy* to deal with major urban development problems (Talbot, 1983, p. viii).

In 1978 three groups—the Center for Environmental Conflict Resolution (Resolve), the Aspen Institute for Humanistic Studies, and the Sierra Club—came together, despite their different focuses, to explore, promote, and develop the field of environmental mediation through a conference (Resolve, 1978). Many other organizations, such as the American Arbitration Association and the National Academy of Conciliators, are currently involved in the training and use of mediation for environmental disputes, as well as the development of informed citizen participation in decision making. Currently eight states plus the District of Columbia have organizations that provide neutral mediation for environmental disputes (Talbot, 1983, p. viii).

Like all other uses of mediation, environmental mediation generally follows the process we have outlined in Chapter Three. Mediation is a way of getting the parties of interest, or those closely involved or affected, to begin working toward an agreement that is acceptable to them. It is a process requiring the participants to negotiate and solve problems in order to reach a set of acceptable and workable agreements. Stage 4, negotiation and decision making, is the crucial stage of environmental mediation. Cormick (1981, p. 3) notes that negotiations can occur without a mediator, but mediation can never occur without negotiation.

Although the basic process of environmental mediation follows the stages outlined in Chapter Three, a unique set of techniques can be used. Mernitz (1980) summarizes these techniques into the following categories: *shuttle diplomacy*, where the mediator holds private caucuses with the participants, bringing offers back and forth as a go-between; *nondirective consensus building*, where education is supplied about consensus itself and group facilitation is offered; *bilateral task force negotiations*, setting educational or awareness-building exercises and subsequent discussions; *dialectic scanning*, the fact-finding and isolation of issues stage, where conflicts are examined for factual misunderstandings and differences in cause-and-effect perceptions or values; and *scoping*, defined by the CEQ, in its 1978 revision of regulations for NEPA, as "an early and open process for determining the scope of issues to be addressed and for identifying the significant issues related to a proposed action" (43 Fed. Reg. 55,978). This scoping process must follow the determination that an environmental impact statement (EIS) will be required; all interested parties must be invited to attend.

While these terms may be helpful to some, they can distort the basic mediation process. Shuttle diplomacy simply requires the mediator to conduct most of the seven-stage process in private caucus rather than in joint sessions. Both nondirective consensus building and bilateral task force negotiations seem similar to what we have called the first stage of the mediation process: creating structure and trust. By getting the participants to share common expectations, terminology, and perspectives, their own structures will become clarified and intragroup trust will be created, as well as a safe forum for intergroup exchange. The Columbia River Symposium, held in June 1982 under the auspices of the Natural Resources Law Institute of Lewis and Clark School, is an example of a program that reflected concepts of consensus building and bilateral task force negotiations. The symposium was not intended as a stage in the mediation process and, thus, there was no expectation that it would result in agreement or resolve the dispute about preservation of the Columbia River Gorge. The conflicts arising from the tension between the felt need to preserve the gorge and expressed intentions to develop part of it present a challenging opportunity for mediation.

Mediation of environmental disputes also involves the use of negotiation during the fourth stage. The EPA has already recognized the need for another method besides litigation to resolve disputes concerning their rule-making function and has recently instituted a negotiation process. The purpose of this demonstration project is to create a set of agreements concerning their rules for cleanup and disposal that is "acceptable to a wide range of interests, more quickly, and without the need for litigation" (Cannon, 1983, p. 11). Because of the Federal Advisory Committee Act (FACA), which applies to all such negotiations, both open and closed sessions must be allowed. The EPA will be using a third-party intervenor-facilitator to conduct these sessions. In accord with our earlier definitions in Chapters Two and Three, we believe this is appropriate for mediation of these rule-making disputes and applaud the EPA for promoting such efforts.

Stage 6 of mediation (legal review), as well as stage 7 (implementation, review, and revision), also has a historical precedent in environmental disputes. A consent decree by the court can be used to ratify a negotiated (mediated) settlement and provide continuing jurisdiction for later enforcement of its terms. Such a consent decree thereby allows for a legal watchdog role over compliance to ensure that the voluntary agreement is acceptable and maintained. A consent decree was issued in the case between the EPA and the NRDC in 1976 (called the Toxics Consent Decree) regarding their dispute over water pollutants. Under this kind of decree, the review and potential revision function in stage 7 is facilitated by the courts. This particular consent decree became the basis for further legislation in 1977, thus showing the potential connection between mediation, litigation, and legislation.

The criteria for success in environmental mediation cases have not been fully developed. The six case studies described by Talbot (1983), however, give a good indication of success. An excellent article by Lee (1982) indicates that the participants' criteria for success may differ from those used by the mediator. He finds that most mediators use at least two criteria as signposts of success: an outcome that is mutually acceptable to the participants and a process that promotes equality, fairness, and uncoerced outcomes. Another criterion, which may not emerge until stage 7 (implementation) is whether the mutually agreeable outcome is practical and able to weather emerging contingencies.

Another way in which mediation has been used in environmental disputes is *after* litigation has occurred. As with all public law litigation, the remedy to the situation does not automatically flow from the right that has been determined by the judge. The court may determine who won the suit, based on the past, yet require *both* parties to draft the decree or order of the court concerning future behavior. According to Chayes (1976, p. 1299):

> Some form of negotiation will almost inevitably ensue upon submission of the draft to the parties for comment. The negotiating process ought to minimize the need for judicial resolution of remedial issues. Each party recognizes that it must make some response to the demands of the other party, for issues left unresolved will be submitted to the court . . . and may result in a solution less acceptable than might be reached by horse-trading.

Postlitigation negotiations could be conducted most constructively with the assistance of a trained mediator.

For environmental disputes that do not fall under the NEPA requirements, there is also a precedent and legislation promoting the use of mediation. In the Coastal Zone Management Act, Section 307, a promise is given that all subsequent federal actions will be consistent with the required and approved State Coastal Management Program. If there is a dispute between state and federal agencies whether such actions are consistent, the matter can be mediated. The mediation process, called *secretarial mediation services,* and mediation sessions are provided under this law by the secretary of the Department of Commerce (15 C.F.R. 930, Subpart G).

Some mediators believe that only a small percentage, perhaps as little as 10 percent, of the environmental cases referred to them can be effectively mediated (Resolve, 1978). This modest success rate may be attributable to the need in environmental mediation cases for all participants to share a similar set of expectations and the requirement that the issues conform to a set of criteria, such as the following guidelines proposed by Jerome T. Barrett, director of professional development for the Federal Mediation and Conciliation Service. These criteria are drawn from the service's extensive work in labor-related disputes but are applicable to environmental disputes (Resolve, 1978, pp. 18-19):

1. Clearly identifiable parties to the dispute with the authority to make changes and to bind others
2. A willingness of all parties to the dispute actually to bargain on at least some of the issues
3. A desire on the part of the bargainers and their constituencies to reach an agreement
4. An understanding and acceptance by the bargainers and their constituencies of the concept of representative bargaining
5. Bargainers who understand and keep current with the parameters of their authority from their constituencies
6. Responsible bargainers who are willing to lead as well as follow their constituency
7. Issues that the parties are able to view not as rights but as implementations of rights
8. Some degree of trust in the bargaining process and in the parties' ability to negotiate successfully

Some mediators simply state that each environmental dispute has its own unique timing for readiness. While mediation may not be needed or wanted at a certain point in time, they argue, it may later look far better as a conflict resolution method when judicial decision making is proferred or looms as a desperate response to the unresolved dispute, as in the case of the Interstate 90 controversy in the Seattle area (Talbot, 1983). If only 10 percent of environmental disputes can be mediated at a given point in time, one cannot necessarily conclude that the remaining 90 percent are permanently unmediable.

As the field of environmental mediation grows, some have urged that only the cases with the greatest likelihood of producing favorable results should be accepted. While this skewing by selection may have been ethically and professionally justifiable early in its development, the field will not progress by holding back, refusing to take risks, and fearing unfavorable conclusions. The pressing urgency of many environmental conflicts, which reject the expensive and time-consuming process of litigation, speaks to the need for private or public mediation centers to take on the hard cases as well as the well-defined simple issues.

By understanding the process of mediation we have proposed, environmental mediators can set up systems to deal with even the most complex cases. To increase the likelihood of success, the following tactics provide mediation teams with expertise on the specific subject being mediated: group facilitation, process observation, participant education, and consensus building. By expanding the timetables or scope of stages 1 and 2 (setting structure; fact finding and isolation of issues), cases of environmental disputes can more easily be prepared for the actual conference-table negotiation and decision making in the fourth stage of the mediation process.

Because most environmental disputes involve vast quantities of technical information, the use of computers to manage, store, and retrieve the data, as well as to make projections, has become commonplace. The outcome from data is only as good as the input and program used, however, so some authors (Straus, 1977) have suggested that participants avoid the "battle of the printout" by negotiating the rules concerning the selection, use, and validation of data and computers *before* commencing the actual mediation. This point cannot be overemphasized: mediating facts is crucial in many environmental disputes that involve scientific uncertainties or future projections. This point is closely connected to the context of the scoping process demanded by NEPA and discussed in this chapter. Straus (1977, pp. 106–107) calls this *data mediation,* but we prefer to see it as part of the rule setting and structuring that must be done in stage 1 in order to avoid nonacceptance of "facts" in stage 2 or continued negotiation about such items during stage 4.

The multiplicity of issues and rights—as well as the number of jurisdictions involved within the United States in the life cycle of anadromous fish (such as salmon and steelhead, which begin their lives in fresh water, migrate to salt water, and return to fresh water to breed)—highlights the need for a better process than litigation for resolution of disputes. The Salmon and Steelhead Enhancement Act of 1980 created an advisory committee (SSAC) that set up a Dispute Resolution Task Team "to assist in developing dispute resolution systems and processes that may be applicable to management of salmon and steelhead fisheries in the Pacific Northwest" (SSAC

Draft on Dispute Resolution). Mediation seems well suited to this group and many others like it across the country that are concerned with complex environmental issues.

The conflicting interests of American Indians, sport fishermen, power companies, residential developers, and the fishing industries concerning anadromous fish may be settled by the use of mediation rather than litigation, yet an ultimate solution to the problem may be hampered by the continuing pollution or degradation of the environment by other interests in still other jurisdictions. The United States may be able to resolve the conflicts regarding fishing quotas and habitat protection in their freshwater breeding grounds and the sea through use of mediation and legislation such as the Salmon and Steelhead Act. However, our regulations will be distorted and undermined if the fish must pass through an ocean contaminated by distant countries that do not respect our environmental regulations and standards.

While environmental mediation is still in its infancy, its heritage from international law and politics can be clearly seen. The underlying issue of many environmental disputes is the potential global effect. The question of how to stop acid rain, pollution that is created in the United States but carried to Canada by weather systems, points to the international cause and effect of many environmental problems and disputes. Our world has but one water and air system. Ultimately we shall recognize that we are all part of the same global ecological network.

International mediators could provide the process to resolve disputes about development and destruction of areas that have not only a national, short-term outcome but a worldwide impact. The Amazon rain forests, for example, are now believed to supply the planet with much of its oxygen. Unless this global interest is considered in the scope of the dispute over slash-and-burn agriculture by including participants from international conservation efforts, the resolution of the dispute through mediation may meet the needs of only the local government, in this case Brazil. Certainly more thought and energy must be given to the international perspective in the near future (Edon, 1971). The issue of living in the "nuclear common world" has been clearly stated by Jonathan Schell (1982, p. 177):

The oneness of the earth as a system of support for life is already visible around us. Today, no matter how strenuously statesmen may assert the "sovereign" power of their nations, the fact is that they are all caught in an increasingly fine mesh of global life, in which the survival of each nation depends on the survival of all.

Mediation is a fresh approach to conflict resolution that can, with further development, help to settle disputes which,if left unresolved, could threaten that fine mesh of life. As Kahn, Brown, and Martel (1976) stated "It may yet turn out that future man will marvel at the paradoxical combination of hubris and modesty of 20th-century man, who, at the same time, so exaggerated his ability to do damage and so underestimated his own ability to adapt to or solve such problems." The application of mediation to national and international environmental disputes is perhaps the most compelling use of the process because of the immediacy of the conflicts and long-term implications of their outcome. Mediation is already working well to provide better decisions and conflict resolution in the basic social unit, the family. It should be refined and adapted for use in the largest social unit: the planetary ecological system itself.

Recommended Reading

"Environmental Mediation." J. L. Watson and L. J. Danielson. *Natural Resources Lawyers*, 1983, *15* (4).
    Gives an excellent summary of the Homestake mining case, and in the process defines the three types of environmental mediation: broad policy issues, mixed policy and site-specific issues, and site-specific issues.

Environmental Mediation: An Effective Answer? Resolve, Center for Environmental Conflict Resolution (Eds.), Palo Alto: Resolve, 1978.
    This report of the 1978 conference co-sponsored by Resolve, the Aspen Institute for Humanistic Studies, and the Sierra

Club Foundation gives readers a general understanding of the issues
in environmental mediation.

Mediation of Environmental Disputes: A Source Book. S. Mernitz.
   New York: Praeger, 1980.
        As the only hardcover book on this subject, it discusses the
nature of environmental disputes, the function of mediation, the
mediator's role and techniques, and the conclusions that can be
reached from reviewing cases.

Settling Things: Six Case Studies in Environmental Mediation. A.
   R. Talbot. Washington, D.C.: The Conservation Foundation and
   The Ford Foundation, 1983.
        The chronological ordering of information in this short book
of environmental mediation histories shows critical points and provides interesting reading.

9

✿ ✿ ✿ ✿ ✿

Education and Training
of Mediators

Training and Format

There is much concern about education and training in mediation. Some believe that mediation is a new profession demanding an approved graduate curriculum and academic prerequisites for entry. Others think that it is a practiced competency or set of skills to be added through continuing education to an existing professional base such as law, counseling, or administration. Some argue that mediation need not be a professional practice and can be offered by lay personnel who have ties to the subject or the setting of the dispute. We should not preclude any of these paths into mediation service until the results of each can be studied and more is known about what works best. (See the discussion of licensure and certification in Chapter Ten).

There appears to be no disagreement, however, about the need for *some* form of education or training by those who serve as mediators. Consensus on the need for mediation education and training does not resolve questions about the prerequisites, the curriculum, and the nature of the study—whether it should be conceptual or experiential, academic or practical. Related to these considerations are the questions of whether one-day training programs are adequate, whether a multiyear course of study is required, and whether there is a need for initial or continuing case supervision and review.

There is ample room for a diversity of training approaches so that those seeking mediation skills and understanding can have a choice of courses and programs. The training of people from the community to help resolve local disputes or people from a work setting to resolve workplace conflicts might be reasonably accomplished in a practical program designed for a one-day format. Such a workshop might introduce basic mediation concepts and skills, particularly for use in existing roles. Similarly, a one-day program should be sufficient to orient lawyers to serve as mediators in minor commercial litigation cases or personal injury suits that are clogging court dockets. Short continuing education and skills-enhancement programs for those already in some form of mediation practice also have a legitimate role.

Intensive two-day to one-week training programs emphasizing participatory exercises and demonstrations of mediation techniques for those with related professional backgrounds are proliferating and are generally well subscribed. These programs fill an important role: orienting professionals to the uniqueness of mediation practice, allowing them to transpose their skills to a mediation format, and introducing them to mediation issues. Those who are experienced in mediation are frequently requested to share what they have learned in their practice with those just beginning. These skill-oriented seminars, workshops, and institutes provide a systematic structure for experienced mediators to demonstrate their styles and share their thinking with others while receiving some recognition and compensation for their time. These programs also facilitate the formulation of mediator networks. Information about available training programs can be obtained from some of the national organizations listed in Resource E at the back of this volume.

Although these workshops provide a valuable training opportunity, they should not be oversold. The time restrictions imposed on a training format of one week or less limit their role to mediation orientation, an introduction to substantive knowledge, and skill refinement. They should not be regarded as comprehensive professional curricula.

A follow-up component to these workshops is needed to help the enrollees establish systems of in-service training, case supervision, or peer review so that the skills learned in the workshops can be applied and honed through supervised practice. Listening to a lecture, reading this book, or participating in a simulation will not instantly transform even a person with considerable aptitude into a mediator. That transformation will come through a combination of understanding, observation, practice, and supervision.

One reason why workshops, seminars, and institutes are offered or accredited by organizations such as the American Arbitration Association or the Academy of Family Mediators and by private mediation trainers is because they fill a void; there are very few academic courses and curricula in mediation. Law schools and graduate schools of counseling, social work, education, administration, management, nursing, and other human service fields are starting to offer courses in conflict resolution. A few degree or certificate curricula in mediation or conflict resolution are now being organized at respected universities, including the Catholic University of America, the University of Colorado, the University of Illinois, and the University of Maryland. Others will surely follow their lead.

The current interest in mediation may stimulate the creation of joint academic programs between schools of law and social work or counseling. They may parallel the development of previous joint programs such as those in law and urban planning, law and business, law and psychology, and law and criminology. These joint-degree programs, after serving their purposes of promoting complementary bodies of knowledge, development of new research and its application, sensitivity to new needs and interests, and preparation of teaching materials, often are replaced with richer offerings in the regular curricula of each of the schools. New majors and separate fields of study are often integrated back into more traditional curricula after they serve similar purposes as those of joint-degree programs. Black studies, women's studies, and environmental studies, for example, are now part of the offerings of many different departments or graduate programs in some universities, though it may have required establishing a separate concentration of courses before they found their rightful place in other curricula.

It is anticipated that more law schools and other graduate and undergraduate departments will offer courses in mediation concepts and skills. This trend may develop as a parallel to separate degree or certificate programs in conflict resolution. In other words, we shall see some students developing an academic specialty in mediation while others study it as an integrated part of public administration, psychology, business, law, education, or human service fields. As this happens, mediation will become more credible and more professionals will become involved in offering mediation services in many different formats and settings. This development will promote mediation services by providing interprofessional knowledge and more intelligent referrals, not only between mediation providers but also from other professionals.

Educational Content

In considering what is appropriate education and training in mediation—whether for an individual wanting to become a mediator, an institution designing a mediation curriculum, or disputants evaluating the choice of a mediator—at least five subjects must be included: understanding conflict, mediation procedure and assumptions, mediation skills, substantive knowledge, and mediation ethics and standards.

Understanding Conflict. Mediation is a holistic approach to conflict resolution. In order to resolve conflicts without the imposition of outside authority, it is important for the mediator to understand the nature of conflict, how it comes into being, its dynamics, how it is manifested in particular disputes, and how it may be managed and resolved. (These subjects are introduced in Chapter Two.) Although a mediator without knowledge of the nature of conflict may be able to help resolve some disputes, the chances for consistently and permanently resolving disputes are greatly enhanced by being able to put the conflict in perspective.

Mediation Procedure and Assumptions. Mediation is a conflict resolution method that is distinct from adversarial resolution, therapy, and the other alternatives discussed in Chapter Two. To promote successful resolution through mediation, the mediator should be familiar with the basic stages of the process discussed in Chapter Three and the basic propositions covered in Chapter One. Though others may define the stages of mediation differently, understanding a stage-by-stage approach and learning the dynamics of mediation, both cognitively and experientially, is an important aspect of mediation education.

Learning about mediation involves two elements. First is the positive aspect of understanding the function of mediation and what needs to be accomplished in each stage. Second is a dissassociation of habits and assumptions fostered by the mediator's original profession. This step requires a change in the internal map that directs us to our philosophical destination. It has, for example, been pointed out that the philosophical map of lawyers includes the assumptions that disputants are adversaries and disputes are resolved by the proper application of legal rules. Riskin (1982, p. 44) refers to these assumptions as the "polar opposites of those which underlie mediation: (1) that all parties can benefit through a creative solution to which each agrees; and (2) that the situation is unique and therefore not to be governed by any general principle except to the extent that the parties accept it." The lawyer's standard philosophical map for resolving conflict, emphasizing a strictly rational outlook, must be changed to a philosophical map more appropriate for mediation. Likewise, the therapist's philosophical map, which emphasizes finding and treating the causes of conflict while allowing individual decisions to be deferred, must be converted to the joint decisions and task orientation of mediation.

Scientists, educators, health care providers, parents, and others who wish to become effective mediators must learn a new map in order to reach their destination. The mediation map may cover the same territory as their familiar map, but the steps to mediation have different landmarks. Accepting a different orientation and learning new procedures for the resolution of conflict is the most important step in the education of a mediator.

Mediation Skills. The level and mixture of skills of those becoming mediators will necessarily vary, as does the skillfulness of experienced mediators. Strength in one skill may compensate for weakness in others and no mediator uniformly masters all possible mediation tools. A mental health professional entering mediation may have well-developed techniques for dealing with anger as well as clinically refined listening skills. A lawyer entering mediation practice may not have developed these skills but should have an equally important capacity for isolating issues, testing reality, assessing needs, and directing negotiations. Educators have good information-sharing and motivational skills; administrators are practiced at clarifying, planning, and budgeting. Each set of experiences and aptitudes brings with it skills helpful for mediation along with undeveloped faculties that may also be useful.

The skill-building component of mediation training must allow flexibility so that each person can concentrate on developing skills that were not emphasized in his or her background and education. An experienced therapist need not relearn skills of active listening and paraphrasing. A lawyer knows how to phrase information-gathering questions and test the information. Although a mediation curriculum may have common elements, regardless of professional background or previous experience, actual training must be fine tuned to complement existing skills. As suggested by Riskin (1982, p. 45), mediation training might nurture a lawyer's emotional faculties and further develop a therapist's cognitive and rational capabilities.

Although each of us has a head start on certain skills and some may have a well-developed facility for mediation skills, these skills have to be applied in a different dynamic package for successful mediation. A successful lawyer must be skillful at developing rapport and gaining the trust of a client. But the same lawyer may have to apply that skill differently when serving two or more parties with conflicting interests. A clergyman adept at helping others to evaluate choices and make decisions may have to apply those skills in a less moralistic manner than would be appropriate in a pastoral counseling setting. For most of those who become mediators, mediation requires a combination of new applications for old skills and the mastering of additional competencies. Again, training that utilizes an interdisciplinary team approach naturally fuses different orientations and skills for the mutual benefit of each training participant.

A group of experienced mediators from different backgrounds was convened by the Association of Family and Conciliation Courts in December 1982 to consider appropriate education and training for mediators. This group composed the following selected list of recommended mediation skills and techniques:

- Listening skills
- Trust- and rapport-building skills
- Interests and needs assessment skills

- Option inventory skills
- Techniques for dealing with anger
- Empowerment skills
- Sensitivity skills
- Refocusing and reframing skills
- Reality-testing skills
- Paraphrasing skills
- Negotiating skills
- Information-sharing skills
- Techniques of breaking deadlocks
- Skills for remaining neutral
- Self-awareness techniques
- Pattern- and stereotype-breaking skills
- Techniques of including other parties
- Humor skills
- Goal-setting skills
- Child interview techniques
- Identifying agenda items and ordering skills
- Strategic-planning skills
- Skills in designing temporary plans
- Rewarding and affirmation techniques
- Skillful use of attorneys and other professionals
- Techniques of building momentum
- Caucusing techniques
- Techniques of balancing power
- Conflict-identifying and analysis skills
- Agreement-writing skills
- Credibility-building skills
- Techniques for developing ground rules
- Grief-counseling techniques
- Referral techniques

The same group listed the following mediation concepts, among others, that should be learned as part of a mediator's education:

- Stages of negotiation
- Nature and role of power (disputants' and mediator's)

- Accepting failure and defining success
- Parameters of professional ethics
- Community standards of reasonableness versus private ordering
- Budgeting
- Responsibility to unrepresented parties
- Interest-based versus positional bargaining
- Timing (fading opportunity)
- Influence of constituencies on parties
- Durability of agreements
- Distributive versus integrative bargaining
- Postmediation processes and follow-up
- Rituals of agreement
- Modeling effective communication

We each tend to do that which we know best. Our style of mediation depends on the emphasis we place on the skills and knowledge with which we are most comfortable. A lawyer is unlikely to mediate exactly like a therapist; a minister will probably not mediate the same as a scientist; and a teacher will not use the identical mediation strategies a union official would employ. Mediators from each of these backgrounds may learn and utilize skills in different ways. This healthy diversity may also be reflected in the structure of mediation training and educational programs.

Substantive Knowledge. Mediators tend to specialize in disputes involving subjects, organizations, or settings that relate to their areas of interest, experience, or expertise. Although refined mediation skills may be effective regardless of the subject or setting, these skills are all the more likely to result in agreement when combined with substantive knowledge of the subject in dispute, the organizational milieu in which it occurs, and comfort with the unique conflict setting.

In order to mediate a labor dispute, the mediator, in addition to conflict resolution skills, should have a working knowledge of labor/management laws and regulations, some knowledge of union organization and dynamics, an understanding of management structure and concerns, and a sense of the relationship between management and the bargaining unit. It would be difficult to mediate an educational dispute involving a learning-impaired student without knowing about the curriculum, child development patterns, the special problems of the learning-impaired child, school district financial data, and the law regarding special education programs.

The group of mediators brought together by the Association of Family and Conciliation Courts in December 1982 also considered the specific concepts and substantive knowledge that mediators should possess for effective child custody and divorce mediation. This list included, in near equal parts, psychological concepts such as "negative intimacy" and also substantive legal knowledge like "tax problems." It is generally impracticable and probably unnecessary that mediators be cross-trained as clinical psychologists and attorneys or scientists or educators or any of the other combinations one could postulate. But the mediator must have a working knowledge of the substantive area and the interpersonal dynamics regarding the dispute in order to help the participants identify the issues, develop options, and recognize the need for consultation with experts or referral to others.

A mediator without a law school education can be knowledgeable enough about tax questions to recognize when an issue exists about capital gains treatment or allocation of income without necessarily being able to advise the parties on how to minimize the tax consequences or structure the agreement for the most favorable tax treatment. A lawyer-mediator can learn to recognize and point out stress-induced or grieving behavior without necessarily knowing how to treat it. Educating mediators to recognize the red flags of many different substantive areas, and to be aware of what can be accomplished by those of different disciplines, should be one of the principal goals of mediation training. Awareness of substantive issues in mediation, rather than proficiency in offering advice or treating the cause of the behavior, is the object of mediation preparation.

Mediation training may provide some skills identified with a therapist or a lawyer and some substantive knowledge of frequently mediated subjects such as divorce, environmental issues, and labor/management relations. Mediators, however, must guard against being seduced into thinking they can practice in these areas beyond that which is needed to help resolve the immediate dispute in mediation. Learning the tricks of the trade does not mean that one knows the trade. Knowing how to listen actively and paraphrase statements of feeling does not imply professional competence to deal with emotional disturbance. Likewise, knowing the basic tax treatment of spousal support as compared to child support does not make one a tax planner. Caution must be exercised by a mediator not to use cross-disciplinary knowledge outside the limited context of mediation. The primary aim should be to help participants develop options and know when to seek expert help.

Mediation Ethics and Standards of Practice. Any training program that purports to prepare people for professional service must imbue in them an understanding of the ethical restraints and standards by which their practice should be guided. Inclusion of ethics and standards in a training curriculum fulfills an obligation owed to the public and a commitment toward the emerging professionalization of mediation.

Those who come to mediation from other professions bring their own traditions for achieving fairness and dignity of practice. These traditions serve as a template that will shape their notions of fair proceedings in mediation. The template will not, however, apply perfectly to mediation; it will require reshaping, polishing, and even redesign. Those who approach the practice of mediation without the experience or training of another profession require an introduction to the importance of self-restraint when dealing with those who are subject to their power of suggestion or vulnerable to their position of authority. Standards of practice provide a shared expectation of competence and fair dealing only if those who provide a related service have some common thread of education, training, and understanding about those expectations.

Mediation, as a hybrid service, does not fit neatly into conventional cubbyholes of professional standards or existing ethical codes. Although existing codes and professional standards may be informative in setting guidelines for the practice of mediation that will help assure ethical and fair relationships with participants and colleagues, mediation is a distinct endeavor with a need for its own ethical code and standards. These standards are discussed in the next chapter.

Recommended Reading

Dispute Resolution Training: State of the Art. C. Gold and R. Lyons (Eds.). New York: American Arbitration Association, 1978.

Selected proceedings of a 1977 conference held in Racine, Wisconsin, on the subject of training "impartial intervenors" for all types of disputes. Contains papers on training for mediating community, labor, and commercial conflicts, including the training provided for Federal Conciliation Service mediators.

"Legal Education and the Dispute Resolution System." A. Sacks. In A. Sacks and F. Sander (Eds.), *The Lawyer's Changing Role in Resolving Disputes.* Cambridge: Harvard Law School, 1982.

A working draft presentation by the former dean of Harvard Law School in which he critically examines the law school curriculum as it relates to training for dispute resolution and suggests changes.

"Training Mediators for Family Dispute Resolution." C. W. Moore. In J. A. Lemmon (Ed.), *Successful Techniques for Mediating Family Breakup.* Mediation Quarterly, no. 2. San Francisco: Jossey-Bass, 1983.

A thoughtful discussion of the training needed in order to provide effective family mediation.

10

✼ ✼ ✼ ✼ ✼

Ethical, Professional, and Legal Issues

The very elements that make mediation so appealing compared to the adversarial model also create potential dangers and raise substantial professional, ethical, and legal issues. Mediation is conducted in private, often with no attorneys present. Because it is not tightly bound by rules of procedure, substantive law, and precedent, the question of whether the process is fair and productive of just results is presented. Because mediation represents an "alternative" to the adversarial system, it lacks the precise and perfected checks and balances that are the principal benefit of the adversary process. The purposeful "alegal" character of mediation creates a constant risk of dominance by the more knowledgeable, powerful, or less emotional party. Because mediation is a new practice that crosses traditional professional boundaries and recognizes the legal, emotional, and technical aspects of conflicts, there are concerns about interdisciplinary cooperation, struggles for territory, and assertions of professional dominance through claims of right, experience, or expertise. Tight economic times may draw marginal practitioners from many fields to what is viewed as a growth industry. Questions of standards, ethics, certification, and licensure are now being voiced, and delicate issues of confidentiality and liability are surfacing. Let us look now at these important issues.

Fairness

There are legitimate concerns that mediation may not be a fair process for some participants and that its widespread use may thwart justice. These concerns merit consideration and mediators should be prepared to address them. We shall attempt to state the concerns and respond to them.

Adversarial traditions and litigation provide a structure for resolving disputes within an exacting set of procedures that have been tested and refined to achieve fairness. Mediation, as an alternative to the adversarial system, is less hemmed in by rules of procedure, substantive law, and precedent. It lacks the precise and perfected checks and balances that are the principal benefit of the adversary process. Although some mediated agreements, such as marital settlements, require court approval, most do not. Even marital settlements are unlikely to be judicially scrutinized in detail because of their consensual nature. Private agreements requiring later enforcement by a court might be subject to judicial review at that time, but the standard of review is generally one of "unconscionability." Courts are appropriately reluctant to set aside or reform private agreements and contracts, so the unconscionability standard provides relief only for the most oppressive or grossly unfair provisions. The private nature of most mediation proceedings also precludes any meaningful public view of the process or evaluation of the result unless a problem of public dimension arises later.

These concerns about fairness, although serious, skirt the overriding feature and redeeming value of mediation—it is a consensual process that seeks self-determined resolutions. Mediation, unlike litigation, may appropriately recognize the collision of "legal" norms with "person-oriented" norms. These personal norms or principles, though not legally valid in court, may be important to the participants in reaching a fair settlement within the context of the issues and characteristics of their unique dispute. The accommodation of these colliding norms may produce an agreement no less principled for the disputants than a litigated result decided only on accepted legal norms or principles. A personal norm that considers fault relevant to the financial outcome of divorce may be

accommodated in mediation, for example, even though this principle is no longer legally relevant in the courts of many states. If it is
relevant in accommodating the parties' personal principles, knowing that fault would not be considered in court, can it be said that
the resulting settlement is less principled or fair? Suppose two
Christian businessmen are in a dispute over the penalties charged
for a late shipment of goods. Is a calculation of the penalty excluding sabbath days from the count of late days unfair because it would
not be calculated in the same way by a court?

The accommodation of these nonlegal principles is one of the
very advantages of private ordering that may make the settlement
more acceptable and lasting for the disputing parties (Mnookin and
Kornhauser, 1979). Mediation, in contrast to litigation, allows consideration of a larger universe of norms and principles and is more
open ended than court proceedings (Gulliver, 1979). The role and
evaluation of norms in dispute resolution is far from a simple matter
of quantitatively comparing court outcomes with those of alternative forms of dispute resolution.

The voiced concern about the fairness aspect of mediated
agreements tends to compare mediation with a romanticized notion
of formal justice. In considering whether mediated settlements will
be fair and just, we must ask "compared to what?" The adversarial
approach to dispute resolution does not require the parties to be
represented by lawyers and many are not. Nor does it impose a
mediator or "audience" when private bargaining is used to resolve
the dispute. It must be remembered that approximately 90 percent of
all cases filed in courts are bargained to an agreement before reaching trial. Many of the remaining cases go by default due to the
defendant's ignorance or lack of resources to prepare a defense.

The question of fairness in the outcome of a dispute should
be asked equally of all forms of dispute resolution, including bargained agreements and litigation. Many disputes resolved outside of
mediation are the result of unequal bargaining power due to different levels of experience, patterns of dominance, different propensi-
ties for risk avoidance, the greater emotional needs of one disputant,
or psychological obstacles in the path to settlement. Should the
matter proceed to litigation, the same items may skew the fairness of
the outcome in court as in the bargaining phase—and in addition

there may be unequal resources to bear the costs of litigation, different levels of sophistication in choosing the best attorneys, and just plain luck as to which judge is assigned to make a decision. These comments are not intended as unique criticisms of our adversarial or judicial systems; no dispute resolution mechanism is devoid of problems concerning fair outcomes, and none of the alternatives is the best for every dispute.

There are several safeguards relating to the fairness of mediation outcomes. The principal safeguard is the presence of a skilled and reasonable mediator—a knowledgeable third party to help the disputants evaluate their relative positions so that they can make reasoned decisions that seem fair to them after considering all relevant factors. The mediator serves as a check, though not necessarily a guarantor, against intimidation and overreaching. The mediator also acts as an agent of reality to help the parties probe whether their positions are realistic and what practical effects will flow from their choice of outcomes. The mediator, though impartial regarding the participants, has a responsibility to promote reasonableness—particularly since the outcome of a conflict may affect other parties, such as the public or the children of divorce. There is a difference between being nonpartisan and being unconcerned.

For some, mediation implies only a process of compromise in which each participant is urged to move toward a center position. Mediators must recognize that the demands and expectations that divide some disputants are so insane or productive of harm or evil, whether by design, emotional blindness, or greed, that no compromise should be made toward their realization. Though most positions are subject to reasonable compromise, some things cannot and should not be compromised. The mediator is there to facilitate the recognition of this possibility, not to hide behind the simplistic rubric that all positions can be compromised. The mediator's role is to guide the process of conflict resolution and management, not to be a magician who makes conflict vanish and produces an agreement in every case.

A second check on the fairness of a mediated agreement is contained in the stage that we have labeled legal review and processing (see Chapter Three). Independent legal review is a necessity in divorce settlements, labor contracts, environmental issues, and other legally oriented and complex disputes. The reviewing attorneys serve as a check to assure that all necessary items have been considered by the participants and that the proposed agreement accurately states their understanding. The reviewing attorneys might inform the individual participants of any other alternatives to the suggested terms and whether the points of agreement fall within acceptable legal norms. These norms are often raised in the context of the likely range of court decisions if agreement is not reached. The likelihood of a different court outcome than the proposed agreement must then be weighed against the costs in time, money, and emotional stress that may result from further negotiation, mediation, or litigation. The basic purpose of this independent legal review is to determine whether the agreement is "fair enough" not to take it back to the drawing board and if all necessary items have been covered.

Every mediated agreement, even if not legally reviewed, should be processed in a manner that allows a double check, a second opinion, or at least the passage of time in order to help avoid impetuous or pressured decisions. This processing may involve consultation with friends, advisers, constituents, or superiors. It may involve a trial implementation, registration, or, in some cases, judicial review.

A third check against an unfair mediation outcome is that mediation, as a cooperative process, serves as a model for future conflict resolution and adjustment between the participants. The participants are much more likely in a mediated situation to review and revise an unfair agreement. We suggest in our seven-stage mediation process (Chapter Three) that mediators make themselves available and encourage periodic review and, where appropriate, revision of the agreement. Most written mediated agreements stipulate that if the participants have any future disputes relating to the terms of the agreement, or if they are unable to reach agreement about revision should the circumstances change, they will resort to mediation. In contrast, the adversarial process tends to exacerbate hostilities and make future cooperation difficult. It is particularly unlikely that a court order or judgment will be changed by later stipulation. The legal doctrine of *res judicata*, except in child custody and domestic support cases, prevents suits for modification of previous judgments. Even in support and child custody cases, rules are imposed requiring a substantial change of circumstance before the matter can be reconsidered.

The concern is voiced that mediation may create a "two-track" system of justice. Informal dispute resolution will be available for poor people and those with small claims and minor disputes; justice according to law and with procedural safeguards will be reserved for the affluent. Ironically, the opposite concern is also leveled that mediation will become an increasingly expensive procedure, precluding its use by the poor and relegating them to traditional dispute resolution processes. Perhaps those who fear that mediation will be foisted on the poor as a litigation substitute are focusing on public mediation programs, while those who fear that the poor will be economically precluded from mediation are referring to private fee-for-service mediation.

These concerns that mediation will only be available for the rich or that the availability of public mediation programs may hinder access to the courts for the less affluent also romanticize litigation and blink at reality. The reality is that the poor have never had equal access to the courts; the current high cost of legal proceedings, coupled with inordinate delays in court dockets, has effectively limited litigation of choice to the wealthy. Interestingly, corporate giants are no more happy with the expense and delay of court proceedings than others, and many corporations and heavy users of the courts have joined the search for alternatives to litigation in resolving disputes between themselves (*Alternatives*, 1983).

The concern that private fee-for-service mediation will not be available for the least affluent is well taken. This concern, however, should not be limited to mediation but should be directed to all civil forms of dispute resolution. The fact that the poor cannot afford the costs of private mediators should parallel concern that the poor cannot afford the cost of private attorneys, therapists, and other professionals who might be able to help them with conflicts. It is easier to be critical of mediation than to eliminate poverty or devise comprehensive mechanisms for more equal access to professional services. Mediation may, indeed, provide a more cost-effective way to subsidize dispute resolution services for the poor while satisfying the affluent as a superior alternative to other dispute resolution mechanisms.

Standards of Practice and Ethical Limitations

As mediation struggles to become a profession, it will be increasingly important that standards be developed to establish minimum acceptable practices and that ethical limits be formulated regarding inappropriate mediator behavior. Public and professional acceptance of the role of mediation will be enhanced once standards of mediation practice are developed and made known.

Distinction Between Standards and Ethics. We have, for convenience, separated standards of practice from ethical limitations. The distinction between standards and ethics may be only academic, but it is helpful for our analysis. An ethical code is generally imposed on members of a professional group by its governing organization or as a condition of licensure or certification. Professional standards may exist outside an ethical code or in its absence and may be subscribed to by practitioners or looked to by the public and the courts as a set of expectations and minimally acceptable common practices for the service offered. The standards protect those served from harm and assure the integrity of the process. Following the standards in a competent manner should also protect the practitioner from legal liability by clarifying the limits of "reasonable care," as that term is used in the courts. We have approached our discussion of ethical limitations as the "do nots" imposed by existing ethical codes and regulations for other professions that either form the background of the mediator or touch upon aspects of mediation practice. We view standards as a positive statement of what is morally and socially expected from the process of mediation and from mediators.

Ethical Limitations. Mediation, as previously discussed, is a hybrid service drawing practitioners from different backgrounds and professions. Lawyers, psychiatrists, psychologists, therapists, social workers, counselors, nurses, arbitrators—all have ethical codes to guide their practices. The lawyer's code of professional responsibility is premised on adversarial procedures and the requirement that a lawyer represent but one side. Medical ethics are geared to diagnoses

of illness and treatment. The codes of various mental health professionals are based on a service orientation of assessment and therapy.
The American Arbitration Association's code of ethics for arbitrators is premised on procedural fairness and arbitrator decision making. It has not yet been determined what parts, if any, of these
separate codes apply to the practice of mediation, which differs to
some extent from the traditional practices of each profession. Each
set of codes implies a statement about the social and institutional
roles and expectations of the professional practice it addresses.
These roles and expectations do not always fit the mediation setting.

The codes for each profession and their official interpretations serve as red flags for mediators from those professions. When
applied to other professional practices, these codes can do little more
than provide a warning of where a mediator can go wrong and
where the dangers lie. They do not provide detailed protocols for
mediation. The existing professional codes transposed to mediation
do not so much furnish a criteria of what is expected as they inform
mediators of what to avoid.

Attorneys have been the most active professional group in
raising ethical questions about mediation. Lawyers consider dispute
resolution to be the business of lawyers. They have observed that
many conflicts that are mediated have a legal context as well as an
emotional or technical aspect. Lawyers, in their zeal to preserve the
adversary system and safeguard the complex checks and balances on
which it rests, have attempted to impose restraints on both lawyers
and nonlawyers who offer mediation services.

Events such as divorce, creation of a partnership, preparation
of a will, drafting of real estate documents, and countless other
dealings between people usually create conflicting interests. Most
transactions involve adverse as well as complementary interests. The
process of dealing with these events need not be adversarial. An
adversarial process tends to emphasize conflicting interests at the
expense of complementary or joint interests. A cooperative process
tends to emphasize complementary interests while overlooking conflicting interests. Both approaches present ethical risks for lawyers
or others serving as mediators. These risks might be minimized by
identifying conflicting interests, managing them through media-

tion, and then urging independent review outside the mediation process before an agreement is completed.

Restraints on Attorneys.

Bar Opinions. The bar is concerned that attorneys not run afoul of the American Bar Association's *Model Code of Professional Responsibility* (1969), particularly canon 5. This canon, which prohibits representation of conflicting interests, presupposes that lawyers function in an adversarial mode. Nonadversarial lawyering is seldom referred to in the code. The code's narrow adversarial model of a lawyer's role denies the reality that many lawyers primarily counsel clients in ways unrelated to legal conflict, courts, or litigation. Lawyers often advise and counsel clients in the context of planning to maximize gain and avoid disputes.

Tension exists between the adversarial norm of the Model Code and the popular perception that lawyers exacerbate conflicts by their adversarial fixation. Bar ethics committees in Boston, Oregon, Maryland, Virginia, Connecticut, and New York City have issued cautious professional responsibility rulings that have allowed mediation by attorneys under circumscribed conditions. Each of these opinions was based on a question concerning divorce mediation. State ethics committees in Minnesota, Washington, Wisconsin, and New Hampshire appear more cautious, if not prohibitive, about an attorney serving as a family mediator, though each of these opinions can be read to indicate that some mediation approaches may provide adequate ethical safeguards.

The message that emerges from the ethics opinion in jurisdictions that allow attorneys to serve as mediators or advise participants before a mediated agreement is finalized is that the participants must be made aware of the attorney's limited role and the risks of mediation. The mediation participants must explicitly understand that a mediating attorney cannot advance either party's interest over the interest of the other and can give only nonpartisan legal advice to each party in the presence of the other. It must be explained that the attorney's role is dependent upon full disclosure of all relevant facts by the participants and that in a divorce case without full disclosure the settlement may be set aside by the court upon the insistence of either party. The participants must be urged to obtain independent review of the agreement and must be aware from the outset that the attorney may not represent any or all of them in any proceeding relating to the conflict or in any subsequent capacity.

New Model Rules of Professional Conduct. The ethical rulings just referred to are based on state adaptations and interpretations of the *Model Code of Professional Responsibility*. The code was approved by the American Bar Association (ABA) in 1969 and now serves as the ethical standard for lawyers in most states, although each state bar is free to write its own code or adopt modifications. The ABA Commission on Evaluation of Professional Standards (popularly referred to as the "Kutak Commission," after its late chairman) drafted a new model code of ethics that, following years of debate, was approved by the ABA in August 1983. The new *Model Rules of Professional Conduct,* unlike the prior code, recognize the distinct function of a lawyer as a "counselor," as well as an "advocate." Rule 2 now divides the lawyer's counseling function into three parts: "adviser," "intermediary," and "evaluation for use by third persons." The adviser role is phrased in terms of advising a single client, though the comment and notes accompanying the proposed rules would not appear to preclude advising a family or serving as adviser to multiple parties. Some attorneys who mediate see themselves as advisers to all participants rather than legally representing them. Mediation, if defined as commonly advising clients rather than representing them, might be allowed within the purview of the proposed rule on the lawyer as adviser.

Serving multiple clients as an intermediary, however, is separately addressed in the new model rules. Rule 2.2, "Intermediary," section (a), sets forth the following conditions that are required before a lawyer may ethically act as an intermediary:

1. The lawyer consults with each client concerning the implications of the common representation, including the advantages and risks involved and the effect on the attorney/client privileges, and obtains each client's consent to the common representation.

2. The lawyer reasonably believes that the matter can be resolved on terms compatible with the clients' best interests, that each client will be able to make adequately informed decisions in the matter, and

that there is little risk of material prejudice to the interests of any of the clients if the contemplated resolution is unsuccessful.

3. The lawyer reasonably believes that the common representation can be undertaken impartially and without improper effect on other responsibilities the lawyer has to any of the clients.

Section 2.2(b) also requires the lawyer acting as intermediary between clients to "consult with each client concerning the decisions to be made and the considerations relevant to making them, so that each client can make adequately informed decisions."

The commission's comment on rule 2.2 states that a lawyer acts as an intermediary when the lawyer "represents" all parties in seeking to establish or adjust a relationship "between clients" on an amicable and mutually advantageous basis. It lists as an example "mediating a dispute between clients" along with other examples, including helping to organize a business between two parties, working out the financial reorganization of an enterprise, and other forms of "common representation." The comment declares "the rule does not apply to a lawyer acting as . . . mediator between or among parties who are not clients of the lawyer, even where the lawyer has been appointed with the concurrence of the parties. In performing such a role the lawyer may be subject to [other] applicable codes of ethics."

This new rule and the accompanying commentary distinguish between serving as an intermediary between clients and serving as a mediator between those who are not clients. The ABA apparently recognizes in the model rules that it does not directly govern lawyers acting as mediators between those who are not represented by the lawyer-mediator as clients. The key word *clients* is used to trigger applicability of the model rules. It is, however, not clear when a lawyer represents participants in mediation such that they become clients and when the participants can seek the lawyer's help as a mediator but never become clients.

Presumably a lawyer who serves as a mediator outside of the law office, gives no legal advice or opinions, and does not draw up an agreement is not acting in any legal capacity and is not then governed by the lawyer's code. This would, however, be a rare case. More often the lawyer would offer impartial legal advice or explain the law to the participants. Does the lawyer-mediator then "represent" the participants as "clients"?

Opinions in Boston, New York City, and Connecticut, which allow lawyer mediation, characterize the lawyer-mediator as representing neither of the parties, although these opinions anticipate and allow the lawyer to give impartial legal advice in the presence of all participants. A similar Oregon opinion that allows impartial lawyer mediation while characterizing the mediator's role as "representing" all participants appears to be a semantic mishap. Bar opinions in states that prohibit lawyers from serving as mediators seem to assume that a lawyer-mediator must represent all the participants as a form of "common representation." Adoption of the new ABA model rules in these states may require a reexamination of their prohibitive bar opinions.

Restraints on Co-mediation Teams. Surprisingly, teaming clinicians with lawyers, in part to prevent either from going beyond his or her field of expertise, seems to present more ethical issues than if either professional proceeds alone. An Oregon Bar Association opinion (1980) indicates that an attorney can cautiously offer solo mediation services without running afoul of ethical restrictions. When the same attorney teams with a mental health professional, however, there are serious concerns about possible violations of canon 3, which requires a lawyer to assist in the prevention of unauthorized law practice and prohibits a lawyer from practicing in partnership or splitting fees with a nonlawyer. It does seem odd that canon 3 restrictions should impede the use of interdisciplinary mediation teams, since one of the very purposes of the team approach is to prevent "unauthorized practice." There are also potential canon 2 problems with solicitation and use of a trade name when a lawyer participates in a divorce mediation center or clinic. These problems can generally be avoided with careful structuring of the practice and sensitivity to the legitimate concerns of the bar, as occurred in the Oregon case.

Restraints on Nonlawyers. A counselor, psychologist, or other nonlawyer who serves as a divorce mediator is not governed by the lawyer's code of professional ethics. If the mediator is a member of another professional discipline, however, he or she will have to look at that profession's code of ethics. These standards are not codified in as much detail as those of lawyers, who thrive on codes and rules, and they provide fewer answers to the unique ethical issues raised by family mediation. Can a therapist serve as a mediator before or after providing services to one or both parties as a therapist? Can a mediator employed by an agency or court ethically comply with an agency or court requirement that the mediator offer a recommendation for an imposed resolution if the participants do not reach agreement? Can a private mediator advertise his or her mediation services along with other services? What is the ethical responsibility of a nonlawyer mediator to know whether a proposed agreement is legally enforceable?

In offering mediation, nonlawyers run the risk of engaging in the unauthorized practice of law, thus subjecting themselves to misdemeanor or contempt charges. The primary issue in unauthorized practice investigations is whether the nonlawyer has engaged in activities properly constituting the practice of law. The cases provide little guidance on what is considered to be the practice of law in this area.

Mental health professionals offering mediation might argue that any legal advice they give and any agreement they help write out in mediation are only "incidental" or necessary to the practice of their own profession and that, therefore, they fall outside the prohibition of unauthorized law practice. This justification has allowed title insurance companies to draft legal documents connected with conveyances, real estate brokers to fill out form documents as part of property transactions, and accountants to advise their clients on tax issues.

It has generally been held that the offering for sale of a prepared lay divorce kit containing forms, explanations for using the forms, and information concerning the relevant divorce law, usually written by an attorney, is not prohibited. Courts in a few states have held to the contrary, though. It has also been held that providing scrivener services—that is, filling in the blanks as requested by divorcing couples without offering individualized legal advice—is not the prohibited practice of law. On the other hand, where nonlawyers offer interviews, explanations, advice, help in selecting the appropriate form, and other assistance to divorcing couples, the services are the unauthorized practice of law, which is enjoinable or punishable. In divorce mediation, nonlawyers should be particularly cautious about preparing comprehensive marital settlement agreements. Drafting such documents for submission to a court for approval has traditionally been the work of attorneys and can be quite technical. To avoid being charged with the practice of law, a nonlawyer should clearly advise each participant to have the agreement reviewed by an attorney *before* signing it and the agreement should not purport to be in final form. The nonlegal nature of the document should be indicated by labeling it a "mediated plan" or "memorandum of agreement."

Attorneys are reluctant to do anything that might appear to promote the unauthorized practice of law. In a 1962 opinion, for example, the Los Angeles County Bar ruled that an attorney could not be retained by a family counseling service to give legal advice to the organization's clients. The committee warned that the attorney might be promoting the unauthorized practice of law by marriage counselors who advised clients with reference to the laws relating to family relationships.

Bar associations, perhaps sensitive to the charge that their policing efforts are motivated more by economic protection of lawyers than by concern for the public good, have issued few formal opinions on the subject nor have they pursued prosecution of nonlawyer mediators. More bar opinions and charges may result as the practice of mediation by nonlawyers grows. The North Carolina State Bar Association (1980), through its Unauthorized Practice of Law Committee, has ruled that a nonprofit organization offering a divorce mediation service requiring participating couples to sign an agreement by which they would be required to submit unresolved disputes to binding arbitration was engaged in the unauthorized practice of law. The New York City Bar Committee (1981), in approving a mediation program undertaken by a nonprofit mental health organization, assumed laymen could perform divorce mediation activities without exercising professional legal judgment and without engaging in the unauthorized practice of law. The committee concluded, however, that it was beyond its jurisdiction to decide whether the mental health professionals in the proposed divorce mediation program would be engaged in the unauthorized practice of law.

Nonlawyer mediators with unique expertise relating to the subject in dispute, the emotional aspects of the conflict, or the dispute resolution process would appear to present a strong case for relaxation of the unauthorized practice of law restrictions. Mediation is truly a different service than that traditionally offered by attorneys. Legal information is only an incidental component of the larger mediation task of helping to resolve conflicts. Mediation may not be less costly in terms of professional fees and is not generally offered as a way to avoid the costs of legal advice. If viewed as a distinct and valuable service in its own right rather than as a substitute for legal advice, mediation complements legal services and should not be considered the unauthorized practice of law. This distinction between mediation practice and legal practice might be made more clear by the formulation of a positive set of practice standards for mediators that recognizes mediation as a separate profession that stands on its own.

Standards of Practice. Standards of practice help clarify the goals of a service, improve its quality, and enhance the public image of the service provider (see Van Hoose and Kottler, 1977, p. 103). One element in the definition of a profession is acceptance and adherence to common standards of practice. It is standards that help distinguish one profession from another and separate professions from trades.

Professional standards are necessary because the results of professional services can only be judged by the integrity of the process and not by immediate outcomes. The services offered cannot be easily weighed or measured and the good or harm that comes from the service will not be fully known until much later, when error or a lack of integrity cannot be readily corrected. The quality of the professional service can probably not be evaluated by the client except by comparing it with the standards established for the practice.

The difficulty of establishing standards of practice for a newly emerging profession is that the standards must emanate from a common perception of the goals of the practice as well as its social role. In order to be coherent and widely accepted, the standards must accurately portray what the practice is all about and what makes it a distinctive service with a need for a separate set of practice standards. Because mediation does not yet have an academic base with an accepted curriculum, nor a dominant professional organization that could declare its purpose or regulate entry to practice, there have been no universally accepted criteria for structuring standards of practice.

Other professions with some nexus to mediation have developed written professional standards. These standards reflect countless hours of committee work, refinement through practice application, and, in some cases, court tests. Mediators and mediation organizations can look to the standards of their profession of origin for a guide to standards for the practice of mediation, but they should not stop there.

Some national associations and a few local organizations of mediators have proposed or adopted a code of professional conduct, either for mediators in general or as standards of practice for mediation specialties. The impact of these mediation standards might depend on whether they are just a matter of personal subscription or whether they are imposed as a requirement for professional affiliation, specialty declaration within a recognized profession like law or counseling, membership within a local organization or network of mediators, employment by an agency or court, licensure, or certification.

Though there are several sets of standards or codes of conduct for mediators now in circulation, two appear to be especially thoughtful as positive statements of what is expected from mediators. The first is the *Code of Professional Conduct for Mediators* developed by Christopher W. Moore and adopted by the Center for Dispute Resolution (1982) in Denver, Colorado. It is a general code applicable to all types of mediation (See Resource D). The second, *Standards of Practice for Divorce Mediators*, is, as its title indicates, directed to the growing specialty of divorce mediation. It was adopted in principle by the Council of Family Law Section of the American Bar Association in 1983 following development by a special task force. The concern for the role of independent legal advice and counsel is, understandably, particularly evident in the bar association standards. Interestingly, the ABA task force standards were initially prepared by Thomas A. Bishop, who was simultaneously appointed to help prepare mediation standards for the Association of Family and Conciliation Courts and for the Academy of Family Mediators. This interlocking type of activity, which is not atypical among the organizations interested in the emerging professional application of mediation, is one way to achieve a common set of expectations and similar standards.

Licensure and Certification

There is currently some regulation of the qualifications of mediators in the public sector. Statutory and administrative requirements exist regarding the credentials and experience for court-connected mediators and other public employees serving as mediators. A master's degree in counseling, social work, or a related field and substantial working experience are required for employment as a family mediator in the courts of California, Connecticut, Nevada, and Oregon. Some states allow certain types of additional experience to be substituted for the required master's degree, and the State of Michigan, in its friends of the court mediation legislation, expressly authorizes lawyers trained in mediation to serve as a friend of the court. (See Comeaux, 1983.) Some administrative rules regulating procedures for mandated mediation for medical malpractice claims, public employee labor disputes, and claims against government bodies establish requirements of education or relevant experience in the subject area in order to qualify as a mediator in these disputes. Similarly, some mediation programs established by court rule to help alleviate congested litigation dockets require that mediators be members of the bar with practice experience or establish their expertise in the subject of the dispute.

There is currently no legal regulation of mediation in the private sector. Although there has been considerable discussion about the need for such regulation, many question whether the public good would be served by regulation of mediation at this time. Before considering the pros and cons of that debate, let us first look at the most common methods for regulating the practice of other professional services.

Licensing Acts. Licensing statutes typically define the professional practice and describe the nature of the activities allowed. A true licensing statute also bans those who are not licensed from practicing the covered profession. Administering the examination and determining qualifications for licensure, as well as the practical task of policing unauthorized practice, is sometimes delegated by the state to a professional organization. This is the case in many states regarding licensing of attorneys. (See Cathcart and Graff, 1978.)

Certification Acts. Certification legislation generally authorizes the use of certain titles or descriptive words to portray the services offered by certified individuals. These acts expressly or by implication proscribe the use of these titles or descriptive words by those who are not certified. Specialty certification sometimes exists within more comprehensive licensed professions. Certification statutes generally provide no criminal sanctions. These acts, as a practical matter, have only an indirect effect in regulating how professionals might advertise or announce themselves and in helping to determine the standard of care that might be imposed in a lawsuit alleging civil liability for negligence. Certification may also be a prerequisite for insurance or third-party payment for services rendered. Recommendations for certification or actual certification may be handled by a state board or agency or, as in the case of licensure, delegated to a professional association.

Other Regulatory Controls. There are a number of other mechanisms that regulate entry into a professional practice or delineate those with certain training and experience. Other methods of regulation and control seldom have as great an impact as licensure and certification. Some state agencies, courts, or private organizations may keep a *registry* of mediators who meet certain minimum requirements for employment or referral of cases. Other agencies, courts, or community organizations may require *subscription* to a standard of practice or code of ethics before they will list or use a mediator. Some governmental departments, private agencies, and professional organizations may *accredit* educational courses or mediation training programs and then require certain accredited courses as a condition of mediation employment or referral. Criteria may also be established for inclusion in a government-sponsored or private *directory* or *listing* of mediation services. (See Milne, 1982.)

Pros and Cons of Regulation. Some would argue that the public has a right to the protection of licensure or certification of mediators. Nonregulation invites charlatans and incompetents of all stripes to offer their services as mediators to an unknowing public that may not have adequate information or criteria to make an intelligent choice of a mediator.

There are, however, substantive, procedural, territorial, and constitutional questions raised about certification and even more about licensure. Carl Rogers (1973) believes that licensure for therapists has had the effect of stagnating professional practice. He states that licensure examination questions are often drawn from material used ten to twenty years earlier and that examiners tend to have been trained fifteen to twenty years earlier. Others argue that licensing systems have the effect of reducing competition and establishing barriers designed to restrict entry to a profession. This criticism flows in part from the observation that licensing legislation is usually proposed and submitted by professional groups that will benefit economically from the licensure (Cathcart and Graff, 1978).

Licensure and certification procedures, to the extent that they are effective, tend to bar some from practice or deny them the same benefits as those who are licensed or certified. These procedures may therefore be challenged as violating the due process clause of the Fourteenth Amendment to the United States Constitution. Frequent challenges have been made of other licensing statutes, subjecting them to court review and occasional declarations of invalidity. (See, generally, Cathcart and Graff, 1978.)

Because the practice of mediation as we know it is still relatively new, we cannot be sure of the exact qualifications necessary for providing the service effectively and assuring protection of the public interest. There are few academic programs in the field of mediation. Only isolated examples of harm from incompetent mediation have been reported. We are witnessing some struggles for mediation turf between established professional associations and new organizations dedicated to promoting the interest of their mediator membership. No single organization currently appears able to provide unity and direction to the profession. For all these reasons, it would appear premature to limit entry into the field by state-sanctioned licensing or certification.

We should welcome the diversity that is emerging as many individuals, agencies, and organizations become involved in offering mediation services. The very real risks of unregulated practice and the few instances of harm and abuse that may result are, at this early stage, outweighed by rewards to the public of diversity of service and consumer choice. After all, one of the basic propositions of mediation is that people can make better decisions about their own lives than can an outside authority (Proposition 3 in Chapter One). Should we not also promote free choice in the selection of a mediator, at least until it is clear that the harm of nonregulation outweighs the benefits of consumer options?

Most efforts to license and certify those who provide other professional services have created bureaucratic structures that have fallen prey to economic self-protection by those who benefit from erecting regulatory fences around their practices. Public sentiment eventually responds with calls for removal of the protection initially intended to benefit the public. The time may soon come when certification or licensure of mediators is necessary to prevent abuses, but there is not yet enough known about mediation to restrict the practice beyond prohibiting aggrandized claims and unethical procedures. This should not be interpreted as an argument against statutory qualifications for those offering public-sector mediation, particularly when the mediation is mandated by statute, regulation, or court rule.

Perhaps the less restrictive steps of establishing mediation registries, requiring subscriptions to acceptable standards of practice, accrediting educational and training programs, and listing the qualifications and experience of mediators could provide adequate public protection until there is more evidence of the need for licensure and more knowledge about what would best protect the public. Additionally, there would appear to be some benefit and little harm in encouraging licensed professions to certify specialists in mediation. The certification could be structured not to bar others from mediating, but the certified specialists would be recognized as having met not only licensure requirements within a traditional profession but also special expertise in the theory and skills of mediation.

Confidentiality

The question of confidentiality arises in two separate contexts. It is important to distinguish between privacy from public disclosure and a privilege against court testimony. A mediator may not share with friends intimate secrets about mediation participants or write about them in a newspaper, even if the mediator could be compelled to reveal the same information in court.

Privacy and Privilege. Mediators are bound not to discuss with other people what is revealed to them in mediation unless such revelations are agreed to by the participants or compelled by a court order or statute. The expectation of privacy arises from the private nature of many disputes subject to mediation, from the professional restraints on the mediator, from statutory provision in some jurisdictions, from common law, from public policy, and often from the contract to mediate. Each of these reasons for the expectation of privacy is separately considered below.

It may be assumed that mediators are bound not to discuss with others what is revealed to them in mediation; however, that does not necessarily mean that comments made during the mediation process are privileged against either of the parties testifying in court about what was said or against the court compelling testimonial disclosure by the mediator. A privilege protecting either or both clients from testifying in court about what was said to a confidant outside of court is a technical matter determined by statutes and court rulings. No evidentiary privilege exists unless created by statute or required by public policy and then only within the strict terms of the statutory wording or the precise purpose of the public policy.

The Need for Privacy. There is general agreement that the success of mediation is dependent upon an expectation of privacy and confidentiality. If the participants do not trust that the mediation is private and that revelations will be held in confidence by the mediator, they may be reserved in revealing relevant information and hesitant to disclose potential accommodations that may appear to compromise earlier positions. It is generally thought that an absence of trust in the privacy of a mediation session "dooms the success of the conference before it begins" (Pottmeyer, 1983).

One of the mediator's tasks is to help the disputants unlock earlier positions preventing settlement and move toward agreement without losing face or feeling embarrassment for backing off from fixed positions. Fear that disclosure of the accommodation will make them appear weak, uncommitted, or insincere may inhibit the give-and-take essential for successful mediation. Participants cannot be assured that mediation will result in settlement. If mediation proceeds under a cloud that what is said may be used adversely in a later battle or court proceeding, necessary candor and willingness to offer compromises or reveal weaknesses cannot reasonably be expected.

Like everything else in mediation, privacy and confidentiality are not absolutes. Labor disputes and public-sector conflicts may not always demand or allow the strict privacy accompanying private disputes. In some neighborhood dispute resolution programs, it is thought that privacy may breed distrust. The San Francisco Community Boards require that all mediation sessions be public and that the terms of mediated agreements be available to all. Public exposure is, however, an exception. (See Vorenberg, 1982, pp. 31–32.) The more commonly held wisdom is expressed by Simkin (1971, p. 33): "Confidential characteristics of the mediator's relationship with the parties are critical to useful performance. To violate a real confidence would destroy the mediator's effectiveness."

In considering whether a mediator from the Federal Mediation and Conciliation Service should be required to testify in an adversary proceeding following unsuccessful mediation, the National Labor Relation's Board has consistently recognized the importance of confidential mediation. In a noted and frequently cited case (*Tomlinson of High Point, Inc.*, 1947, p. 688), the board stated its reason for not requiring the mediator to testify:

> The inevitable result would be that the usefulness of the Conciliation Service in the settlement of future disputes would be seriously impaired, if not destroyed. The resultant injury to the public interest would clearly outweigh the benefit to be derived from making their testimony available in particular cases.

Professional Standards and Confidentiality. The professional codes and standards of practice of professions that contribute to mediation, as discussed in the previous section, emphasize the importance of privacy and the protection of confidentiality. These codes may or may not apply when a person trained in a traditional

profession offers mediation. If in doubt, most professionals will
proceed cautiously and follow the restrictions imposed by their professional background—their profession of origin.

The new *Model Rules of Professional Conduct* adopted by
the American Bar Association in 1983 continue to require lawyers to
preserve the confidences and secrets of a client with one principal
exception to prevent criminal acts "likely to result in imminent
death or substantial bodily harm" (American Bar Association, 1983,
1-6(b)(1)). Even this concession to prevent death or serious bodily
harm has been a subject of great controversy among lawyers. The
Principles of Medical Ethics adopted by the American Psychiatric
Association (1973) promote confidentiality as follows: "A physician
may not reveal the confidences entrusted to him in the course of
medical attendance or the deficiencies he may observe in the character of patients unless he is required to do so by law or unless it
becomes necessary in order to protect the welfare of the individual or
of the community" (section VI).

The American Association for Marriage and Family Therapy
recently approved a new set of ethical principles (1982) requiring
that "family therapists respect both the law and the rights of clients
and safeguard client confidences as permitted by law" (section IV). A
code of ethics has been adopted by the National Association of Social Workers (1980) that contains admonitions about the protection
of privacy. Enforcement of confidentiality through the use of malpractice suits against social workers has, however, proved difficult.
(See *Martino* v. *Family Services Agency of Adams County*, 1983,
p. 2311.) The code of ethics of the American Personnel and Guidance
Association (1974) has restrictions intended to preserve confidentiality, including one to the effect that the counseling relationship and
information resulting therefrom shall be kept confidential, consistent with the obligations of the member as a professional person.

Canon VI of the *Code of Ethics for Arbitrators in Commercial
Disputes* (American Arbitration Association, 1977) provides that "an
arbitrator should be faithful to the relationship of trust and confidentiality inherent in that office." Subsection B under canon VI goes
on to state: "Unless otherwise agreed by the parties or required by
applicable rules of law, an arbitrator should keep confidential all
matters relating to the arbitration proceedings and decisions." The

Code of Professional Conduct for Labor Mediators (1971), adopted jointly by the Federal Mediation and Conciliation Service and the several state agencies represented by the Association of Labor Mediation Agencies, recognizes the importance of privacy: "Confidential information required by the mediator should not be disclosed to others for any purpose or in a legal proceeding or be used directly or indirectly for the personal benefit or profit of the mediator" (section 5). The progress made toward reaching settlement of the labor dispute is accorded a lesser degree of privacy: "It is recognized that labor disputes are settled at the bargaining table; however, the mediator may release appropriate information with due regard (1) to the desires of the parties, (2) to whether that information will assist or impede the settlement of the dispute, and (3) to the needs of an informed public" (section 4). The Academy of Family Mediators (1982), as the leading organization representing divorce mediators, has proposed standards that specify the mediator's duty to protect the privacy and confidentiality of the mediation process. This duty is expressly limited by the mediator's "inability to bind third parties in the absence of any absolute privilege" (section 3(b)).

Statutory and Common Law Privileges. Lawyers, physicians, psychologists, social workers, nurses, the clergy, and certain other professionals may have the benefit in their work of privileges of confidentiality protected by statute. For example, a physician/patient privilege was created by statute in New York in 1828 (New York Civil Practice Act, 1920, sections 352 and 354), and most states have since passed similar legislation. (See the listing of statutory enactments in "Confidential Communications to a Psychotherapist," 1952, p. 385, n. 7.) The coverage of these statutes varies from state to state. (See "Privileged Communications," 1971, which collects and analyzes state statutes creating a privilege for mental health professionals.)

Although professional privileges are generally a matter of statutory creation, some courts have been willing, as a matter of public policy, to recognize an evidentiary privilege in the absence of a statute. The test most commonly used by the courts to determine whether information communicated in a helping relationship should be barred from courtroom exposure is a four-part inquiry developed by Dean Wigmore (1935, p. 527):

1. The communication must have been imparted in confidence that it would not be disclosed to others.
2. The preservation of secrecy must be essential to the success of the relationship.
3. The relationship must be one that society wishes to foster and protect.
4. Any injury to the relationship caused by disclosure must outweigh the expected benefit to be derived from compelling disclosure.

In other than mediation cases, courts faced with a request for privilege in the absence of a protective statute have most often held that the benefits of compelling disclosure were greater than the injury to the professional relationship and the privilege has been denied (see "Underprivileged Communications," 1973). The only two court decisions known to have weighed the injury to the mediation process against the benefit from compelling disclosure, as suggested by Wigmore, have both ruled to protect the confidentiality of mediation from courtroom disclosures.

The Ninth U.S. Circuit Court of Appeals was presented a classic situation where the mediator's testimony was crucial in an unfair labor practice case to determine which of the adverse sides was telling the truth about what went on at the mediation sessions. The appellate court affirmed a trial court order refusing to require the federal mediator to testify. The court considered Wigmore's test of harm to the cause of truth versus injury to a greater public interest (in this case mediation) and ruled in favor of upholding the confidentiality of mediation. (See *National Labor Relations Board* v. *Macaluso*, 1980.) The court in this National Labor Relations Board case confirmed the importance that mediation participants "must feel free to talk without any fear that the conciliator may subsequently make disclosures as a witness in some other proceeding, to the possible disadvantage of a party to the conference" (p. 55). The court concluded: "The complete exclusion of mediator testimony is necessary to the preservation of an effective system of labor mediation, and . . . labor mediation is essential to continued industrial stability, a public interest sufficiently great to outweigh the interest in obtaining every person's evidence" (p. 56).

In *Adler* v. *Adams* (1979), the United States District Court for the Western District of Washington issued an order to protect from disclosure the testimony and notes of private mediators who had earlier helped resolve an environmental dispute. The court held that "requiring a mediator to make such disclosure would severely inhibit the proper performance of his or her duties, and thereby undercut the effectiveness of the mediation process. There is a substantial public interest in fostering effective mediation techniques in settlement of disputes" (p. 3). The court did, however, require the mediators to produce documents that the participants had presented at those mediation sessions open to the public or furnished to the mediator by sources not party to the mediation.

Limits on Testimonial Privilege. A testimonial privilege protects the confiding party against court disclosure of what was said only if the statements were necessary for the rendition of the professional service that the privilege protects. If our definition of mediation as a nontherapeutic process is accepted, for example, the privilege protecting the confidentiality of therapeutic services would never attach. Likewise, if an attorney does not purport to be practicing law while offering mediation services, the attorney/client privilege would not exist. Courts have ruled that an attorney acting as a friend, business adviser, estate executor, or negotiator does not come within the statutory privilege protecting the attorney/client relationship. (See, for example, *Myles and Resiser Co.* v. *Loew's, Inc.,* 1948.) Nor does the attorney/client privilege apply in a court proceeding between people who had earlier been jointly represented by the same attorney. This latter rule would appear to doom application of the attorney/client privilege in most cases of lawyer mediation.

It should also be noted that the privilege against courtroom disclosure belongs to the client and not to the professional provider. The client may waive the privilege. In other words, if the client of a lawyer or therapist chooses to have the information made available in a court proceeding—or more accurately does not object to testimony about the information—the lawyer or therapist cannot invoke the privilege.

Statements made in the presence of an adverse party also defeat most traditional privileges. In mediation, even if it were characterized as a legal, therapeutic, or other privileged relationship, the presence of an adverse party who may be on the other side of a court proceeding would effectively void the privilege. Statements made in the presence of an adverse party are generally not privileged because the lips of the adverse party are not sealed from that which they hear from their opponent. If the adverse party is able to testify about what was stated, there is no policy served by preventing others present from testifying about what was said. Again we must distinguish between privacy from general public disclosure by the mediator, which is to be expected, and a privilege against court testimony, which is defeated by the presence of an adverse party. (See Cleary and others, 1972, pp. 189–190.)

Similarly, if the otherwise privileged communication is knowingly made in the presence of people not party or necessary to the session, then the information cannot be privileged. (See Cleary and others, 1972, p. 187.) Thus the information presented at public sessions in the environmental mediation case of *Adler* v. *Adams* could not be privileged, even though the information provided in private sessions with the mediators was protected. There must be a reasonable expectation of confidentiality before it exists.

Settlement Confidentiality. Another basis for keeping statements made during mediation out of the courts is that offers of settlement and statements and evidence of conduct during negotiations for settlement are generally inadmissible, even though the common law rule may have been to the contrary (Cleary and others, 1972, pp. 663–666). It would follow that if mediation is a type of settlement negotiation between the parties, statements made to facilitate the mediated settlement should be protected. A statute could define mediation as a settlement process and expressly declare it to be public policy that discussions during mediation be confidential and inadmissible. Such a statute might clarify the considerable uncertainty existing in some jurisdictions on this issue of whether mediation fits the settlement provisions of the confidentiality rules.

Even in the absence of new legislation, the existing public policy of promoting private settlement of potential litigation might be persuasive to a court considering the issue of admissibility of testimony revealing what was said during mediation. The court would have to weigh the benefit to justice in obtaining the testimony against the injury to the process of mediation through fear of later disclosure. (See, generally, Waltz and Huston, 1979.)

The modern evidentiary rule that bars offers of compromise, as well as evidence of conduct or statements made in compromise negotiations (*Federal Rules of Evidence* 408, 1975), is generally qualified to allow use of evidence discoverable by other means than what was revealed during negotiations. In other words, the policy is to prevent a participant from immunizing otherwise available evidence by presenting it during mediation. If, for example, evidence of child abuse already existed, it does not become inadmissible because it is additionally blurted out during custody mediation. There is also a question whether statements made in mediation are generally protected against disclosure in a subsequent criminal prosecution (McGinness and Cinquegrama, 1982).

Contract Confidentiality. Most private mediators require their clients to sign an agreement expressly providing that the mediation sessions will be confidential and that the mediator will not be called to testify about what is said or to give any professional opinion related to the case in court. A court would not necessarily be bound to honor this private contract, though it may be persuaded by public policy considerations to do so.

At least one appellate opinion, *Simrin* v. *Simrin* (1965), has held enforceable an express agreement that communications made during marriage counseling would be privileged and that neither spouse would call the counselor at a divorce trial, even though there was no direct statutory protection. The wife argued that to hold her to her bargain with her husband and the counselor, a rabbi, would sanction a contract to suppress evidence contrary to public policy promoting the admissibility of evidence relevant to child custody. The California Court of Appeals recognized that "for the unwary spouse who speaks freely, repudiation [of the confidentiality agreement] would prove a trap; for the wily, a vehicle for making self-serving declarations" (p. 95). The court compared the public policy favoring marriage counseling to the general evidentiary policy protecting "statements that are made in offers of compromise and to avoid or settle litigation, which are not admissible in evidence" (p. 95).

Other courts have implied an agreement to be bound by mediation confidentiality if the unwritten confidential policy was reasonably known to the participants. (See *National Labor Relations Board* v. *Macaluso*, 1980.) A court could also hold that a signatory to the contract to mediate in confidence was equitably estopped from calling the mediator to testify or that it will not compel the mediator, a nonlitigant, to breach a contract. One former spouse could sue the other for breach of the mediation contract in a separate proceeding if damages could be proved. Perhaps one of the principal values of such a contract provision for confidentiality is the moral constraint it places on each party to honor their commitment and recognize the importance of confidentiality, even if mediation does not result in a complete settlement.

Mediation Statutes and Court Rules. Traditional professional privileges do not assure an evidentiary privilege for the confidentiality of mediation, and there are not enough favorable court decisions to guarantee mediation confidentiality. Until mediation becomes a distinct and licensed profession, it is unlikely that a general statutory privilege will exist parallel to those for other professions dependent on trust. Many existing statutory privileges are contained in licensing legislation. (See "Privileged Communications," 1971.)

The legislature could, however, create a privilege specifically designed to shield mediation confidentiality. When mediation is sanctioned or compelled by statute, the statute may provide for the privacy of mediation sessions and also create a special privilege against testimony in court of what is revealed in mediation. Oregon's new mediation statute, although appearing in the code under the category of custody and visitation mediation, broadly provides that "all communications, verbal or written, made in mediation proceedings shall be confidential" (Oregon H.B. 2362, 1983). Florida's mediation statute says that "all verbal or written communication in mediation or conciliation proceedings shall be confidential and inadmissible as evidence in any subsequent legal proceedings, unless both parties agree otherwise" (Florida Statutes, Section 61.21(3), 1982). The 1981 New York Dispute Resolution law provides:

All memoranda, work products, or case files of a
mediator are confidential and not subject to disclosure

in any judicial or administrative proceeding. Any communication relating to the subject matter of the resolution made during the resolution process by any participant, mediator, or any other person present at the dispute resolution shall be a confidential communication. [Chapter 847, section 849(b) (6)]

Similarly, a 1982 Michigan statute declares that

a communication between a domestic relations mediator and a party to a domestic relations mediation is confidential. The secrecy of the communication shall be preserved inviolate as a privileged communication. The communication shall not be admitted in evidence in any proceeding. The same protection shall be given to communications between the parties in the presence of the mediator. [Michigan H.B. 4870, 1982]

California, which enacted the first statute mandating mediation of custody disputes in 1981, appears to provide double protection for mediation confidentiality. The California statute, Civil Code §4607(c), states:

Mediation proceedings shall be held in private and shall be confidential, and all communications, verbal or written, from the parties to the mediator made in a proceeding pursuant to this section shall be deemed to be *official information* within the meaning of Section 1040 of the Evidence Code. [Emphasis added.]

In addition to the express privacy and confidentiality of California custody mediation proceedings, "official information," as referred to in section 1040 of the California Evidence Code, cannot be disclosed if an authorized official refuses disclosure. Unlike other privileges, this cannot be waived by the person who made the statements, provided there is good reason to refuse disclosure. This provision has been viewed by a California appellate court as protecting the confidentiality of the parties' mediation communications from disclosure by cross-examination of the mediator. (See *McLaughlin* v. *Superior Court*, 1983.)

Other states, such as Washington, have a statute protecting a "public officer" from courtroom examination of a "communication made to him in official confidence" (Washington Revised Code, Section 5, 60.060(5), 1974). It has been reasoned that this statute would be applicable to court-connected mediation, even if established by local court rule in the absence of an authorizing state statute (Pottmeyer, 1983).

The U.S. Department of Justice Community Relations Service (CRS), which mediates public interest conflicts and community disputes, has federal statutory protection of confidentiality in its mediation sessions:

> The activities of all officers and employees of the Service in providing conciliation assistance shall be conducted in confidence and without publicity, and the Service shall hold confidential any information acquired in the regular performance of its duties upon the understanding that it would be so held. [United States Code 42, Section 200g-2(b)]

This statutory protection has been upheld in the federal courts. (See *City of Port Arthur, Texas* v. *United States*, 1980.)

Courts generally have the power to control the procedures necessary to carry out their functions and by which they make decisions, including evidentiary decisions. Several local trial court jurisdictions have developed court rules for the mediation of domestic relations cases and minor civil disputes. (See Comeaux, 1983.) These local court rules may furnish the details necessary to implement state legislation on mediation or fill the void in the absence of any applicable legislation.

The local mediation rules may also clarify the confidentiality of court-connected or court-inspired mediation programs. The local rules of the State Circuit Court in Portland, Oregon, for example, establish mandatory custody mediation. The court's rule 6 provides a more comprehensive mediation "privilege" than that allowed for existing statutory privileges:

> All mediation proceedings shall be private and all communications made shall be confidential.

> A spouse or any other individual engaged in mediation proceedings shall not be examined in any civil or criminal action as to such communications and such communications shall not be used in any civil or criminal action without the consent of the parties to the mediation. Exceptions to testimonial privilege otherwise applicable under ORS 40.225 to 40.295 [lawyer/client, physician/patient, and other statutory privileges] do not apply to communications made confidential under this subsection. [Circuit Court of the State of Oregon for the County of Multnomah–Dept. of Domestic Relations, October 22, 1982]

It is possible that local court rules may conflict with state statutes regarding confidentiality in mediation. The local rule, as in Portland, may indicate that the local trial judges will afford greater confidentiality to communications in mediation than required by state statutes. This local exercise of discretion based on the policy of encouraging mediation is not likely to be overruled by appellate court decision. The Supreme Court of Arizona upheld a Conciliation Court policy that refused to make information obtained through court-connected counseling available to a trial court, even if disclosure was jointly authorized by the counseling participants. There was no statute making the information privileged. The Arizona Supreme Court recognized the inherent power of the local court to refuse disclosure if deemed necessary to fulfill its functions. (See *Fenton* v. *Howard*, 1978.)

On the other hand, a court rule that is more restrictive of confidentiality than that allowed by statute could be more easily challenged. The state mediation statute may expressly allow a local rule option on confidentiality, provided the local option does not violate other statutes or constitutional prohibitions. (See the discussion of *McLaughlin* v. *Superior Court*, 1983.)

Federal courts also have local rules and some have established mediation programs by such local rule. The United States District Court for the Western District of Washington in Seattle, for example, has created mandatory mediation in certain civil cases. Its rules specifically provide for confidentiality of the mediation proceedings and the mediator's memorandum.

Confidentiality Between Parties. A particularly sensitive issue of confidentiality arises when the mediator caucuses with each side in the absence of the other. The purpose of such caucusing is to allow each side to reveal to the mediator information they would not want to disclose to the other, to allow the mediator to discuss matters that would be uncomfortable to state to the parties when together, and to interpret the concerns and perspective of each side to the other.

Individual caucusing is most common in labor mediation, environmental mediation, and the mediation of international disputes. Shuttle mediation, described in the previous chapter, by definition depends on individual caucusing. The mediator can talk separately to each participant and not reveal what is said to the other only if both explicitly agree to that process. Some mediators who use caucusing are skilled and accustomed to maintaining trust on both sides. They claim caucusing is an important aid in moving disputants through an impasse. The keys appear to be a clear understanding at the outset of whether caucusing will be permitted and the mediator's ability to judge when the level of trust allows it.

Caucusing is fraught with confidentiality questions and dangers, however. It is most difficult for the mediator to maintain the appearance of absolute impartiality when it is known that the mediator is party to information about the dispute that is not shared by each side. This information may be quantitative data relevant to the conflict or subjective opinions regarding one side's bargaining or settlement position. A mediation participant who does not share the "secret" information may perceive partiality or a liaison between the mediator and the other side. Assuming that normally the mediator caucuses separately with each side, the disputant who shares private information may worry about the mediator disclosing it to the opposing side. If the information appears to have been revealed or used adversely to their position, the feeling of betrayal will, of course, totally frustrate the mediation.

Some mediators caucus with each side only if it is agreed that information revealed during the caucus will be shared at the next joint meeting. This approach can also create problems of confidentiality because it is sometimes hard to enforce the mutuality of revelations if during a caucus one of the disputants blurts information but insists on keeping it confidential or disagrees with the way in which the mediator represents the caucus discussion to the other side. The participants not present during the caucus may be naturally suspicious and continue to doubt whether all known information from the caucus has been revealed.

The *Code of Professional Conduct for Labor Mediators,* previously referred to, covers caucusing and separate meetings as follows: "Bargaining positions, proposals, or suggestions given to the mediator in confidence during the course of bargaining for his sole information should not be disclosed to the other party without first securing permission from the party or person who gave it to him" (section 5). This provision appears to restate the problem rather than offering any guidance on how the benefit of caucusing can be reconciled with the difficulty of the nonmutuality of private information disclosed to the mediator.

Opinion Testimony and Recommendations. An issue related to that of confidentiality is opinion testimony of the mediator regarding recommendations for resolution of the dispute. If the mediation does not result in a settlement agreement, may the mediator be allowed or compelled to offer a recommendation to a court or administrative agency regarding how the dispute should be resolved? The mediator may be in a unique position to recommend an imposed outcome because of likely expertise in the subject of dispute combined with inside knowledge of facts and feelings revealed during mediation. This dilemma is most apparent in child custody mediation but may also arise in other conflicts, such as the disputed value of goods, nuclear plant locations, school closures, and in countless other situations.

The consensus among mediators appears to confirm that the trust and candor required in mediation are unlikely to exist if the participants know the mediator may be formulating an opinion or recommendation that will be communicated to a judge or tribunal. The recommendation of the mediator, particularly in a child custody and visitation case, would generally be given such great weight that the mediator, in effect, would be switching roles from decision facilitator to decision maker. The confusion and suspicion created by this crossover role taint the validity, effectiveness, and integrity of the mediation process.

The participants may, in some circumstances, agree or contract for the mediator to decide the matter if they are unable to do so or to testify as to a recommendation. Using the informal, consensual process of mediation with no evidentiary or procedural rules as the basis for an imposed decision does, however, create a considerable risk that the more clever or sophisticated participant may distort or manipulate the mediation in order to influence the mediator's opinion.

A combined process of mediation followed by arbitration, all performed by one person, has been used with some success in labor conflicts. This "med-arb" approach may work best when the participants are of relatively equal bargaining experience and the efficiency of a combined procedure outweighs the inhibiting or strategic effect of the mediator's anticipated role change. Some have also argued for use of the mediator "switchover" role, from mediator to court custody expert, when it becomes necessary to decide temporary child custody after all else has failed.

The California statute that mandates mediation in all contested child custody cases allows the mediator to make recommendations to the court if such a procedure is consistent with local court rules. (See California Civil Code 460-7 (e).) This statutory policy represents a compromise between those counties, most notably Los Angeles, where the court absolutely prohibits its mediators from crossing over to serve as custody investigators and other California counties, like San Francisco and San Mateo, where the mediator is asked by the court to recommend a temporary custody order if the parties cannot agree. (See McIsaac, 1981.) The California State Statute also makes all mandated custody mediations private and confidential. (See California Civil Code 4607(c).) Some California jurisdictions interpreted these provisions to allow the mediator to recommend a custody arrangement to the court but to bar either side from questioning the mediator on the reasons behind the recommendation.

When this policy was challenged by a parent in San Mateo County, the California Supreme Court stayed the proceeding and asked the First District Court of Appeals to rule on the practice. The appellate court ruled that the San Mateo policy was unconstitutional. The mediator could testify on the custody recommendation without contravening the provision for confidentiality, but if the mediator could not be questioned or cross-examined on his or her decision, this would be in violation of constitutional guarantees of a fair trial and a right to cross-examine adverse witnesses. The court-connected mediator could make a custody recommendation to the court only if subject to cross-examination. (See *McLaughlin* v. *Superior Court*, 1983).

It is only fair that a mediator not be allowed to recommend a custody decision to the court without the test of cross-examination. The mediator-investigator, in the absence of cross-examination, may base the recommendation on bias, ignorance, or disprovable facts. The court's opinion in *McLaughlin* appears, however, to miss the central issue of mediation confidentiality. The real question is not cross-examination but whether the mediator should be allowed to testify under any conditions. If the mediator is allowed to testify, confidentiality is effectively lost.

The *McLaughlin* case, as well as accepted evidentiary rules and notions of due process, requires that if the mediator is to make a custody recommendation, the mediator can be examined by the adversely affected party regarding the reasons for the recommendation. If the mediator is so questioned, the adversely affected party doing the questioning could be held to have waived the objections to the revelations made by the mediator in court. The other party, for whom the recommendation was favorable, would hardly be expected to object. In other words, the adversely affected party would be compelled to cross-examine the mediator and thus open the door to all the facts revealed during mediation.

In addition to statutory construction arguments, a challenge to the mediator's recommendation and testimony could be based on the due process argument that because the California legislation mandates mediation in all contested custody cases, allowing the mediator to make a recommendation and testify creates an untenable Hobson's choice for divorcing parents: either refrain from being candid in mediation discussions or reveal relevant confidences knowing that they can be used later against your individual interests. This challenge has been countered with the argument that parties to a court-compelled mediation are unlikely to reveal confidences that would threaten their desired custody resolution, whether or not those confidences would be revealed in court.

As the use of mediation increases, there will probably be a greater incidence of mediators called to testify about statements made during mediation. Passage and clarification of specific statutory privileges for communications made during mediation would promote the practice, protect the parties, and avoid traps for the unwary.

Work-Product Restrictions. In the *McLaughlin* case, the mediator was a court employee expected by the terms of employment to testify in court should mediation not produce agreement. Mediators, private or publicly employed, may be subpoenaed to testify about their opinions regarding the appropriate outcome of a case they unsuccessfully mediated. Apart from the considerations of confidentiality previously discussed, there is also an objection that may be asserted, at least by private mediators, based on the work-product doctrine.

The work-product doctrine was initially formulated to protect attorneys from discovery of their opinions or thoughts regarding a case being prepared for trial and has since been expanded to apply to other professionals (Saltzburg, 1980). The doctrine only protects the mental impressions, ideas, theories, and strategies of a professional. The facts underlying those impressions and the specific information gathered in mediation are not protected by the work-product doctrine, though they may be shielded by other doctrines of privacy and confidentality discussed above. (See *Hickman* v. *Taylor*, 1947.) The work-product "privilege," unlike most of the privacy protections previously discussed, belongs to the professional provider and can be waived only by that person. Opinions are the principal product of many professionals and therefore receive substantial legal protection. (See *United States* v. *Pfiger, Inc.*, 1977.)

Liability

Claims Against Mediators. There are very few claims against mediators and no reported cases in which a mediator has been successfully sued for damages regarding mediation services. This contrast to the experience of soaring claims against many other providers of professional services is probably attributable in part to the fact that mediation as a professional practice is relatively new and in part to the nature of the mediation process. Mediation produces a consensual result reflecting the participants' joint determination of what is fair and appropriate. Participants are generally satisfied with mediation services (see Chapter One). Lawsuits and claims are the result of dissatisfaction.

Mediation is not yet a common enough practice to generate a volume of cases that would produce some lawsuits as a matter of probability. Evidence casting doubt on the reasonableness of a particular mediation result or the integrity of the mediator is not likely to come to light until some time after the mediation is concluded. The revelation of mediator impropriety and the development of a large enough number of cases to produce some small percentage of troublesome results or litigious clients is probably but a question of time. There is also, as yet, no established standard to which mediation services can be compared for purposes of easily establishing liability.

The potential liability of the mediator to a participant may arise from a number of different legal theories. A mediator could conceivably be sued for fraud, false advertising, breach of contract, invasion of privacy, defamation, outrageous conduct, breach of fiduciary duty, and professional negligence or malpractice. One event or set of facts may lead to liability, or at least a lawsuit, on several different legal theories or causes of action. The two that are most likely to be the basis of a legal claim against a mediator are breach of contract and professional malpractice. These two causes of action, as potentially applicable to mediators, are discussed below.

Contract Liability. In offering and contracting for the provision of mediation services a mediator must be cautious not to make any implied or expressed promises about the results. If a mediator indicates in the offer or contract for services that mediation will be cheaper, better, or faster than other alternatives such as litigation or arbitration, the mediator may be liable if the promise is not kept. Since there can be no assurance that mediation will be better than the alternatives in any specific case, such representations should be avoided. The current tendency to oversell mediation could easily result in disappointed participants and antagonistic attorneys and other professionals prepared to assist in taming the practice of mediation through lawsuits.

The agreement to mediate should clearly state that no promises as to the outcome of mediation or the success of the process are expressed or implied and that the participants understand that they might be able to claim more for themselves in an adversarial proceeding than they are likely to obtain through mediation. Any implied or expressed promise that mediation will be better or produce a more favorable result could subject the mediator to liability for breach of that contractual promise. (See *Boecher* v. *Borth,* 1976; Prosser, 1971.)

Some contractual obligations are hard to avoid when providing mediation and may be implied as an imposed standard of practice. For example, a mediator, or the agency for which the mediator works, may, in effect, enter into a contract with the participants that the mediation will be private and confidential unless agreed to the contrary. The participants may sue if the contract, expressed or implied, is breached. In a reported Illinois case, a client of an agency social worker sued the social worker and the agency for revealing confidences to others in violation of an implied contract for confidentiality, allowing a conflict of interest to develop, and incompetently performing counseling services. The suit was allowed to proceed only on the claim of breach of contract because of the revelation of information given in confidence. (See *Martino* v. *Family Services Agency of Adams County,* 1983.) As discussed in a preceding section, no guarantee of absolute confidentiality can be made for mediation sessions. The mediator is, however, contractually and ethically bound not to reveal confidences without the permission of the participants or upon court order or by demand of law.

Rather than risk an implied contract based on false expectations or promising more than can be delivered, the mediator should use a written contract to limit liability. This contract for employment of the mediator may incorporate mediation guidelines or rules. The contract, or the contract and rules together, should outline the process to be used in the mediation, the role of the mediator, the risks and limitations of mediation, the need for outside review and independent legal advice, the obligations of the participants, the basis for determination of any fees or costs, and the obligation of participants for payment. (See Resource A: Employment Agreement and Resource B: Mediation Guidelines.)

Malpractice Liability. Mediator liability based on allegations of professional negligence, or malpractice, is the liability claim most likely to be encountered by a mediator. Malpractice claims generally arise under the law of torts and require proof on four elements: a duty owed to the participants by the mediator; a breach of the duty by failure to comply with acceptable standards of practice; damages measurable in money; and a causal relationship between the failure to exercise an acceptable standard of practice and the alleged damages. Proof of all four elements is necessary. Adequate proof may be difficult in a claim against a mediator.

Duty and Breach. The mediator's duty arises out of the agreement, expressed or implied, to provide competent mediation services. In other words, the law may require that any professional service offered be performed competently. Competence is generally defined as compliance with existing professional standards of care for the service offered. The first problem for the claimant in a malpractice case against a mediator would be to produce proof of what is an acceptable standard of care in the practice of mediation. As our earlier discussion of standards of practice indicated, there are no universally accepted criteria for structuring standards of mediation practice because the goals of mediation and its social role are just now being formulated. Ironically, the first successful malpractice case against a mediator may mark the establishment of mediation as a recognized profession.

If the mediator is a member of a professional organization that has promulgated standards of practice, or if the mediator has subscribed to established standards, or if standards have been prescribed for the mediator by the terms of the mediator's licensure, certification, employment, or referral, then proof of the applicable standard and the consequent duty owed is made easier. As a general rule, proof of the applicable standard of care, as well as its breach, is presented through expert testimony. Because of the newly emerging nature of mediation as a distinct practice, qualified experts may be hard to find and differences of opinion are to be expected.

The mediator may be subject to liability, even in the absence of expert testimony, if the mediator's conduct is clearly unreasonable in risking harm to the participants. According to the *Restatement (Second) of Torts* (1965):

> An act may be negligent if it is done without the competence which the reasonable man in the actor's vision would realize is necessary to prevent causing unreasonable risk of harm to another. . . . This is true . . . where the actor, by professing competence, induces another to accept his services or otherwise subject himself to the acts. [Section 299 and Comment c]

If the mediator purports to have special knowledge or experience in the subject of the mediated conflict, the mediator may be held to a higher standard of care relating to that subject. In other words, a mediator's self-designation as having special expertise in the law relating to family disputes, or in the phases of child development, such that a divorcing couple might reasonably rely on the mediator's expertise and advice in making their own joint decisions, could give rise to a claim that the mediator had a duty to provide correct information on which the couple could rely. The same could be true if participants in an environmental dispute rely for the resolution of their conflict on the purported expertise of the mediator concerning toxic wastes, or if an educator mediating a dispute on special education provides erroneous information about the content or benefits of an alternative learning program chosen as a resolution by the participants because of the mediator's expertise. The mediator must be cautious when providing information or advice and should always urge the participants to obtain independent counsel on any subject beyond the mediator's expertise. In our increasingly complex world a mediator may be held negligent for failure to urge the participants to consult with experts or obtain special information when relevant or necessary to formulate alternatives for resolution of conflicts. The same challenge of specialization and expertise is currently facing lawyers, physicians, and professionals of all types.

Physicians and other health care providers have been held to the duty of informing their patients about the risks in the service provided. Though this duty to inform of risk was originally limited to medical procedures and advice, it has since been expanded to require attorneys to reveal the risks of a trial as compared to its alternatives and would logically require any professional offering a service to reveal the risks involved. The standards discussed in the preceding section and set forth in Resource D at the back of the book, as well as many of the bar association rulings on ethics, would clearly require a mediator to advise the participants of the risks of proceeding with mediation rather than the other conflict resolution procedures available. There is no reason to think that all mediators would not be held to such a duty and that liability might not follow from its breach.

A mediator who drafts a settlement agreement for the participants could be held to a requirement that the draft be an accurate reflection of the stipulations made during mediation and that it be drawn skillfully enough to effectuate the participants' intended purpose. Drafting settlement agreements can be risky business. Again the mediator would be wise to make it clear that it is the responsibility of the participants to have any proposed agreement reviewed by independent counsel before signing it. In any event, no agreement should be offered to the participants for their signature without the opportunity for them to read and consider it at their leisure outside the mediation setting. Any agreement drafted by a mediator who is not an attorney should not purport to be in legal form and should be labeled a "memorandum on points of agreement" or a "mediated plan," rather than designated as a final settlement.

Damages and Causation. Even if a disgruntled mediation participant could establish that a mediator had a duty of care which was breached and that the mediator therefore committed professional malpractice or negligence, there are still two additional interrelated requirements. The intertwined elements of damage and causation require proof of measurable damage that can be equated to dollars and that this damage would not have occurred but for the negligence or malpractice of the mediator. These necessary elements of damages and causation may be particularly difficult to prove in a case involving mediation.

The damages cannot be mere conjecture or speculation. It is the claimant's burden to establish the injury sustained and the value of that injury or loss in terms of dollars. What the claimant might have obtained by resolution of the dispute in some manner other than mediation or what economic consequence may have flowed from any alleged negligence of the mediator is more likely than not to be a matter of speculation and conjecture. Any damages sustained because of the mediator's conduct or malfeasance may be more of an emotional loss and annoyance than a loss measurable in dollars.

The necessary element that would probably be most difficult to prove in a negligence action against a mediator is that of causation. The claimant must establish that any damages or loss sustained would not have occurred but for the negligence or malfeasance of the mediator. Proving what would have happened in the absence of mediation is difficult. It would be hard to establish what precisely would have happened in litigation as an alternative to mediation, for example, and equally challenging to prove that the claimant would have been better off negotiating a resolution outside of mediation. If the mediator is careful not to guarantee any specific or more favorable result than could be obtained by alternatives to mediation, it would be most difficult to prove that any alleged damages were caused by the mediator's action. Even a claim of unequal bargaining power and overreaching, unchecked by the mediator during the mediation, would not be proof that the same unequal power would not have resulted in a similar or worse outcome in litigation or adversarial negotiations. (See the previous discussion of fairness.)

If the claimed damages are sustained after independent review of the agreement or after the mediator has urged such a review, it would be even harder to fix the causative blame on the mediator. On the other hand, a mediator who allows the parties to sign an agreement without an admonition of the importance of independent review and counsel may have trouble escaping a claim that poor advice during mediation or the allowance of overreaching or unfair bargaining during mediation was the cause of provable damages.

One of the more likely claims to arise from mediation is that if the mediation is unsuccessful in resolving the dispute, the time passed in mediation may preclude pursuing meaningful alternatives because of the expiration of a statute of limitations, a change in the facts, or an accumulation of more damages due to the passage of time. Again, if the mediator has advised the participants of the risks, urged them to consult with others during and after the mediation, and had the participants sign a contract acknowledging these factors, it would be difficult to prove that any damages were caused by the mediator. This precautionary safeguard by the mediator would also make it clear that the participants in mediation assume the risks incurred so that they will not be heard to complain later.

The only reported case in which a mediator was sued for malpractice nicely illustrates several of the preceding points. In the case of *Lange* v. *Marshall* (1981), a Missouri Court of Appeals had occasion to consider the liability of an attorney who undertook the mediation of a divorce settlement for two of his friends who had been married twenty-five years. After signing the settlement agreement, which was pending before a judge for approval, Mrs. Lange had second thoughts about the settlement terms and obtained an independent lawyer who eventually obtained a more favorable divorce settlement for her. Mrs. Lange sued the mediator, claiming he was negligent in not inquiring further as to the financial worth of her former husband, failing to help her negotiate a better settlement, not advising her that she could get more if she litigated the matter, and not fully and fairly disclosing her rights as to marital property, custody, and maintenance. The case went to a jury that returned a verdict against the mediator in the amount of $74,000.

On the mediator's appeal of the jury verdict, the court of appeals assumed for purposes of its opinion that the mediator owed a duty to the participants that was breached by his failure to do one or more of the things about which Mrs. Lange complained. The court held, however, that Mrs. Lange did not meet her burden as a claimant in establishing that the negligence of the mediator actually caused the economic damages she claimed to have suffered in the way of lost support payments, fees for accountants and private investigators, lost taxes, medical costs and other expenses, as well as legal fees—all incurred after she obtained her own lawyer and engaged in the lengthy litigation eventually leading to a more favorable settlement. The court pointed out that there was no evidence that these expenses would not have been incurred anyway or that her former husband would have agreed to a different settlement had the mediator done the things he was charged with not doing. If anything, the court found the evidence to the contrary. The court noted that Mrs. Lange engaged in ten months of heated litigation with Mr. Lange

following her repudiation of the mediated settlement and that she
could not prove that this litigation and the expenses she incurred
would not have happened "but for" the alleged negligence of the
mediator:

> [Mr. Lange] testified that he intended to be fair with
> the plaintiff but that her idea of fairness, and her attor-
> ney's idea of fairness, did not comport with his. . . . It is
> the rankest conjecture and speculation to conclude
> that Ralph Lange's willingness to settle the marital
> affairs without litigation on the basis of the original
> [mediated] settlement established his willingness to
> settle without litigation at a higher figure acceptable
> to plaintiff. . . . The parties agreed that defendant was
> not representing plaintiff as an advocate but in a me-
> diation position. [p. 239]

Insurance. The preceding discussion of the mediator's potential liability may paint a gloomier picture than is warranted by the
limited number of actual claims for liability that have been asserted
against mediators. The potential for claims does, however, exist. It
would be naive to think that the early euphoria for mediation, the
high expectations created by media coverage, and the inflated claims
of some mediators will not give way to criticism and disappoint-
ment in some cases. As mediation becomes a recognized professional
practice with an established set of standards, it will probably attract
more of the malpractice litigation zeal that has both plagued and
improved other professional practices.

Even the expense of successfully defending malpractice claims
may be an economically crippling blow to mediators or an agency
with which they are associated. Thoughtful mediation techniques,
as urged throughout this book, as well as a preventive practice orientation, can minimize the risks for mediators. There can, of course, be
no guarantee against error and no assurance that a claim could not
be asserted even in the absence of error.

Mediators are urged to protect themselves with some form of
liability or malpractice insurance. Many insurance companies and
programs that insure the mediator's profession of origin against
malpractice claims will cover a claim arising from the practice of
mediation. Some insurance policies may not cover a nontraditional

practice, however, or may preclude coverage by reasoning that a lawyer, therapist, nurse, or other insured professional is not practicing within the professional range of services for which the insurance was contracted. Some insurance companies have indicated a willingness to issue an inexpensive rider to their existing malpractice insurance policies specifically to cover the risks of mediation. Other companies have indicated, in response to inquiries, that their existing policies, at least for attorneys and therapists, would cover mediation claims. Mediators would be wise to check their individual policy and confirm coverage with the insurance carrier.

Several companies now offer liability insurance for mediators through membership in some of the mediation organizations and professional associations listed in Resource E at the back of the book. The cost of this insurance is quite modest because of the low claim experience to date. Mediators are urged to contact these organizations to obtain more information about the insurance they make available to their membership.

Recommended Reading

Fairness

"A Comparative Theory of Dispute Institutions in Society." R. L. Abel. *Law and Society,* Winter 1973, *8,* 235–240.
    The role of norms in dispute resolution is discussed as a distinguishing feature of different dispute-processing mechanisms.

Disputes and Negotiations: A Cross-Cultural Perspective. P. H. Gulliver. New York: Academic Press, 1979.
    In chap. 7, Gulliver discusses the role of the mediator and on p. 223 focuses on the mediator as an "enunciator" of norms relevant to the dispute.

Justice Without Law? Resolving Disputes Without Lawyers. J. S. Auerbach. New York: Oxford University Press, 1983.
    A valuable and penetrating, if somewhat cynical, historical analysis of alternative dispute resolution. Many of the concerns stated in this section are attributable to Auerbach.

Standards of Practice and Ethical Limitations

Ethical and Legal Issues in Counseling and Psychotherapy. W. Van
  Hoose and J. Kottler. San Francisco: Jossey-Bass, 1977.
    A good text on the theoretical and practical considerations of
ethical practice and legal limitations for counselors. Chapter 6
specifically addresses professional and legal regulation.

"Professional Responsibility Problems of Divorce Mediation." L. J.
  Silberman. *Family Law Quarterly,* Summer 1982, *16,* 107–145.
    An excellent and comprehensive analysis of ethical and legal
limitations on lawyer and nonlawyer mediators. Much of our discussion in this section was drawn from Silberman's thoughtful
analysis.

Confidentiality

Confidentiality in Social Work: Issues and Principles. S. Wilson.
  New York: Free Press, 1978.
    A comprehensive examination of confidentiality for social
workers with a practice-oriented discussion of legal and policy implications applicable by analogy to mediation.

"Privileged Communications: A Case by Case Approach." *Maine
  Law Review,* 1971, *23,* 443–462.
    This law review note collects all the statutes establishing evi-
dentiary privileges for the helping professions and proposes a statutory approach that would deal with claims of privilege in a more
uniform way based on the nature of the professional relationship
rather than the specific profession involved.

Liability

*Legal Liability in Psychotherapy: A Practitioner's Guide to Risk
  Management.* B. Schutz. San Francisco: Jossey-Bass, 1982.
    Contains pertinent legal information and offers suggestions
for managing the risk of legal liability without sacrificing clinical
effectiveness.

11

✖ ✖ ✖ ✖ ✖

Specific Considerations
in Setting Up
a Mediation Service

The first task of a person who wishes to provide mediation services is to define the desired clientele, or conflict situations, and determine the sector (public or private) where services will be provided. Because each sector is different in scope, complexity, and implications for service delivery, each is discussed here separately. Information regarding physical arrangements, however, and the need for record-keeping and liability (see Chapter Six), are common in both settings. Mediation is a new field, and new service delivery systems and styles are developing. Mediation services are not hampered by tradition or legislation as are many other helping professions. We want to stress the importance of keeping a consumer awareness in the provision of services, while not neglecting the very real needs of mediators to make a living and enjoy good working conditions.

The following ideas are merely suggestions that may help newly trained mediators in defining their practice and offering mediation services. We strongly recommend the completion of an academic or skill-training program (see Chapter Nine) as a prerequisite for providing mediation, no matter which conflicts or clientele will be addressed, since this training will provide a starting point for understanding not only mediation itself but the service delivery systems that already exist.

Private Practice

Private practice involves a verbal or written contractual relationship between the mediator (service provider) and the mediation participants (recipient). A fee is paid directly to the mediator for the provision of services, and the practice, as a business, reports and pays taxes on the income generated by this activity. The practice may or may not have employees, but it must always keep records of financial transactions and must be efficiently run in order to be profitable.

Most private practices receive no governmental or special grant money to provide certain services to a particular clientele. In public-sector or institutional practices, however, there are two possible contractual arrangements: One is between the recipient of the service and the institution, the other between the institution and the service provider. Occasionally there is a third contractual arrangement. The government funding or grant source contracts with the institution to provide services to a certain population in a certain way.

Private mediation practices can do business in several different business entities or structures. Mediators may do business by themselves as sole proprietorships in order to retain total independence, or they can band together with others to form business entities ranging from loose professional associations to partnerships, or professional corporations, and in some instances nonprofit corporations. All state and some local governments have requirements for the formulation, registration, and internal structure of these various business entities, as well as for sole proprietorships. Many communities require a business license for private professional practices. We suggest that the reader get reliable information from an attorney regarding the applicable laws, regulations, and ordinances, as well as their implications and consequences, before hanging out a shingle and starting to mediate.

The selection of a name is an important consideration. If you are a mediator in a sole proprietorship, you have the option of doing business under just your own name or under an assumed business name (a DBA—"doing business as . . ."). Attorneys may be precluded from using an assumed business name (see Chapter Ten). Some partnerships and most corporate structures do business under a business name, which you may need to register with your state and local authorities. The title of your business or private practice should convey information about what you do for whom or give potential recipients a feeling that sets their expectation. Specific rules and limitations govern the use of assumed names or designations by attorneys.

DBAs or business names that highlight the conflict situation to be mediated will often lead potential clients to your practice, since they are well aware of the problem but may not be sure which process they want. Thus a mediator in a sole proprietorship who wants to specialize in tenant/landlord disputes might want to be indexed in the Yellow Pages and other directories under the DBA of "Housing Dispute Mediation Service." Mediators who do not wish to limit their practice might pick up a neutral DBA, such as "East Anglia Mediation Unit," or simply use their own name.

Private practices have the advantage that they can be constituted in a manner that is helpful to the practitioner. Mediators can include as many or as few dispute areas as their expertise and interest allow. They can choose whether or not to include others to make it a group private practice. They can choose the target population for ease, location, and ability to pay.

Private mediation practices are most likely to be utilized by those who, for reasons relating to quality, anonymity, or status, do not wish to use public-sector services, some of which would undoubtedly be less expensive than the private practice. For the same reason of expense, private practitioners are not likely to deal with the same socioeconomic or ethnic groups as will mediators working in court-mandated or state-subsidized agencies. While some mediators may see this built-in economic elitism as a favorable reason to select private practice, there are disadvantages. Private practice can be financially risky and stressful; the pace at which you may have to work to meet overhead costs, including advertising and case-finding activities, may make private practice a disillusionment.

Many other professionals have had to come to grips with these hard realities. Often they use private practice as a part-time supplement to their existing public-sector contracts or full-time jobs, some of which are themselves none too stable because of changing governmental priorities. This "mixed" practice is one way that a sole proprietor or small partnership business entity can imitate the usual protective maneuvers of large corporations—to diversify income sources so that the loss of one will not devastate the entire business.

The importance of referrals cannot be overemphasized in the establishment of private practices. (See Chapter Twelve for a discussion.) Moreover, private practices often have to form advertising and public relations campaigns in order to let other professions and the public know about the practice and where the service is located. Pressman and Siegler (1983) suggest some basic case-finding and advertising strategies based on the practice's financial goals and target populations or situations. Each population may require a different advertising strategy: newspaper ads, printed announcements, individually typed letters to potential referral resources, direct-mail ads, brochures, membership in business and professional organizations, and direct contact.

Private practices have the advantages of greater control, more flexibility in daily scheduling, and a wider range of functions that must be performed. It is up to the individual to determine exactly how beneficial these factors are for his or her situation.

In the private sector, the charging of fees for periodic mediation services is usually structured either as a cash transaction prior to the beginning of the sessions or an advance payment, based on anticipated length, that is put in an escrow account (Coogler, 1978). In the latter method, any unused portion can be refunded, and additional prepayments may be required as the mediation process continues. Both methods are usually based on an hourly fee determined by the mediator's costs, the client's ability to pay, or some compromise between the two, such as a sliding fee scale with a minimum amount fixed to overhead costs. Some mediators are willing to accept national barter system credits or equivalent trades in goods and services. Any such trades should be structured into a written contract that specifies not only the object or service being provided but also any deadlines for completion. All such financial arrangements should be written on, or attached to, the employment agreement (agreement to mediate) and accurately stated in professional disclosure statements or promotional material.

Public Sector

Private-sector mediation is only one alternative, however. Currently mediation is being provided in public-sector agencies or institutions for such conflict situations as divorce and custody disputes (McIsaac, 1983), tenant/landlord problems, and neighborhood disputes. Conciliation and juvenile court workers, social workers, and counselors, as well as public administrators, department supervisors, and others, need to be trained in order to enhance their theoretical knowledge and skill application, since mediation rather than litigation is beginning to be used through family courts as an alternative for minor criminal cases (Salius, 1983) and also in juvenile courts (Vorenberg, 1982).

Because most public agencies follow the third-party payment arrangement discussed earlier, mediators working for public services may never have to deal with payment issues directly, as do private-sector mediators. And because public-sector mediation services are often subsidized by grant money, they may be better able to offer mediation clinics providing parts of stage 1 and stage 2 in a large group setting, thus reducing agency time and participant cost.

Since most entitlement programs and state benefit programs have committees that arbitrate disputes between potential recipients and the staff regarding eligibility, there may be an increasing tendency to rely on public-sector mediation as a substitute for existing appeal mechanisms. Any such recourse to mediation should be done in such a way that the neutrality of the mediators is ensured and the expense to the public minimized. This might best be accomplished by creating a centralized state or federal Mediation Exchange, which would send mediators to the multiplicity of public agencies, either regularly or as needed, to help with consumer complaints, appeals processes, and internal decision making.

The structure of the organization in which mediation is provided will determine its effectiveness and methodology (Kochan and

Jick, 1978). Mediators must be aware of all these issues before deciding which setting is best for their own skills and career aspirations.

Environments for Mediation

Mediation does not require a special setting as do some other professions, although the setting must allow privacy. Since the only "tools" required are the mediator's own expertise in communication techniques, personal authority, and some helpful papers or worksheets, the mediator's motto could be said to be "Have Process—Will Travel."

Mediation is mobile, and marathon or crisis-style mediation can be provided in the participant's usual environment, such as home, office, or school. An excellent example of the use of mediation in a typical environment is the racial conflict avoided in a school building described by Lincoln (1981).

The ideal location is a quiet, neutral place that holds no particular meaning for either participant. The criteria for evaluating the suitability of a location can be framed into the following questions:

1. *Is it quiet and uninterrupted?* Jangling telephones, noise from other people, and sudden interruptions create tension and break down important concentration and communication.
2. *Does it have negative or biased connotations?* If one participant has bad associations with the location or thinks of it as someone else's space, he or she may feel threatened, defensive, or inhibited.
3. *Is it comfortable?* Does it have soft but adequate lighting, soft chairs, enough space so no one feels cramped, unpretentious decorations, coordinating colors (preferably cooler hues)—the appropriate style to match the participants' sense of your professional status and their expectations?
4. *Is access easy?* Will it be a problem to find the location or nearby parking? Will it present major inconveniences for one or both participants? Can the mediator make sure it is opened and ready prior to the session? What about wheelchair access?
5. *Is it available for continued and convenient scheduling?* Will the scheduling of future sessions depend solely on securing this place again?

6. *Is the cost prohibitive?* Are the costs involved in using this space reasonable? Will high costs be added onto the fee and passed on to the participants directly or indirectly?
7. *Does it have space for waiting and caucusing?* Mediators in marathon or crisis sessions may need to have auxiliary rooms where private sessions can be held.
8. *Are nearby restrooms and restaurant facilities available?* Participants' physical needs must be met, especially in marathon sessions.
9. *Is the space safe for participants and mediator?* Are there adequate locks, outdoor lighting, smoke detectors, and police and emergency protection available?

Mediation is a less formal process than litigation, and this difference should be reflected in the environment. However, the space should also convey the symbols of the mediator's job to lead, facilitate, and ultimately guide the process. Thus the accoutrements of the place should not attempt to imitate the traditional legal setting (unless the mediator also happens to be an attorney or judge). Although desks and conference tables should not be used to impress the participants or keep them at a distance, the mediator must physically indicate his or her status as a professional, not a peer. Participants must be provided with equal accommodations and should not be expected to share seating with each other.

Ideally the mediator should be situated so that both participants can be seen and spoken to without moving. We find that soft chairs (with the mediator's chair distinguished from the others by a variation of pattern, size, or color), arranged in a triangle, with a small coffee table in the center, form the best pattern. Small couches, slightly angled but facing each other, allow more room and suggest more freedom. Another chair can be provided at the end of the couches or chairs to accommodate advocates and attorneys or another person brought in to provide additional information. An excellent discussion of mediation seating arrangements around a conference table is provided by the Neighborhood Justice Center of Atlanta (1982) and by Filley (1975).

Participants' reactions to the environment are based on their expectations about mediation and colored by their cultural and learned perceptions of self. Modern, downtown, high-tech buildings and furnishings may give young professional mediators more status and authority in their own eyes but may be interpreted as cold, "ritzy," or intimidating for participants who come from less urbane surroundings. Mehrabian (1976, pp. 148–150) suggests that clients who have dealt with a professional who is just starting a practice in a warm, relaxed environment often react unfavorably to a change to a colder, more "professional" style. While most mediation cases do not involve continuing services, the implication seems clear that mediators may need to find a place and style that suits their own sense of self in order to avoid constant changes suggesting ambitious upward mobility.

Because mediation is a process that can be practiced without many expensive facilities, mediators may want to consider time-sharing an office space with another professional to reduce overhead costs and put community resources to better use. Some counselors, therapists, or lawyers may have offices that meet the criteria expressed earlier and can be rented by the hour once a mediation case is scheduled. In this way, a mediator starting to build a practice need not incur expenses until there is income yet can still have a pleasant setting for participants. If a mediator has several time-shared offices of this sort, he or she can offer potential clients the convenience of picking the closest office in a metropolitan area. In this way, too, mediators can "ride a circuit" to nearby counties or areas that would otherwise be unable to sustain a full-time mediation practice.

Environments are important whether mediation is done in public agencies or in private practice. Public-sector mediators may want to route client flow in such a way that mediation participants who are waiting for caucuses to end or for joint sessions to resume will not have to return to a noisy, public waiting area. Sensitivity to the waiting participant's need to have a quiet place to reflect on issues is particularly necessary when caucusing is used.

Often waiting rooms in public agencies are too small or too large and do not permit tension-reducing conversation among people who have arrived together. Lamps and chairs (not couches) arranged in an L shape or other conversation-promoting positions will help even large public agencies seem more humane and are naturally important in private practice too.

We have covered only the basic environment common to all types of mediation cases. Mediation services geared to particular ethnic or socioeconomic groups may need to be advised further by interior design consultants and other experts regarding the level of comfort or stress these groups may experience in certain physical settings. (See Chapter Thirteen for further comments.) The Recommended Reading at the end of the chapter offers further insight into the interesting dynamics of physical surroundings and their influence on interpersonal relations.

Scheduling of Sessions

The use of time during and between mediation sessions is of crucial importance to the efficacy of the mediation process. Several factors must be considered in setting up a schedule of sessions. The situational context of the disputed issues has perhaps the biggest effect on the pace of the mediation process.

Sometimes one or both participants have arbitrary deadlines for closure of mediation imposed on them, such as an impending court hearing, a board meeting by which a decision must be reached, or a calendar date for tax purposes. Often the participants have their own personal timetables by which they will evaluate the efficacy of mediation, such as an anniversary of the relationship or a desire to have the matter settled before summer vacation. Timetables, whether internal or external, should be made explicit in the first session and then brought to the participants' attention periodically as the mediation progresses. Such timetables can motivate participants to bring out underlying conflicts and speed decision making.

Haynes (1981) and others (Neighborhood Justice Center of Atlanta, 1982) recommend a scheduling model that requires individual caucus sessions between the mediator and each participant. While this model is helpful for understanding the positions and internal conflicts of each participant, it can be an additional expense in time and money and is not absolutely necessary in all cases. Such sessions can be offered as an option during the initial structuring and rule setting of the first session (stage 1) and left to the discretion of either the participants or the mediator.

Mediation sessions are often held during or after the participants' regularly scheduled workday. Many participants, especially in emotionally draining disputes such as divorce or custody cases, must have enough emotional and physical energy left at the end of a mediation session to address the needs of their children or their other responsibilities. Marathon sessions are therefore to be avoided as a general rule. Decisions and concessions made at the end of such marathons are often more a product of a desire to end the session than they are germane to the real intentions and abilities of the participants.

As for the length of each session, in contradiction to Haynes's (1981) view, we think the duration of each session in periodic scheduling should be kept to a maximum time with a little flexibility built in. Most people cannot concentrate beyond their "seatability factor"—that is, how long their bodies feel comfortable without stretching, standing, or going to the bathroom. While this factor can be accounted for by periodic rest breaks, general energy levels cannot.

We have found that one-hour sessions are too short to allow participants time to establish rapport and settle into the tasks of each stage of the immediate process. Yet real productivity in a session decreases after two hours. We therefore tell participants that the sessions will last two hours, remind them of the impending time limit, and evaluate the state of each participant and the content fifteen minutes before the anticipated end. Controlling the topic of discussion to prevent its running more than a half-hour over the two-hour limit is an acquired skill that is essential. As postulated in "Murphy's Law and Counseling" (Pratt, 1982, p. 217):

- *First Law of Remaining Time:* If there is a significant breakthrough, it will occur during the last five minutes of a session.
- *Second Law of Remaining Time:* This will occur only when you cannot run overtime.

It is well for mediators to remember this professional joke and plan sufficient flex-time at the end of each session to come to a definite endpoint of discussion. The mediator must model respect for imposed limits if the participants are to follow that example in their own communication patterns.

If extra time is needed at the end of the first session, the mediator may want to reconfirm a policy of charging for extra time in half-hour increments, starting with the next overrun. This added economic incentive to conclude on time motivates participants to get into the subject matter quickly in the subsequent session. Mediators may also want to consider a policy stating that time allocated for a session but not needed because of efficient negotiation is positively rewarded by refunding or reallocating the money. This policy requires extensive recording and bookkeeping, however, and the unused appointment time is lost to the mediator. Thus it is reasonable to require full payment even when the session finishes early.

The number of sessions needed in periodic mediation and the intervals between sessions are also important for an effective mediation process. If the intervals are too short, the participants become exhausted by the emotional demands and feel overburdened by mediation. If they are scheduled too far in the future, however, sessions become disjointed and too much time is spent in each session regaining rapport and refreshing memories through review. Unless the arbitrary deadlines mentioned earlier demand otherwise, weekly sessions are the most advantageous.

Mediators should make this schedule definitive, and it should be clearly addressed in promotional and structuring material during stage 1. Three-way power struggles regarding the scheduling of the next session can inhibit progress by reinstituting a win/lose competition between participants, yet some accommodations must be made for participants who are juggling other activities or competing demands for time while also mediating. Mediators must determine their own availability and then be flexible. Intervals of longer than two weeks may have to be seen as constituting an impasse, however, since they seriously interfere with the continuity of the process. Recalcitrant participants must then decide whether to reconsider their time commitments or suffer a setback in mediation, which may end up throwing the issues into litigation or arbitration.

Some situations, as noted earlier, require that mediation be done in a single marathon session. Sometimes the rationale is that the participants will not willingly return once they have left. Other times the reasons are financial—when expensive time is being allocated to mediation rather than the participants' usual work, the participants, and even the whole system, can suffer economically from that loss of productivity and earning. Whatever the reason, the mediator should set up sessions that correspond with the nature of the issues. Marriages were not made in a day, and families cannot be restructured coherently in that amount of time. However, certain critical issues can be resolved within eight hours. Many situations only need the resolution of a single conflict in order for the participants to reestablish a working relationship. If marathon or crisis mediation is successful, other issues can be decided at later meetings that do not require the mediator's attendance, although the mediator should set up a plan for such subsequent meetings.

The weekly sessions mentioned earlier may be inappropriate if the situation being mediated involves imminent threat to the survival, safety, or security of the participants. Such cases can be handled on a crisis scheduling basis by attempting to isolate and mediate only the issues that relate directly to the threat, while reserving other issues for the more relaxed pace of weekly sessions.

Consider the case of a tenant's eviction by a landlord. Here the mediator, who has been called by the tenant two days before the eviction notice specifies that forcible removal from the premises can be undertaken, may want to speed the intake and introduction stage by calling the landlord, explaining the tenant's willingness to discuss problems (and perhaps even pay the costs) through mediation, and inviting the landlord to come in that day. Another example of crisis scheduling is a custody dispute where the husband has threatened to take physical custody of the child by force. In this case, the mediator's action depends on the contacting party's permission and help in obtaining the necessary information to make a contact. This kind of crisis scheduling should be used with discretion, of course, and reserved for only those cases where dealing with the immediate threat will allow for continued communication and mediation of all issues.

Scheduling must also involve the efficacy of the mediator. Mediators should remember to schedule time slots to relax and refresh themselves after each session. This time is very important, when caseloads increase, to prevent a mediator's version of "counselor burnout" (Watkins, 1983; Maher, 1983). If the standard mediation appointment is two hours, the appointment calendar should reserve three hours: two hours for the session, a half-hour runover allowance for the participants, and a half-hour for the mediator's own personal needs. Paperwork and administrative concerns should not be allowed to use up all the time between clients. If the mediator is to work all day, the ideal timing of sessions would be: 9:00 A.M. to 12:00 noon, 1:00 to 4:00 P.M., and a choice between 4:00 to 7:00 P.M. or 7:00 P.M. to 10:00 P.M. Since participants often must schedule their sessions for times when they are not committed to work outside the home, mediation can easily be scheduled to fit both the participants' and the mediator's needs by setting the first time slot at 4:00 to 6:00 P.M.

For effective use of the mediator's energy, no more than two three-hour appointment slots should be scheduled back to back in one time period without an additional one-hour break. Part-time and weekend times such as Saturday morning, 10:00 A.M. to 12:00 noon, show that mediation sessions can be customized to a balanced personal and professional life. Mediators who are moonlighting from other jobs or want to work around their childcare needs often find such scheduling a help. In this sense mediation reflects a holistic approach and the information-processing future of work in post-industrial society described by Toffler (1981). Mediation as a profession can weather the current storm of social and economic upheaval and redefinition with flexibility and personal choice. The scheduling of sessions and the provision of services can reflect the basic intentions of the mediation process—to empower people to select options that fit uniquely for *them.*

Recommended Reading

General

Business Plan for Small Service Firms. Management Aids 2.022. Education Division, Office of Management Assistance, U.S. Small Business Administration. Fort Worth, Tex.: Small Business Administration, 1980.

One of many publications that can help professionals become familiar with the choices and processes involved in starting a small business.

*The Independent Practitioner: Practice Management for the Allied
   Health Professional.* R. M. Pressman and R. Siegler. Homewood,
   Ill.: Dow Jones-Irwin, 1983.

   While written primarily for medical professionals, this book
analyzes the business aspects of a private practice, such as how to set
up and maintain corporate and client recordkeeping systems.

*Private Practice Handbook: The Tools, Tactics and Techniques for
   Successful Practice Development.* (2nd ed.) C. H. Browning. Los
   Alamitos, Calif.: Duncliff's International, 1983.

   A pragmatic approach to many aspects of setting up and
maintaining a private practice.

Environments for Mediation

The Hidden Dimension. E. T. Hall. Garden City: Doubleday, 1966.

   A classic introduction to the world of space and physical
setting as a powerful tool in communication.

*Public Places and Private Spaces: The Psychology of Work, Play
   and Living Environments.* A. Mehrabian. New York: Basic
   Books, 1976.

   A compendium of ideas for the effective arrangements of
space.

12

Receiving and Making Referrals

Referral is a crucial aspect of practicing mediation successfully—not only referral of participants to mediation but also referral to other helping professionals. Mediators are to some degree specialists and are often not the first resource that comes to the mind of prospective participants when problems arise. This is especially true today, since mediation as a concept is still emerging. Although it is becoming better known through mandatory state programs such as California's Conciliation Court system, and through more and more media exposure, mediation is still far from a household word.

Thus mediators must educate other helpers, as well as prospective clients and constituencies, about the value of mediation. Other systems, institutions, and private practitioners in law, medicine, business, counseling, therapy, social work, education, and religious ministries must be informed about the process and expectations of mediation, since these persons represent the primary contact for those who are experiencing interpersonal conflict, disputes, or a need for more effective decision making. In return, mediators should make use of other agencies, professions, and programs to meet the expressed or implied needs of the participants who are experiencing personal turmoil and stress.

Referrals from Others

Because mediation is a general process, mediators must first designate the specific boundaries of their practice, based on their personal expertise and interest as well as the inherent or expressed needs of the institution, community, or prospective clientele. Information about these limits should be sent, along with other information about the mediation process, to fellow professionals and the heads of organizations concerned with the subject. If the mediator wants to provide services for neighborhood disputes, for example, the materials should specify the kind of problems that will be resolved—such as tenant/landlord issues, building and zoning disputes, children's vandalism, dogs, garbage, noise, cars, parking, lawns, construction and appearance of houses and outbuildings, and intrusion between neighbors.

The materials sent to potential referral resources must be explicit regarding criteria for using the mediation service. Thus mediators in a large business organization should inform department heads and personnel leaders whether only certain members or classifications of employees can use the mediator to resolve their conflicts. It should also be explained whether the participants must be authorrized representatives of factions or subgroups or whether they can participate as individuals attempting to resolve their personal conflicts.

In every case, the information circulated to potential referral sources should include a professional disclosure statement concerning the mediator's view of mediation, education and employment record, current status, relevant publications, and professional affiliations. In divorce and custody mediation practices, marital and parental status should be mentioned.

Printed materials and individual cover letters are often not enough to stimulate good referrals to a mediator. Most professionals and administrators, even if they believe in a certain approach, hesitate to send one of their own clients unless they themselves have had ample opportunity to meet with the mediator personally and discuss issues. They may also feel inclined to refer if a respected colleague has expressed highly favorable reviews prior to a referral. The problem then becomes one of making the most of the mediator's often limited time to develop opportunities for such discussion.

Professionals who work together, in shared clinic settings, in loose affiliations, or in departmental groupings, often have routine staff or board of directors meetings. Mediators can ask to attend them. A simple ten-minute presentation of theory, with concrete examples of successful mediation followed by question and answer time and appropriate handouts, can create interest and understanding without impinging on the supervisor's or professionals' time and concentration. Getting the business manager, secretary, or executive director to put you on the agenda may not prove easy, however.

While such meetings are helpful, they do not often augment your case-finding activities; they should bring in referrals, but they can only be used infrequently, often only once a year. The biggest barrier to referral, if those who listened to your presentation approve of mediation as you have presented it, is *ease* in referring. Having preprinted materials to hand to disputants and prospective participants, as well as the knowledge that their own people will be given preference when it comes to scheduling mediation, are added incentives to refer.

From the mediator's point of view, such prescreened participants are the easiest to work with, simply because they come to the first session (or first contact) with a more appropriate set of expectations and intentions than do walk-ins. To gain these referrals, however, the mediator must supply the referral source with specific criteria for screening. In divorce mediation cases, these criteria may include a conclusive and permanent decision by at least one (or even both) of the spouses to end the relationship and a motivation to participate for reasons beyond mere expediency or reduced costs. For mediation services in large corporations, the immediate supervisor should review the situation with the disputants before contacting the mediator.

It is human nature even for professionals and supervisors to distort the reality of their own failures by stating that the service they provided was not the best one for the problem while referring the person with the problem to another type of service. Unfortunately, mediators can inherit many an awkward case this way. Haynes (1981, p. 48) warns against mediators accepting such premature referrals motivated by a counselor's or therapist's feeling of stalemate or failure in divorce counseling. We would like to think that referrals are made in order to meet the clients' needs better rather than to relieve a professional of a difficult case or even perhaps to discredit mediation by sending an impossible case doomed to failure because the participants are not yet ready. Mediators must verify that all the cases they accept from referral sources have their primary origin in interpersonal conflict rather than mental distress requiring therapy. At least in the beginning, you may ask other referral sources to contact you directly *before* referring, so that you can evaluate the appropriateness before involving the disputants. This step will help to build trust and rapport between you and the referral source.

Building professional networks is never easy—old boy affiliations can run deep, and territorial encroachment by mediators in conflicts formerly the domain of a single profession can be seen as real threats to income and establishment. Developing solid professional networks among first-line workers as well as those in higher positions can help break down these artificial distinctions, thus providing better service to people with problems.

Public-sector agencies providing mediation services to clients with the same problem (family disputes, custody decisions, tenant/landlord arguments, or education conflicts) should have an especially well-developed reciprocal referral system with private-sector mediators. Often because of more effective advertising or better visibility, a private mediator attracts cases that, owing to lack of money or special needs, should be transferred to a public agency that can provide similar mediation services. Likewise, public agencies may want to recommend private mediators, especially when confidentiality needs, complexity, or sophistication of the situation or the participants warrant. There should be no competition for case finding and referrals if both public and private mediation services are well conceived and executed. Mediation is not a duplication of services already being provided by other professions; rather, it is a new alternative within the total service delivery system. This perception must be conveyed to other helping agencies and professionals in the community in order to build solid referral networks that can give prospective cases appropriate help.

An additional source of cases is self-referral—a term commonly used when a prospective participant has already determined the need for mediation services and is attempting to locate them. Self-referrals usually require more time in stage 1 in order to explain basic terminology (such as the difference between mediation and arbitration or between mediators and ombudsmen) and also to describe mediation's relationship to the legal or hierarchical chain of command in which they may find themselves. Self-referrals often express a great sense of relief in finding you, since they usually have done a lot of searching and tend to be highly motivated.

Self-referrals can be promoted by adequate, yet unostentatious, advertisement of your services. In-house newsletters, descriptive ads in newspapers and professional or trade publications, listings in community resource directories, and even Yellow Page listings can help guide people to you. It is important that your service be listed properly. Persons experiencing a certain problem, such as a custody dispute, will be caught by direct use of that term in the listing or advertisement. It is always surprising how many people turn to such listings as a first recourse and how few helping agencies or professionals design their material for quick recognition. (Conciliation Court Services is an excellent example of an incomprehensible title to many persons who therefore overlook it during the stress of divorce.) Many persons contacting you from clearly defined listings may require information and referral (see the next section) or may be deemed inappropriate cases. If your listing has eased the self-referral process for even one in ten contacts, however, the expenditure is probably justifiable.

Referring Inappropriate Cases

Depending on the type of mediation practice you have, you may need to refer people who have contacted you to other services that will be more helpful to their circumstances. Potential cases may be inappropriate either because the case does not fall within the scope of your practice or because it is not yet ready to mediate.

If you think the case falls into the latter category, you may want to explain your perception of the participants' unreadiness and refer the case to other services or aid as a temporary measure. An example would be when a woman contacts you regarding divorce mediation while her husband is in jail or is in another state looking for a job. If the husband's condition is temporary and she thinks he would be receptive to a voluntary process emphasizing fairness and mutual accommodation, then the case is appropriate and may be accepted when he returns. If the husband's condition is not temporary or he is not receptive to mediation, the wife should be referred to a conciliation court, mental health center, or private practitioner for help in dealing with the emotional and pragmatic issues surrounding divorce.

This receiving, evaluating, and disseminating of information is often referred to as *information and referral* (I and R). The assessment of the case's need is only done to determine the most appropriate referral resource. Mediators who spend time on the phone or in person doing I and R work may either want to note it on a contact sheet or on a special I and R list that can be easily tabulated for type of problem, recommended referral, and time spent.

In order to match the contact person's need with the appropriate service, mediators need extensive knowledge of their own community resources. A sizable amount of information must be received and given in order to make I and R callers want to wade further into the often murky waters of public-sector help. Some communities have realized the need for a centralized approach to this I and R function, due to the frequency of changes in personnel, locations, phone numbers, and entrance requirements of referral resources. A contact that requires I and R work often necessitates at least twenty minutes worth of assessment of the need and explanation of possible options. Many mediators in private practice find that such calls demand too much time and immediately refer the caller to a crisis line, government switchboard, advocacy program, or institution designated to provide I and R.

Many callers investigating mediation have multiple problems, only one of which can be effectively mediated. Trying to extricate the appropriate problem from the tangled web requires patience and empathy. Mediators may wish to use telephone screening devices, such as taped messages that describe the kind of cases that are handled, or secretaries who can screen incoming calls. One telephone number can be for random incoming calls while another number can be given to professional members of the referral network as well as ongoing mediation participants.

Occasionally cases appear to be appropriate to your mediation practice, yet the potential participants turn out to be unable or unwilling to follow the mediation process or your office procedures. Sometimes this failure is due to the absence of nonverbal signals in telephone contacts or incomplete coverage of necessary data. Sometimes it is due to the disputant's resistance to start resolving disputes or deal with underlying conflicts. An excellent review of resistance that manifests itself in the first visit is described by Anderson and Stewart (1983). Cases involving participants with emotional or physical handicaps may be appropriate but may need to be referred to services through other agencies better equipped to handle their uniqueness. A case comes to mind of a man diagnosed as paranoid schizophrenic who could maintain a rational demeanor in a short phone conversation but could not control his rage against an absent (and illusory) antagonist while in the presence of the mediator. A referral back to his usual therapist, with an offer to mediate any disputes verified by the therapist, would be the best course.

While such cases are highly unusual, any professional who deals with the public encounters them sooner or later. Some mediators require a short preliminary interview or one-hour personal consultation with the participants before scheduling a full mediation session to ensure having an additional opportunity to evaluate personally the appropriateness of a potential case. This evaluation will determine the subsequent referral or termination of the case.

All referrals, even for inappropriate cases, require sufficient rapport and concrete information, such as telephone numbers, driving instructions, and names, in order to make the referral seem like a real option to the person contacting you. If people sense your frustration and hurry, they will not act upon your information, nor will they do so if it seems vague or incomplete. In summary, then, despite the very real problems, administratively and economically, of spending time talking to people who will not become mediation participants, mediators, like all helping professionals, have an ethical responsibility to guide troubled people to the right services.

Auxiliary Services

As participants come to mediation sessions and explore their conflicts and issues, new aspects of their problems are often discovered. These new dimensions, while off the main issues involved in the manifest or underlying conflicts, should be further explored. However, it can distort the mediation process to try to create deeper awareness and commitment to change during the sessions themselves.

A good example is the fictional custody conflict case in Chapter Five involving Bob and Rhonda. Rhonda's relationship and lack of true independence from her mother is an issue that a perceptive therapist or counselor would want her to explore. Rhonda's delayed break from her family of origin has set up conditions that could preclude further development in her current family unless Rhonda realizes this fact and changes her relationship with her mother as well as her perception of herself. Unless she is helped to recognize and accept this pattern, she is likely to continue her dependency and allow too much intrusion by her mother into the next stage of her own family—the postdivorce, reconstructed family. Awareness of personal and family developmental issues can certainly be sparked by ample emotional discovery in mediation of all types, but it cannot be adequately addressed in that setting. Rhonda will need far more time and encouragement than the mediator can provide in order to build her self-confidence and break the cycle.

Business and workplace mediation can bring to light latent internal conflicts regarding self-perceptions about success/failure, power/helplessness, independence/dependence, and other dichotomies promoted in our competitive society. Although these conflicts may not be as acute as the feelings that arise during divorce, a participant expressing conflict on these issues should be referred for growth-enhancing help.

When red herrings, obvious perceptual errors, and extensive underlying conflicts about tangential issues arise during the course of mediation, mediators must be bold enough to confront and explain their own perceptions of the participant's need and then make a referral for help. As mentioned in earlier chapters, the participants in mediation are often in crisis or at least under considerable stress—a time when there is great motivation to change and seek professional help. The mediator must seize the opportunity to direct the participant to auxiliary help. How to do so effectively is the subject of this section.

As noted earlier the mediator must have sufficient rapport with the participant to effect a referral that the participant will actualize. Particularly if the conflict produces defenses against unacceptable perceptions, the mediator's style and timing are of utmost importance in maintaining a clear channel of communication. No matter how accurate the mediator's view of the problem requiring help, however, or how skillfully the mediator is able to share this information, participants will not seek outside help unless they can acknowledge the *need* for it. Sometimes that acknowledgment can be brought about by discussion and questioning. The following dialogue shows a mediator trying to normalize the tangential problems and the need for additional services for a couple in divorce mediation:

Preparatory Statement for Referral

Mediator: Now that the mediated agreement is being signed, I'd like to share with you some general trends following divorce.

Normalizing the Need for Additional Services

Many former clients have told me they feel a need for a support group in order to build new friendships that are not couple-oriented and get some practical suggestions on how to handle being single again. Other clients have told me that they really need some long-term help sorting out their feelings about the opposite sex and the meaning of marriage *before* they try it again.

Using a Written Take-Home Tool

I'm handing you a brief list of common reactions that tell you when the *emotional* divorce is finally over. It has some suggested readings that may be helpful to you, either now or in a year or two.

Personalizing the Need

Based on what I've heard in mediation about your individual concerns, I've checked certain items on your sheets that I think will really help you in particular.

Open Questions About the Issue: ("Soft" Confrontation)

[*Turns to woman.*] Linda, since this is your second marriage that is ending in divorce, I'm wondering if you've become aware of any patterns that seem to be emerging. Have you discovered anything that seems to be interfering with maintaining a close relationship with men?

Confirmation by Client

Linda: Well, yeah, I guess so. I just don't know if I can change it though.

Normalizing and Rewarding

Mediator: Well, sometimes it takes a lot of work and time to get beyond the things we tell ourselves or that we've learned. I'd really like to help you with these concerns, because you've made such an effort to be open, honest, and progressive during mediation.

Making the Referral

I'm not really set up to do that kind of work, but I know a person, Susan Brown, who is in an agency about two miles from here, who would really be the person to talk with about this kind of thing. I've referred other participants to her, and I've always gotten good reports back. [*Normalizing the need.*]

Stressing Details and Convenience

Here, I'll write her name and number on your postdivorce sheet. [*While writing.*] She's a lady I'd trust to send my own family to. Do you know where the big mall is on Murray Road? Well, she's in an office there, upstairs. [*Personalizing the referral.*] It's very private and your kids could go to the show while you see her.

Reflection

[*Turns to man.*] Lee, one of the things you've expressed during the sessions is your need to progress in your career. Have you seen a connection between your drive to succeed and the need to restructure your family through divorce?

Defensive Reaction to Unwanted Perception

Lee: No, I don't really think there's any connection. I've done my part.

Accepting Unreadiness

Mediator: All right. At some point in the future, particularly before you become seriously involved with another woman, you may want to look at this issue again.

Normalizing the Problem

Many men find themselves caught between trying to do what their job demands and yet knowing that leaves little time or energy for their home life. If you ever find yourself in that bind, you may want to contact a counselor. [*Personalizing the referral.*] If you're in this area, give me a call and I'd be happy to refer you to a person I know and trust. [*Keeping the door open for recontact.*]

Participants must not only be aware of the issue for which a referral is being made but also believe that the referral resource being suggested is capable of helping them with that issue. Many people hold strong convictions regarding the inability of one or another professional group to help. Some write off all psychiatrists, all lawyers, all social workers as unctious and ineffective. Sometimes this belief is based on past experience or learning. Sometimes it is only a mask for a fear that they themselves are beyond hope, "just made that way," or unable to change or accept help from anyone. Sometimes shame and doubt mingle into a perception that "anybody who goes to a counselor is crazy—I'm not crazy, so I won't go." The mediator must probe these perceptions gently but firmly in order to determine whether the participant is willing to forgo them and take a risk based on trust in the mediator. Asking about their past experiences with helpers can bring to light the origin of such perceptions.

While the preceding dialogue shows a referral at the very end of mediation, a mediator should not wait until the last session if the need for referral is urgent. If the participant is calling too frequently between sessions, having a lot of scheduling difficulties, becoming verbally (or nonverbally) angry, crying or withdrawing too frequently during sessions, or comes to the session late or inebriated, it may indicate active resistance and a need for auxiliary services to probe the underlying conflicts.

Using a prior example discussed in Chapter Four, auxiliary services for the fifty-year-old woman experiencing general adaptation syndrome may include a referral to the local Displaced Homemaker's program for career counseling, job skills training, and emotional support, as well as referral to a family counselor or parent education program to help her deal more effectively with the adolescent children. She may also have, even without referral by the mediator, sought guidance and strength from a rabbi, minister, priest, or other spiritual leader or group. She may not be aware of a homemaker program that could give her practical help with household responsibilities during her temporary breakdown. She may need to be given the telephone number of the suicide prevention or crisis line to help her make it through the night.

Books and handouts can serve as an intermediary move before actual referral. By suggesting popular books, you can give the mediation participant a chance to acknowledge the issues privately without direct confrontation or embarrassment. Book lists are helpful, but having a lending library and giving the participant the appropriate material during a break or convenient time (with a proviso to return it by next session), can do much to reduce defensive behavior and pave the way for a successful referral.

Providing auxiliary referrals for tangential services is an important function of maintaining a caring, yet controlled, mediation process. It relieves the mediator of wearing too many hats during mediation sessions, yet it facilitates the mediator's professional responsibility to be sensitive to the participant's expressed or implicit needs.

Recommended Reading

On Becoming a Counselor: A Basic Guide for Non-Professional Counselors. E. Kennedy. New York: Continuum Publishing, 1980.

An excellent chapter on problems that helpers find when making referrals and how to handle them.

The Helping Relationship: Process and Skills. L. Brammer. Englewood Cliffs, N.J.: Prentice-Hall, 1973.

Contains a very short but excellent summary of ten basic principles for making referrals.

Legal Interviewing and Counseling: A Client-Centered Approach. D. A. Binder and S. C. Price. St. Paul: West, 1977.

Excellent section on referrals for client assistance and for evaluative purposes.

13

✖ ✖ ✖ ✖ ✖

Dealing
with Special Concerns

No matter what clientele or conflict situation mediators work with, the issues of the participants' background and perceptual world, which is derived from the ethnicity and socioeconomic status of the original family, are important factors in the provision and accept-ability of both the mediation services and the stages of the process itself. All mediation participants, whatever the context, are coping with their own, and perhaps the other participant's, attitudes and behavior regarding personal power, manipulation, persuasion, and coercion. Certain conflict situations require the mediator's under-standing and sensitivity to the climate for depression and suicide. These tangential issues should be considered part of the mediator's training. Much has been written on these topics, enough to require a separate review, but we have tried to narrow the subject to the essen-tials in this chapter. Thus we offer the following discussion as a brief overview.

Ethnic and Sociocultural Perspectives

How a potential participant receives the offer of mediation and relates to the goals, process steps, and mediator's role and tech-niques has a great deal to do with the ethnic and socioeconomic lessons the person has learned before mediation (Hall, 1976). Many of the conflicts that could be mediated relate centrally to these perceptions (see Chapter Eight).

Many private mediators often come from and design their services for the ethnic assumptions and principles of the British-American and Jewish middle to upper socioeconomic groups (McGill and Pearce, 1982; Herz and Rosen, 1982). They do so because of the cultural perceptions and value systems inherent in these subcultures (Spiegel, 1982) regarding the nature of conflict and the use of professional services to resolve it. Mediation as a conflict resolution process is universal and comprehensible to people of many different cultural and ethnic views, but it must be provided in such a way that it is consistent with their beliefs and traditions.

Coogler (1979) has suggested that mediation can be made useful to members of the low-income socioeconomic group by modifying fee and appointment schedules and making an effort to understand the participants' language and reading level, family structure and values, network system, and desire for minimal formalities. Mediators working with tenant/landlord conflicts, neighborhood disputes, community justice or police and crisis programs, as well as family and divorce conflicts or domestic violence, should heed Coogler's concepts when devising their service delivery system.

Obviously the poor cannot afford expensive mediation any more than they can afford expensive litigation and adjudication in the courts. For mediation to become a real option for a sizable percentage of the population, the public sector or some philanthropic organization must underwrite the costs of mediation. Although mediators who wish to address the needs of the poor can minimize their overhead costs by office sharing and other cost-saving maneuvers, mediation will continue to be for the privileged until it is made mandatory through subsidized public agencies. (See Chapter Eleven for a discussion of private and public-sector mediation.)

The setting of appointments in a mediation service is influenced by the participants' ethnic perceptions. While the American middle class has adopted much of the British and German emphasis on punctuality and measured time as an important commodity ("Time is money"), this outlook tends to produce a future rather than past or present orientation and a mechanistic, clock-and-calendar approach to time (Spiegel, 1982). This approach is compatible with the stated propositions and process of mediation, which is basically involved with planning for the future. This emphasis on the future is not so strong in other ethnic cultures, however; people coming from rural cultures—such as many Irish and Italians (Spiegel, 1982), American Indians and Alaskan natives (Attneave, 1982), Afro-Americans (Pinderhughes, 1982), and Cubans (Bernal, 1982)—are oriented much more around the present, or even the past, as compared to cultures where clocks, mechanization, compulsory education, and industrial reality have required *deferred* gratification and punctuality. The pace of life, the value of minutes and hours, and the life-styles lived by mediation participants directly affect their punctuality as well as their willingness to plan for contingencies in the future. The mediator should take these differences into account. Rules or guidelines, which are the mediator's explicit expectations regarding appointments, lost time, and scheduling pace, should be modified according to these cultural perspectives.

Many widely diverse cultures, including blacks and Afro-Americans, Puerto Ricans and Asians, have a system of honor, obligation, or respect that dictates "my word is my bond." These concepts rule their relationships. People from these cultural traditions do not relate well to printed information or written contracts that specify every possible issue or contingency. They regard the need for such materials as an insult at worst and superfluous at best.

Mediators working with people of German (Winawer-Steiner and Wetzel, 1982, pp. 263–265), British (McGill and Pearce, 1982, p. 472), or Norwegian extraction (Midelfort and Midelfort, 1982, p. 443) will want to use clarity and brevity along with precision and objectivity in written communication, since these are cultural values. Jewish families, however, may reject "brief, logical explanations and solutions to problems in favor of more complex feeling-oriented ones" (Herz and Rosen, 1982, p. 388). Mediators should be aware of these attitudes toward written communication by different ethnic groups and apply their knowledge in mediation, particularly in stage 5 (clarification and writing a plan).

Many ethnic groups regard any intervention by mediators, counselors, and other helping professionals as an explicit expression of their personal failure and will voluntarily agree to such intrusion only in the most dire circumstances. Members of French

Canadian families, for example, often use defense mechanisms (see Chapter Four) to defend against this perception of failure. The mediator must help them see that the problem-solving stage and homework tasks assigned are "duties," in order to bring their cultural values of persistence and endurance to bear (Langelier, 1982). Many cultures share this perception of failure and embarrassment. Bringing problems to an outsider is often considered shameful by Asian family members, and shame is a dominant cultural motivator (Shon and Ja, 1982).

Assuming that the participants from ethnic backgrounds have agreed to mediate, the ethnic dimension still affects their expectations of the mediator. After suffering the indignities of coming to outsiders in order to be told what to do, they feel confused when the mediator then takes a neutral role and asks the participants themselves to make decisions.

The use of mediation is favored in cultures where conflict itself is unacceptable, since mediation is a simpler, faster way to resolve disputes. Widely diverse ethnic groups, from Iranians (Jalali, 1982, pp. 293–294) to Norwegians (Midelfort and Midelfort, 1982, pp. 446–447), have strong cultural traditions and almost automatic acceptance of mediation. Cultures in which face saving and not backing down are important values find mediation a great help so long as it is provided with attention to other cultural norms (not supplanting traditional authority, for example).

Table 11 summarizes the most relevant ethnic issues for mediators. It is based on the references and recommended readings and should be used only as a clue to anticipated problems in providing mediation services to such participants. Mediators working with family-related conflicts should pursue further information regarding typical ethnic family structures and values before mediation.

Depression and Suicide

Not every case that is mediated is a cause for concern about a participant becoming depressed or despondent to the point of considering suicide. Nevertheless, mediators should be alert to the signs of severe depression that go beyond the usual grief and loss process described in Chapter Four. We believe that mediators who work

Table 11. Cross-Comparison of Ethnic Perspectives for Mediators.

Reaction	American Indian/Alaskan Native	Black Afro-American	Mexican	Puerto Rican/Cuban	Asian	Franco-American/French Canadian	British	Irish	German	Greek	Italian	Jewish	Polish	Norwegian	Vietnamese	Iranian
Reaction to need for outside help from professionals																
Feels shame, sense of failure, personal weakness		*			*	*	*	*	*	*		*	*		*	*
Distrusts agencies and helping systems in general	*	*		*										*		*
Feels a threat to personal authority/family hierarchy			*		*	*			*	*	*		*		*	*
Turns first to members of own community	*	*	*		*	*	*		*	*	*		*	*		*
Distrustful of many related questions					*	*			*	*						*
Reaction to interpersonal conflict																
Denies the conflict until manifest conflict behavior is intolerable						*	*		*				*			
Accepts the conflict but feels helpless to act	*			*								*				
Represses anger and other negative feelings			*		*	*	*	*	*		*	*	*	*	*	
Uses explosive verbal/nonverbal communication, then begins problem solving		*		*						*	*					*
Reaction to time and schedules																
Future orientation							*		*			*				
Present orientation	*	*	*													
Past orientation					*	*		*		*			*	*	*	*

Punctual, expects to start and end on time					*	*	*		*			*		*		
Clocktime less important; "forgets" to cancel or reschedule	*	*	*	*							*				*	
Works well with crisis/marathon style done at home				*											*	
Needs many appointments to avoid rushing awareness/ information release					*	*	*							*		
Reaction to mediator's credentials																
Questions education and experience to determine quality							*					*				
Relies on others within the subgroup for referral	*		*		*					*	*		*		*	
Accepts the mediator as an expert			*	*	*	*		*		*				*		
Mediator must prove ability, trustworthiness							*		*			*	*			
Reaction to mediator's role, techniques																
Unused to intrafamilial equality in decision making		*	*	*	*	*		*	*	*	*		*		*	*
Gives complete information, helps professional							*		*			*				
Asks mediator for advice as higher authority			*		*			*		*	*			*		
Complies in sessions but may undermine decisions later			*		*				*	*						*
Prefers more affective than contractual tone			*	*							*	*				
Needs action-oriented pace				*												
Reaction to fees																
Unwilling to pay before services are given or approved as "right"									*		*	*				
Pays grudgingly due to ambivalence										*						
Pays regularly					*		*	*	*					*		
Does not accept "charity"; if can't pay in full, will find another service		*												*	*	
Fees are understood, acceptable, but prefers third-party reimbursement	*						*									

with cases that dynamically affect a participant's self-concept and self-worth must be aware of this problem and also be prepared to intervene effectively.

There are many excellent treatises, theories, and popular books (Cammer, 1969) concerning severe depression. While many of them offer useful perspectives, we find *reality therapy* (Glasser, 1981) to be the most consistent with the philosophy and practice of mediation for this issue. In this view, depression is a set of behavior that is created and manifested to remove the internal conflict by eliciting help from others or attempting to change the world. Glasser sees the depressed person as one who is actively creating behavior, or "depressing," in order to elicit responses from others that will change the world sufficiently to alleviate the internal conflict the "depressor" feels. Sometimes the act of depressing gets us what we need. More often, though, depressing is a self-defeating strategy because other people avoid, underrespond or overreact to the person who is exhibiting it.

Depression is a reaction to a perception of powerlessness and hopelessness. According to John Jung (1978, p. 129):

> The concept of learned helplessness, developed by Seligman, is a related idea that suggests that the repeated inability to influence outcomes will instill a state of passivity in an organism. . . . Learned helplessness also weakens motivation to perform as well as creates emotional disruption that may eventually become depression.

Certainly a sense of helplessness, if not a cause, is a result of severe depression and can be learned through our social interactions in the world (Dweck and Licht, 1980).

Because it is linked to a sense of powerlessness, there is a much higher incidence of clinical depression among certain subcultures, minorities, and women. It is often a more socially acceptable way of dealing with anger and rage than other destructive behavior and thus has been promoted by society at large; people who are busy depressing are immobilized and do not, in fact, rock the boat or change their corner of the world. Indeed, people who are severely depressed are made even more powerless to act constructively to help themselves by being given potent psychoactive drugs and shock therapy. At the farthest end of the intervention continuum, the most severely depressed are simply removed from society and put into mental health institutions. While these later measures may be effective in keeping a person alive, they must be questioned as to their effectiveness in helping the individual deal with an already lowered self-concept or temporary depression. Mediators should not promote such measures for people who are only experiencing transitory depression brought about by situational factors such as divorce or workplace dispute.

The following common symptoms of severe depression could lead to suicidal behavior if no intervention is provided: loss of appetite, suppression of sexual urges, impairment in digestion and elimination, confusion and disorientation, inability to perform routine tasks, lowered attention to grooming, memory blackouts, withdrawal from usual relationships and activities, and physical isolation. No factor by itself is a complete indicator, and each of these symptoms has its own continuum of severity, so mediators are advised to look at the gestalt of the *person* rather than merely summing up these signs.

Perhaps the easiest way to determine an individual's potential for becoming severely depressed or suicidal is to review other evaluative criteria mentioned in this book. The mediator should look first at the general area of conflict being mediated. Family-related mediation generally has much more impact on people's views of themselves than do most employee/employer or tenant/landlord problems. A sole proprietor who has created a business out of hard work and deferment of personal needs may have a greater self-involvement in a civil rights dispute with an employee than would a representative of a large corporation, however, because that sole proprietor has more to lose personally. One way to assess this potential is to determine the level of loss the participant is experiencing. The greater the self-involvement, the more unique the loss; and the more final the loss, the more potential there is for serious depression and suicidal behavior.

The next area to look at is the constellation of conflicts the person is experiencing. There is more potential for depression and suicide when the conflicts are of the avoidance/avoidance or the approach/avoidance type, since in the former case the person feels trapped and powerless to escape and in the latter case feels frustrated, confused, and often angry at himself or others for creating the conflict. Underlying conflicts that linger unresolved, or even unacknowledged, past the resolution of the manifest conflict are the raw material for future problems such as depression. The person has, presumably, been taken through a conflict resolution process that removed or managed the manifest conflict, thus taking away social legitimacy for *feeling* the underlying conflict, let alone resolving it. The person then tells himself, "I've been through (mediation, arbitration, conciliation, negotiation, counseling), so I *shouldn't* be feeling this way"—an attitude that can start the typical downward spiral of self-deprecation, shame, and despair often seen as a prelude to severe depression or suicide. Therefore the more effective the conflict resolver is at acknowledging and resolving the underlying conflicts, the less likely this spiral is to be set into motion.

Another factor to look at when evaluating a participant's likelihood of severe depression or suicide is to itemize triggering events—anniversaries, birthdays, phrases, gestures, and the like that hold a special or intimate meaning for the participant. These triggering events often release a flood of memories or remind the person of the loss. Mediators can sensitize participants ahead of time by legitimizing feelings before they happen, planning for special dates, and reminding participants not to operate out of former habits and expectations. Also, mediators can strategically time their follow-up evaluations for those peak points or dates. (See Chapter Three for a discussion of follow-up procedures.)

Although not all cases involve such strong emotions, the mediator may be the only professional to whom a participant will relate concerns and feelings. If you see symptoms of moderate to severe depression, if one participant mentions perceptions and concerns about the other, if you become aware of a participant's underlying mental or emotional conflicts, if participants call you before or after mediation saying they are depressed or thinking about suicide, how should you handle it? When a mediator learns of the conditions and symptoms mentioned earlier (excluding an overt plea for help or threat), the best course is to educate the person, providing a perspective for reevaluation of feelings and thoughts. A well-timed and well-executed referral for additional services of a specially trained professional can be the most effective tool (see Chapter Twelve). Drawing out the fears and conflicts requires expertise in handling them. If you do not possess sufficient skill or do not wish to take on the often lengthy process of helping a depressed individual, use your rapport to facilitate the referral and gather enough information to assess the appropriate service need.

If you are being given this information by another participant or relation, remember that you can effectively deal only with the one with whom you are communicating directly. Thus if a former wife in a custody mediation case is worried about the husband, educate the *woman* about the symptoms of depression and suicide and *her* role in getting the man the help he needs. Her rapport and interactions with the man are far more vital than yours to his future actions; she probably has far more practical knowledge of the man's circumstances, resources, and capabilities than you do. She must be helped to discover her feelings and determine what his behavior means to her. She should be encouraged to discuss her feelings of guilt and powerlessness with a professional as a way of helping her through the stress of aiding him.

If you receive a call from the depressed person expressing concern about depression, the techniques of verbal reward, reflection, and questioning will help you determine:

1. Whether the person is severely depressed to the point of interrupting basic survival behavior of eating, sleeping, and elimination
2. Whether the person has someone to contact who can take on continuing responsibility for him
3. Whether the depression is chronic or situational and the duration of this acute phase
4. What level of help (telephone or other crisis service, long-term counseling, admittance to a regular or mental hospital) the person is willing to consider and accept voluntarily
5. Whether suicide has been contemplated or attempted
6. Where the person is now—address and phone number

When the person says, "I've thought about ending it all" or "I'm going to find a way to stop all this," it is important for the mediator to acknowledge the possibility of suicide and discover whether the person has a specific suicide plan. The following dialogue will give you some indication of a typical telephone exchange:

Tom: I feel so damned depressed I can't take it anymore.

Mediator: Have you been thinking about suicide?

Tom: Sure, I've thought about it. . . .

Mediator: Have you tried it?

Tom: No, not yet. . . .

Mediator: Do you have something with you right now that you're thinking about using?

Tom: No, no . . . I don't think I could use a gun. . . .

Mediator: That's good. I don't want you to. And I'm *sure* you don't really want to stop living. You just want the pain you're feeling to stop. There are other ways besides killing yourself. I know you're feeling pretty helpless and hopeless right now, and that's why I'm glad you've called and why I want you to stay on the phone with me for a while. There *are* ways to help you, but first you've got to promise me that you're not going to kill yourself or hang up right now. Can you promise me?

Tom: [*Crying.*] Yes, I guess so.

Mediator: It's all right to feel what you're feeling, Tom. I'm just going to keep talking to you for a while. . . .

You should not try to resolve the problem at this point. No matter how well conceived and appropriate your plans may be later on, they can only overwhelm the person now and augment the fear of inadequacy. Keep to the realm of feelings. Encourage the suicidal person to talk about feelings: legitimizing them, making behavioral contracts for the immediate future (such as what he is going to do after your phone call), and encouraging the person to rely on ingrained habits or social forms (getting up at the usual time, personal grooming, going to work on time) to maintain a reality base. Never do anything—such as calling another person or sending a crisis team or police officer—without first suggesting the idea and getting a verbal statement that the suicidal person will allow it and cooperate. To do otherwise will break off all rapport and trust, and the person's negative reactions may be generalized to all helping professionals.

Referrals to others, while perhaps needed, will not be actualized by a person at this point and may also break down the necessary rapport ("He wants to get rid of me by sending me to a shrink!") or heighten existing fears. While the person who receives a suicide call must act responsively and responsibly, he or she is *not* totally responsible for whether that person lives or dies. Many people who work with suicide threats believe it helps to tell the person that suicide *is* an option and that the helper will not stop them but will encourage them to pursue other avenues. Naturally, when someone is incapacitated by a chemical substance or self-inflicted wound, the call itself is confirmation of the person's desire to be rescued and continue living. In this case the helper must call upon all resources to preserve life.

To sum up, mediation holds the potential for aggravating internal conflicts involving a participant's self-worth and ability to get out of a bad situation. Because of this, mediators must be aware of the signs of depression that could lead to suicidal thoughts or actions. They must be sufficiently trained and ready to act effectively should a seriously depressed or suicidal participant, or former client, contact them with an overt or unexpressed request for help.

Resistance

Every practicing mediator knows that most participants will, at some point in the mediation process, show resistance to the demands of the process. This behavior can be expressed by such actions as verbal withdrawal from negotiation, late arrival to sessions, attempts to reopen closed issues, inability to choose between options, and hostility aimed at the other participant or the mediator. Each of these actions requires a repertoire of responses by a skilled mediator. We have discussed these techniques in several chapters, particularly Chapters Three, Eight, and Nine. In this section we highlight the general categories of resistance and connect them to the seven-stage mediation process outlined in Chapter Three.

Resistance is very similar to the defense mechanisms described in Chapter Four. By acting resistant, participants are expressing a desire for the world to change in order to meet their perceived needs. They are unwilling to set unwanted or uncomfortable limits on their own behavior. Sometimes resistance is the behavioral manifestation of an internal conflict of the approach/ avoidance or avoidance/avoidance type (see Chapter Two). When there is a potential for change, you will usually see resistance. It is an attempt by one or both of the participants to undermine any effort, decision, or behavior that would promote the mutually approved goal determined earlier. The one demonstrating resistance has reassessed the situation and now perceives the formerly acceptable goal as a threat.

The initial contact is a point at which resistance to mediation can first appear. The potential client calls to inquire about services but is unwilling to set an appointment; the caller cannot commit to a time without checking first with another friend or helper (who will not be a mediation participant). In the former case, mediators can ease the reluctance by offering a consultation without obligation to continue, a shorter commitment of time, and perhaps even a reduction in the basic hourly cost. With these three pragmatic barriers removed, reluctant clients may be able to overcome their resistance and take a risk.

Based on the categories that Anderson and Stewart (1983) have noted in family therapy, mediators may expect this resistance at the initial contact to be couched in one of the following terms:

- Problem 1: It's not my fault that mediation is needed.
- Problem 2: I want mediation, but the other participant doesn't.
- Problem 3: I'll mediate with some but not all of the potential participants.
- Problem 4: Another person told me to set an appointment, but I don't think mediation will work.
- Problem 5: I'm not sure the mediator is competent (or adequately credentialed, or the right age, or the right marital status).

For each of these problems there is a range of responses that can help lessen the resistance. The reader is referred to the work of Anderson and Stewart (1983) for more information on specific techniques.

During the first and second stages of mediation, the following types of resistance often surface. One or both of the participants:

- Say that all the problems and conflicts are resolved
- Cannot focus on the relevant past
- Will only focus on the past, not the future
- Will not talk in the session
- Battle for dominance verbally
- Unexpectedly reschedule or cancel
- Arrive late or inebriated
- Fail to perform assigned tasks or bring in materials

Remember that the resistance a mediator sees in all stages is a mirror of the issues that must be resolved or managed. None of the behavior should be answered with an emotional response or be taken personally by the mediator. As a general rule, such resistance should be talked about openly in joint session before returning to the other points at issue. Strict adherence to any rules that were accepted earlier is imperative, but the mediator should try to refocus discussion whenever possible rather than call an impasse.

At stage 4, negotiation and decision making, mediators can often expect one of the participants to announce that he or she wishes to withdraw from mediation because (1) mediation is not working or (2) the mediator is biased or incompetent. Mediators can legitimize this announcement before it happens. They should tell participants in stage 1, or as a preliminary statement to the session, that such a response is natural and the participant should talk about such issues in a private caucus or telephone conversation *before* withdrawing from mediation. The mediator can discover the participant's internal conflict in this way and perhaps relabel the issue or change the participant's perception of dread, threat, failure, or frustration.

Moore (1983b, pp. 416–429) has reviewed the literature and suggests that there are four basic patterns mediators can follow to move participants from resistant stances during negotiation and decision making (stage 4):

1. Incremental convergence
2. A delay of agreement, then a leap to a package settlement
3. Development of a consensual formula or agreement in principle
4. Procedural means to reach agreements

The first pattern is called for when positional bargaining has been primarily used. The second method is often used when there has been a high demand and few concessions or when a weak participant wishes to prove a point but still settle the matter. The third method involves getting consensus on the general and then moving to the specific. The fourth method of procedural moves includes the procedural timeline, referral for arbitration and litigation, and arbitrary decision-making methods such as splitting the difference and flipping a coin. Another variation is for the participants to agree to postpone, avoid, or drop an issue altogether. All these methods rely for their effectiveness on proper timing.

At stage 4 the resistance is likely to be aimed at the procedural level of the mediation session itself, as a diversion to shift attention from the true issues and onto the less threatening aspects of mediation. Although mediators should deal with the underlying conflicts, they may want to start with the procedural problems by creating agreement on the agenda of each session in regard to which issues to discuss. Moore (1983b) summarizes the literature and discusses the following approaches to agenda development: ad hoc; simple agenda; alternating choices; ranking according to importance; the principled agenda; less difficult items first; building-block or contingent agenda; and trade-offs or packaging.

Mediation sessions that have gone smoothly, with little resistance, until stage 5 (clarification and writing a plan) may flare up in moments over the proposed wording of the mediated plan. Rather than stifle such controversy, it is important to remind the participants that they are doing exactly the right thing. Such verbal rewards, together with strict control by the mediator over the protocol of who speaks uninterruptedly, will keep such turning points from escalating into walkouts. Reframing the issues, clarifying the specific disagreements or disputed wording, reminding participants not to sign a document that will not be upheld—all are useful techniques.

A common response from participants who seek outside counsel from lawyers or therapists at stage 6 is: "My attorney (or social worker and so forth) says I shouldn't sign this." The mediator can get the participant to voice the fear (either in joint or private session) by asking, "What are you afraid will happen if you do?" After the explanation is provided, the mediator can then inquire, "What safeguard could be built into the mediated plan to prevent this?" The suggested antidote can be discussed in joint session while the mediator, acting as an agent of reality, reminds them first of all the time and money they have invested and then of the typical consequences of not coming to agreement through mediation. If the resistance is still strong, the mediator can call an impasse or suggest an adjournment to consider it further.

Additional sources of resistance can be created by other institutions, helping agencies, and larger systems that must either ratify the mediated plan (stage 6: legal review and processing) or can undermine the effectiveness of the agreements. For example, mediation of disputes regarding the exclusive use of certain trails for snowmobiles or cross-country skiers within a designated federal scenic area can only be effective if the administrating body, in this case the Department of Agriculture, has a policy of regional autonomy as well as support for mediated plans. In divorce disputes, the best mediated settlement will not be ratified by the courts unless resistance by judges to mediation is reduced by legislation or precedence; the local court judges must be educated to the process in order to evaluate and ratify it.

Overcoming resistance by participants as well as outside entities is perhaps the most challenging aspect for development of effective mediation services. We realize this discussion is but the tip of the iceberg and look forward to further professional research and development that will elaborate specific techniques.

Recommended Reading

Ethnic and Sociocultural Perspectives

Ethnicity and Family Therapy. M. McGoldrick, J. K. Pearce, and J.
   Giordiano (Eds.). New York: Guilford Press, 1982.
      A unique collection of articles outlining the history of ethnic
groups, the nature of their family structures and values, and the
interaction between these factors and the agent of change.

The Personnel and Guidance Journal, April 1983, *61* (8).
   Special issue on international guidance and counseling.
      A compendium of articles concerning the unique aspects of
cross-cultural perspectives, as well as views about counseling from
other nations directly applicable to mediation.

Perspectives on Cross-Cultural Communication. C. H. Dodd. Du-
   buque: Kendall/Hunt, 1977.
      A basic conceptual framework that synthesizes relevant find-
ings from anthropology, linguistics, sociology, speech communication, political science, and mass communication.

Resistance

Mastering Resistance: A Practical Guide to Family Therapy. C.
   Anderson and S. Stewart. New York: Guilford Press, 1983.
      Based on family therapy but offers many definitions and
techniques directly applicable to mediation.

Power: The Inner Experience. D. C. McClelland. New York: Irving-
   ton, 1975.
      An excellent background work that presents useful classifica-
tions of power.

✳ ✳ ✳ ✳ ✳

Conclusion

In this book we have discussed the practice of mediation, as well as its philosophical, psychological, legal, and social foundations. We have explored the nature of conflict and have outlined a seven-stage mediation process for the resolution of many types of conflicts. We have compared mediation with other methods of conflict resolution and have described various styles of mediation. Professional and legal issues have been raised and some answers suggested. Education and training considerations have been discussed, as well as concrete suggestions for developing a mediation service. We have attempted to offer a comprehensive guide to the theory and practice of effective conflict resolution.

Throughout this book we have limited our references to mediation as an "alternative" dispute resolution process or as a less expensive substitute for litigation. An alternative implies a deviation from the norm. Our society can no longer afford to consider litigation the norm. Mediation is premised on the desirability of decision by consent, not on the imposition of authority, as in litigation. We, as mediators, can facilitate a norm that promotes cooperation and self-determination rather than coercion and imposed decisions. The proper role for litigation is that of last resort when all consensual forms of dispute resolution have been reasonably exhausted. Only then is the alternative of litigation justified.

The uses of mediation we have outlined primarily relate to the resolution of disputes between individuals and small groups. The principles applicable to consensual resolution of disputes in these small-scale situations are similar to those used to nonviolently resolve conflicts between nations. It is even more important for nations to consider consensual peacemaking the norm, compared to war or the threat of war, than it is for individuals to consider mediation the norm, compared to litigation or the threat of it. We can only hope that as the value of developing and considering creative options for consensual resolution of personal disputes is increasingly promoted, the decreasing use of coercion and force in international conflicts will follow.

Resources

A. Employment Agreement
B. Mediation Guidelines
C. Mediated Custody and Child Support Plan
D. Code of Professional Conduct for Mediators
E. Selected List of National Organizations

DIVORCE & CUSTODY MEDIATION SERVICE

JOINT CUSTODY • DIVORCE & SEPARATION AGREEMENTS • CUSTODY MEDIATION

ALISON Y. TAYLOR, M.A. • Mediator/Counselor

We, the undersigned, hereby agree to have_____
provide mediation services to us. The mediator has provided us with a
Professional Disclosure Statement and has explained the mediation process
to us. We understand and agree to the Mediation Guidelines (attached), which
are part of this contract.

Costs for mediation services will be charged at $_____per_____.
Payments will be made ____by each participant equally for half of all charges.
                       ____by one participant for all charges_____.

To make payments for the above charges, I/we agree to use:

___Cash, money order, or cashier's check, payable at the start of sessions.
___A prepaid escrow account; $_____, paid on_____, will
   be credited to our account; any unused portion will be returned.
   Subsequent payments will be made_____.
___A third-party payer_____.
___Business Exchange (BX) credits.
___Trades in needed goods or services (specify).

It is anticipated that sessions will begin on_____
and will be held_____until mediation is completed or a withdrawal
or impasse is declared. It is anticipated that approximately_____
sessions will be needed. Sessions will last approximately_____hours;
extra time beyond 10 minutes may be charged at the half hourly rate above.

Because of the extensive participant review and revision, we agree to hold
the mediator harmless against errors, omissions, or future negative consequences stemming from the provision of the mediation process or the preparation of the Mediated Plan. We understand that the mediator cannot
guarantee the outcome or success of that plan.

Any further mediation required or desired following the signing of the
Mediated Plan will be provided upon the terms and conditions agreed to at
that time.

Participants will not require the mediator to testify in any subsequent
court proceedings regarding the subject of this mediation, nor will they
allow the mediator's notes or case records to be brought into such proceedings.

We agree to the above terms:

_____   _____
_____   _____

Mediator_____

DIVORCE & CUSTODY MEDIATION SERVICE

JOINT CUSTODY • DIVORCE & SEPARATION AGREEMENTS • CUSTODY MEDIATION

ALISON Y. TAYLOR, M.A. • Mediator/Counselor

1. Both participants agree voluntarily to cooperate with the mediation process by reducing poor communication patterns such as personal attacks and angry outbursts and by staying with the issues at hand. Both will actively participate in the search for fair and workable options.

2. During the sessions the participants will work to resolve only those issues which are as yet undecided or in dispute in the following areas:
____Physical separation   ____Child custody   ____Spousal support
____Property settlement   ____Visitation   ____Contingency plans
____Money tax planning   ____Child support   ____Legal processes
____Other:

3. Participants will hold private sessions (caucus) with the mediator when mutually requested in order to improve the mediator's understanding of the participant's position. Information gained through private session may be shared in joint sessions, unless the participant wishes it to be kept confidential.

4. The mediator will keep track of the issues which are <u>open</u> (unresolved) and <u>closed</u> (where a tentative decision acceptable to all has been reached). Reversals in positions will be fully explored so that decisions will not be made just to "get it over with" or to relieve uncomfortable feelings.

5. The mediation process will be determined to be at an impasse if:

    a. The mediator declares it because of:
       1. Noncompliance with the rules
       2. Incomplete participation
       3. Lack of personal readiness
    b. A participant declares an impasse and the mediator agrees (preceding reasons).
    c. Three sessions have produced no substantial progress.

6. An impasse will be handled in one or more of these ways:
    a. Complete termination of the case by the mediator.
    b. Participants must receive other services (counseling, legal).
    c. Specific events must occur before proceeding (relocation, job).
    d. Participants reschedule when ready to resume.
    e. Participants withdraw from mediation in writing.

7. Participants will be prompt and will call if they expect to be more than 10 minutes late. Cancellation or rescheduling requires at least _____hours prior notice, or a one-hour charge may be made against the account.

8. Each participant will supply all information requested by the mediator in order to discuss open issues, reopen closed issues, or determine appropriate options. Incomplete disclosure may invalidate agreements.

9. Children, or other persons directly affected by the issues being mediated, will be brought into joint sessions if the mediator finds their presence necessary. Advocates and attorneys may be present as long as their involvement promotes the mediation process and as long as the mediator and other participants have been given prior notice.

10. Between mediation sessions and before finalizing an agreement, participants are encouraged to consult with attorneys regarding their legal rights and obligations.

11. If a trial period is needed to determine the appropriateness of an option, the participants will record its terms in written form prior to its start and will continue or suspend mediation during the trial period as the mediator determines. Such trial periods will not prejudice later agreements or decisions.

12. The first draft of the Mediated Plan, while still unsigned, will be considered a working copy for the purposes of participant review and revision. Participants will not ask the mediator to testify in any legal proceedings regarding the issues involved in mediation. No sound or video recording of the session will be made without prior consent of the mediator and other participants.

13. Both participants agree to suspend or refrain from starting court proceedings against each other for issues related to those in mediation while sessions are in progress or until (1) the Mediation Plan has been signed by both; (2) a participant has withdrawn in writing; (3) the mediator has declared an impasse. Exceptions: restraining orders; petition for dissolution.

14. In all issues the best interest of the participants' children will be the primary consideration for selection of options.

These rules have been explained to me and I agree to abide by them:

_____   _____

_____   _____

I have explained these rules to the participants and they have agreed by their signatures that I have witnessed:

_____

_____

Resource C. Mediated Custody and Child Support Plan.

We, John and Jane Doe, are husband and wife. We were
married on March 1, 1967, and have one child of our marriage,
John Jr., who is nine years old.

Irreconcilable differences have arisen between us causing
the irremediable breakdown of our marriage. We have physically
separated, and have lived apart approximately one year. We
have mutually decided to divorce.

During the year we have lived apart we continued to share
parenting of John Jr., and cooperated in providing for his needs.
He appears to have adjusted well to the existing situation.
We each have a significant nuturing relationship with him that
is important to all of us.

We each believe the other to be a fit parent. We want
to continue to share responsibility for our son's physical care,
and for major decisions about his health, education, welfare,
and discipline. We will cooperate together to minimize
disruptions to his life. We will seek joint legal and joint
physical custody of John Jr. We want to remain flexible, yet
provide all of us reasonable schedules and prior notice of
necessary changes. Our primary concern has been and will
continue to be the best interests of John Jr., considering
the reality of our divorce.

We have reached this plan voluntarily through the process
of mediation which was provided by the mediator signed below.
We understand the mediator was not representing either or both
of us. We consulted with private attorneys before we signed
this mediated plan.

In order to accomplish the divorce, we agree as follows:

CUSTODY

1. We will both share joint physical and legal custody of
   John Jr.

ALTERNATING RESIDENCES

2. John Jr. will live with each parent on an approximately
   equal basis. He will live with each parent for two
   weeks at a time, starting with Jane on the first Sunday
   after this mediated plan is signed. The switch of

residences will occur no later than 6 p.m. every other
Sunday, and the parent with whom he will live will be
responsible for picking him up at the prearranged time.

VISITATION

3. John Jr. will visit the parent with whom he is not living
    at least one evening a week, between 5 p.m. and 8 p.m.
    The parent he is visiting will be responsible for John
    Jr.'s transportation to and from the other parent's
    residence.

PARENTAL RESPONSIBILITY

4. The parent who has physical care of John Jr. will be
    responsible for everyday decisions about his care,
    including medical and dental services, as long as
    these are consistent with the major decisions which
    both parents will make together about his education,
    religious, cultural and artistic training, and non-
    emergency health services. In order to make informal
    joint decisions each will share school and medical
    records, and notice of meetings. The parents will confer
    about John Jr.'s needs, growth and care, and discuss
    schedule changes on a regular basis, no less than once
    a month.

MODIFICATION BY AGREEMENT

5. Each parent will be open to possible changes by mutual
    agreement so that John Jr. can receive the maximum
    benefit of care, love, concern and special benefits
    from both parents.

6. Each parent agrees to promote respect and affection for
    the other parent, and to allow and support each parent's
    unique style of parenting.

HOLIDAYS AND VACATIONS

7. Holidays and school recesses will not require any
    schedule changes except for the following:

PARENT	EVENT
Jane	Mother's Day
John	Father's Day
Jane	Week before Christmas and Christmas Eve

PARENT	EVENT
John	Christmas Day - noon through next week
Jane	Day before through Thanksgiving Day 2 p.m.
John	Thanksgiving Day 2 p.m. through 10 p.m.

John Jr. will be with each parent alternating years for his birthday, and will alternate years for a one-day "tax holiday" if needed by parents to establish Head-of-Household status. Each parent will have John Jr. live with them for six weeks during the summer recess of school, unless they decide to continue the usual schedule, decisions regarding the summer schedule will be made each March.

ANNUAL REVIEW

8. John and Jane will confer once every year between spring school break and summer to review the custody plan in light of John Jr.'s age, needs, abilities progress and preferences. They will review the environment and care each parent can provide.

DEATH OF PARENTS

9. If either parent should die before John Jr. becomes 21 years old, the surviving parent will take full custody and provide for John Jr. until he is 21. Should both parents die before that time without remarrying, John Jr.'s aunt, Mary Smith, will assume custody acting as guardian according to the spirit of this mediated plan and the Will of the last surviving parent. If one or both parents remarry and John Jr. developed a significant positive relationship with either or both, John Jr.'s future living arrangements will take into account such relationship(s) and John Jr.'s preference.

CHANGE OF CIRCUMSTANCES

10. The above agreements will not be substantially changed by subsequent remarriage or co-habitation of one or both parents. Should John or Jane's change of employment or residence seriously affect John Jr.'s school district or the joint physical custody schedule outlined earlier, both parents agree to use every effort to minimize his disruption, and to maintain as close to equal time of

physical custody as possible; if equal custody is
unworkable or disruptive to John Jr., the parents agree
to work together to revise this plan to maximize John
Jr.'s relationship with both parents.

SUBSTITUTE CARE

11. The parent with whom John Jr. is staying is responsible
for providing supervision, or for arranging, transporting
and paying for substitute care which is acceptable to
both parents. Each parent intends to minimize the amount
of time John Jr. will be cared for by substitute care
providers during their scheduled time with John Jr.

CHILD SUPPORT

12. By the third day of every month each parent will deposit
an amount of money for support of John Jr. in a joint
checking account which requires both their signatures.
This money will be restricted to payment and reimbursement
of expenses for John Jr.'s support, including but not
limited to: food, clothing, shelter, transportation,
educational costs and supplies, recreational opportunities,
toys and major gifts, lessons, cultural events, substitute
care, grooming, allowances, medical care and health
insurance. John and Jane will share these costs pro-
portioned to their gross income over $10,000 for the
previous year, but no less than $200 per month total
contribution by both parents. Each will discuss
anticipated changes in John Jr.'s need and their ability
to pay.

SUPPORT CONTINUATION

13. This child support will continue until John Jr. is 18
years of age, or has graduated from high school. It may
be continued by mutual consent of John and Jane until
age 21 if he is continuing his education by attending
full-time a school, college, or university, or a technical
or vocational program designed to prepare him for gainful
employment. The parents will make such a decision by no
later than six months before his entrance in such high
education, and will determine at that time the conditions
and arrangements for the use of such support money by
John Jr.

ANNUITY TRUST

14. Each parent will contribute a total of $100 per month to a tax-deferred annuity or trust account, based on the same formula explained in paragraph #12. The income and principal of this annuity is to be used for John Jr's support in the event of his parents' deaths, or as support, tuition, and other expenses for higher education as outlined above.

FUTURE CONFLICT RESOLUTION

15. John and Jane will attempt to avoid further disputes. Should disputes arise or changes be required, or breaches of this plan occur they agree to submit such issues to mediation as a first recourse, and to follow the mediation process to its conclusion before starting any post-decree relief or modification by the court.

SUBMISSION TO COURT

16. John and Jane will have their separate attorneys negotiate the distribution of marital property, the determination of spousal support and other necessary decisions, and will ask them to present this plan to the court for approval.

Resource D. Code of Professional Conduct for Mediators.

Preamble

Mediation is an approach to conflict resolution in which an impartial third party intervenes in a dispute with the consent of the parties, to aid and assist them in reaching a mutually satisfactory settlement to issues in dispute.

Mediation is a profession with ethical responsibilities and duties. Those who engage in the practice of mediation must be dedicated to the principle that all disputants have a right to negotiate and attempt to determine the outcome of their own conflicts. They must be aware that their duties and obligations relate to the parties who engage their services, to the mediation process, to other mediators, to the agencies which administer the practice of mediation, and to the general public.

Mediators are often professionals (attorneys, therapists, social workers) who have obligations under other codes of ethics. This code is not to be construed as a competitive code of behavior but as additional guidelines for professionals performing mediation. When *mediating*, professionals will be bound by the ethical guidelines of this code.

This code is not designed to override or supersede any laws or government regulations which prescribe responsibilities of mediators and others in the helping professions. It is a personal code relating to the conduct of the individual mediator and is intended to establish principles applicable to all professional mediators employed by private, city, state, or federal agencies.

1. *The Responsibility of the Mediator to the Parties*

The primary responsibility for the resolution of a dispute rests upon the parties themselves. The mediator at all times should recognize that the agreements reached in negotiations are voluntarily made by the parties. It is the mediator's responsibility to assist the disputants in reaching a settlement. At no time should a mediator coerce a party into agreement. Mediators should not attempt to make a substantive decision for the parties. Parties may, however, agree to solicit a recommendation for settlement from the mediator.

It is desirable that agreement be reached by negotiations without a mediator's assistance. Intervention by a mediator can be initiated by the parties themselves or by a mediator. The decision to mediate rests with the parties, except where mediation is mandated by legislation, court order, or contract.

Expenses of Mediation—Mediators will inform all parties of the cost of mediation services prior to a mediator's intervention. Parties should be able to estimate the total cost of the service in relation to that of other dispute resolution procedures.

Reprinted with permission of the Center for Dispute Resolution, Denver, Colo. (copyright © 1982).

Ideally, when costs are involved, the mediator should attempt to have
parties agree to bear the costs of mediation equitably. Where this is not
possible, all parties should reach agreement as to payment.

2. *Responsibility of the Mediator Toward the Mediation Process*

Negotiation is an established procedure in our society as a means of resolving disputes. The process of mediation involves a third party intervention
into negotiations to assist in the development of alternative solutions that
parties will voluntarily accept as a basis for settlement. Pressures which
jeopardize voluntary action and agreement by the parties should not be a
part of mediation.

The Mediation Process—Mediation is a participatory process. A mediator is obliged to educate the parties and involve them in the mediation
process. A mediator should consider that such education and involvement
are important not only to the resolution of a current dispute, but will also
better qualify the parties to handle future conflicts in a more creative and
productive manner.

Appropriateness of Mediation—Mediation is not a panacea for all
types of conflicts. Mediators should be aware of all procedures for dispute
resolution and under what conditions each is most effective. Mediators are
obliged to educate participants as to their procedural options and help them
make wise decisions as to the most appropriate procedures. The procedures
should clearly match the type of outcome which is desired by the parties.

Mediator's Role—The mediator must not consider himself or herself
limited to keeping the peace or regulating conflict at the bargaining table.
His or her role should be one of an active resource person upon whom the
parties may draw and, when appropriate, he or she should be prepared to
provide both procedural and substantive suggestions and alternatives which
will assist the parties in successful negotiations.

Since the status, experience, and ability of the mediator lend weight
to his or her suggestions and recommendations, he or she should evaluate
carefully the effect of his or her interventions or proposals and accept full
responsibility for their honesty and merit.

Since mediation is a voluntary process, the acceptability of the mediator by the parties as a person of integrity, objectivity, and fairness is
absolutely essential for the effective performance of mediation procedures.
The manner in which the mediator carries out professional duties and responsibilities will measure his or her usefulness as a mediator. The quality
of character as well as intellectual, emotional, social, and technical attributes will reveal themselves in the conduct of the mediator and in his or her
oral and written communications with the parties, other mediators, and the
public.

Publicity and Advertising—A mediator should not make any false,
misleading, or unfair statement or claim as to the mediation process, costs,
and benefits, and as to his or her role, skills, and qualifications.

Neutrality—A mediator should determine and reveal all monetary,
psychological, emotional, associational, or authoritative affiliations that he
or she has with any of the parties to a dispute that might cause a conflict of

interest or affect the perceived or actual neutrality of the professional in the performance of duties. If the mediator or any one of the major parties feels that the mediator's background will have or has had a potential to bias his or her performance, the mediator should disqualify himself or herself from performing a mediation service.

Impartiality—The mediator is obligated during the performance of professional services to maintain a posture of impartiality toward all involved parties. Impartiality means freedom from bias or favoritism either in word or action. Impartiality implies a commitment to aid all parties as opposed to a single party in reaching a mutually satisfactory agreement. Impartiality means that a mediator will not play an adversarial role in the process of dispute resolution.

Confidentiality—Information received by a mediator in confidence, private session, caucus, or joint session with the disputants is confidential and should not be revealed to parties outside of the negotiations. Information received in caucus is not to be revealed in joint session without receiving prior permission from the party or person from whom the information was received.

The following exceptions shall be applied to the confidentiality rule: In the event of child abuse by one or more disputants or in a case where a mediator discovers that a probable crime will be committed that may result in drastic psychological or physical harm to another person, the mediator is obligated to report these actions to the appropriate agencies.

Use of Information—Because information revealed in mediation is confidential and the success of the process may depend on this confidentiality, mediators should inform and gain consent from participants that information divulged in the process of mediation will not be used by the parties in any future adversarial proceedings.

The mediator is also obligated to resist disclosure of confidential information in an adversarial process. He or she will refuse to voluntarily testify in any subsequent court proceedings and will resist to the best of his or her ability the subpoena of either his or her notes or person. This provision may be waived by the consent of all parties involved.

Empowerment—In the event a party needs either additional information or assistance in order for the negotiations to proceed in a fair and orderly manner or for an agreement to be reached that is fair, equitable, and has the capacity to hold over time, the mediator is obligated to refer the party to resources—either data or persons—who may facilitate the process.

Psychological Well-Being—If a mediator discovers that a party needs psychological help either prior to or during mediation, he or she will make appropriate referrals. Mediators recognize that mediation is not an appropriate substitute for therapy and shall refer parties to the appropriate procedure. Mediation shall not be conducted with parties who are either intoxicated or who have major psychological disorders which seriously impair their judgment.

The Law—Mediators are not lawyers. At no time will a mediator offer legal advice to parties in dispute. Mediators will refer parties to appropriate attorneys for legal advice. This same code of conduct applies to mediators who are themselves trained in the law. The role of an impartial mediator should not be confused with that of an attorney who is an advocate for a client.

NOTE: The authors must take exception to the above paragraph. Lawyers may serve as mediators and may provide impartial legal advice to the parties together. We offer the following substitute wording: At no time will a mediator who is not a lawyer offer legal advice. Mediators will urge parties to separately consult with independent attorneys for legal advice. The role of a mediator should not be confused with that of an attorney who represents a client as an advocate. A lawyer-mediator should not represent either party during or after the mediation process.

The Settlement—The goal of negotiation and mediation is a settlement that is seen as fair and equitable by all parties. The mediator's responsibility to the parties is to help them reach this kind of settlement. Whenever possible, a mediator should develop a written statement that documents the agreements reached in mediation.

A mediator's satisfaction with the agreement is secondary to that of the parties.

In the event that an agreement is reached which a mediator feels (1) is illegal, (2) is grossly inequitable to one or more parties, (3) is the result of false information, (4) is the result of bad faith bargaining, (5) is impossible to enforce, or (6) does not look like it will hold over time, the mediator may pursue any or all of the following alternatives:

1. Inform the parties of the difficulties which the mediator sees in the agreement.
2. Inform the parties of the difficulties and make suggestions which would remedy the problems.
3. Withdraw as mediator without disclosing to either party the particular reasons for his or her withdrawal.
4. Withdraw as mediator but disclose in writing to both parties the reasons for such action.
5. Withdraw as mediator and reveal publicly the general reason for taking such action (bad faith bargaining, unreasonable settlement, illegality, etc.).

Termination of Mediation—In the event that the parties cannot reach an agreement even with the assistance of a mediator, it is the responsibility of the mediator to make them aware of the deadlock and suggest that the negotiations be terminated. A mediator is obligated to inform the parties when a final impasse has occurred and to refer them to other means of dispute resolution. A mediator should not prolong unproductive discussions that result in increased time, emotional, and monetary costs for the parties.

3. The Responsibility of the Mediator Toward Other Mediators

A mediator should not enter any dispute which is being mediated by another mediator or mediators without first conferring with the person or persons conducting such mediation. The mediator should not intercede in a dispute merely because another mediator may also be participating. Conversely, it should not be assumed that the lack of mediation participation by one mediator indicates a need for participation by another mediator.

In those situations where more than one mediator is participating in a particular case, each mediator has a responsibility to keep the others informed of developments essential to cooperative effort and should extend every possible courtesy to his or her co-mediator.

During mediation, the mediator should carefully avoid any appearance of disagreement with or criticism of his or her co-mediator. Discussions as to what positions and actions mediators should take in particular cases should not violate principles of confidentiality.

4. *The Responsibility of the Mediator Toward His or Her Agency and Profession*

Mediators frequently work for agencies that are responsible for providing mediation assistance to parties in dispute. The mediator must recognize that as an employee of said agencies, he or she is their representative and that his or her work will not be judged solely on an individual basis but as a representative of an organization. Any improper conduct or professional shortcoming, therefore, reflects not only on the individual mediator but upon the employer and as such jeopardizes the effectiveness of the agency, other agencies, and the acceptability of the mediation process itself.

The mediator should not use his or her position for personal gain or advantage, nor should he or she engage in any employment, activity, or enterprise which will conflict with his or her work as a mediator.

Mediators should not accept any money or thing of value for the performance of services—other than a regular salary or mutually agreed upon fee—or incur obligations to any party which might interfere with the impartial performance of his or her duties.

Training and Education—Mediators learn their trade through a variety of avenues—formal education, training programs, workshops, practical experience, and supervision. A mediator has the responsibility to constantly upgrade his or her skills and theoretical grounding and shall endeavor to better himself or herself and the profession by seeking some form of further education in the negotiation and mediation process each year that he or she is in practice.

A mediator should promote the profession and make contributions to the field by encouraging and participating in research, publishing, or other forms of professional and public education.

Expertise—Mediators should perform their services only in those areas of mediation where they are qualified either by experience or training. A mediator should not attempt to mediate in a field where he or she is unprepared and where there is risk of psychological, financial, legal, or physical damage to one of the parties due to the mediator's lack of background.

A mediator is obligated to seek a co-mediator trained in the necessary discipline or refer cases to other mediators who are trained in the required field of expertise when he or she does not possess the required skills.

Voluntary Services—A mediator is obligated to perform some voluntary service each year of practice to provide assistance to those who cannot afford to pay for mediation and to promote the field. It is left up to the individual mediator to determine the amount and kind of service to be rendered for the good of the profession and society.

A mediator should cooperate with his or her own and other agencies in establishing and maintaining the quality, qualifications, and standards of the profession. Mediators should participate in individual and agency evaluations and should be supervised either by an agency, a mutually agreed upon peer, or the professional organization's Board of Ethics. A mediator involved in any breach of this code of conduct should notify his or her agency of said breach. Mediators hearing of violations of this code of ethics should also report said information to their agency or the Board of Ethics.

5. The Responsibility of the Mediator Toward the Public and Other Unrepresented Parties

Negotiation is in essence a private, voluntary process. The primary purpose of mediation is to assist the parties to achieve a settlement. Such assistance does not abrogate the rights of the parties to resort to economic, social, psychological, and legal sanctions. However, the mediation process may include a responsibility of the mediator to assert the interest of the public or other unrepresented parties in order that a particular dispute be settled; that costs or damages be alleviated; and that normal life be resumed. Mediators should question agreements that are not in the interest of the public or unrepresented parties whose interests and needs should be and are not being considered at the table. Mediators may and should raise questions as to whether other parties' interests or the parties themselves should be at the negotiating table. It is understood, however, that the mediator does not regulate or control any of the content of a negotiated agreement.

Publicity shall not be used by a mediator to enhance his or her position. Where two or more mediators are mediating a dispute, public information should be handled by a mutually agreeable procedure.

Resource E. Selected List of National Organizations.

The following organizations can provide further information regarding training for mediators, conferences, publications, liability insurance, and the location of local mediation programs. This list is by no means exhaustive. We have not attempted to list the many specialized training organizations and regional, state, and local associations, councils, and networks that provide mediation training and contacts, nor does this list include all the offices and institutes providing mediation services.

Academy of Family Mediators
P.O. Box 246
Claremont, CA 91711
(714) 626-0590

Founded in 1981, the academy has established educational and experience criteria for various levels of membership. It accredits mediation training programs, promotes professional mediation standards, publishes a directory and newsletter, and sponsors publication of *Mediation Quarterly*.

American Arbitration Association
140 South 51st Street
New York, NY 10020
(212) 484-3235

Founded in 1926 to provide services and training in arbitration, mediation, and negotiation, the AAA has twenty-four regional offices located throughout the United States. The association handles a wide variety of disputes including labor, consumer, commercial, family, and environmental issues. The AAA publishes periodicals and maintains the Eastman Arbitration Library in its New York headquarters.

American Bar Association
Special Committee on Alternative Means of Dispute Resolution
1800 M Street, NW
Washington, D.C. 20036
(202) 331-2258

Established by the ABA in 1976 to serve as a national clearinghouse on mediation and arbitration activity, the special committee sponsors conferences and workshops, provides information on other conferences and organizations, and publishes a wide variety of information: a national program directory, a law school directory, a bibliography, a quarterly newsletter, and other publications.

Association of Family and Conciliation Courts
c/o Oregon Health Sciences University
Department of Psychiatry
Gaines Hall-149
3181 S.W. Sam Jackson Park Rd.
Portland, OR 97201
(503) 220-5651

This international association of judges, court administrators, lawyers, mediators, and mental health professionals, established in 1963, assists jurisdictions interested in establishing court-connected counseling and mediation services, conducts semiannual conferences and workshops, and publishes the *Conciliation Courts Review*, the *Joint Custody Handbook*, and numerous brochures on divorce. It also sponsors research on divorce mediation and child support.

The Conservation Foundation
1717 Massachusetts Avenue, NW
Washington, D.C. 20036
(202) 797-4300

Established in 1948, The Conservation Foundation since 1976 has been involved in promoting the mediation of environmental disputes. In 1981 the Center for Environmental Conflict Resolution (Resolve) became part of the foundation and enhanced its mediation activities. The foundation sponsors research and acts as an information center.

Council of Better Business Bureaus
1515 Wilson Blvd.
Arlington, VA 22209
(703) 276-0100

In its continuing effort to enhance communication and resolve disputes between consumers and business, the BBB has become increasingly involved in the promotion of mediation programs. It functions as an information outlet and has local offices throughout the country.

Family Mediation Association
5530 Wisconsin Avenue
Suite 1250
Chevy Chase, MD 20815
(301) 530-1220

Founded in 1974 by O. J. Coogler, author of *Structured Mediation in Divorce Settlements*, the association conducts training programs throughout the country, has initiated a national certification program for family mediators, publishes a quarterly newsletter (*The Family Mediator*), and engages in public education programs on family mediation.

Federal Mediation and Conciliation Service
2100 K Street, NW
Washington, D.C. 20427
(202) 653-5300

Established in 1947 by the Labor Management Relations Act (Taft-Hartley Act), this service employs over two hundred mediators in eighty field offices throughout the country. It facilitates voluntary negotiations and mediation in labor disputes.

National Academy of Conciliators
1133 Fifteenth Street, NW
Suite 1250
Washington, D.C. 20005
(202) 654-6515
800-638-8242

The National Academy of Conciliators is a public service corporation founded to foster alternatives to litigation in the settlement of disputes, primarily construction industry disputes. The academy seeks to help disputing parties reach expeditious and reasonable solutions to their conflicts through the use of third-party neutrals trained in conciliation, mediation, and arbitration techniques. The academy provides training as well as contacts, information, publications, and direct service.

National Institute for Dispute Resolution
1901 L Street N.W., Suite 600
Washington, D.C. 20036
(202) 466-4764

A private, non-profit organization, began operations in 1983 with $6 million in grants provided by several major foundations. The Institute's purpose is to help support, examine, and promote ways of settling disputes without litigation. NIDR provides grants as well as technical information to assist organizations and individuals interested in using dispute resolution methods for settling conflicts.

National Peace Academy Campaign
110 Maryland Avenue, NE
Suite 409
Washington, D.C. 20006
(202) 546-9500

Established in 1979 by an act of Congress, this organization seeks to establish the U.S. Academy of Peace and Conflict Resolution—an academy for the education and promotion of global peace through techniques such as mediation and other alternatives. If established, the academy will offer masters programs, internships, and seminars for consumers, businesses, and government officials.

Society of Professionals in Dispute Resolution (SPIDR)
American Arbitration Association
1730 Rhode Island Avenue, NW
Washington, D.C. 20036
(202) 296-8510

This organization is composed of professional neutrals in the United States and Canada. Members include mediators, fact finders, arbitrators, and trial examiners. There is a special emphasis on labor management but recently the society has become involved in other civil matters, including family and business disputes. It conducts an annual meeting and publishes its annual proceedings and periodic newsletters; the society also holds regional meetings.

※ ※ ※ ※ ※

References

Abel, R. L. "A Comparative Theory of Dispute Institutions in Society." *Law and Society*, 1973, *8*, 235–240.

Abel, R. L. (Ed.). *The Politics of Informal Justice*. 2 vols. New York: Academic Press, 1982.

Academy of Family Mediators. "Standards for Mediation." Unpublished manuscript, 1982.

Adler v. *Adams*. U.S. Dist. Ct., West. Dist. of Wash. at Seattle, No. 675-73(2), Magistrates Order on Motion to Quash Subpoena for Protective Order, May 3, 1979, aff., June 7, 1979.

Alper, B., and Nichols, L. *Beyond the Courtroom*. Lexington, Mass.: Heath, 1981.

Alternatives to the High Cost of Litigation. Monthly reports. New York: Law and Business, Inc., 1983.

American Arbitration Association and American Bar Association. *Code of Ethics for Arbitrators in Commercial Disputes*. New York: American Arbitration Association, 1977.

American Association for Marriage and Family Therapy. *Ethical Principles for Family Therapists*. Washington, D.C.: American Association for Marriage and Family Therapy, 1982.

American Bar Association. *Model Code of Professional Responsibility*. Chicago: American Bar Association, 1969.

359

American Bar Association. *Alternative Means of Family Dispute Resolution.* Chicago: American Bar Association, 1982.

American Bar Association. *Model Rules of Professional Conduct.* Chicago: American Bar Association, 1983.

American Personnel and Guidance Association. *Code of Ethics.* Alexandria, Va.: American Personnel and Guidance Association, 1974.

American Psychiatric Association. *The Principles of Medical Ethics.* Washington, D.C.: American Psychiatric Association, 1973.

Anderson, C., and Stewart, S. *Mastering Resistance: A Practical Guide to Family Therapy.* New York: Guilford Press, 1983.

Association of Family and Conciliation Courts. "Mediator Standards and Certification." Task group report presented to Association of Family and Conciliation Courts Conference, San Diego, December 1982.

Attneave, C. "American Indians and Alaska Native Families: Emigrants in Their Own Homeland." In M. McGoldrick, J.K. Pearce, and J. Giordiano (Eds.), *Ethnicity and Family Therapy.* New York: Guilford Press, 1982.

Auerbach, J. S. *Justice Without Law? Resolving Disputes Without Lawyers.* New York: Oxford University Press, 1983.

Bahr, S. "Mediation Is the Answer: Why Couples Are So Positive About This Route to Divorce." *Family Advocate,* 1981, *3 (4),* 32–35.

Bandler, R., Grinder, J., and Satir, V. *Changing with Families.* Palo Alto: Science and Behavior Books, 1976.

Bandura, A. *Principles of Behavior Modification.* New York: Holt, Rinehart and Winston, 1969.

Barker, L. *Listening Behavior.* Englewood Cliffs, N.J.: Prentice-Hall, 1971.

Bateman, B. *So You're Going to a Hearing: Preparing for a Public Law 94-142 Due Process Hearing.* Northbrook, Ill.: Hubbard Scientific, 1980.

Beavers, W. R. "Healthy, Midrange, and Severely Dysfunctional Families." In F. Walsh (Ed.), *Normal Family Processes.* New York: Guilford Press, 1982.

Bellack, L., and Baker, S. S. *Reading Faces.* New York: Holt, Rinehart and Winston, 1981.

Bellman, H., and others. "Environmental Conflict Resolution: Practitioner's Perspective of an Emerging Field." *Environmental Consensus,* Winter 1981, pp. 1-7.

Bellow, G., and Moulton, B. *The Lawyering Process.* Mineola, N.Y.: Foundation Press, 1981.

Benjamin, A. *The Helping Interview.* (2nd ed.) Boston: Houghton Mifflin, 1974.

Bernal, G. "Cuban Families." In M. McGoldrick, J. K. Pearce, and J. Giordiano (Eds.), *Ethnicity and Family Therapy.* New York: Guilford Press, 1982.

Berne, E. *The Mind in Action.* New York: Simon & Schuster, 1947.

Berne, E. *Games People Play: The Psychology of Human Relationships.* New York: Grove Press, 1964.

Bienenfeld, F. *Child Custody Mediation: Techniques for Counselors, Attorneys and Parents.* Palo Alto: Science and Behavior Books, 1983.

Binder, D. A., and Price, S. C. *Legal Interviewing and Counseling: A Client-Centered Approach.* St. Paul: West, 1977.

Birnbach, L. (Ed.). *The Official Preppy Handbook.* New York: Workman, 1980.

Black, M., and Joffee, W. "A Lawyer/Therapist Team Approach to Divorce." *Conciliation Courts Review,* 1978, *16* (1), 1-5.

Boecher v. *Borth.* 51 App. Div. 2d 598, 377 N.Y.S.2d 781 (New York, 1976).

Boulding, K. E. *Conflict and Defense: A General Theory.* New York: Harper & Row, 1962.

Brammer, L. M. *The Helping Relationship: Process and Skills.* Englewood Cliffs, N.J.: Prentice-Hall, 1973.

Brown, D. "Divorce and Family Mediation: History, Review, Future Directions." *Conciliation Courts Review,* 1982, *20* (2), 1-37.

Brunner, H. E. *The Mediator: A Study of the Central Doctrine of the Christian Faith.* Philadelphia: Westminster Press, 1947.

Bullmer, K. *The Art of Empathy: A Manual for Improving Accuracy of Interpersonal Perception.* New York: Human Sciences Press, 1975.

Burger, W. "Our Vicious Legal Spiral." *Judges Journal,* 1977, *16* (4), 22-24.

Burger, W. "Isn't There a Better Way?" *American Bar Association Journal*, 1982, *68*, 274–277.

Burgess, H. *The Foothills Water Treatment Project: A Case Study of Environmental Mediation*. Boston: Department of Planning, Massachusetts Institute of Technology, 1980.

Buzzard, L. "Alternative Dispute Resolution: Who's in Charge of Mediation?" Transcript of a program presented by American Bar Association, Young Lawyers Division and Special Committee on Alternative Means of Dispute Resolution, Chicago, January 1982, pp. 45–51.

California Civil Code. Section 4607(c) (1980).

"Calm After the Storm: Grandmother of Environmental Lawsuits Settled by Mediation." *Environmental Law Reporter*, 1981, *11*, 1074–1077.

Cammer, L. *Up from Depression*. New York: Pocket Books, 1969.

Cannon, J. A. "Negotiated Rulemaking: EPA's Current Initiative." *Environmental Analyst*, May 1983, pp. 10–12.

Carkhuff, R. R. *The Art of Problem-Solving: A Guide for Developing Problem-Solving Skills for Parents, Teachers, Counselors, and Administrators*. Amherst, Mass.: Human Resource Development Press, 1973.

Cathcart, J., and Graff, P. "Occupational Licensing: Factoring It Out." *Pacific Law Journal*, 1978, *9*, 147–163.

Center for Dispute Resolution. *Code of Professional Conduct for Mediators*. Denver: Center for Dispute Resolution, 1982.

Chambers, D. L. "The Coming Curtailment of Compulsory Child Support." *Michigan Law Review*, 1982, *80* (8), 1614–1634.

Chayes, A. "The Role of the Judge in Public Law Litigation." *Harvard Law Review*, 1976, *89*, 1281–1316.

Children's Hearing Project. *Program Description*. (Photocopied text.) Cambridge, Mass.: Massachusetts Advocacy Center, 1982.

City of Port Arthur, Texas v. *United States*. No. 80-0648, District of Columbia, Nov. 12, 1980.

Cleary, E. W., and others (Eds.). *McCormick's Handbook of the Law of Evidence*. St. Paul: West, 1972.

Cohen, J. A. "Chinese Mediation on the Eve of Modernization." *California Law Review*, 1966, *54* (2), 1201–1226.

Colgrove, M., Bloomfield, H. H., and McWilliams, P. *How to Survive the Loss of a Love: 58 Things to Do When There Is Nothing to Be Done.* New York: Bantam Books, 1976.

Combs, A. W., Avilia, D. L., and Purkey, W. W. *Helping Relationships: Basic Concepts for the Helping Professions.* Boston: Allyn & Bacon, 1971.

Comeaux, E. A. "A Guide to Implementing Divorce Mediation in the Public Sector." *Conciliation Courts Review,* 1983, *21* (2), 1–25.

"Confidential Communications to a Psychotherapist." *Northwestern University Law Review,* 1952, *47,* 384–389.

Coogler, O. J. *Structured Mediation in Divorce Settlements.* Lexington, Mass.: Heath, 1978.

Coogler, O. J. "Divorce Mediation for 'Low Income' Families: A Proposed Model." *Conciliation Court Review,* 1979, *17* (1) 21–26.

Cook, R., Rochl, J., and Shepard, D. *Executive Summary Final Report.* Washington, D.C.: Neighborhood Justice Field Institute, U.S. Department of Justice, 1980.

Cormick, G. W. "Environmental Mediation in the U.S.: Experience and Future Directions." Paper presented at the annual meeting of the American Association for the Advancement of Science, Toronto, 1981. (Available from the Institute for Environmental Mediation, Seattle.)

Cormier, W. H., and Cormier, L. S. *Interviewing Strategies for Helpers: A Guide to Assessment, Treatment and Evaluation.* Monterey: Brooks/Cole, 1979.

Coser, L. *Functions of Social Conflict.* New York: Free Press, 1956.

Council of Family Law Section of the American Bar Association. *Standards of Practice for Divorce Mediators.* Chicago: American Bar Association, 1983.

Crouch, R. E. "Divorce Mediation and Legal Ethics." *Family Law Quarterly,* 1982, *16* (3), 219–250.

Curran, B. *The Legal Needs of the Public: The Final Report of a National Survey.* Washington, D.C.: Bar Association Foundation, 1977.

Davidson, H., Ray, L., and Horowitz, R. (Eds.). *Alternative Means of Family Dispute Resolution.* Washington, D.C.: American Bar Association, 1982.

Deutsch, M. *The Resolution of Conflict*. New Haven: Yale University Press, 1973.

Doo, L. W. "Dispute Settlement in Chinese-American Communities." *American Journal of Comparative Law*, 1973, *21*, 627–663.

Dweck, C., and Licht, B. "Learned Helplessness." In J. Garber and E. P. Seligman (Eds.), *Human Helplessness: Theory and Applications*. New York: Academic Press, 1980.

Edon, A. "Past Failures and Successes in Peacemaking with Suggestions for the Future." In E. B. Tomkins (Ed.), *Peaceful Change in Modern Society*. Stanford: Hoover Institution Press, 1971.

Ekman, P., and Friesen, W. V. *Unmasking the Face: A Guide to Recognizing Emotions from Facial Clues*. Englewood Cliffs, N.J.: Prentice-Hall, 1975.

Ellis, A. *Reason and Emotion in Psychotherapy*. New York: Lyle Stuart, 1962.

Ellis, A., and Harper, R. *A New Guide to Rational Living*. New York: Wilshire, 1975.

Elson, H. M. "Setting Up a Private 'Mediation' Practice." In H. Davidson, L. Ray, and R. Horowitz (Eds.), *Alternative Means of Family Dispute Resolution*. Washington, D.C.: American Bar Association, 1982.

Epstein, N. B., Bishop, D. S., and Baldwin, L. M. "McMaster Model of Family Functioning: A View of the Normal Family." In F. Walsh (Ed.), *Normal Family Processes*. New York: Guilford Press, 1982.

Erikson, E. H. *Identity, Youth and Crisis*. New York: Norton, 1968.

Erikson, E. H. (Ed.). *Adulthood: Essays*. New York: Norton, 1978.

Fast, J. *Body Language*. New York: Evans, 1970.

Federal Mediation and Conciliation Service and Association of Labor Mediation Agencies. *Code of Professional Conduct for Labor Mediators*. Washington, D.C.: Government Printing Office, 1971.

Federal Rules of Evidence. New York: Matthew Bender, 1975.

Feeley, M. M. *The Process Is the Punishment: Handling Cases in a Lower Criminal Court*. New York: Russell Sage Foundation, 1979.

Fellers, P. *One Earth, One Family: Peace Education*. (Photocopied text from course curriculum.) Portland, Ore.: Holy Redeemer School, 1982.

Felstiner, W., and Drew, A. "European Alternatives to Criminal Trials: What We Can Learn." *Judges Journal,* 1978, *17* (3), 18–24.

Fenton v. *Howard.* 118 A.2, 119, 575 P.2d 318 (Arizona, 1978).

Festinger, L. *Conflict, Decision, and Dissonance.* Stanford: Stanford University Press, 1964.

Filley, A. C. *Interpersonal Conflict Resolution.* Glenview, Ill.: Scott, Foresman, 1975.

Fisher, R. *International Mediation: A Working Guide.* New York: International Peace Academy, 1978.

Fisher, R., and Ury, W. *Getting to Yes.* New York: Penguin Books, 1983.

Florida Statutes. Section 61.21(3), Chapters 82–96 (1982).

Folberg, J. "Divorce Mediation." *Family Law Newsletter,* 1981, *4,* 1–2.

Folberg, J. "Issues and Trends in the Law of Joint Custody." In J. Folberg (Ed.), *Joint Custody and Shared Parenting.* Washington, D.C.: Bureau of National Affairs, 1984.

Folberg, J., and Milne, A. (Eds.). *Divorce Mediation: Theory and Practice.* New York: Guilford Press, in press.

Folberg, J., and Taylor, A. "Client Interviewing and Counseling." In J. Folberg and others (Eds.), *Civil Litigation Manual.* Vol. 1. Portland: Oregon State Bar, 1982.

Fox, W. M. "Why We Should Abandon Maslow's Need Hierarchy Theory." *Journal of Humanistic Education and Development,* 1982, *21* (1), 29–32.

Frankl, V. E. *Man's Search for Meaning.* New York: Pocket Books, 1963. (Originally published 1939.)

Franks, M. "How to Calculate Child Support." *Case and Comment,* 1981, *86,* 3–9.

Freed, D. J. "Equitable Distribution as of December 1982." *Family Law Reporter,* January 11, 1983, *9* (10), 4001–4007.

Freeman, D. R. *Marital Crisis and Short-Term Counseling: A Casebook.* New York: Free Press, 1982.

Freeman, H. A. *Legal Interviewing and Counseling: Cases with Comments.* St. Paul: West, 1964.

Fuller, L. "Collective Bargaining and the Arbitrator." *Wisconsin Law Review*, 1963, pp. 3–46.

Fuller, L. "Mediation—Its Forms and Functions." *Southern California Law Review*, 1971, *44*, 305–339.

Gallant, C. B. *Mediation in Special Education Disputes.* Washington, D. C.: National Association of Social Workers, 1982.

Galper, M. *Joint Custody and Co-Parenting.* Philadelphia: Running Press, 1980.

Gardner, R. A. *The Parents' Book About Divorce.* New York: Bantam Books, 1979.

Gardner, R. A. *Family Evaluation in Child Custody Litigation.* Cresskill, N. J.: Creative Therapeutics, 1982.

Gibbs, W. "The Kpelle Moot: A Therapeutic Model for Informal Justice Settlement." *Africa*, 1963, *33*, 1–11.

Ginsberg, R. B. "American Bar Association Delegation Visits the People's Republic of China," *American Bar Association Journal*, 1978, *64*, 1516–1525.

Glasser, W. *Reality Therapy: A New Approach to Psychiatry.* New York: Harper & Row, 1965.

Glasser, W. *Positive Addiction.* New York: Harper & Row, 1976.

Glasser, W. *Stations of the Mind: New Directions for Reality Therapy.* New York: Harper & Row, 1981.

Goffman, E. *Behavior in Public Places: Notes on the Social Organization of Gatherings.* New York: Free Press, 1963.

Gold, C., and Lyons, R. (Eds.). *Dispute Resolution Training: State of the Art.* New York: American Arbitration Association, 1978.

Gold, L. "The Psychological Context of the Interdisciplinary Co-Mediator Team Model in Marital Dissolution." *Conciliation Courts Review*, 1982, *20* (2), 45–53.

Goldsmith, J. "The Postdivorce Family System." In F. Walsh (Ed.), *Normal Family Processes.* New York: Guilford Press, 1982.

Golten, R. J. "Mediation: A 'Sellout' for Conservation Advocates, or a Bargain?" *Environmental Professional*, 1980, *2*, 62–66.

Gulliver, P. H. *Disputes and Negotiations: A Cross-Cultural Perspective.* New York: Academic Press, 1979.

Haley, J. *Problem-Solving Therapy.* San Francisco: Jossey-Bass, 1976.

Haley, J. "The Myth of the Reluctant Litigant." *Journal of Japanese Studies,* 1978, *4,* 359–390.

Hall, E. T. *The Hidden Dimension.* Garden City: Doubleday, 1966.

Hall, E. T. *Beyond Culture.* Garden City: Anchor Press, 1976.

Hallett, K. *A Guide for Single Parents: Transactional Analysis for People in Crisis.* Millbrae, Calif.: Celestial Arts, 1974.

Harrington, C. "Delegalization Reform Movements: A Historical Analysis." In R. Abel (Ed.), *The Politics of Informal Justice.* Vol. 1. New York: Academic Press, 1982.

Harter, P. J. "EPA's Regulatory Negotiation Will Provide Opportunity for Direct Participation in Development of a Regulation." *Environmental Law Reporter,* 1983, *13,* 10202–10203.

Hayes, J. R. *The Complete Problem Solver.* Philadelphia: Franklin Institute Press, 1981.

Haynes, J. M. *Divorce Mediation: A Practical Guide for Therapists and Counselors.* New York: Springer, 1981.

Haynes, J. M. "Fighting Fair" [book review]. *Fair Share,* November 1983.

Henderson, D. C. *Conciliation and Japanese Law: Tokugawa and Modern.* Seattle: University of Washington Press, 1965.

Herz, F. M., and Rosen, E. J. "Jewish Families." In M. McGoldrick, J. K. Pearce, and J. Giordiano (Eds.), *Ethnicity and Family Therapy.* New York: Guilford Press, 1982.

Hickman v. *Taylor* 329 U.S. 495 (1947).

Himes, J. S. *Conflict and Conflict Management.* Athens: University of Georgia Press, 1980.

Holmes, T. H., and Rahe, R. H. "Social Readjustment Rating Scale." *Journal of Psychosomatic Research,* 1967, *2,* 216.

Howard, J. W. "Adjudication Considered as a Process of Conflict Resolution: A Variation on Separation of Powers." *Journal of Public Law,* 1969, *18,* 339–370.

Huntington, D. "Divorce and the Developmental Needs of Children." *Mediation of Child Custody and Visitation Disputes.* Transcripts from the Vallambrosa Retreat, September 1981. Los Angeles: California Chapter, Association of Family and Conciliation Courts, Institute for Training and Research, 1982.

Illich, J. *The Art and Skill of Successful Negotiation.* Englewood Cliffs, N.J.: Prentice-Hall, 1973.

Irving, H. H. *Divorce Mediation.* Toronto: Personal Library Publishers, 1980.

Irving, H., and others. "A Study of Conciliation Counseling in the Family Court of Toronto: Implications for Socio-Legal Practice." In H. Irving (Ed.), *Family Law: An Inter-Disciplinary Perspective.* Toronto: Carswell, 1981.

Jackson, E. N. *Understanding Grief: Its Roots, Dynamics, and Treatment.* New York: Abingdon Press, 1957.

Jalali, B. "Iranian Families." In M. McGoldrick, J. K. Pearce, and J. Giordiano (Eds.), *Ethnicity and Family Therapy.* New York: Guilford Press, 1982.

Jandt, F. E. *Conflict Resolution Through Communication.* New York: Harper & Row, 1973.

Janis, I. L., and Mann, L. *Decision Making: A Psychological Analysis of Conflict, Choice, and Commitment.* New York: Free Press, 1977.

Joint Committee of the American Arbitration Association and the American Bar Association. *Code of Ethics for Arbitrators in Commercial Disputes.* New York: American Arbitration Association, 1977.

Jung, J. *Understanding Human Motivation: A Cognitive Approach.* New York: Macmillan, 1978.

Kahn, H., Brown, W., and Martel, L. *The Next Two Hundred Years: A Scenario for America and the World.* New York: Morrow, 1976.

Kavalec, M. L. *Description: Community-Youth Mediation Program.* (Photocopied text.) Cleveland, Ohio: Community-Youth Mediation Program, 1983.

Kelly, J. "Mediation and Psychotherapy: Distinguishing the Differences." *Mediation Quarterly,* 1983, *1,* 33–44.

Kelly, J., Zlatchin, C., and Shawn, J. "Divorce Mediation: An Emerging Field." In C. Ewing (Ed.), *Psychology, Psychiatry and the Law: A Clinical and Forensic Handbook.* Sarasota: Professional Resource Exchange, 1984.

Kemp, C. G. *Intangibles in Counseling.* Boston: Houghton Mifflin, 1967.

Kennedy, E. *On Becoming a Counselor: A Basic Guide for Non-Professional Counselors.* New York: Continuum Publishing, 1980.

Kennedy, E. M. "Equal Justice and the Problem of Access." *Loyola of Los Angeles Law Review*, 1978, *11*, 485–491.

Kessler, S. "Counselor as Mediator." *Personnel and Guidance Journal*, 1979, *58* (3), 94–196.

Knapp, M. *Non-Verbal Communication in Human Interaction*. New York: Holt, Rinehart and Winston, 1972.

Kochan, T., and Jick, T. "The Public Sector Mediation Process." *Journal of Conflict Resolution*, 1978, *22* (2), 209–240.

Koopman, E. J., and Hunt, E. J. "Family Mediation: Issues in Defining, Educating and Implementing a New and Needed Profession." Unpublished manuscript, Institute of Child Study, Department of Human Development, University of Maryland, 1982.

Krause, H. D. *Family Law in a Nutshell*. St. Paul: West, 1977.

Krause, H. D. *Child Support in America: The Legal Perspective*. Charlottesville, Va.: Michie, 1981.

Kressel, K., and others. "Mandated Negotiations in Divorce and Labor Disputes: A Comparison." *Conciliation Courts Review*, 1977, *15* (2), 9–12.

Kressel, K., and others. "A Typology of Divorcing Couples: Implications for Mediation and the Divorce Process." *Family Process*, 1980, *19* (2), 101–116.

Kübler-Ross, E. *Death: The Final Stage of Growth*. Englewood Cliffs, N.J.: Prentice-Hall, 1975.

Lange v. *Marshall*. 622 S.W.2d 237 (Missouri Appeals, 1981).

Langelier, R. "French Canadian Families." In M. McGoldrick, J. K. Pearce, and J. Giordiano (Eds.), *Ethnicity and Family Therapy*. New York: Guilford Press, 1982.

Lee, K. N. "Defining Success in Environmental Dispute Resolution." *Resolve*, 1982, *1*, 3–4.

Levinson, D., and others. *Seasons of a Man's Life*. New York: Knopf, 1978.

Lieberman, J. K. *The Litigious Society*. New York: Basic Books, 1981.

Lincoln, W. F. "Mediation: A Transferable Process for the Prevention and Resolution of Racial Conflict in Public Secondary Schools." Written with assistance of the National Institute of Education (NIE-P-76-0155). San Francisco: American Intermediation Service (National Center for Collaborative Planning and Community Service), 1981.

Los Angeles County Bar Association. Committee on Legal Ethics, Opinions, No. 270, 1962.

McEwen, C., and Maimon, R. "Mediation and Judicial Legitimacy: Achieving Compliance Through Consent." Unpublished manuscript, University of Maine Law School, 1982.

McGill, D., and Pearce, J. K. "British Families." In M. McGoldrick, J. K. Pearce, and J. Giordiano (Eds.), *Ethnicity and Family Therapy*. New York: Guilford Press, 1982.

McGinness, P. E., and Cinquegrama, R. J. "Legal Issues Arising in Mediation: The Boston Municipal Court Mediation Program." *Massachusetts Law Review*, 1982, *67* (3), 123-136.

McGoldrick, M., and Carter, E. A. "Forming a Remarried Family." In E. Carter and M. McGoldrick (Eds.), *The Family Life Cycle*. New York: Gardner Press, 1980.

McGoldrick, M., and Carter, E. A. "The Family Life Cycle." In F. Walsh (Ed.), *Normal Family Processes*. New York: Guilford Press, 1982.

McGoldrick, M., Pearce, J. K., and Giordiano, J. (Eds.). *Ethnicity and Family Therapy*. New York: Guilford Press, 1982.

McIsaac, H. "Mandatory Conciliation Custody/Visitation Matters: California's Bold Stroke." *Conciliation Courts Review*, 1981, *19* (2), 73-51.

McIsaac, H. "Court-Connected Mediation." *Conciliation Courts Review*, 1983, *21* (2), 49-59.

Mack, R. W., and Snyder, R. C. "An Analysis of Social Conflict— Toward An Overview and Synthesis." In F. Jandt (Ed.), *Conflict Resolution Through Communication*. New York: Harper & Row, 1973.

McLaughlin v. *Superior Court.* 140 C.A.3d 473, 189 Cal. Rptr. 479 (California, 1983).

Maggiolo, W. *Techniques of Mediation in Labor Disputes.* Dobbs Ferry, N.Y.: Oceana Publications, 1972.

Maher, E. L. "Burnout and Commitment: A Theoretical Alternative."*Personnel and Guidance Journal,* March 1983, *61* (7) 390-393

Martino v. *Family Services Agency of Adams County.* 9 *Family Law Reporter* 2311 (1983).

Maslow, A. H. *Motivation and Personality.* New York: Harper & Row, 1954.

Massengill, A. D. "Mediation Models: An Integrated Approach." In H. Davidson, L. Ray, and R. Horowitz (Eds.), *Alternative Means of Family Dispute Resolution.* Washington, D. C.: American Bar Association, 1982.

Mehrabian, A. *Public Places and Private Spaces: The Psychology of Work, Play and Living Environments.* New York: Basic Books, 1976.

Mernitz, S. *Mediation of Environmental Disputes: A Source Book.* New York: Praeger, 1980.

Merry, S. E. "The Social Organization of Mediation in Non-Industrial Societies: Implications for Informal Community Justice in America." In R. Abel (Ed.), *The Politics of Informal Justice.* Vol. 2. New York: Academic Press, 1982.

Metzner, D., and Reasbeck, S. "Getting Past the Impasse." *Newsletter of the California Chapter, Association of Family and Conciliation Courts,* Winter 1982, pp. 4–5.

Midelfort, C. F., and Midelfort, H. C. "Norwegian Families." In M. McGoldrick, J. K. Pearce, and J. Giordiano (Eds.), *Ethnicity and Family Therapy.* New York: Guilford Press, 1982.

Milne, A. "Divorce Mediation—An Overview of Current Approaches." Paper presented at the winter meeting of the Association of Family and Conciliation Courts, Fort Lauderdale, December 3, 1981.

Milne, A. "Divorce Mediation—Shall We Sanction the Practice?" Paper presented at the American Bar Association National Conference on Alternative Family Dispute Resolution, Arlington, Va., August 1982.

Milne, A. "Divorce Mediation: The State of the Art." *Mediation Quarterly,* 1983, *1,* 15–31.

Minuchin, S. *Families and Family Therapy.* Cambridge, Mass.: Harvard University Press, 1974.

Mnookin, R., and Kornhauser, L. "Bargaining in the Shadow of the Law: The Case of Divorce." *Yale Law Journal,* 1979, *88,* 950–997.

Molloy, J. T. *Dress for Success.* New York: Warner Books, 1976.

Montalvo, B. "Interpersonal Arrangements in Disrupted Families." In F. Walsh (Ed.), *Normal Family Processes.* New York: Guilford Press, 1982.

Moore, C. W. "A General Theory of Mediation: Dynamics, Strategies and Moves." Unpublished doctoral dissertation, Department of Sociology, Rutgers University, 1983a. Available through University Microfilms International, Ann Arbor, Mich.

Moore, C. W. "Training Mediators for Family Dispute Resolution." In J. A. Lemmon (Ed.). *Successful Techniques for Mediating Family Breakup.* Mediation Quarterly, no. 2. San Francisco: Jossey-Bass, 1983b.

Myles and Resiser Co. v. *Loew's, Inc.* 194 Misc. 119, 81 N.Y.S.2d 861 (New York, 1948).

Nader, L. (Ed.). *Law in Culture and Society.* Chicago: Aldine, 1969.

Nader, L. "Disputing Without the Force of Law." *Yale Law Journal,* 1979, *88,* 998-1021.

Nader, L. (Ed.). *No Access to Law—Alternatives to the American Judicial System.* New York: Academic Press, 1980.

Nader, L., and Todd, H. F. (Eds.). *The Disputing Process: Law in Ten Societies.* New York: Columbia University Press, 1978.

Napolitane, C., and Pelligrino, V. *Living and Loving After Divorce.* New York: Rawson, Wade, 1977.

National Association of Social Workers. *Code of Ethics.* Washington, D. C.: National Association of Social Workers, 1980.

National Labor Relations Board v. *Macaluso, Inc.* 618 F.2d 51 (9th Cir. 1980).

Neighborhood Justice Center of Atlanta (NJCA). *Dispute Resolution in Education: The NJCA Mediation Model.* (Training manual for workshop.) Atlanta: Neighborhood Justice Center of Atlanta, 1982.

New York City Bar Association. Committee on Professional and Judicial Ethics, Opinion No. 80-23, February 27, 1981.

New York Civil Practice Act. Sections 352 and 354 (1920).

New York Dispute Resolution Law. Chapter 847, section 849(b) (6) (1981).

Nierenberg, G. I. *Fundamentals of Negotiating.* New York: Hawthorn Books, 1973.

Nierenberg, G. I., and Calero, H. H. *How to Read a Person Like a Book.* New York: Pocket Books, 1973.

Nierenberg, G. I., and Calero, H. H. *Meta-Talk: The Guide to Hidden Meanings in Conversation.* New York: Cornerstone Library, 1980.

North Carolina State Bar Association. "Committee Reports: Unauthorized Practice of Law." *North Carolina State Bar Quarterly*, September 1980, pp. 4–5, 7.

Okun, B. F. *Effective Helping: Interviewing and Counseling Techniques.* (2nd ed.) Monterey: Brooks/Cole, 1982.

Ordione, G. S. "Arbitration and Mediation Among Early Quakers." *Arbitration Journal*, 1954, *9*, 161–66.

Oregon Bar Association. Committee on Legal Ethics, Proposed Opinion No. 70-46, April 2, 1980.

Oregon H.B. 2362. Oregon Legislative Assembly, 62nd Legislature (1983).

Parker, A. O. "A Comparison of Divorce Mediation Versus Lawyer Adversary Processes and the Relationship to Marital Separation Factors." Unpublished doctoral dissertation, Department of Counseling, University of North Carolina, 1980.

Patterson, C. H. *Theories of Counseling and Psychotherapy.* (2nd ed.) New York: Harper & Row, 1973.

Pearson, J., and Thoennes, N. "Divorce Mediation: Strengths and Weaknesses over Time." In H. Davidson, L. Ray, and R. Horowitz (Eds.), *Alternative Means of Family Dispute Resolution.* Washington, D. C.: American Bar Association, 1982.

Pinderhughes, E. "Afro-American Families and the Victim System." In M. McGoldrick, J. K. Pearce, and J. Giordiano (Eds.), *Ethnicity and Family Therapy.* New York: Guilford Press, 1982.

Portland, Oregon. State Circuit Court, Rules.

Pospisil, L. "Legal Levels and Multiplicity of Legal Systems in Human Societies." *Conflict Resolution*, 1967, *11* (1), 2–26.

Pottmeyer, T. "The Confidentiality of Child Custody Mediation." *Washington State Bar News*, February 1983, pp. 12–17.

Pratt, G. W. "Murphy's Law and Counseling." *Personnel and Guidance Journal*, 1982, *61* (4), 217–219.

Pressman, R. M., and Siegler, R. *The Independent Practitioner: Practice Management for the Allied Health Professional.* Homewood, Ill.: Dow Jones-Irwin, 1983.

"Privileged Communications: A Case by Case Approach." *Maine Law Review*, 1971, *23*, 443–462.

Prosser, W. *Law of Torts.* (4th ed.) St. Paul: West, 1971.

Resolve Center for Environmental Conflict Resolution. *Environmental Mediation: An Effective Answer?* Palo Alto: Resolve, 1978.

Restatement (Second) of Torts. St. Paul: American Law Institute Publishers, 1965.

Ricci, I. *Mom's House, Dad's House: Making Shared Custody Work.* New York: Macmillan, 1980.

Richardson, L. F. (Ed.). *Statistics of Deadly Quarrels.* Chicago: Quadrangle Press, 1960.

Riskin, L. "Mediation and Lawyers." *Ohio State Law Journal,* 1982, *43,* 29–60.

Rogers, C. "Some New Challenges." *American Psychologist,* 1973, *28* (5), 379–387.

Rosenberg, M. "Let's Everybody Litigate?" *Texas Law Review,* 1972, *50,* 1349–1368.

Rummel, R. J. *Understanding Conflict and War.* Vols. 1 and 2. New York: Wiley, 1976.

Sacks, A. "Legal Education and the Dispute Resolution System." Unpublished working paper prepared for the National Conference on the Lawyer's Changing Role in Resolving Disputes, Harvard Law School, Cambridge, Mass., October 1982.

Salius, A. J. (Ed.). "Program Description: Services Provided in Minor Criminal Cases in the Geographical Area Courts." Unpublished training material, Family Division, Superior Court, State of Connecticut, 1983.

Salmon and Steelhead Advisory Committee. "Draft: Dispute Resolution Plan." Unpublished manuscript.

Saltzburg, S. "Privileges and Professionals: Lawyers and Psychiatrists." *Virginia Law Review,* 1980, *66* (1), 597–650.

Sander, F. "Varieties of Dispute Processing." *Federal Rules Decisions,* 1976, *70,* 111–133.

Sander, F. "Developments in Judicial Administration." *Federal Rules Decisions,* 1977, *80,* 186–190.

Sander, F. "Alternatives to the Courts." Unpublished working paper prepared for the National Conference on the Lawyer's Changing Role in Resolving Disputes, Harvard Law School, Cambridge, Mass., October 1982.

Saposnek, D. T. *Mediating Child Custody Disputes: A Systematic Guide for Family Therapists, Court Counselors, Attorneys, and Judges.* San Francisco: Jossey-Bass, 1983.

Sarat, A., and Grossman, J. "Courts and Conflict Resolution: Problems in the Mobilization of Adjudication." *American Political Science Review*, 1975, *69*, 1200–1217.

Satir, V. *Conjoint Family Therapy*. (Rev. ed.) Palo Alto: Science and Behavior Books, 1967.

Satir, V. *Peoplemaking*. Palo Alto: Science and Behavior Books, 1972.

Schafer, W. *Stress, Distress, and Growth*. Davis, Calif.: Responsible Action, 1978.

Schaffer, T. L. *Legal Interviewing and Counseling*. St. Paul: West, 1976.

Schell, J. *The Fate of the Earth*. New York: Knopf, 1982.

Schimazu, I. "Japanese Perspectives on the Procedural Aspects of Marriage Dissolution." Paper presented at Fourth World Conference of the International Society of Family Law, Harvard Law School, Cambridge, Mass., June 1982.

Schreiber, F. B. *Instructor's Manual for Domestic Disturbances: Officer Safety and Calming Techniques*. St. Cloud, Minn.: Center for Criminal Justice, St. Cloud University, 1979.

Seattle, Washington. United States District Court for the Western District of Washington, Local Rules, CR 1(d) (2) (E) (3-4).

Shear, L. E. "Developing Parental Responsibility Schedules." *Newsletter of the California Chapter, Association of Family and Conciliation Courts*, Summer 1982, pp. 1–3.

Sheehy, G. *Passages*. New York: Bantam Books, 1978.

Sheehy, G. *Pathfinders*. New York: Morrow, 1981.

Shon, S. P., and Ja, D. Y. "Asian Families." In M. McGoldrick, J. K. Pearce, and J. Giordiano (Eds.), *Ethnicity and Family Therapy*. New York: Guilford Press, 1982.

Shonholtz, R. *The Ethics and Values of Community Boards: Developing Concept Tools for the Work of Community Members*. (Photocopied text.) San Francisco: Communitv Board Program, 1981. Available through the Community Board Program, 149 Ninth Street, San Francisco, Calif. 94104.

Shonholtz, R. "New Justice Theories and Practices." Paper presented at the annual meeting of the Law and Society Association, Denver, June 1983.

Silberman, L. J. "Professional Responsibility Problems of Divorce Mediation." *Family Law Quarterly*, Summer 1982, *16*, 107–145.

Simkin, W. E. *Mediation and the Dynamics of Collective Bargaining.* Washington, D. C.: Bureau of National Affairs, 1971.

Simrin v. *Simrin.* 233 C.A.2d 90, 43 Cal. Rptr. 376 (California, 1965).

Skinner, B. F. *The Behavior of Organisms.* New York: Appleton-Century-Crofts, 1938.

Skinner, B. F. *Science and Human Behavior.* New York: Macmillan, 1953.

Spiegel, J. "An Ecological Model of Ethnic Families." In M. McGoldrick, J. K. Pearce, and J. Giordiano (Eds.), *Ethnicity and Family Therapy.* New York: Guilford Press, 1982.

Statsky, W. *Domestic Relations.* St. Paul: West, 1978.

Straus, D. B. "Mediating Environmental Trade-Offs." *Arbitration Journal,* 1977, *32* (2), 96–110.

Talbot, A. R. *Settling Things: Six Case Studies in Environmental Mediation.* Washington, D.C.: The Conservation Foundation and The Ford Foundation, 1983.

Taylor, A. "Toward a Comprehensive Theory of Mediation." *Conciliation Courts Review,* 1981, *19* (1), 1–12.

Thompson, W. N. *The Process of Persuasion: Principles and Readings.* New York: Harper & Row, 1975.

Toffler, A. *The Third Wave.* New York: Bantam Books, 1981.

In re Tomlinson of High Point, Inc. 74 National Labor Relations Board 681 (1947).

"Underprivileged Communications: Extension of the Psychotherapist-Patient Privilege to Patients of Psychiatric Social Workers." *California Law Review,* 1973, *61,* 1050–1071.

Uniform Marriage and Divorce Act. Chicago: National Conference of Commissioners on Uniform State Laws, 1979.

United States Code 42. Section 200g-2(b) (1976).

United States v. *Pfiger, Inc.* 560 F.2d 326 (8th Cir. 1977).

University of Wisconsin Dispute Processing Research Program. *Report.* Madison: University of Wisconsin Press, 1983.

Van Hoose, W., and Kottler, J. *Ethical and Legal Issues in Counseling and Psychotherapy.* San Francisco: Jossey-Bass, 1977.

Vaughn, B., and Hunter, L. *Selected Readings in Environmental Conflict Management.* Palo Alto: Resolve, Center for Environmental Conflict Resolution, 1978.

Vorenberg, E. W. "State of the Art Survey of Dispute Resolution Programs Involving Juveniles." Dispute Resolution Papers, Series 1, American Bar Association, Special Committee on Alternative Means of Dispute Resolution (Division of Public Service Activities), July 1982.

Vroom, P., Fossett, D., and Wakefield, R. "Mediation: The Wave of the Future." *American Family*, 1981, *4*, 12–15.

Wallerstein, J. S. "The Child's Response to Divorce: The Family's Response and the Assessment of Children's Needs." *Mediation of Child Custody and Visitation Disputes.* (Transcripts from the Vallambrosa Retreat, September 1981.) California Chapter, Association of Family and Conciliation Courts, Institute for Training and Research, 1982.

Wallerstein, J. S., and Kelly, J. B. *Surviving the Breakup: How Children and Parents Cope with Divorce.* New York: Basic Books, 1980.

Walsh, F. "Conceptualizations of Normal Family Functioning." In F. Walsh (Ed.), *Normal Family Processes.* New York: Guilford Press, 1982.

Walton, R., and McKersie, R. *A Behavioral Theory of Labor Negotiations.* New York: McGraw-Hill, 1965.

Waltz, R., and Huston, J. "The Rules of Evidence in Settlement." *Litigation*, 1979, *5* (1), 1–22.

Ware, C. *Sharing Parenthood After Divorce: An Enlightened Custody Guide for Mothers, Fathers, and Kids.* New York: Viking Press, 1982.

Warren, C. "The Hopeful Future of Mediation: Resolving Environmental Disputes Outside the Courts." In *Environmental Mediation: An Effective Alternative?* Palo Alto: Resolve, Center for Environmental Conflict Resolution, 1978.

Washington Revised Code. Section 5, 60.060(5) (1974).

Watkins, C. E. "Burnout in Counseling Practice: Some Potential Professional and Personal Hazards of Becoming a Counselor." *Personnel and Guidance Journal*, 1983, *61* (5), 304–308.

Watson, A. S. *The Lawyer in the Interviewing and Counseling Process.* Indianapolis: Bobbs-Merrill, 1976.

Wicker, T. *A Time to Die.* New York: Ballantine Books, 1975.

Wigmore, S. *A Student's Textbook of the Law of Evidence.* Brooklyn: Foundation Press, 1935.

Williams, G. R. *Legal Negotiation and Settlement.* St. Paul: West, 1983.

Winawer-Steiner, H., and Wetzel, N. A. "German Families." In M. McGoldrick, J. K. Pearce, and J. Giordiano (Eds.), *Ethnicity and Family Therapy*. New York: Guilford Press, 1982.

Wiseman, J., and Fiske, J. "Lawyer-Therapist Team as Mediator in a Marital Crisis." *Social Work*, 1980, *25*, 442–450.

Wood, J. *How Do You Feel? A Guide to Your Emotions*. Englewood Cliffs, N.J.: Prentice-Hall, 1974.

Woolfolk, R. L., and Richardson, F. C. *Stress, Sanity and Survival*. New York: Monarch, 1978.

Woolley, P. *The Custody Handbook*. New York: Summit Books, 1979.

Yaffe, J. *So Sue Me! The Story of a Community Court*. New York: Saturday Review Press, 1972.

Index

Depression: analysis of, 321, 324–329; grief linked to, 97; referral for, 327, 329; symptoms of severe, 325; telephone calls from person in, 327–329; triggering events for, 326

Deutsch, M., ix–x, 7, 13, 23–24, 28, 30, 36–37, 223, 364

Dialectic scanning, in environmental mediation, 225

Direct-conflict couples, 167, 183

Directive demand, in communication, 107

Directive statements, in communication, 109

Discussion of positions, in introduction stage, 42

Disengaged-conflict couples, 167, 183

Displacement, in divorce disputes, 162–163

Dispute Resolution Act of 1980, 5–6

Disputes, conflicts distinct from, 19

District of Columbia: environmental mediation in, 224; special education mediation in, 199

Divorce mediation: for child custody and visitation, 179–184, 189; and child support, 169–172; disputes and decisions in, 161–168, 188; financial decisions in, 168–179, 188; and financial disclosure, 168–169, 178; and property division, 175–179; for spousal support, 172–175; unequal power in, 184–186

Divorce Mediation Worksheet, 126

Dodd, C. H., 334

Dollard's research, 20–21

Doo, L. W., 3, 364

Drew, A., 28, 365

Due process hearing, and educational mediation, 197, 199

Dweck, C., 324, 364

E

Edon, A., 230, 364

Education. *See* Training and education

Educational mediation: analysis of, 196–203; and closing buildings, 201; and desegregation, 202; examples of, 197–198; for handicapped students, 196–200

Ekman, P., 118, 364

Ellis, A., 80–82, 83, 95, 364

Elson, H. M., 134, 364

Empathy, and counseling, 87–89, 98

Employment agreement, in introduction stage, 43–44

Ending statement, definitive, for divorce, 163–164, 165, 183

Energy Supply and Environmental Coordination Act, 219

Enmeshed couples, 164–165, 182, 183

Environmental mediation: analysis of, 217–231; benefits of, 220–221; empowered representatives for, 223; international, 230–231; issues for, 221–222; postlitigation, 227; process of, 224–225; and state activity, 219; success criteria in, 226–228; tactics in, 229

Environmental Protection Agency (EPA), 219–220, 225–226

Epstein, N. B., 27n, 31, 364

Erikson, E. H., 158, 159n, 364

Ethical issues: analysis of, 244–290; of confidentiality, 263–280, 290; and liability, 280–289, 290; and limitations on mediators, 250–252, 290; and restraints on attorneys, 252–255; and restraints on nonlawyers, 255–258; standards of practice distinct from, 250

Ethnic and sociocultural perspectives, and mediation, 318–323, 334

Explanatory statements, in communication, 107

F

Facial expression, in communication, 118–120

Fact finding and issue isolation, as mediation stage, 47–49

Fairfax County, Virginia, mediation study in, 12

Fairness: of access to mediation, 249–250; issue of, 245–250, 289; norms in, 245–246; safeguards for, 247–249; and unconscionability standard, 245

Families: continuum of, 153–154; and developmental stages, 154, 158–161, 187; interpersonal arrangements among, 155–157; life chronology for, 160; strategic model of, 149, 186; structural theory of, 148–149; systems view of, 150–153

Family and kinship circles, mediation's roots in, 2

Family mediation, and normal structures and processes, 148–157, 187

Family Mediation Association, 5, 136, 356

Family Mediation Center, impact of, 11

Fast, J., 118, 129, 364

Federal Advisory Committee Act (FACA), 226

Federal Insecticide, Fungicide, and Rodenticide Act, 219

Federal Law Enforcement Assistance Administration, 5

Federal Mediation and Conciliation Service (FMCS), 5, 131, 227–228, 265, 357, 364; and Code of Professional Conduct for Labor Mediators, 267, 277, 364

Feeley, M. M., 214, 364

Feelings: categories of, 88; and counseling, 87–89, 98; words for, 87–88

Fellers, P., 200–201, 364–365

Felstiner, W., 28, 365

Fenton v. *Howard*, and confidentiality, 275, 365

Festinger, L., 79–80, 365

Filley, A. C., 297, 365

Fisher, R., 7, 30, 37, 57, 139, 365

Fiske, J., 146, 378

Florida: mediation statute in, 272; special education mediation in, 199

Florida Statutes, 272, 365

Folberg, J., 11, 128, 171, 184, 188, 189, 365

Follow-up, in implementation stage, 66–68

Ford Foundation, 224

Fossett, D., 2, 6, 377

Fox, W. M., 77, 365

Frankl, V. E., 77, 365

Franks, M., 171, 365

Freed, D. J., 177, 365

Freeman, H. A., 74, 365

Freud, S., 74–75

Friesen, W. V., 118, 364

Fuller, L., 4, 7, 17, 132, 366

G

Galanter, M., 7

Gallant, C. B., 13, 199, 200, 366

Galper, M., 127, 189, 366

Geisler, J., xv

General adaptation syndrome, and stress, 94

General Motors, 131

Georgia, special education mediation in, 199

Gibbs, W., 2, 366

Ginsberg, R. B., 2, 366

Glasser, W., xv, 75, 77–79, 83, 98, 149, 324, 366

Goffman, E., 117, 366

Gold, C., 243, 366

Gold, L., 140, 146, 366

Goldsmith, J., 154, 366

Golten, R. J., 220, 366

Graff, P., 261, 262, 362

Grief, and counseling, 96–97, 99

Grinder, J., 101, 102, 360

Grossman, J., 28, 374

Guideline review, in introduction stage, 42–43, 47

Gulliver, P. H., 2, 6, 16, 246, 289, 366

H

Haley, J., 2, 149, 186, 187, 366–367

Hall, E. T., 123, 129, 304, 318, 367

Hallett, K., 75, 367

Hamberger, S., xv

Hand gestures, in communication, 122–123

Index

Rationalization, and communication, 90
Reaction formation, and communication, 91
Reality therapy, for depression, 324
Reassurance, in introduction stage, 46
Referrals: analysis of, 305–317; to auxiliary services, 311–317; to books for loan, 316; criteria for screening, 307; for depression, 327, 329; of inappropriate cases, 309–311; information and referral (I and R) process in, 310; normalizing dialogue for, 313–315; from others, 294, 306–309; premature, 307–308; from professional networks, 308; and resistance, 311; self-, 308–309
Reflection, in communication, 107, 112–115
Reframing: in family mediation, 153; in introduction stage, 46–47
Rehabilitation Act of 1973, Section 504 of, 198
Resistance: analysis of, 329–333, 334; and communication, 91; in divorce mediation, 163; expressions of, 329, 330, 331; moving participants from, 332; and referrals, 311; at stages of mediation, 330–333
Resolve. *See* Center for Environmental Conflict Resolution
Resource, Conservation, and Recovery Act, 219
Review and revision stage, and fairness, 248–249
Review session: in implementation stage, 69–70
Reward and redirection, in communication, 108
Ricci, I., 189, 374
Richardson, F. C., 92, 99, 378
Richardson, L. F., 20, 374
Riskin, L., 237, 238, 374
Rochl, J., 13, 363
Rockefeller Foundation, 224
Rocky Mountain Center for the Environment (ROMCOE), 6
Rogers, C., 262, 374
Rosen, E. J., 319, 320, 367
Rosenberg, M., 4, 374
Rummel, R. J., 21–23, 24, 37, 374

S

Sacks, A., 243, 374
Safe Drinking Water Act, 219
Salius, A. J., 207, 295, 374
Salmon and Steelhead Advisory Committee (SSAC), 229–230, 374
Salmon and Steelhead Enhancement Act of 1980, 229–230
Saltzburg, S., 280, 374
San Francisco County: and confidentiality, 278; neighborhood mediation in, 195, 265
San Mateo County, and confidentiality, 278–279
Sander, F., 4, 7, 17, 214, 243, 374
Saposnek, D. T., 189, 374
Sarat, A., 28, 374
Satir, V., 29, 101, 102, 126, 160, 184, 187, 360, 375
Schafer, W., 94, 97, 99, 375
Schaffer, T. L., 124, 375
Schell, J., 230–231, 375
Schimazu, I., 2, 375
Schreiber, F. B., 139, 206, 375
Schutz, B., 290
Scoping, in environmental mediation, 222, 225, 229
Scotland, youth mediation in, 207
Secretarial mediation services, and environmental mediation, 227
Seligman, E. P., 324
Shawn, J., 146, 368
Shear, L. E., 126, 375
Sheehy, G., 158, 375
Shepard, D., 13, 363
Shon, S. P., 321, 375
Shonholtz, R., 6, 138, 195, 375
Siegler, R., 294, 304, 373
Sierra Club, 219, 224
Sierra Club Foundation, 231–232
Silberman, L. J., 290, 375
Silence, in communication, 109